D0782115

"Mary Healy's commentary demonstrates tl. ...., is a living word that addressed an ancient community in crisis and continues to speak to the issues of our time. Readers will benefit from Healy's firm grasp of the history of the interpretation of Hebrews and the applications of this homily for today."

—**James W. Thompson**, Abilene Christian University

"The Letter to the Hebrews is one of the richest and yet least understood of the New Testament writings. The arguments are complex and deeply rooted in the Old Testament. This commentary uses the best of Catholic teaching and biblical scholarship to illuminate some of the key teachings of Hebrews in a way that Catholics can appreciate and apply to their own understanding of Jesus Christ."

—**Fr. Mitch Pacwa, SJ**, St. Paul Center for Biblical Theology, Steubenville, Ohio

"One of the most frequent requests I get for Bible study is for a good commentary. I enthusiastically endorse the Catholic Commentary on Sacred Scripture series. In this volume, Dr. Healy demonstrates her giftedness at taking complex ideas and presenting them in an understandable and practical way. Her writing draws readers into the text in a heartwarming way. I enjoyed this commentary, and I know my students will as well."

—**Jeff Cavins**, founder, The Great Adventure Catholic Bible Study System

Praise for the Catholic Commentary on Sacred Scripture

"By bringing together historical background, exegetical interpretation, Church tradition, theological reflection, and pastoral application, this series promises to enkindle thoughtful discussion about the implications of the New Testament for lived Christian faith in the Church today. Its accessible format and multi-angled approach offer a model for teaching and ministry."

—**Katherine Hayes**, Seminary of the Immaculate Conception

"This could be the first commentary read by a pastor preparing a text and could be read easily by a Sunday school teacher preparing a text, and it would be an excellent commentary for a college Bible class. . . . The Catholic Commentary on Sacred Scripture will prove itself to be a reliable, Catholic—but ecumenically open and respectful—commentary."

—**Scot McKnight**, *Jesus Creed* blog

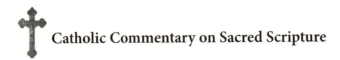 Catholic Commentary on Sacred Scripture

Hebrews

Mary Healy

Baker Academic
a division of Baker Publishing Group
Grand Rapids, Michigan

© 2016 by Mary Healy

Published by Baker Academic
a division of Baker Publishing Group
P.O. Box 6287, Grand Rapids, MI 49516-6287
www.bakeracademic.com

Printed in the United States of America

Library of Congress Cataloging-in-Publication Data
Names: Healy, Mary, 1964– author.
Title: Hebrews / Mary Healy.
Description: Grand Rapids : Baker Academic, 2016. | Series: Catholic commentary on sacred scripture | Includes bibliographical references and index.
Identifiers: LCCN 2016001366 | ISBN 9780801036033 (pbk.)
Subjects: LCSH: Bible. Hebrews—Commentaries. | Catholic Church—Doctrines.
Classification: LCC BS2775.53 .H425 2016 | DDC 227/.87077—dc23
LC record available at http://lccn.loc.gov/2016001366

Printed with Ecclesiastical Permission
Most Reverend Earl Boyea, Bishop of Lansing
February 23, 2015

16 17 18 19 20 21 22   7 6 5 4 3 2 1

Contents

Illustrations

Editors' Preface

The Church has always venerated the divine Scriptures just as she venerates the body of the Lord. . . . All the preaching of the Church should be nourished and governed by Sacred Scripture. For in the sacred books, the Father who is in heaven meets His children with great love and speaks with them; and the power and goodness in the word of God is so great that it stands as the support and energy of the Church, the strength of faith for her sons and daughters, the food of the soul, a pure and perennial fountain of spiritual life.

Second Vatican Council, Dei Verbum 21

Were not our hearts burning within us while he spoke to us on the way and opened the scriptures to us?

Luke 24:32

The Catholic Commentary on Sacred Scripture aims to serve the ministry of the Word of God in the life and mission of the Church. Since Vatican Council II, there has been an increasing hunger among Catholics to study Scripture in depth and in a way that reveals its relationship to liturgy, evangelization, catechesis, theology, and personal and communal life. This series responds to that desire by providing accessible yet substantive commentary on each book of the New Testament, drawn from the best of contemporary biblical scholarship as well as the rich treasury of the Church's tradition. These volumes seek to offer scholarship illumined by faith, in the conviction that the ultimate aim of biblical interpretation is to discover what God has revealed and is still speaking through the sacred text. Central to our approach are the principles taught by Vatican II: first, the use of historical and literary methods to discern what the biblical authors intended to express; second, prayerful theological reflection to understand the sacred text "in accord with the same Spirit by whom it was written"—that is, in light of the content and unity of the whole Scripture, the living tradition of the Church, and the analogy of faith (*Dei Verbum* 12).

The Catholic Commentary on Sacred Scripture is written for those engaged in or training for pastoral ministry and others interested in studying Scripture to understand their faith more deeply, to nourish their spiritual life, or to share the good news with others. With this in mind, the authors focus on the meaning of the text for faith and life rather than on the technical questions that occupy scholars, and they explain the Bible in ordinary language that does not require translation for preaching and catechesis. Although this series is written from the perspective of Catholic faith, its authors draw on the interpretation of Protestant and Orthodox scholars and hope these volumes will serve Christians of other traditions as well.

A variety of features are designed to make the commentary as useful as possible. Each volume includes the biblical text of the New American Bible, Revised Edition (NABRE), the translation approved for liturgical use in the United States. In order to serve readers who use other translations, the most important differences between the NABRE and other widely used translations (RSV, NRSV, JB, NJB, and NIV) are noted and explained. Each unit of the biblical text is followed by a list of references to relevant Scripture passages, Catechism sections, and uses in the Roman Lectionary. The exegesis that follows aims to explain in a clear and engaging way the meaning of the text in its original historical context as well as its perennial meaning for Christians. Reflection and Application sections help readers apply Scripture to Christian life today by responding to questions that the text raises, offering spiritual interpretations drawn from Christian tradition or providing suggestions for the use of the biblical text in catechesis, preaching, or other forms of pastoral ministry.

Interspersed throughout the commentary are Biblical Background sidebars that present historical, literary, or theological information, and Living Tradition sidebars that offer pertinent material from the postbiblical Christian tradition, including quotations from Church documents and from the writings of saints and Church Fathers. The Biblical Background sidebars are indicated by a photo of urns that were excavated in Jerusalem, signifying the importance of historical study in understanding the sacred text. The Living Tradition sidebars are indicated by an image of Eadwine, a twelfth-century monk and scribe, signifying the growth in the Church's understanding that comes by the grace of the Holy Spirit as believers study and ponder the word of God in their hearts (see *Dei Verbum* 8).

Maps and a glossary are included in each volume for easy reference. The glossary explains key terms from the biblical text as well as theological or exegetical terms, which are marked in the commentary with a cross (†). A list of suggested resources, an index of pastoral topics, and an index of sidebars are included to enhance the usefulness of these volumes. Further resources, including questions for reflection or discussion, can be found at the series website, www.CatholicScriptureCommentary.com.

It is our desire and prayer that these volumes be of service so that more and more "the word of the Lord may speed forward and be glorified" (2 Thess 3:1) in the Church and throughout the world.

Peter S. Williamson
Mary Healy
Kevin Perrotta

Note to Readers

The New American Bible, Revised Edition differs slightly from most English translations in its verse numbering of Psalms and certain other parts of the Old Testament. For instance, Ps 51:4 in the NABRE is Ps 51:2 in other translations; Mal 3:19 in the NABRE is Mal 4:1 in other translations. Readers who use different translations are advised to keep this in mind when looking up Old Testament cross-references given in the commentary.

The NABRE (2011) was a revision of the NAB Old Testament only; thus where this commentary cites the New Testament it will refer to the NAB rather than the NABRE.

Abbreviations

†	indicates that the definition of a term appears in the glossary
ACCS 10	*Ancient Christian Commentary on Scripture: New Testament 10, Hebrews*, edited by Erik M. Heen and Philip D. W. Krey (Downers Grove, IL: InterVarsity, 2005)
ANF	*Ante-Nicene Fathers: The Writings of the Fathers down to A.D. 325*, edited by Alexander Roberts and James Donaldson (Buffalo, NY: Christian Literature Publishing, 1885)
c.	circa
Catechism	*Catechism of the Catholic Church*, 2nd ed. (New York: Doubleday, 2003)
cf.	compare
ESV	English Standard Version
JB	Jerusalem Bible
KJV	King James Version
Lectionary	*The Lectionary for Mass*, 1988/2000 USA ed. (Washington, DC: Confraternity of Christian Doctrine)
LXX	†Septuagint
NAB	New American Bible
NABRE	New American Bible, Revised Edition (2011)
NIV	New International Version
NJB	New Jerusalem Bible
NPNF	*Nicene and Post-Nicene Fathers*, edited by Philip Schaff and Henry Wace (Buffalo, NY: Christian Literature Publishing, 1890)
NRSV	New Revised Standard Version
NT	New Testament
OT	Old Testament
RSV	Revised Standard Version
RSV-CE	Catholic Edition of the Revised Standard Version (Ignatius Bible)
v(v).	verse(s)

Books of the Old Testament

Gen	Genesis	Tob	Tobit	Ezek	Ezekiel
Exod	Exodus	Jdt	Judith	Dan	Daniel
Lev	Leviticus	Esther	Esther	Hosea	Hosea
Num	Numbers	1 Macc	1 Maccabees	Joel	Joel
Deut	Deuteronomy	2 Macc	2 Maccabees	Amos	Amos
Josh	Joshua	Job	Job	Obad	Obadiah
Judg	Judges	Ps	Psalm/Psalms	Jon	Jonah
Ruth	Ruth	Prov	Proverbs	Mic	Micah
1 Sam	1 Samuel	Eccles	Ecclesiastes	Nah	Nahum
2 Sam	2 Samuel	Song	Song of Songs	Hab	Habakkuk
1 Kings	1 Kings	Wis	Wisdom	Zeph	Zephaniah
2 Kings	2 Kings	Sir	Sirach	Hag	Haggai
1 Chron	1 Chronicles	Isa	Isaiah	Zech	Zechariah
2 Chron	2 Chronicles	Jer	Jeremiah	Mal	Malachi
Ezra	Ezra	Lam	Lamentations		
Neh	Nehemiah	Bar	Baruch		

Books of the New Testament

Matt	Matthew	1 Tim	1 Timothy
Mark	Mark	2 Tim	2 Timothy
Luke	Luke	Titus	Titus
John	John	Philem	Philemon
Acts	Acts	Heb	Hebrews
Rom	Romans	James	James
1 Cor	1 Corinthians	1 Pet	1 Peter
2 Cor	2 Corinthians	2 Pet	2 Peter
Gal	Galatians	1 John	1 John
Eph	Ephesians	2 John	2 John
Phil	Philippians	3 John	3 John
Col	Colossians	Jude	Jude
1 Thess	1 Thessalonians	Rev	Revelation
2 Thess	2 Thessalonians		

Introduction

What is the meaning of Christ's death on the cross? And what does it have to do with us? Of all the books of the New Testament, the Letter to the Hebrews offers the most profound and penetrating exploration of this mystery that lies at the heart of Christian faith. Yet Hebrews is in many respects the enigma of the New Testament. The author has left us no byline and few clues as to his identity. This "letter" is actually a homily within a letter, written to unspecified addressees in an unidentified setting at an unknown time. Not surprisingly, it was one of the last books to be universally accepted as part of the New Testament canon. But the early Church recognized this book as a magnificent reflection, inspired by the Holy Spirit, on Christ's †paschal mystery as the culmination of God's plan of salvation, the fulfillment of all that was hidden in the words, deeds, and rites of the old covenant.

For readers today, Hebrews presents special challenges. Its vocabulary is difficult, its structure complex, its logic not always easy to follow. The thought world of Hebrews, with its intense interest in priesthood, †tabernacle, ritual purity, and blood sacrifice, is foreign to most people of the twenty-first century. Many Catholics are familiar only with the short passages that appear in the Sunday lectionary, extracted from the context into which they are so carefully woven. Yet the effort to engage this biblical book in detail and understand it as a carefully constructed whole yields rich rewards. Hebrews is no abstract, dry treatise of theological speculation. It is a window opening onto the event at the center of all history, the act of love in which Christ died for us. The more one studies this letter, the more one finds that it illuminates and transforms our understanding of who God is, what he has done for us, and how we are to live as Christians today.

The purpose of this commentary is to make Hebrews accessible to readers by unpacking the meaning of each passage in light of the whole letter and especially in light of the Old Testament figures and prophecies that for the author are the indispensable background for understanding the fulfillment of God's plan in Christ. In keeping with the aims of the Catholic Commentary on Sacred Scripture, the goal is not merely to describe what Hebrews says about divine realities but also to understand *the realities themselves* in light of what Hebrews says about them. This commentary reads Hebrews from the heart of the Church, drawing from the insights of contemporary biblical scholars as well as Church Fathers, saints, and Church documents.

Who Wrote Hebrews?

Hebrews is the only book of the New Testament that is formally anonymous; that is, neither the letter itself nor a heading above it in the earliest manuscripts names an author. But this does not preclude our making some educated guesses. Taking a brief look at the various hypotheses that have been proposed can sharpen our understanding of the letter's audience, purpose, and historical setting.

Is Paul the Author?

Hebrews has traditionally been grouped with the Letters of Paul, although Church Fathers from early on recognized that it does not readily fit this categorization. The question of authorship had immense importance for the early Church because it was tied to the question of which books belonged to the New Testament canon (which was not settled until the late fourth century). The Church regarded only "apostolic" writings—those written by an apostle or a close associate of an apostle—as canonical. Was Hebrews apostolic?

The Western Fathers were reluctant to ascribe Hebrews to Paul. The Eastern Fathers were more inclined to accept Pauline authorship, at least in a broad sense. St. Clement of Alexandria (c. 150–215) claimed that Paul originally wrote the letter in the Hebrew language, and then Luke translated and published it in Greek. To explain why Paul does not name himself as in all his other letters, Clement opined that "in sending it to the Hebrews, who were prejudiced and suspicious of him, he wisely did not wish to repel them at the very beginning by giving his name."[1] Origen (184–253) noted that Hebrews resembles the theology of Paul at many

---

1. Eusebius, *Ecclesiastical History* 6.14.2. Clement also quotes his predecessor Pantaenus (died c. 200) as ascribing Hebrews to Paul.

points, but that its Greek diction is more elegant and polished than the apostle's. He concluded that Hebrews expresses the thought of Paul, but as written down by someone else, presumably a student of Paul's who remembered his teachings.[2]

Through the influence of St. Jerome (c. 347–420) and St. Augustine (354–430), the Western Church came to accept the Eastern view, assuming some form of Pauline authorship while still classifying Hebrews separately from the other thirteen Letters of Paul.[3] Thus by the late fourth century the churches universally came to recognize Hebrews as apostolic and canonical, but without formally settling the question of authorship.

What are the reasons for doubting Paul's authorship?

First, the thirteen Pauline Letters explicitly identify Paul as the author (always as the very first word in the epistle), whereas Hebrews names no author. Further, Hebrews lacks Paul's characteristic greeting, "grace and peace," which appears in all thirteen letters, and it contains none of his typical autobiographical remarks.[4]

Second, the vocabulary and style are markedly different from Paul's. Many of Paul's favorite expressions are absent, such as "the gospel," "Christ Jesus," "chosen," "fulfill," "build up," and "justify." Whereas Paul, in his zeal to get his point across, often disregards fine points of grammar or style, sometimes shifting abruptly from one topic to another or breaking off in midsentence, Hebrews is a polished, finely crafted work of literary art. Some, like Clement, hypothesize that Paul authored an original Hebrew-language version that someone else then translated into Greek, but this is unconvincing, given Hebrews' many striking Greek expressions and wordplays that work only in Greek.[5] Moreover, in several places the argument depends on a turn of phrase that does not exist in the Hebrew Old Testament but is present in the Greek †Septuagint.[6]

Third, Hebrews quotes Scripture in a way different from Paul. Whereas Paul usually introduces quotations with "it is written" or "scripture says," Hebrews emphasizes Scripture as God's *speech* in the present: God says (1:5) or Christ says (2:11–13) or the Spirit says (3:7; 10:15).

2. Eusebius, *Ecclesiastical History* 6.25.11–13.

3. Both Jerome (*Epistle* 129.3) and Augustine (*Forgiveness of Sins* 1.50) acknowledge Hebrews as belonging in some sense to the Pauline Letters but withhold judgment on the question of authorship. See F. F. Bruce, *The Epistle to the Hebrews*, rev. ed., New International Commentary on the New Testament (Grand Rapids: Eerdmans, 2012), 17.

4. See Luke Timothy Johnson, *Hebrews: A Commentary*, New Testament Library (Louisville: Westminster John Knox, 2006), 40.

5. See George Milligan, *The Theology of the Epistle to the Hebrews: With a Critical Introduction* (Edinburgh: T&T Clark, 1899), 17.

6. A prominent example is the reflection in Heb 10:5 on a quotation from Ps 40:7 (Ps 39:7 LXX), "a body you prepared for me," whereas the Hebrew text reads, "you opened my ears."

Fourth, the theology of Hebrews, though having many points of contact with that of Paul, is strikingly unique. Only Hebrews refers to Christ as "high priest." Whereas Paul often speaks of redemption as our being "justified by faith," Hebrews uses terms taken from the sacrificial rites of the temple: we are "cleansed," "sprinkled clean," "made perfect." Whereas Paul speaks of the law of Moses primarily as a moral code, Hebrews focuses on its ritual prescriptions. Whereas Christ's resurrection is central to Paul's theology, Hebrews mentions the resurrection only obliquely and focuses instead on Jesus' exaltation at the right hand of God.

It should be noted, however, that these differences are not contradictions. Hebrews and Paul agree on the essential content of Christian revelation: Jesus Christ is the image of God through whom the world was created (Heb 1:1–3; 1 Cor 8:6; Col 1:15–16), the savior who took on our human flesh (Heb 2:14–16; Rom 8:3), who died for our sins once and for all (Heb 9:26; Rom 6:9–10), who humbled himself and then was brought back from the dead and glorified at God's right hand (Heb 2:9; 13:20; Phil 2:8–9); he is the mediator of the new covenant (Heb 9:15; 1 Cor 11:25) who continues to intercede for us (Heb 7:25; Rom 8:34), who empowers us to practice faith, hope, and love (Heb 10:22–24; 1 Cor 13:13), and who will come again to complete the work of salvation (Heb 9:28; 1 Cor 1:7; Titus 2:13).[7]

Finally, perhaps the strongest objection to Pauline authorship is that the author of Hebrews counts himself among those who had received the gospel secondhand; he says the good news was "announced originally through the Lord, [and] was confirmed for us by those who had heard" (Heb 2:3). This is in sharp contrast with Paul, who considered the chief credential of his apostleship to be the fact that he had received the gospel directly from the risen Lord: "I did not receive it from a human being, nor was I taught it, but it came through a revelation of Jesus Christ" (Gal 1:12).

Who Else Might Have Written Hebrews?

Other candidates that have been proposed include Luke, Barnabas, Silas, Apollos, Priscilla, and Clement of Rome. But each of these suggestions runs into problems. Luke's writing is only superficially similar to Hebrews, and it is highly unlikely that the author of Hebrews was a Gentile, as Luke was. There is no evidence that Barnabas was a writer, or even an eloquent preacher (see Acts 14:12). It is doubtful that either he or Silas, leaders in the early Jerusalem church (Acts 4:36; 15:22), would have had the advanced training in Greek †rhetoric that

---

7. See Milligan, *Hebrews*, 199.

the author of Hebrews evidently had. The Priscilla theory runs into difficulties at Hebrews 11:32, where the author refers to himself using a masculine participle. Clement lacks the theological profundity of Hebrews and views the priesthood and the relationship of the Old and New Testaments differently.

Among these guesses, Apollos has perhaps the greatest claim to plausibility. Luke tells us that Apollos was a Jew from Alexandria, "an eloquent speaker, . . . an authority on the scriptures . . . with ardent spirit," who spoke "boldly" (Acts 18:24–26)—all qualities that match the Letter to the Hebrews. Alexandria was home to the kind of Jewish Platonism exemplified by the first-century philosopher Philo, to which Hebrews has some resemblances. Apollos argued vigorously from the Scriptures that the Messiah is Jesus (Acts 18:28), which is just what Hebrews does. Apollos was known to Paul yet independent of him (1 Cor 3:4) and was likely acquainted with Timothy, who is mentioned in Hebrews 13:23 (1 Cor 16:10–12). Hebrews' unusual reference to "baptisms" in the plural (Heb 6:2) could be explained by Apollos at first knowing only the baptism of John, then being more fully instructed in Christian baptism (Acts 18:25–26). But despite all these intriguing points of contact, the Apollos theory remains speculative. The complete absence of any confirming tradition counts against it. Unfortunately, we have no known writings of Apollos with which to compare Hebrews, as we have for Paul and Clement.

Despite our natural curiosity, and despite nearly two millennia of diligent scholarly detective work, the writer to the Hebrews has managed to keep his desired anonymity. We are not really any closer to an answer than was Origen, who famously wrote in the third century, "As to who actually wrote the epistle, God knows the truth of the matter."[8]

Destination

Hebrews ends like a letter (13:22–25), but it does not begin like one.[9] It lacks the customary greeting of an ancient letter, naming the sender, the recipients, and their location. But the heading "To the Hebrews" appears above it on the oldest surviving copy, dating to around AD 200,[10] and nearly all subsequent copies. This label was probably added by an early scribe because the letter was

---

8. Quoted from Origin's homilies on Hebrews (which have not survived) in Eusebius, *Ecclesiastical History* 6.25.14.

9. Bruce, *Hebrews*, 3. This is the reverse of the Letter of James, which begins but does not end like a letter. Likewise, the First Letter of John lacks both an epistolary beginning and ending.

10. This priceless artifact of early Christianity, Papyrus 46, contains the Letters of Paul, with Hebrews placed between Romans and 1 Corinthians. Today most of the Hebrews portion is housed in the University of Michigan library.

evidently written for a community of Jewish Christians. However, it is unlikely that they were "Hebrews" in the usual New Testament sense (Acts 6:1; Phil 3:5)—that is, Jewish Christians who spoke Hebrew (or †Aramaic) as opposed to "†Hellenists," Jewish Christians who were raised outside Palestine and whose mother tongue was Greek. This letter was clearly written for those who used the †Septuagint and who could appreciate sophisticated Greek rhetoric and figures of speech. Ironically, the Letter to the Hebrews could more accurately be called the Homily to the Hellenists.

A few hints about the identity of the recipients can be gleaned from the letter. They were Jewish Christians who formed a definite community or local church (see 13:17). Some scholars have proposed that they were Gentiles, but this suggestion is unconvincing, given the Jewish premises on which the whole argument is based and the intimate familiarity with Jewish rituals and customs that is assumed throughout.[11] Others have suggested that they had been influenced by the Essenes, the Jewish sect that produced the Dead Sea Scrolls at Qumran, which is possible but not provable.[12] Although they had been Christian for some years (10:32), they had not yet come to the maturity that could be expected; they needed "milk, [and] not solid food" (5:12–14). However, they were generous and hospitable (6:10). In the past they had experienced severe persecution (10:32–34), but not to the point of martyrdom (12:4). Most significantly for the author, they had become slack in their Christian commitment and were in danger of falling away from Christ (2:1; 3:12; 4:11; 10:35; 13:9). They seem to have been tempted to revert to the Old Testament way of relating to God, centered on the temple sacrifices.

As for the location of the community, the two best possibilities are Jerusalem or Rome. Other proposals include Alexandria, Caesarea, Antioch, Ephesus, and Colossae.

Jerusalem?

Some scholars have focused on Jerusalem or another locale in Palestine as the most likely place to find the deep attachment to the Jewish sacrificial rites that Hebrews presumes. It is also the most likely site for a fully Jewish church, rather than the mixed Jewish-Gentile churches that Paul had founded throughout the empire.

On the other hand, it is hard to imagine how a Hellenist like the author of Hebrews could write to the mother church at Jerusalem with as much authority

11. See Bruce, *Hebrews*, 5–6.
12. Ibid., 7–8.

Fig. 1. Possible locations of the community addressed in Hebrews

as he does (see 5:12; 13:17). It is even harder to see why he would write in Greek.[13] Besides, the Jerusalem church did in fact have members who had "resisted to the point of shedding blood" (12:4): namely, Stephen and James (Acts 7:58–60; 12:2). Even several decades after Jesus' ascension, it also surely had members who had heard the gospel from the Lord in person and not only through the testimony of others (see 2:3). Finally, Hebrews assumes knowledge of the sacrificial rites but not firsthand familiarity with the temple (in contrast, for instance, to Stephen's speech in Acts 7); it says much about the wilderness tabernacle but never actually mentions the temple.

Rome?

The majority of scholars locate the community in Rome or elsewhere in Italy. This would make good sense of the note at the end of the letter: "Those from Italy send you greetings" (13:24). This note could mean the author is writing *from* Italy, but more naturally it means he is writing *to* Italy from some other place where there are Italian Christians who want to greet their compatriots. The earliest known quotation from Hebrews appears in the letter known as

---

13. The letter seems to be addressed to a Greek-speaking church, but according to Acts 6, Hebrews and Hellenists were closely intermingled in the Jerusalem church.

1 Clement, which comes from Rome. The Roman church did experience horrific persecution under Emperor Nero in AD 64. However, the remark that "you have not yet resisted to the shedding of blood" would hardly fit those who had lived through that bloodbath; thus it is likely that Hebrews was written to Rome only if it was written prior to AD 64. The "great contest of suffering" (10:32) could then refer to bitter opposition from fellow Jews or to the expulsion of Jews from Rome by Emperor Claudius in AD 49 (see Acts 18:2), which may have been due to inter-Jewish strife over the spread of Christianity.[14]

On the other hand, the Roman church was a mixed Jewish-Gentile community, whereas Hebrews seems to be addressed to a purely Jewish church. It is possible, however, that there was a smaller Jewish Christian community at Rome, perhaps founded by the "travelers from Rome" who were among the crowd when the Spirit descended at Pentecost, who heard Peter's speech and were baptized (Acts 2:10, 41). In the end, Rome remains the best hypothesis but far from proven.

Date

Some scholars hold that Hebrews was written in the 80s or 90s, but the evidence better fits a date before the calamity of AD 70, when Roman armies utterly demolished Jerusalem and killed or enslaved hundreds of thousands of Jews. In several places the author writes of the †levitical priestly ministry as if it were still going on: "Every priest stands daily at his ministry, offering frequently those same sacrifices that can never take away sins" (10:11; see 9:6–9; 10:1–3). It is possible that this is a "literary present tense" to make the Old Testament more vivid.[15] However, the whole argument of Hebrews "is better adapted to the state of mind which would exist before, rather than after, the overthrow of Jewish national hopes and expectations in the terrible catastrophe of 70 AD."[16] Moreover, the author writes that the old covenant is close to disappearing but has not yet vanished away (8:13), wording that would makes less sense after AD 70.

If the Rome hypothesis is correct, then the letter was almost certainly written between the expulsion of Jews in AD 49 and the persecution under Nero in AD 64. Since the author speaks of their former sufferings as long past (10:32), a

---

14. The second-century Roman historian Suetonius wrote that the expulsion was due to "disturbances at the instigation of Chrestus" (*Life of Claudius* 25). "Chrestus" is probably a misspelling of "Christus," the Latin name for Christ.

15. Clement of Rome and Justin Martyr, for instance, wrote in the present tense of temple activities long after the temple was gone.

16. Milligan, *Hebrews*, 51.

date closer to the latter is more likely. In the early to mid-60s it would not have required any special foresight to see further persecution looming on the horizon. It is also likely that the author knew of Jesus' prophecy of the destruction of the temple (Matt 24:1–2; Mark 13:1–2; Luke 19:44). Perhaps he even took note of the approaching fortieth year since the Lord's passion around AD 30 and saw a spiritual connection between that time period and the Israelites' forty years of testing in the wilderness (3:10, 17; see comments on 3:9–10).

Literary Form and Features

Hebrews is clearly a composition intended for oral delivery.[17] The author himself calls it a "word of exhortation" (13:22 NRSV)—the same term used for a synagogue sermon by Paul in Acts 13:15.[18] Hebrews nearly always uses verbs for speaking and hearing rather than writing: "About this we have much to say . . . you have become sluggish in hearing" (5:11); "What more shall I say?" (11:32; see 6:9; 8:1). The preacher alternates between doctrine and moral exhortation in a way masterfully designed to hold listeners' attention and drives his points home with colorful metaphors and word pictures. His intention may have been that the letter be read aloud by a skilled orator in the church to which it was sent. The homily would have taken about forty-five minutes to deliver orally.

Besides containing the finest Greek in the entire Bible,[19] Hebrews has the richest vocabulary—1,038 different words, of which 154 are not found elsewhere in the New Testament and 10 are not found anywhere in prior Greek literature.[20] Hebrews also employs an impressive array of literary devices, most of which are, unfortunately, invisible to those reading it in translation. An incomplete list includes alliteration (repeating initial letters: 1:1; 4:16; 11:17), assonance (repeating vowel sounds for near-rhymes: 5:8; 6:20), anaphora (repeating a word in successive sentences: chapter 11), antithesis (contrasting opposites: 7:23–24), †chiasm (repeating elements in reverse sequence: 2:18; 13:4), paranomasia (wordplay: 5:8; 7:9; 9:16), litotes (understatement using a double negative: 6:10; 11:16), and rhetorical questions (1:5, 13–14; 2:2–3).[21]

17. This commentary will, accordingly, refer to "the author" and "the preacher" interchangeably.
18. The Greek phrase is the same in both passages (*logos tēs paraklēseōs*), but the NAB translates it as "message of encouragement" in Heb 13:22.
19. See Ben Witherington III, *Letters and Homilies for Jewish Christians: A Socio-Rhetorical Commentary on Hebrews, James and Jude* (Downers Grove, IL: IVP Academic, 2007), 39.
20. Paul Ellingworth, *The Epistle to the Hebrews: A Commentary on the Greek Text*, New International Greek Testament Commentary (Grand Rapids: Eerdmans, 1993), 12–13.
21. See Harold W. Attridge, *The Epistle to the Hebrews: A Commentary on the Epistle to the Hebrews*, ed. Helmut Koester, Hermeneia (Philadelphia: Fortress, 1989), 20–21; Johnson, *Hebrews*, 8.

Structure

There is little agreement on the overall structure of Hebrews; in fact, there are almost as many proposed outlines as there are commentators.[22] Because ancient Greek writing did not include section headings, chapter or verse numbers, or even punctuation, it is often very difficult to decide where one section ends and another begins. In fact, it is a mistake to divide sections too sharply, since our author often uses a bridge passage to serve as both the conclusion of one section and the beginning of another. Moreover, he does not develop his argument in the way we are used to, proceeding in orderly steps from A to B to C. His logic is, rather, spiral. He returns to the same themes again and again, each time with a slightly different emphasis and at a deeper level. For instance, he first introduces the revolutionary idea that Jesus is a high priest at 2:17–3:1, then returns to it at 4:14–16 and again at 5:10, and finally develops it in depth in chapters 7–10. And he continually alternates theological discourse with practical exhortations that remind readers how doctrine must be applied to life.

Like every early Christian homily, Hebrews is essentially a work of biblical interpretation. Passages from the Old Testament are the pillars on which the author builds his whole argument concerning the glorious majesty and atoning work of Christ. Seven primary reflections on biblical passages (interwoven with other quotations or allusions that amplify their meaning) provide the basic structure:[23]

Heb 1:5–2:4	"You are my son. . . . Sit at my right hand"	A chain of passages framed by Ps 2:7 and Ps 110:1
Heb 2:5–18	"What is man that you are mindful of him . . . ?"	Ps 8:4–6
Heb 3–4	"Oh, that today you would hear his voice"	Ps 95:7–11
Heb 5–7	"You are a priest forever"	Ps 110:4
Heb 8–10	"I will conclude a new covenant"	Jer 31:31–34
Heb 11	"My just one shall live by faith" (Heb 10:38)	Hab 2:2–4
Heb 12–13	"Do not lose heart when reproved by him"	Prov 3:11

All but the last three of these passages are from the Psalms. For Hebrews, the Psalms are pivotal in God's unfolding revelation: originating in the time

22. Johnson (*Hebrews*, 11–15) describes three general approaches to outlining Hebrews: the topical approach, which merely lists topics in order; the †chiastic approach (exemplified by Albert Vanhoye), which views the composition as forming concentric circles around a central point; and the rhetorical approach (taken by Johnson), which views Hebrews as an argument structured according to the rules of classical rhetoric.

23. This structure is adapted in part from William L. Lane, *Hebrews 1–8*, Word Biblical Commentary 47A (Nashville: Thomas Nelson, 1991), cxiv–cxv, based on a paper by J. Walters; and Richard N. Longenecker, *Biblical Exegesis in the Apostolic Period* (Grand Rapids: Eerdmans, 1999), 156. For a more detailed outline, see "Outline of Hebrews," which follows this introduction.

of David, they both hint at the incompleteness of what God had done earlier through Moses and point forward to God's ultimate purposes in Christ.

Theological Themes

As a theologian the author of Hebrews is remarkably original and bold. Whereas for other New Testament authors the primary biblical prototype for our salvation is the exodus (the source of key themes like redemption, ransom, deliverance from slavery into freedom, lamb of God), Hebrews views salvation from the perspective of the Jewish solemnity of †Yom Kippur, the Day of Atonement, when the high priest would enter into the †Holy of Holies, making †atonement for sins by sprinkling the blood of a sacrificed bull and goat. Whereas other New Testament writings speak of Jesus as Messiah-King (like David and Solomon of old), a redeemer and lawgiver (like Moses), and the founder of a new humanity (like Adam),[24] Hebrews speaks of Jesus as the *high priest* (like Aaron) who offers †sacrifice to God to expiate the sins of the people.

Brief as it is, this homily-within-a-letter has made an incalculable contribution to the Christian understanding of Jesus, his †paschal mystery, and the Church. The major themes developed in Hebrews can be summarized under the following headings.

Jesus Our High Priest

Among the New Testament books, Hebrews is unique in calling Christ a priest.[25] It is not hard to see why no other New Testament author uses this term for Christ. In a Jewish context, "priest" meant something very specific: a descendant of Aaron who offered animal sacrifices in the Jerusalem temple in accord with the Mosaic law. Obviously, Jesus fit none of those characteristics. In a Gentile context, "priest" denoted pagan priests who sacrificed to idols, even further removed from Jesus' identity and role. But through an inspired interpretation of Psalm 110, Hebrews shows how Christ is indeed high priest in a way that fulfills and infinitely surpasses the †levitical priesthood. He ministers not in the earthly temple but in God's heavenly sanctuary (8:1–2). He is the priest who uniquely offers *himself* in sacrifice—both the offerer and the offering, priest and victim. Because he perfectly fulfilled God's will and was raised up to indestructible life, his sacrifice never needs to be repeated (7:16;

---

24. See, for instance, Matt 27:37; John 1:41, 49; Gal 4:5; Titus 2:14; Rom 5:14; 1 Cor 15:45.
25. The Greek term is *hiereus*, used in the Septuagint to translate the Hebrew *kohen*.

9:12; 10:10). It is the single, once-for-all sacrifice that cleanses God's people of sin and makes us worthy to be in his presence forever.

Solidarity with Sinners

Hebrews exalts the divinity of Christ in the highest terms possible.[26] He is the eternal Son through whom God created the universe, the radiance of God's glory, the heir of all things who sustains the whole universe in being (1:2–3), the divine king whose throne stands forever (1:8). Yet at the same time Hebrews emphasizes Christ's radical solidarity with those he came to save. He "had to become like his brothers in every way, that he might be a merciful and faithful high priest" (2:17). He shared our human frailty, though without sin: he experienced temptation (2:18; 4:15), suffering with cries and tears (5:7–8), insult (11:26), and death (2:9). Hebrews even makes the extraordinary statement that the eternal Son "learned obedience from what he suffered" (5:8). Jesus is able to be a high priest full of *com-passion* because he has literally *suffered with* us. He comes to our side in times of trial as one who knows our human experience from within.

Because of his identity as both God and man, Jesus alone is qualified to be a priest in the fullest sense: he is the perfect mediator, able to represent God to man and man to God. He is therefore the mediator of the new and everlasting †covenant (8:8–13), which overcomes the failures of the former covenant and gives God's people access to all the blessings promised by God.

The Power of Christ's Death

At the heart of the message of Hebrews is the explosive power that flows from the event at the center of all history: Jesus' self-offering on the cross. Hebrews conveys this central truth through a multipronged contrast with the Jewish sacrificial rites. Because those former rites deal only with ritual purification, they "cannot perfect the worshiper in conscience but only in matters of food and drink and various ritual washings" (9:9–10). The fact that the priests continued to perform these rites year after year (9:6) showed that they had no lasting effect. The history of Israel only confirmed that animal sacrifices were powerless to overcome the evil that perpetually rises up within the human heart (10:4).

Jesus, in contrast, offered not a helpless animal but *himself* (9:14), his own life freely laid down in obedience to God—a gift of infinitely greater value than

---

26. New Testament texts comparable to Heb 1 are the prologue of the Gospel of John (1:1–18) and the Christ hymn of Col 1:15–20 (see also Eph 1:20–23; Phil 2:6–11).

animal sacrifices. Through his agonizing passion and death, he offered the Father the limitless love, trust, and obedience that God deserved but had never received from humanity (10:6–7). In passing through death to divine glory, his human nature was "perfected"—transformed by divine life—and so also the human nature of the "many children" whom he is bringing to glory (2:10; 7:28; 10:14).

Hebrews affirms that by Christ's passion those who share in him have been changed from within (10:22), radically and permanently. This means that the Christian life does not consist in acquiring a holiness we do not have, but rather in appropriating and more deeply living the holiness we have already been given (10:10). So we are invited to a relationship with God that is filled with confident hope and free from the burden of guilt and sin. Our whole life is qualified to be a priestly life, in which all our actions and sufferings are offered as "a sacrifice of praise" that is pleasing to God (13:15–16).

Old and New

For Hebrews, as for the early Church in general, the deepest meaning of the Old Testament is found in Christ. Not only the prophecies but also the laws, rituals, prayers, persons, saving events, and †eschatological hopes of Israel all point forward to the glorious culmination of God's plan in Christ. This is not a matter of ignoring the literal sense of the text but of going beyond it to the ultimate intention of the divine Author. The old covenant with its great institutions of †Torah and temple was a marvelous gift from God. But now in the radiant light of Christ all that belongs to the former age is seen as preparatory and provisional, an anticipation pointing forward to the full consummation.

Hebrews expresses the relation between the old and new by proclaiming in a myriad of ways that what we possess in Christ is "greater" or "more" than what came before. Jesus is worthy of more glory than Moses (3:3); he passed through a greater tabernacle (9:11); his blood speaks more eloquently than that of Abel and purifies us much more than the blood of goats and bulls (9:13–14; 12:24). We have better things related to salvation (6:9), a better covenant enacted on better promises (7:22; 8:6), a better hope, sanctuary, homeland, and resurrection (7:19; 9:24; 11:16, 35).

To say all this is not to break with the Old Testament, since as Hebrews points out, the Old Testament itself asserts its own incomplete status and foretells something better.[27] If Joshua had given the Israelites rest, God would not

---

27. See James Thompson, "The New Is Better: A Neglected Aspect of the Hermeneutics of Hebrews," *Catholic Biblical Quarterly* 73 (2011): 547–61.

have spoken afterward of another rest (4:8). If perfection had come through the levitical priesthood, Scripture would not have foretold another priest (7:11). If the first covenant had been faultless, there would have been no promise of a second (8:7). Before Christ came, Israel's history was something of an unfinished puzzle, an unsolved conundrum. Now, in Christ, God has fully revealed his purposes, and all history can be recognized as one great plan of salvation.

Hebrews' way of reading the Old Testament is known as †typological interpretation: the former things are understood as †types, or prototypes, that foreshadow Christ and the realities of the new covenant. This approach, which is common to all the New Testament authors, is sometimes compared with that of Philo of Alexandria, a near contemporary. But there is a radical difference between the two. Whereas Philo sees biblical characters and events as allegories representing timeless, abstract ideas, Hebrews sees them as part of a divine plan in which God's earlier deeds foreshadow his greater acts in the fullness of time.[28] For Hebrews, the old covenant types point both *forward* in time to Christ and *upward* to transcendent divine realities. A good illustration of the difference is the way Philo and Hebrews interpret the priest Melchizedek (see Gen 14:18–20). For Philo, Melchizedek represents Reason, an abstract ideal.[29] For Hebrews, Melchizedek prefigures Jesus Christ, the great high priest who has entered into God's true sanctuary in heaven.

The Pilgrim Church

Hebrews provides unique insights into the Church, especially around the theme of pilgrimage. A pilgrim is someone on a journey toward a sacred place. Although Hebrews never uses the word "pilgrim," it powerfully conveys a vision of God's people as pilgrims traveling toward the holy city, the heavenly Jerusalem.[30] In chapters 3–4 Hebrews invites Christians to identify with the Israelites journeying through the desert toward the promised land. It constantly portrays the Christian life as dynamic, a life in movement. We are to approach the throne of grace (4:16; 10:22), persevere in running the race (12:1), make straight paths (12:13), come to Mount Zion (12:22), and go to Jesus (13:13). And we are warned not to drift away (2:1), fall away (3:12), be carried away (13:9), or be weary or lame (12:12–13). The key qualities that are needed for such a journey are *faith* and *endurance*, to which we are exhorted throughout

---

28. Bruce, *Hebrews*, 27–28; Longenecker, *Biblical Exegesis*, 153–55.
29. Philo, *Allegorical Interpretation* 3.82.
30. See Johnson, *Hebrews*, 9.

the letter but especially in chapters 11–12. Hebrews is thus a primary source of a theme that is prominent in the documents of Vatican Council II, especially *Lumen Gentium*: the Church as a pilgrim people, always in movement, having not yet arrived at our heavenly destination.[31]

Drawing Near to God

Among the many exhortations in Hebrews, two verbs stand out: *draw near* (or approach, 4:16; 7:25; 10:22; 11:6) and *enter in* to God's presence (4:11; 6:19–20; see 10:19). These terms may not convey much to us, but for Jews steeped in Scripture they were extraordinary. The Old Testament emphasizes the radical inability of sinful human beings to draw near and enter God's holy presence. Ever since the fall, when Adam and Eve were banished from the garden where they had walked with God (Gen 3:23), sin had remained a barrier that blocked access to God (see Isa 59:2). Through Abraham, and later Moses, God initiated a relationship with his people and made his dwelling place in their midst. Yet part of the role of priests and Levites who ministered at the †sanctuary was to insure that the Israelites *not* draw too near to God (Exod 19:12; Num 1:51–53). Only the high priest would dare enter into God's presence, and he only once a year. Yet Israel's worship instilled a deep longing for God's presence, as the Psalms attest: "My soul yearns and pines / for the courts of the LORD. / My heart and flesh cry out / for the living God" (Ps 84:3; see also Ps 27:4). In light of this background, the appeals of Hebrews take on new significance. Jesus has overcome the barrier between God and man, not by diminishing the holiness of God but by removing sin from sinners. This is why we are invited to draw near with the confidence of children approaching their heavenly Father, knowing we have been totally cleansed by the blood of Jesus and may ask for whatever we need (4:16; 10:19).

Hebrews for Today

Hebrews was written to a community of Christians who were struggling. They had had times of fervor in the past but had become discouraged in the midst of a hostile culture with the threat of further persecution. Some had stopped regularly attending the †liturgy, and some were even tempted to abandon the faith. As readers will recognize, this situation is not unlike that of the Church in the Western world today. In such times, the message of Hebrews is both

---

31. See sections 7, 21, 48–50.

bracing and encouraging. Hold fast to your faith in Christ! Do not throw away your confidence; it will have great reward (3:6, 14; 10:35). Do not be among those who draw back and perish (10:39). Do not grow weary, but keep your eyes fixed on Jesus, the leader and perfecter of faith (12:1–2).

More than any other book of the New Testament, Hebrews makes us aware of the unlimited efficacy of Christ's death on the cross, the once-for-all sacrifice that is continually made present to us anew in the Eucharist (13:10). In that act of love, Jesus reversed the whole history of human sin and rebellion against God. He destroyed the power of the devil and freed "those who through fear of death had been subject to slavery all their life" (2:14–15). He sanctified and "made perfect forever" those who believe in him (10:10, 14), opened the "new and living way" for us to enter into God's presence (10:20), and made us heirs of an "unshakable kingdom" (12:28). He equipped us with everything we need to do what is pleasing to God (13:21). To read and study Hebrews prayerfully is to have one's life transformed by entering into the reality of these gifts that are already ours. We are then strengthened to respond in the exemplary way that Hebrews sums up in 10:19–25: draw near to God with a sincere heart and absolute trust, hold unwaveringly to our confession in Christ, rouse one another to love and good works, participate in the liturgy and Christian fellowship, and encourage one another as the day of the Lord draws near.

Outline of Hebrews

Prologue: God has spoken to us through the Son (1:1–4)

   I. "You are my son. . . . Sit at my right hand" (1:5–2:4)

      A. The Son's superiority to the angels (1:5–14)

      B. Exhortation to pay heed (2:1–4)

  II. "What is man that you are mindful of him?" (2:5–18)

      A. The Son's self-abasement lower than the angels (2:5–9)

      B. The Son's solidarity with weak humanity (2:10–18)

 III. "Oh, that today you would hear his voice" (3:1–4:13)

      A. Warning not to harden your hearts (3:1–19)

      B. Exhortation to enter God's rest (4:1–11)

      C. God's living and effective word (4:12–13)

 IV. "You are a priest forever" (4:14–7:28)

      A. Jesus the compassionate high priest (4:14–16)

      B. Jesus appointed to the order of Melchizedek (5:1–10)

      C. Exhortation to grow to maturity (5:11–6:12)

      D. Exhortation to trust God's unchangeable promise and oath (6:13–20)

      E. Melchizedek superior to Levi (7:1–10)

      F. Jesus the high priest forever (7:11–28)

  V. "I will conclude a new covenant" (8:1–10:18)

      A. The earthly tabernacle and the true tabernacle in heaven (8:1–6)

      B. The failed old covenant and the promise of the new (8:7–13)

      C. The powerless rites of the old covenant and tabernacle (9:1–10)

      D. The power of Christ's blood (9:11–14)

      E. The covenant renewed and fulfilled (9:15–22)

F. Christ's all-sufficient sacrifice in the true tabernacle (9:23–28)

G. Christ's perfect fulfillment of God's will (10:1–10)

H. Christ's followers made perfect forever (10:11–18)

VI. "My just one shall live by faith" (10:19–11:40)

A. Exhortation to confidence, faith, and fervor (10:19–25)

B. Warning not to fall away (10:26–31)

C. Exhortation to endurance (10:32–39)

D. Old covenant heroes who lived by faith (11:1–40)

VII. "Do not lose heart" (12:1–13:21)

A. Exhortation to endurance (12:1–13)

B. Warning not to be unfaithful to the grace of God (12:14–29)

C. Exhortation to offer sacrifices pleasing to God (13:1–19)

D. Blessing (13:20–21)

Epistolary ending (13:22–25)

God's Final Word

Hebrews 1:1–4

Hebrews opens with a magnificent prologue (1:1–4) that elegantly sums up the key themes of the homily. In Greek the prologue is a single long sentence, containing some of the most refined Greek in the New Testament. It sets forth the plan of God in two stages: the past, in which God spoke to his people Israel in partial and piecemeal ways; and the present, in which he has spoken his final and definitive word through his Son. The Son is the center of the whole plan of salvation, the key that unlocks the meaning of all that God has done until now. In seven phrases the prologue describes the Son's divine majesty, his work of redemption, and his glorious exaltation. But surprisingly, he is not named. Every Christian reader of Hebrews knows well who is being described, but we have to wait until 2:9 for the first mention of his name, Jesus.

The prologue hints at three exalted roles of the Son that will be further explained in the letter. First, he is the *prophet* surpassing all other prophets, through whom God speaks his final and definitive word (v. 2). Second, he is a *priest* in that he accomplished the priestly ministry of cleansing God's people from sins (v. 3). Finally, he is *king* in that he takes up his throne at God's right hand, the place of highest royal authority (v. 3).[1] These prerogatives show that the Son is infinitely superior to the angels, the highest-ranking creatures (v. 4). For readers today who have inherited two millennia of Christian teaching, it

---

1. For an exposition of the inner unity of Christ's role as priest and king and his identity as firstborn Son in Hebrews, see Scott Hahn, *Kinship by Covenant: A Canonical Approach to the Fulfillment of God's Promises*, Anchor Yale Bible Reference Library (New Haven: Yale University Press, 2009), 278–79.

is easy to overlook how astounding these statements are. Hebrews is speaking of Jesus of Nazareth, a Jewish rabbi from Galilee who had suffered a Roman criminal execution only a few decades before—and it ascribes to him a role in the creation of the universe![2]

God Has Spoken through His Son (1:1–4)

[1]In times past, God spoke in partial and various ways to our ancestors through the prophets; [2]in these last days, he spoke to us through a son, whom he made heir of all things and through whom he created the universe,

[3]who is the refulgence of his glory,
the very imprint of his being,
and who sustains all things by his mighty word.
When he had accomplished purification from sins,
he took his seat at the right hand of the Majesty on high,
[4]as far superior to the angels
as the name he has inherited is more excellent than theirs.

OT: Ps 2:8; 110:1
NT: Matt 22:44; John 1:3; 2 Cor 4:4; Eph 1:20–21; Phil 2:9; Col 1:15–16
Catechism: God's one single word, 65–66, 101–4, 241; Jesus at God's right hand, 659–67
Lectionary: 1:1–6: Christmas Mass during the Day

1:1   The prologue begins with a dramatic claim: all God's **past** revelation, and indeed all history, have come to their culmination. History is now divided in two: the former age, in which **God spoke** in fragmentary and varied ways (the old †covenant), and the final time, in which he has spoken once and for all in his Son (the new covenant). In drawing this contrast, Hebrews affirms two truths that will be foundational for the whole letter. First, God's revelation of himself to his people Israel was a wonderful and unique privilege. The very fact that God, the creator of the universe, took the initiative to speak with human beings evokes awe and gratitude. But second, what God has now done in Christ infinitely surpasses what he had done before. All his previous revelation was a preliminary stage in the plan, marvelous in itself but imperfect, like a series of Rembrandt sketches that depict the subject in rough outline, only as preparation for the magnificent full-color painting.

2. Luke Timothy Johnson, *Hebrews: A Commentary*, New Testament Library (Louisville: Westminster John Knox, 2006), 68.

The theme of God *speaking* will run like a thread through Hebrews. When introducing biblical quotations, instead of saying "it is written," Hebrews will invariably use phrases like "God says" or "he has promised."[3] Scripture is not confined to the dusty pages of ancient manuscripts; it is a living and active word through which God continues to speak, addressing his people personally here and now (see 3:7; 4:12).

The Greek word for **ancestors** is literally "fathers," referring to both the †patriarchs of Israel and all generations of Israelite men and women, whom not only Jews but also Gentile Christians can count as their spiritual ancestors (see 1 Cor 10:1). By using this familial term, Hebrews introduces the theme of the family of God into which all believers are welcomed (see 2:11–12, 17; 12:7–9). "Our fathers" also reaffirms the continuity between the old covenant and the new: it is the same God who speaks, and the same people of God, Israel and now the Church, who are addressed by him.

Throughout salvation history God revealed himself **through the prophets**, including Abraham, Moses, and the writing prophets like Isaiah and Jeremiah. But this revelation was given **in partial and various ways**. It came in a variety of forms—through oracles, dreams, visions, prophetic gestures, signs, and miracles. Each prophet had certain unique insights into God's character and plan. Hosea, for instance, understood God's spousal love for his people; Isaiah had a profound awareness of God's holiness; Jeremiah foresaw the new covenant that God would establish.[4] But each prophet's knowledge was incomplete; each grasped only a part of divine revelation. The Son, in contrast, *is* that revelation in its fullness. The superiority of Christ does not diminish esteem for the former covenant; in fact, it enhances it, because now we see how carefully and patiently God had been preparing his people for his final gift.

The author calls the times in which he is writing **these last days**. This does **1:2** not mean that he mistakenly thought the world was about to end and Jesus would come in glory within a few short days or years. Rather, he is drawing on the biblical theme of the "last days" (Isa 2:2; Hosea 3:5; Dan 10:14)—the time when God would decisively intervene in history to restore the fortunes of his people and bring his plan to completion. Hebrews, like the rest of the New Testament, proclaims that with the coming of Christ the last days have arrived—the final stage of salvation history, in which all God's promises find their fulfillment.

3. See, for instance, 1:5, 6; 2:12; 3:15; 4:3; 5:5; 6:13–14; 8:8; 10:15; 12:26.
4. See William Barclay, *The Letter to the Hebrews*, rev. ed., Daily Study Bible Series (Philadelphia: Westminster, 1976), 13.

That Christ is **a son** places him in an entirely different category from the prophets, who were God's servants and messengers.[5] Hebrews wants to ensure that "son of God" is understood in the highest theological sense, since the term could mean various things in a biblical context. In the Old Testament the people of Israel collectively were designated God's son, or God's children (Exod 4:22; Deut 14:1; Hosea 11:1). The king of Israel was understood to be God's son by adoption (2 Sam 7:12–14; Ps 89:27–28). And the angels, members of the heavenly court, were called "sons of God" (Job 1:6; Ps 29:1; 89:7). But Christ's sonship is utterly unique, and Hebrews will now show how this is so in seven clauses, each spelling out a distinct aspect of the Son's nature and work.[6]

The first clause asserts that the Son has been **made** (or "appointed," RSV) **heir of all things**. In the ancient world as now, being a son is equivalent to being an heir (see Gal 4:7); sons could expect to inherit a share of their father's property. This phrase echoes a promise made in Psalm 2, a royal psalm that together with Psalm 110 will play a key role throughout the letter. In Psalm 2:8 God says to the king descended from David, "Ask it of me, / and I will give you the nations as your inheritance, / and, as your possession, the ends of the earth." This promise comes right after the declaration that the king is God's son (Ps 2:7). Hebrews proclaims that the promise is now superabundantly fulfilled in Jesus, who has inherited not just an earthly territory but the entire created universe. As will later become clear, Christ's followers will share in his inheritance (6:12; 9:15; see Rom 8:17), participating in his kingly rule over all creation (see Matt 25:34).

When did the Son receive this inheritance? Although the author does not say explicitly, he is probably referring to Jesus' resurrection and ascension to the Father's right hand (see v. 3). The risen Jesus has, in his humanity, been exalted as Lord over all (see Phil 2:9–11).

The second clause moves backward in time, from the end to the beginning: through him God **created the universe** (literally, "the ages"). The Son is the Omega, the heir of all things at the end, because he is the Alpha, the one through whom all things were created in the beginning.[7] This statement echoes Old Testament texts that depict God's Wisdom as present with him in the beginning and playing a role in the creation of all things (Prov 8:22–31; Wis 8:3–6; Sir 24:1–12). The early Church identified God's Wisdom as the preexistent Christ:

5. A similar contrast between prophets (servants) and the Son is made by Jesus in the parable of the wicked tenants (Mark 12:2–6).

6. See John P. Meier, *The Mission of Christ and His Church: Studies in Christology and Ecclesiology*, Good News Studies 30 (Wilmington, DE: Michael Glazier, 1990), 75.

7. See ibid., 80.

Christian the Brightness of God's Glory

LIVING TRADITION

St. Gregory of Nyssa (c. 335–c. 395), like many other Church Fathers, found the prologue of Hebrews a powerful tool for combating heresies that denied the divinity of Christ. He wrote,

> As the radiance of light sheds its brilliance from the whole of the sun's disk . . . so too all the glory that the Father has is shed by means of the brightness that comes from it, that is, by [Christ] the true Light. Just as the ray is from the sun—for there would be no ray if there were no sun—so the sun does not exist by itself without the ray of brightness that is shed from it. So the apostle conveyed to us the continuity and eternity of the existence that the Only Begotten has from the Father, calling the Son "the brightness of God's glory."[a]

a. *Against Eunomius* 8.1 (translation adapted from ACCS 10).

"All things came to be through him, / and without him nothing came to be" (John 1:3; see 1 Cor 8:6; Col 1:16).

The third clause differs from the others in that it speaks not of Christ's work **1:3** in the created realm, but of his eternal divine nature. He is the **refulgence** (or "radiance," NIV) of God's **glory** and **the very imprint of his being**. Again Hebrews is borrowing language from the book of Wisdom (see Wis 7:26). God's "glory" is the visible manifestation of his awesome majesty. During the exodus it took the form of a luminous cloud, the sign of God's presence in the midst of his people (Exod 16:10; 24:17–18). At Christ's transfiguration it was manifest in the light radiating from his face, again in the midst of a cloud (Matt 17:2–5). Hebrews affirms that the Son *is* the radiance that shines forth eternally from the inner being of God; he is God made visible.

The word for "very imprint"[8] in Greek is *charaktēr*, which refers to the impression that a stamp or seal makes on a soft surface. In the ancient world, coins were made by stamping hot metal with a die on which a portrait had been engraved; the coin would bear the exact impression (*charaktēr*) of the die. The Son, then, is the exact representation of the Father. To see Jesus is to see exactly what God is like (see John 14:9; Col 1:15). In the fullest sense of the term, Jesus has the "character" of his Father.

From this point on in the prologue, the Son is the subject of the verbs—actions that further establish his divine status. The fourth clause returns to

8. Other possible translations are "stamp" (RSV), "exact imprint" (NRSV), "exact representation" (NIV), "impress" (NJB), "perfect copy" (JB).

the idea of creation: the Son **sustains all things by his mighty word**. That is, he continues at every moment to uphold all things in existence; the universe is entirely dependent on him. In the biblical view, creation is not a onetime event that occurred eons ago, in which God set things in motion and then left the world to its own devices. Rather, God continues to lovingly sustain and care for what he has made. As God created all things not by exerting effort but simply by a word (Gen 1), so the Son continues to hold all things in existence by the power of his word.

The fifth clause speaks for the first time of the event that is at the heart of the Letter to the Hebrews: Jesus' †sacrifice of himself on the cross. Here the cross is mentioned only obliquely, in terms that call to mind the Old Testament rite in which the high priest would sprinkle "the blood of purification of sins" on the altar (Exod 30:10 †LXX; see also Lev 16:19). That Jesus **accomplished purification from sins** also hints at a theme that Hebrews will later develop in full: Jesus is the great high priest who alone has brought about the total, once-for-all cleansing from sin that the earthly priests could not achieve (Heb 9:13–14).[9]

The sixth clause describes the final stage of Christ's redemptive work: after his passion and resurrection he **took his seat at the right hand of the Majesty on high**. The mention of God's "right hand" alludes to Psalm 110, which along with Psalm 2 will recur like a refrain throughout Hebrews.[10] In Psalm 110:1 God assures the Davidic king that he will enjoy divine protection and victory over his enemies: "Sit at my right hand, / while I make your enemies your footstool." God's right hand is not, of course, a physical location but rather the position of highest honor and authority. Jesus, in his trial before the Sanhedrin, had announced that this psalm is fulfilled in himself: "From this time on the Son of Man will be seated at the right hand of the power of God" (Luke 22:69). Hebrews will later show the significance of the fact that as high priest, Christ is *seated* rather than standing in the presence of God (10:11–14).

1:4   The prologue concludes by affirming the result of Jesus' enthronement: he has become **as far superior to the angels as the name he has inherited is more excellent than theirs**. This seventh and last clause introduces the theme of the next section of the letter (vv. 5–13): Jesus' superiority over the angels. But it raises two interpretive questions. First, how can the divine Son, the radiance of the Father's glory, *become* superior to the angels?[11] After all, they were created through him. Second, what is the name that he has inherited?

---

9. The same word "purification" (Greek *katharismos*) is often used in the Septuagint for the priestly work of atonement (Exod 29:36; 30:10) and ritual cleansing (Lev 14:32; see also Luke 2:22; 5:14).

10. Hebrews quotes or alludes to Ps 110 in 1:13; 5:6, 10; 6:20; 7:3, 11, 15, 17, 21; 8:1; 10:12.

11. The NAB omits the Greek participle "having become" (*genomenos*).

What's in a Name?

BIBLICAL BACKGROUND

In biblical tradition a name is not merely a label but the expression of a person's very identity—so much so that a change of name indicates a change in one's identity or destiny (Gen 17:5, 15; 32:29; Isa 62:2). God's name, then, is in a sense equivalent to God himself. The fact that God revealed his name to Israel, through Moses at the burning bush (Exod 3:15), was recognized as a marvelous privilege. It meant that God made himself accessible; he entered into a personal relationship with his people. The temple is the place where God's name—his very presence—dwelt among his people (Deut 12:11).

In 2 Samuel 7, a passage that is a backdrop for Hebrews 1, there is a play on the word "name." Through the prophet Nathan, God promised David "a great name" (v. 9 RSV), meaning lasting renown, and foretold that David's son would build "a house for my name" (v. 13)—that is, a temple in which God himself would be present. David then praised God by recounting how God had made "a name for himself" (v. 23 NRSV) through all the mighty deeds that he has done for Israel.

On one level, God's promise was fulfilled in the establishment of David's royal dynasty, beginning with his son Solomon, and Solomon's construction of the temple in Jerusalem (1 Kings 8:20; 9:3). But it is superabundantly fulfilled, according to Hebrews, in David's descendant Jesus, who at his ascension is enthroned as God's heir, inheriting God's own name and royal authority over the whole universe.

The first question will be answered in 2:7–9, which explains that by becoming man, the Son made himself "for a little while lower than the angels." In his incarnation he subjected himself to the lowliness and frailty of human nature; in his ascension to God's glory he has now been exalted *as man* over even the highest of heavenly beings.

The answer to the second question is based on the biblical mindset in which a name has great significance (see sidebar, "What's in a Name?"). A name is not merely a convenient label; it is the expression of a person's identity and role (Gen 27:36; Exod 2:10). Some scholars interpret the name Jesus has inherited as his title "Son" or "firstborn Son" (vv. 5–6). But it more likely refers to God's own divine name, †Yahweh, which he revealed to Moses at the burning bush (Exod 3:14–15; see also John 17:11–12). In the Greek Old Testament, "Yahweh" was translated as "the Lord."[12] Thus Hebrews is expressing in its own way the

---

12. Many English translations of the Old Testament put "the Lord" in small caps wherever it renders the Hebrew "†YHWH."

Church's earliest summary of the good news: "Jesus Christ is Lord" (Phil 2:10–11; see Rom 10:9). As man, Christ "inherited" this divine title at his resurrection and ascension to God's right hand.

Reflection and Application (1:1–4)

God spoke to us in a Son. As Christians, we are used to the idea that God has spoken—so much so that we can easily take it for granted. But the early Church never lost its amazement and wonder that the living God, the creator of heaven and earth, had stooped down to speak lovingly to his creatures. For first-century Jews, who regarded the age of the prophets as having ended four centuries previously (see 1 Macc 9:27), the Christian proclamation was all the more astonishing: God is speaking no longer through various messengers but now in the very person of his Son. As the Gospel of John expresses it, Jesus not only speaks the word of God, he *is* the Word of God (John 1:1)—the fullness of all that the Father has to say to us.

Two conclusions can be drawn from the fact that God has spoken to us in Jesus. First, because Jesus is alive, God continues to speak to us in him. As the Catechism says, "God, who spoke in the past, continues to converse with the Spouse of his beloved Son" (79, quoting *Dei Verbum* 8). He addresses both the Church as a whole and each of us personally: "In the sacred books, the Father who is in heaven meets his children with great love and speaks with them" (*Dei Verbum* 21). This may lead us to ask: How attentively do we listen to God's voice, especially as it comes to us in the Scriptures? Do we thirst for, study, reflect on, and treasure the word of God, as did the ancient Israelites (Ps 1:2–3; 19:8–12)?

Second, because God's word is divine, it has power. This is evident in the Gospels' portrayal of Jesus (see Luke 4:36). No one who encountered Jesus ever left his presence unchanged. They left no longer deaf, or leprous, or burdened with guilt, or dead; or they left conflicted (Matt 16:22), or pierced with conviction of sin (Luke 5:4–8), or fuming with rage because their hearts were hardened (Mark 3:1–6), or full of joy (Luke 19:37). If we keep this in mind as we study the Letter to the Hebrews, we will find it leading us into a life-transforming dialogue with the living God. Even when nothing seems to happen, if we are reading Scripture attentively and prayerfully, we are being changed. For "the word of God is living and effective, sharper than any two-edged sword, penetrating even between soul and spirit, joints and marrow, and able to discern reflections and thoughts of the heart" (Heb 4:12).

Far Superior to the Angels

Hebrews 1:5–14

The prologue of Hebrews gave one of the most exalted descriptions of Christ in the New Testament. In the next section (vv. 5–14) the author sets out to show that what he says about the Son is not a departure from God's previous revelation but is in full accord with it. As the prologue described the Son in seven clauses (vv. 2–4), this section provides scriptural support for those claims with seven Old Testament quotations. Such a string of related citations, known as a †catena (the Latin word for "chain"), was a common feature of biblical interpretation in the ancient world.[1]

The last line of the prologue set the stage for this new section by announcing that the Son is "far superior to the angels" and "the name he has inherited is more excellent than theirs" (v. 4). The seven biblical quotations elaborate on those statements, showing that Jesus' "name" (i.e., his identity) is none other than that of God himself: he is the Son (v. 5), God with God (vv. 8–9), creator of the universe and Lord (v. 10), seated in majesty at God's right hand (v. 13).[2] The first quotation is from Psalm 2, and the last is from Psalm 110—the two key psalms that anchor Hebrews' whole argument concerning Jesus' identity and role. Both are prefaced by a question, "To which of the angels did God ever say . . . ?" (vv. 5, 13), forming a frame that unites the whole section.

---

1. See, for instance, the Qumran documents *4QFlorilegium* and *4QTestimonia*. A New Testament example is Rom 3:10–18.
2. Albert Vanhoye, *A Different Priest: The Letter to the Hebrews*, trans. Leo Arnold, Series Rhetorica Semitica (Miami: Convivium, 2011), 26.

This section contains affirmations about Christ that may at first seem unfamiliar or abstract to Christians today. But these are crucial as the prelude to chapter 2, which emphasizes Jesus' humanity, his closeness to us as our friend and brother. It is only by first understanding Jesus' divine majesty as the eternal Son of the Father that we can fully grasp what it means that he has made himself one of us.

The Supremacy of the Son (1:5–6)

---

[5]For to which of the angels did God ever say:

> "You are my son; this day I have begotten you"?

Or again:

> "I will be a father to him, and he shall be a son to me"?

[6]And again, when he leads the first-born into the world, he says:

> "Let all the angels of God worship him."

OT: Ps 2:7; 2 Sam 7:14; Deut 32:43; Ps 97:7
NT: Acts 2:33–35; 13:33; Rom 8:29; Col 1:15, 18; Rev 1:5
Catechism: Christ and his angels, 331–33; Jesus as Lord, 446–51

1:5   The section opens with a rhetorical question, picking up the theme of God "speaking" from verse 1: **For to which of the angels did God ever say . . . ?** The implied answer is: To none of them! Hebrews now recounts what God has "said" regarding his Son in the form of seven biblical quotations. Most of them are from the Psalms, the prayer book that formed the heart of Israel's worship.

The first two quotations are from Psalm 2:7 and 2 Samuel 7:14, passages that figured prominently in the messianic hopes of Israel. Both are divine pronouncements in which God promises special favor to the son of David. When the Davidic monarchy collapsed in the sixth century BC, these promises seemed to have failed. But the Jews began to interpret these passages as prophecies pointing to the †messiah, a future descendant of David who would revive the royal dynasty and restore peace and prosperity to Israel (Isa 9:5–6; Jer 23:5; Ezek 34:23–24; Hosea 3:5).

Psalm 2 is a royal psalm originally composed for the coronation of a Davidic king. The psalm depicts hostile nations that conspire against the Lord and his "anointed one," the king. In response, God laughs from heaven at these futile

42

plots and pronounces a solemn decree: **You are my son; this day I have begotten you**. This declaration did not mean the king was physically begotten by God, as in pagan mythology, but that he was adopted by God, uniquely chosen to rule over the whole earth as God's heir and royal representative (Ps 2:8–11). "This day" was the day of his enthronement as king.

The phrase **or again** introduces the next link in the chain, 2 Samuel 7:14. This verse is from Nathan's prophecy to David after David confided his desire to build the Lord a "house" (i.e., a temple). Nathan reveals that not David but his son will build the temple, and that God will bestow such favor on David's royal heir that his kingdom and throne will last forever. In words similar to Psalm 2:7, God promises, **I will be a father to him, and he shall be a son to me**.

Both of these texts were foundational in the preaching of the early Church, which saw in Jesus a fulfillment that far exceeded anything Israel had anticipated. Jesus is the son of David in his earthly lineage (Matt 1:1; Luke 1:31–32; Rom 1:3). At the same time he is Son of God, not in a merely adoptive sense like the Davidic kings but in a unique and eternal relationship with the Father. The Gospels record two key moments in Jesus' life, his baptism and transfiguration, when the Father bears witness to Jesus in words echoing Psalm 2: "You are my beloved Son . . ." "This is my Son . . ." (Luke 3:22; 9:35 ESV). But Hebrews, like other New Testament writers, probably interprets "this day" (or "today") in Psalm 2:7 as referring especially to the day of Jesus' resurrection, when he enters into his royal inheritance as Lord of the whole universe (see Acts 13:32–33; Rom 1:3–4).

The third citation is introduced with an explanatory phrase: **when he** (God) **leads the first-born into the world**.[3] It is not clear what event this refers to. Some interpreters (including St. John Chrysostom) think it refers to Christ's incarnation; others (including St. Jerome and St. Gregory of Nyssa) to his second coming.[4] But more likely the author is still speaking of the same event envisaged in verses 3–5: Jesus' resurrection and exaltation to glory, when he is led triumphant by the Father into the presence of all the angelic hosts.

As God's firstborn, Jesus has the status of eldest son, the status that was all-important in the biblical world. A firstborn son received his father's greatest blessing and a double share of the inheritance (Gen 27:19; Deut 21:17). God

1:6

---

3. The Greek term for "world" here is not the usual term, *kosmos*, but *oikoumenē*, meaning "inhabited world." It reoccurs at 2:5, where it clearly refers to the new creation that has begun with Christ's resurrection: "the *oikoumenē* to come, of which we are speaking." See Vanhoye, *A Different Priest*, 81.

4. See Philip Edgcumbe Hughes, *A Commentary on the Epistle to the Hebrews* (Grand Rapids: Eerdmans, 1977), 48; Luke Timothy Johnson, *Hebrews: A Commentary*, New Testament Library (Louisville: Westminster John Knox, 2006), 78–79; Vanhoye, *A Different Priest*, 81.

had chosen Israel as his firstborn son among all the nations (Exod 4:22), a privilege that was embodied in the king. In Psalm 89:28 God declares of the Davidic king, "I myself make him the firstborn, / Most High over the kings of the earth." Now Jesus is revealed as the definitive Davidic king, God's firstborn. His status is unique; however, God has other sons and daughters (see 2:11), and in fact a major theme of Hebrews will be that through Christ's death and resurrection all who believe in him are given a share in his privileges. Other New Testament writings express a similar idea by calling Jesus the "firstborn from the dead" (Col 1:18; Rev 1:5) and the "firstborn among many brothers" (Rom 8:29; see also Gal 4:4–6). Later Hebrews will go a step further and apply the term "firstborn" not only to Christ but to all those redeemed by him (12:23).

In the third biblical quotation God instructs the heavenly hosts how to respond to the presence of his firstborn: **Let all the angels of God worship him**. This is a powerful assertion of the divine status of the Son: he is worthy of worship, the homage that is due to God alone. As Hebrews will later describe in detail (12:18–24), there is a heavenly †liturgy going on, an eternal angelic chorus of worship that all the redeemed are invited to join, celebrating the victory won by Christ.

This quotation seems to be a combination of Deuteronomy 32:43 and Psalm 97:7 in their †Septuagint translations.[5] Deuteronomy 32 presents the song of Moses, Moses' last words to the Israelites as they were about to enter the promised land. In this song Moses prophesies the eventual defeat of Israel's enemies and God's deliverance of his people. In the final, climactic line he sings, "Rejoice with him, you heavens, and let all the sons of God worship him." "Sons of God" is a common biblical expression for angels;[6] thus Moses is summoning even the angelic hosts to honor God for the great victory he has won for his people. Hebrews quotes this scripture well aware of its broader context, which evokes the whole story of Israel's wanderings in the desert and entrance into the promised land. As Hebrews will proceed to show, these former events prefigure the new and greater exodus and the inheritance into which Jesus will lead his people (3:7–4:11). Thus although in context "worship him" refers to worshiping God, Hebrews interprets "him" as rightly applying to the Son, before whom the angels must bow in adoration.

---

5. As is often the case, the Septuagint translation of both of these texts differs somewhat from the original Hebrew (and thus from the NABRE and all standard English translations, which are based on the Hebrew). The Septuagint occasionally gives an interpretive paraphrase, and in some cases it translates a different version of the Hebrew text than the ones extant today. Readers should note that most of the Psalms in the Septuagint are numbered differently from the Hebrew (e.g., Ps 97 is Ps 96 LXX). This commentary uses the NABRE numbering system, which is based on the Hebrew, even when referring to the LXX translation of a psalm.

6. See Job 1:6; 2:1; Ps 29:1; 89:7.

The Role of Angels

The prominence of angels in Hebrews 1:5–14 raises a question: What is the big deal about angels? Why does Hebrews deem it necessary to spend so much time proving Jesus' superiority to them? Most Christians do not think much about angels, though angel fads periodically arise. But for the ancient Jews, angels had a lofty role as God's agents (Exod 14:19; Num 22:22), mediators of the covenant and the law (Acts 7:53; Gal 3:19; Heb 2:2), protectors of nations (Dan 12:1; Sir 17:14), and members of the heavenly court or entourage surrounding God (Job 2:1; Ps 89:6; Tob 12:15). Speculation about angels had developed into an entire angelology offering details about their nature, their various ranks, and their intervention in human affairs both for good and for evil.[a] The danger in this preoccupation was to exalt angels to the level of God himself, forgetting that they are created beings. Some people even fell into the temptation to worship angels (see Col 2:18)—an error that still exists in some quarters today, though perhaps a more common mistake is to neglect the role of angels altogether. Hebrews, like other New Testament writings, affirms the reality of angels and their noble functions but also their subordinate status to Jesus. As created beings, they are servants who worship the Son and do his bidding.

a. Among Jewish †intertestamental writings on angels, see, e.g., *Jubilees* 2:2; 35:17; *1 Enoch* 9:3; 12:2; 20:5; 71:1; *2 Enoch* 22:6; 29:1; *Testament of Levi* 18:5; 4 Macc 4:10–11; and from Qumran the *Songs of the Sabbath Sacrifice* (4Q400–407; 11Q17).

Psalm 97 is a song of praise proclaiming God's exaltation "above all gods"—that is, over idols, angels, and anything else that human beings are tempted to worship. Rather, let us worship God! For Hebrews, it is a further confirmation that Jesus is rightly given the worship that belongs to God alone.

The Servants and the Son (1:7–12)

⁷Of the angels he says:

> "He makes his angels winds
>   and his ministers a fiery flame";

⁸but of the Son:

> "Your throne, O God, stands forever and ever;
>   and a righteous scepter is the scepter of your kingdom.

> ⁹You loved justice and hated wickedness;
>   therefore God, your God, anointed you
>   with the oil of gladness above your companions";

¹⁰and:

> "At the beginning, O Lord, you established the earth,
>   and the heavens are the works of your hands.
> ¹¹They will perish, but you remain;
>   and they will all grow old like a garment.
> ¹²You will roll them up like a cloak,
>   and like a garment they will be changed.
> But you are the same, and your years will have no end."

OT: Ps 45:7–8; 102:26–28; 104:4; Isa 34:4; 61:1–3
NT: Luke 4:18; Acts 10:38; Heb 12:26–27; 13:8
Catechism: Christ the King, 668–72, 2816–21; God alone IS, 212–13

The chain of quotations continues with three scriptures that deepen the contrast between the angels and the Son. According to Jewish faith, there is an infinite gulf between God and all that is not God. Even angels belong to the created order. But the Son, as Hebrews proceeds to show from the Jewish Scriptures, does not. Here the chain builds to a breathtaking crescendo as the Son is for the first time addressed directly and unequivocally as "God" (v. 8).

1:7   The fourth link in the chain is from the †Septuagint version of Psalm 104:4. This psalm is a hymn praising God for his sovereignty over all creation. With poetic eloquence the psalmist declares the transcendence of the one God in contrast to misguided pagan beliefs. The forces of nature are not gods; they are merely created elements totally under God's control. God robes himself in light and travels on the wings of the wind (Ps 104:2–3); he even **makes his angels winds and his ministers a fiery flame**.[7] This imagery emphasizes the subservient role of angels as they carry out their assignments in the visible world. Their involvement in natural phenomena is at God's behest and under his governance. In quoting this line, Hebrews sets the stage for a further dramatic contrast with the Son.

1:8–9   In the fifth citation Hebrews turns to Psalm 45, a psalm composed for a royal wedding and later interpreted as a messianic prophecy. In it the psalmist extols the king's godlike virtues and wondrous deeds. Although the king is human—"the most handsome of men" (Ps 45:3)—the psalmist takes poetic

---

7. The Hebrew text of Ps 104:4 can be translated as "You make the winds your messengers; flaming fire, your ministers," as in the NABRE, or with the subjects and predicates reversed, as the Septuagint renders it.

license to boldly address him as "God" (Ps 45:7):[8] **Your throne, O God, stands forever and ever; and a righteous scepter is the scepter of your kingdom.**[9] But for Hebrews, it is Jesus who fits this royal portrait in its most literal sense. Jesus is the Davidic Messiah-King whose "throne" will endure forever. Jesus demonstrated his righteousness by embracing the Father's will during his whole life and especially in his passion; he showed that he **loved justice and hated wickedness** by choosing to obey God rather than to sin (4:15; 10:7–10). A scepter is a symbol of royal authority; Jesus has taken up his royal authority through his resurrection from the dead (1:3). And he can in the fullest sense be called *God*.

This verse is one of the few New Testament texts where "God" (Greek *ho theos*) refers to Jesus rather than to the Father.[10] Yet by including the next line of the psalm, Hebrews also clarifies that the Son is distinct from God the Father: **therefore God, your God, anointed you with the oil of gladness above your companions** (Ps 45:8). It is God who has raised Jesus to his exalted status. The Greek word for "anointed" (*echrisen*) refers to the anointing rite by which Israelite kings were installed in office. Since the word "Christ" comes from this verb and means "anointed one" (as the Hebrew equivalent, "Messiah," comes from the Hebrew verb for "anoint"), the phrase could be rendered "God, your God, has made you Messiah." The "oil of gladness" alludes to the Holy Spirit, who descended on Jesus at his baptism and "anointed" him for his messianic mission (Luke 4:18; Acts 10:38; see Isa 61:1–3), as the Spirit had rushed upon David when he was anointed king (1 Sam 16:12–13). The "companions" of the Messiah-King, as Hebrews will later make clear, are Christians.[11]

With this psalm the author resolves a difficulty that may have arisen for some of the Jewish Christians in his audience. For Jews, the most unshakable conviction of faith was that God is one and there is none like him (see Deut 6:4; Isa 46:9; Jer 10:6–7). How then can anyone attribute divine prerogatives to Christ? Like the Gospel of John (1:1–4), Hebrews overcomes this dilemma by showing that Scripture itself affirms that the Son is distinct from God the Father yet mysteriously one with him. There are not two Gods. The revelation of Christ's divinity thus in no way detracts from the absolute oneness of God.

---

8. Scripture occasionally applies the title "God" to human beings in a hyperbolic or analogical sense: Exod 4:16; 7:1; Ps 82:6.

9. Some scholars hold that the first phrase should be translated as "Your throne is God." However, as Vanhoye points out, such a position "is untenable, for it presents God as a seat on which the king is sitting!" (*A Different Priest*, 83). There is no support for such a view anywhere in Scripture. Moreover, Hebrews presents the Son as sitting at the right hand of *God's* throne (8:1).

10. Others are John 1:1, 18; 20:28; Rom 9:5; 2 Thess 1:12; Titus 3:4; 2 Pet 1:1.

11. The same term *metochoi* ("companions, participants, sharers") is used of Christians in 3:1, 14; 6:4.

These affirmations are part of the foundation for later Trinitarian theology, which affirmed that God is three persons in one divine nature.[12]

1:10–12   The sixth citation is from Psalm 102:26–28. This psalm is a declaration of faith in God's transcendence over all the troubles and uncertainties of earthly life. In contrast to the instability of the created world, God is eternal and unchanging: **They will perish, but you remain; and they will all grow old like a garment. . . . But you are the same, and your years will have no end**.

Hebrews' use of this psalm is striking. As in verse 6, it cites a scripture about †Yahweh, the God of Israel, and simply takes for granted that this text refers to Jesus. Our author's reasoning seems to be this: You saw above that Psalm 2 calls the messiah God's *son*, and that Psalm 45 calls him *God* and ascribes to him attributes that can belong to God alone. So you must recognize that Jesus, the Messiah whose reign "stands forever and ever" (v. 8), cannot be other than the God whose "years will have no end" (v. 12)!

The Psalms thereby provide biblical support for the statement in the prologue that the Son was active in the creation of the universe (1:2). Psalm 102 shows, moreover, that the Son will be active in the *end* of the universe, when heaven and earth **will grow old like a garment** and **you** (the Son) **will roll them up like a cloak**. This anticipates the theme of †eschatological judgment and cosmic upheaval at the end of Hebrews (12:26–27; see Isa 34:4). But since the Son is always "the same" and "will have no end," those who are faithful to him have nothing to fear, since they have something that will endure forever. As Hebrews will later declare, "Jesus Christ is the same yesterday, today, and forever" (13:8).

The King at God's Right Hand (1:13–14)

---

[13]**But to which of the angels has he ever said:**

> **"Sit at my right hand**
> **until I make your enemies your footstool"?**

[14]**Are they not all ministering spirits sent to serve, for the sake of those who are to inherit salvation?**

OT: Ps 103:20–21; 110:1
NT: Mark 12:35–37; 14:62; 1 Cor 15:24–28
Catechism: Jesus at God's right hand, 659–67; angels in the life of the Church, 334–36

12. See George H. Guthrie, "Hebrews," in *Commentary on the New Testament Use of the Old Testament*, ed. G. K. Beale and D. A. Carson (Grand Rapids: Baker Academic, 2007), 939.

The chain of scriptures concludes by repeating the rhetorical question of **1:13** verse 5 (**To which of the angels . . . ?**) and quoting from Psalm 110, the final link summing up Scripture's testimony to the preeminence of Jesus. Whereas the angels are servants, the firstborn Son is the heir apparent, the crown prince who by God's decree inherits the whole universe.

The verse quoted here, Psalm 110:1, is the Old Testament passage cited more often than any other in the New Testament.[13] For the early Church, it was foundational to understanding Jesus' exaltation as Lord. The Christian interpretation of this verse originated with Jesus himself, who in the Gospels uses it to demonstrate that the Messiah is greater than David (Mark 12:35–37). As usual, Hebrews cites the verse having the whole psalm in mind and hinting at a host of themes that will be unfolded later in the letter: priesthood, Melchizedek, victory over enemies, judgment, and a divine origin before the creation of the world. The psalm is strategically placed here, where it ends the chain of quotations and prepares for the whole argument concerning Christ's eternal priesthood in Hebrews 3–10.

Fig. 2. Twelfth-century image of Christ Pantocrator, or Ruler of All, located in Sant'Angelo Abbey in Capua, Italy.

According to its heading, Psalm 110 is "a psalm of David"—that is, sung by David the musician-king.[14] The psalm portrays David delivering a solemn oracle at the coronation of his son Solomon: "The LORD says to my lord, '**Sit at my right hand until I make your enemies your footstool**'" (Ps 110:1 NRSV). "The LORD" refers to God; "my lord" is a title of respect for the king. God invites the king to take the position of

13. It is quoted in Matt 22:44; Mark 12:36; Luke 20:42; Acts 2:34–35; Heb 1:13; and alluded to in Matt 26:64; Mark 14:62; 16:19; Luke 22:69; Acts 7:55–56; Rom 8:34; 1 Cor 15:25; Eph 1:20–22; Col 3:1; Heb 1:3; 8:1; 10:12–13; 1 Pet 3:22.

14. Some scholars hold that the original meaning of the superscription was not "a psalm *of* David" (i.e., written by David) but rather "a psalm *for* David" (i.e., dedicated to the Davidic king, or to be sung by the Davidic king, or authorized to be included in the Davidic collection of psalms). Whatever the relative merits of these hypotheses, Hebrews' interpretation relies on the meaning of the text as it was understood in the author's day.

highest honor and authority, ruling over not only Israel but all nations "across the wide earth" (Ps 110:6), while God himself conquers the king's enemies.

No such promise was ever made to an angel, as Jews familiar with the Old Testament knew well. But it was made to the son of David and is fulfilled in Jesus, the descendant of David who is exalted forever at the Father's right hand. Christ still has "enemies"—hostile forces that resist his lordship and harass his people. But there will come a day when all his enemies are visibly subjected to him and he hands over to the Father the world he has redeemed, as Paul proclaims in 1 Corinthians 15:24–28.[15]

1:14   The section ends with one more rhetorical question, describing the true role of the angels: **Are they not all ministering spirits sent to serve, for the sake of those who are to inherit salvation?** Their subordination to Christ has already been made clear; now Hebrews declares that their service is for the sake of human beings. The angels honor Christ by helping his people attain salvation—deliverance from evil of every kind and access to the presence of God. This unexpected priority given to lowly human beings will be further spelled out in chapter 2.

15. See Hughes, *Hebrews*, 70.

A Little Lower Than the Angels

Hebrews 2:1–18

Hebrews 1 was a powerful demonstration of Christ's divinity through the testimony of Scripture. Chapter 2, in contrast, will demonstrate Christ's full humanity, his likeness to us in all things but sin. The Son, who is by nature infinitely superior to the angels, was for a little while, through his incarnation and his passion, made *lower* than the angels. Only when the Son's divine majesty is fully recognized can the magnitude of his self-abasement be grasped. It is his union with both God and human beings that uniquely qualifies Christ to be the great high priest, the mediator between God and man.

But before proceeding with this doctrinal exposition, the author pauses for a brief exhortation to readers (2:1–4), urging them to respond appropriately to God's revelation of the Son. It is characteristic of Hebrews to alternate doctrine with what might be called "life application," usually in the form of an exhortation. Hebrews 2:1–14 is the first of these exhortations.[1] They are not interruptions but an essential part of the overall purpose of the letter. For Hebrews, as for the whole New Testament, *doctrine* is inseparably united with *life*. If we understand who Christ is and what he has done for us, then we begin to understand how we ought to conduct ourselves in response to "so great a salvation" (2:3). Conversely, the holy way of life to which we are called is possible only insofar as we receive and appropriate the truth of the gospel. Hebrews makes clear that theology is not abstract theory but lived reality.

1. The others are 3:12–4:3; 4:14–16; 5:11–6:8; 10:32–39; 12:3–17, 25–29.

A Call to Pay Attention (2:1–4)

---

¹Therefore, we must attend all the more to what we have heard, so that we may not be carried away. ²For if the word announced through angels proved firm, and every transgression and disobedience received its just recompense, ³how shall we escape if we ignore so great a salvation? Announced originally through the Lord, it was confirmed for us by those who had heard. ⁴God added his testimony by signs, wonders, various acts of power, and distribution of the gifts of the holy Spirit according to his will.

OT: Deut 4:9
NT: Mark 16:17–20; Acts 7:53; 10:39; 2 Cor 12:12; Gal 3:19
Catechism: miracles, 156, 547–49; gifts of the Spirit, 799–800, 2003

2:1   The exhortation begins with **therefore**, signaling that it directly follows from the doctrine presented in chapter 1. How are **we**, the ones "who are to inherit salvation" (1:14), to respond to such a great gift? We must, first of all, **attend all the more to what we have heard**. In emphasizing our obligation to attend to what we have heard, Hebrews draws on a theme that was foundational to Israel's faith. The covenant response that God required of his people is summed up in Deuteronomy 6:4, the passage known as the †Great Shema: "Hear, O Israel. . . ." Jesus too emphasized the vital importance of attentive listening: "Hear this! . . . Whoever has ears to hear ought to hear. . . . Take care what you hear . . ." (Mark 4:3, 9, 24). To "hear" God's word means to listen not only with the ears but also with the heart, to reflect on it, believe it, and obey it.

The reason for paying such close attention is **so that we may not be carried away**, or better, "drift away." This phrase suggests the idea of a boat drifting away from its moorings and floating downstream with the current. It is a strong warning of the risk of coasting in the spiritual life and thus eventually falling away from Christ. The author speaks here not of renouncing Christ outright but of something more subtle and dangerous: through complacency and apathy, Christians can gradually lose sight of the gift they have received and, ultimately, forfeit it. The letter will be peppered with many similar admonitions: Take care not to "fall away" (3:12 RSV), "fall" (4:11), "become sluggish" (5:11), "throw away your confidence" (10:35), or "be led away" (13:9 RSV). A corresponding metaphor will explain what can *prevent* us from drifting away: an "anchor of the soul" (6:19).

2:2   The next sentence drives home the gravity of the warning by a contrast between angels and Christ like that of chapter 1: **For if the word announced**

through angels proved firm . . . This form of argument is known as *a fortiori* or, among the ancient rabbis, †*qal wahomer* (Hebrew for "light and heavy"), and usually takes the form "If X is true for the lesser, then how much more for the greater." The word announced through angels is Old Testament revelation, especially the Torah, the law that was given through Moses at Mount Sinai. Although angels are not mentioned in the Sinai narrative, later Jewish thought held that the law was transmitted by angels (Acts 7:38, 53; Gal 3:19).[2] The law was God's gift to his people, his holy and just instruction as to how to remain in life-giving communion with him and with one another.

The law was "firm" in that it was legally binding. As the Old Testament makes abundantly clear, **every transgression and disobedience**—that is, every infraction of the law, whether inadvertent or willful—**received its just recompense**. The Greek word for "recompense" can also be translated "reward" (as in 10:35) and implies that moral conduct, whether good or evil, has consequences. The †Torah narrates many striking incidents of the recompense for sin, especially sins of willful rebellion.[3] In a sense, the entire Torah is a record of God's educational program by which he taught his people the real and momentous consequences of their choices for good or evil (see Deut 30:19).

Since sin led to such grave consequences in the old covenant, **how shall we** 2:3 **escape if we ignore so great a salvation?** The point is not that in Christ we have been given a stricter moral code with even harsher penalties. Rather, the point is that we have been offered a *salvation that delivers* us from the penalty for sin. If we reject the means that God himself has given to save us from the consequences of sin, how can we possibly escape those consequences? The far greater mercy now offered entails a corresponding responsibility for us: it is a call to a decision. This recalls Jesus' warning that it will be more tolerable for pagan cities like Sodom and Gomorrah on the day of judgment than for those who spurn the gospel (Matt 10:14–15; see 11:20–24). The admonition is all the more sobering in that it refers not to outright rejection but to simple negligence—the opposite of the attentiveness called for in verse 1.[4] This warning will be repeated near the end of Hebrews, at 12:25.

The good news of salvation was **announced originally through the Lord**— that is, by Jesus in his preaching and ministry. Hebrews calls Jesus "the Lord" (*ho kyrios*), the title used in the †Septuagint to translate the holy name of God.

2. This tradition may have developed partly on the basis of the account of the "angel of the LORD" appearing to Moses in the burning bush (Exod 3:2).

3. See, for instance, Lev 10:1–2; Num 11:33; 16:31–33; 20:12; 21:6; 25:1–9.

4. The same Greek word for "ignore" is used by Jesus for those who ignored the king's invitation to a wedding feast (Matt 22:5).

St. Irenaeus on the Handing Down of Christian Testimony

LIVING TRADITION

St. Irenaeus of Lyons, a second-century bishop, was taught by St. Polycarp, who had in turn learned the gospel from the apostle John. Irenaeus exemplifies the attitude of diligent attentiveness described in Hebrews 2:1–4:

> I remember the events of that time more clearly than those of recent years. For what boys learn grows with their mind and becomes joined to it; so that I am able to describe the very place in which the blessed Polycarp sat as he discoursed, and his goings out and his comings in, and the manner of his life, and his physical appearance, and his discourses to the people, and the accounts that he gave of his conversation with John and with the others who had seen the Lord. And as he remembered their words, and what he heard from them concerning the Lord, and concerning his miracles and his teaching, having received them from eyewitnesses of the Word of life, Polycarp related all things in harmony with the Scriptures. These things being told me by the mercy of God, I listened to them attentively, noting them down, not on paper, but in my heart. And continually, through God's grace, I recall them faithfully.[a]

a. Quoted in Eusebius, *Ecclesiastical History* 5.20.6–7 (translation adapted from *NPNF* II, vol. 1).

With this title the greatness of the gospel in comparison with the old law stands out even more clearly. The law was "announced through angels" (v. 2)—a wonderful, sublime gift—but how much greater is a message spoken in person by the Lord himself.

Although the original readers of Hebrews, like readers today, were not eyewitnesses to Jesus' earthly ministry, the gospel was passed down to them by those **who had heard** it directly from the lips of Jesus. The writer of Hebrews includes himself among this second generation of Christians who learned from the teaching of the apostles.[5] The authenticity of the message is **confirmed** by the testimony of witnesses going back to Jesus himself. The Greek word for "confirmed" (*bebaioō*) is related to "firm" (*bebaios*) in verse 2, implying that the gospel is as reliable and binding as the law of Moses.

2:4   The preaching of the good news of Christ is not merely in words. As Christians proclaim the gospel, **God** adds his own **testimony** in the form of miracles that confirm the truth of the message. Jesus had commanded his apostles not

5. "Second generation" here does not necessarily mean a younger generation, but rather those who received the gospel secondhand.

Signs, Wonders, and Acts of Power in the Early Church

LIVING
TRADITION

St. Irenaeus, quoted in the previous sidebar, also described the evangelistic impact of the many miracles done by Christians in his time:

> Those who are in truth [Jesus'] disciples, receiving grace from him, perform [miracles] in his name so as to promote the welfare of others, according to the gift that each has received from him. For some truly drive out devils, so that those who have been cleansed from evil spirits frequently believe and join themselves to the Church. Others have foreknowledge of things to come: they see visions, and utter prophetic words. Still others heal the sick by laying their hands upon them, and they are made whole. Yes, moreover . . . the dead even have been raised up, and remained among us for many years. And what more shall I say? It is impossible to name the number of the gifts which the Church throughout the whole world has received from God in the name of Jesus Christ who was crucified under Pontius Pilate, and which she exerts day by day for the benefit of the Gentiles, neither practicing deception on anyone, nor taking any reward from them on account of such miraculous works. For as she has received freely from God, freely also does she minister.[a]

St. Augustine, writing in the early fifth century, also recounts numerous miraculous healings, some of which he personally witnessed, which were "wrought in the name of Christ, whether by his sacraments or by the prayers or relics of his saints."[b]

a. *Against Heresies* 2.32.4 (translation adapted from *ANF*, vol. 1).
b. *The City of God* 22.8.

---

only to preach but also to "cure the sick, raise the dead, cleanse lepers, drive out demons" (Matt 10:8; see Mark 16:17–18), and Acts records numerous **signs, wonders**, and **acts of power** worked by the early Christians in Jesus' name.[6] Paul uses the same three terms to describe the deeds that mark an authentic apostle (2 Cor 12:12). The miracles are "signs" because they *signify* or point beyond themselves to Jesus and his ultimate victory over sin, sickness, and death. They are "wonders" in that they call forth a response of wonder, awe, praise, and gratitude, just as did the healings done by Jesus in his earthly ministry.[7] They are "acts of power" (Greek *dynameis*, usually translated "miracles") in that they show forth the mighty power of God.

6. Acts 2:43; 4:30; 5:12; 6:8; 8:13; 14:3; 15:12; see also Rom 15:19.
7. See Mark 5:19–20; 7:37; Luke 13:13, 17; 18:43; 19:37–39; John 9:38.

Gifts Distributed by the Holy Spirit

LIVING TRADITION

The Second Vatican Council affirmed the importance of the charisms distributed by the Spirit to the faithful for the building up of the Church (*Lumen Gentium* 12):

> It is not only through the sacraments and the ministries of the Church that the Holy Spirit sanctifies and leads the people of God and enriches it with virtues, but, "allotting his gifts to everyone according as He wills" (1 Cor 12:11), He distributes special graces among the faithful of every rank. By these gifts He makes them fit and ready to undertake the various tasks and offices that contribute to the renewal and building up of the Church, according to the words of the Apostle: "The manifestation of the Spirit is given to everyone for profit" (1 Cor 12:7). These charisms, whether they be the more outstanding or the more simple and widely diffused, are to be received with thanksgiving and consolation, for they are perfectly suited to and useful for the needs of the Church.

God also confirms the truth of the gospel by the **distribution of the gifts of the holy Spirit according to his will**.[8] This statement takes for granted that the readers of Hebrews, like other early Christians (1 Cor 1:5–7; Gal 3:5), had experienced the Spirit's power through his impartation of gifts. As Paul explains in detail in 1 Corinthians 12–14, each of these Spirit-bestowed gifts, or charisms, contributes in a unique way to the Church's mission. They may include prophecy, tongues, or healings; or natural gifts such as teaching or hospitality raised to a supernatural efficacy (see Rom 12:4–8; Eph 4:11–12). The charisms contribute to the work of evangelization by manifesting in a powerful way the reality and presence of God in the world.

Reflection and Application (2:1–4)

Like many other New Testament passages, Hebrews 2:3–4 emphasizes that the gospel is to be proclaimed not in words only, but also in signs, wonders, healings, and the manifestation of other supernatural charisms by which God confirms the truth of the words.[9] Such miracles demonstrate that Jesus Christ is alive and really has won the victory over sin and death; they reveal God's

---

8. The NAB does not capitalize "holy," presumably to suggest that Holy Spirit was not yet a fixed title for the Third Person of the Trinity. The earliest New Testament manuscripts are written in all capital letters; lowercase lettering was a later invention.

9. See Matt 10:7–8; Mark 16:20; Acts 8:6; 1 Cor 2:4; 4:20; 14:24–25; 2 Cor 12:12.

love and dispose people's hearts to believe the good news. Throughout Church history countless missionaries and evangelists have stirred up faith in Christ by doing miracles in Christ's name, including Saints Anthony of the Desert, Patrick, Benedict, Bernard, Anthony of Padua, Margaret of Castello, Catherine of Siena, Vincent Ferrer, Francis Xavier, Teresa of Avila, Padre Pio, and André Bessette. Such miracles continue to take place today, perhaps in greater numbers than ever before.[10] As the Church responds to the call to the new evangelization, seeking to renew Christian faith in the post-Christian culture of the West, an essential ingredient is the rediscovery and pursuit of this heritage of divine charisms, given by the Spirit for the building up of the Church.

The Self-Abasement of the Son (2:5–9)

⁵For it was not to angels that he subjected the world to come, of which we are speaking. ⁶Instead, someone has testified somewhere:

"What is man that you are mindful of him,
    or the son of man that you care for him?
⁷You made him for a little while lower than the angels;
    you crowned him with glory and honor,
⁸subjecting all things under his feet."

In "subjecting" all things [to him], he left nothing not "subject to him." Yet at present we do not see "all things subject to him," ⁹but we do see Jesus "crowned with glory and honor" because he suffered death, he who "for a little while" was made "lower than the angels," that by the grace of God he might taste death for everyone.

OT: Gen 1:28; Ps 8:5–7
NT: 1 Cor 15:27; Eph 1:22; 1 Pet 3:22
Catechism: Jesus tasted death, 624; God's care for man, 2567

Following the exhortation in 2:1–4, Hebrews resumes its doctrinal exposition, showing how the Old Testament bears witness to Jesus. Whereas chapter 1 focused on the Son's preeminence over the angels, this section shows how the Son was made *lower* than the angels. Hebrews does this through an interpretation of Psalm 8—a psalm that Jewish tradition had not viewed as messianic—in light of Christ.

10. See the hundreds of contemporary testimonies collected by Craig Keener in his two-volume *Miracles: The Credibility of the New Testament Accounts* (Grand Rapids: Baker Academic, 2011).

2:5   Our author, or more precisely, preacher, is **speaking** about **the world to come**—a phrase that may make us think of heaven. But biblically, "the world to come" is the new creation that begins with God's decisive intervention in history, when he accomplishes all that he promised to do for his people. And for the New Testament, the good news is that in Jesus the world to come *has come!* It awaits its full consummation at the end of history but in a mysterious way is already present now: it is both *already* and *not yet.*[11] This is why Hebrews says that we are in "these last days" (1:2) and have already experienced "the powers of the age to come" (6:5), though we still look forward to the "city . . . that is to come" (13:14). In the former age God had, according to Jewish tradition, given **angels** a certain authority over earthly affairs.[12] But not so in the world to come. Rather, it is human beings who will rule (see 1 Cor 6:3), as a quote from the Psalms will show.

2:6   The vague phrase **Someone has testified somewhere** is the author's tongue-in-cheek way of bringing up a biblical text that both he and his readers know quite well (see 4:4). The text he quotes is from Psalm 8, a psalm that expresses wonder at the majesty of creation and the exalted position God has given to man in the cosmos. But Hebrews will find in it a deeper meaning beyond what the psalmist intended. The psalmist, reflecting on the creation story in Genesis, marvels at God's tender care for humanity. When we gaze on the splendor of the sun, moon, and stars, we may well wonder, **What is man that you are mindful of him, or the son of man that you care for him?** Yet throughout Scripture it is evident that God is specially mindful of the human beings created in his image and of the †covenant he has made with them (see Gen 8:1; 9:15). "Son of man" is a way of referring to a human being, descended from Adam.[13] But as the Gospels record, it was also Jesus' characteristic way of referring to himself, and this will prove significant for the interpretation of the psalm.

2:7–8a   The psalm continues, **You made him for a little while** (or "a little") **lower than the angels**. In this line the †Septuagint differs slightly from the original Hebrew, which says literally, "You have made him little less than the gods."[14] The Septuagint interpreted "the gods" to mean the angelic beings who surround God in his heavenly retinue. The point is that at creation God endowed human beings with a dignity only a little lower than that of the angels, the highest

---

11. See Philip Edgcumbe Hughes, *A Commentary on the Epistle to the Hebrews* (Grand Rapids: Eerdmans, 1977), 82.

12. See Deut 32:8 LXX; Dan 10:20; 12:1; Sir 17:14; Acts 7:53; Gal 3:19. See sidebar, "The Role of Angels," p. 45.

13. The Hebrew phrase "son of man" is *ben-adam*, which could be translated "son of Adam."

14. The Hebrew term *elohim* can mean "God," "a god," or "the gods," the latter referring, in this context, to heavenly beings or angels.

created beings. The Greek term for "for a little while" can also mean "a little"—
a double meaning that Hebrews will use to good effect.[15] Hebrews also plays
on the double meaning of "man" (Greek *anthrōpos*), which can refer either to
humanity in general or to an individual human being.

**You crowned him with glory and honor, subjecting all things under his
feet**. As Genesis affirms, God made human beings the crown of creation and
gave them royal authority over other creatures: "Fill the earth and subdue it.
Have dominion over the fish of the sea, the birds of the air, and all the living
things that crawl on the earth" (Gen 1:28). Even though this dominion was
disturbed by the fall (Gen 3), the psalm implies that God did not abandon his
purposes for humanity.

These lofty statements, however, seem to fly in the face of human experience. **2:8b–9**
Hebrews affirms the simple logic that **in "subjecting" all things** to man—as
both Psalm 8 and Genesis 1 affirm—God **left nothing not "subject to him."**
Yet if anything is obvious, it is that much of the created world is *not* subject to
human dominion. Otherwise there would be no disease, no famine, no natural
disasters. We do not even have dominion over ourselves, much less the rest of
creation. Thus it is evident that God's original intention for human dominion,
as expressed in Genesis 1 and Psalm 8, has not yet been fulfilled.

Now the author clinches his argument: on one level the psalm is speaking
of humanity in general, but in the fullest sense it applies only to Christ as *the*
man, the new Adam in whom God's original plan for humanity is restored and
perfected.[16] Who is crowned with glory in the fullest sense and given royal
authority over all creation? The Messiah, risen from the dead and exalted as
Lord of the universe! **At present we do not see** the world subject to man, but
we **do see Jesus "crowned with glory and honor" because he suffered death**.
In Jesus we see already fulfilled what will one day be the glorious destiny of
all humanity.

This is the first mention in Hebrews of the name Jesus, the human name that
accents his solidarity with us.[17] We "see" him, of course, with the eyes of faith.
And in the risen Jesus, clothed with divine majesty, we can already glimpse our
own glorious destiny. Hebrews strengthens this interpretation of the psalm by
taking "a little" in its temporal sense: the Son in his incarnation and passion

15. The NIV translates with the spatial meaning, "a little"; the RSV, NRSV, and NJB choose the
temporal meaning.
16. See James D. G. Dunn, *Christology in the Making: A New Testament Inquiry into the Origins of
the Doctrine of the Incarnation* (Philadelphia: Westminster, 1980), 109–11. Other New Testament texts
applying Ps 8:6 to Jesus are 1 Cor 15:27; Eph 1:22; 1 Pet 3:22.
17. Jesus' name in Hebrew is *Yeshua*, a shortened form of "Joshua" (*Yehoshua*); in Greek both are
spelled *Iēsous*.

lowered himself **for a little while** to a status **lower than** the angels. He became a flesh-and-blood human being who experienced the same weaknesses and sufferings that all of us experience. But because of his obedience even unto death, as Paul says, "God greatly exalted him" (Phil 2:9). That God subjected "all things under his feet" ties in perfectly with Psalm 110, the messianic psalm quoted above, where God tells the messiah, "Sit at my right hand / until I make your enemies your footstool" (Heb 1:13). Psalm 8, a hymn on God's marvelous plan for humanity, has thus become a prophecy of the humiliation and glorification of Jesus. Its deepest meaning has been brought to light by the gospel.

The end of the section broaches a topic that will occupy center stage in Hebrews: the reason the Son accepted the humble status of a human being was precisely so that **by the grace of God he might taste death for everyone**. To say that his death is "for" everyone is to hint at the theme of †atonement, a sacrificial suffering on behalf of others. "Taste death" calls to mind the event that brought death into the world in the first place: the original sin, in which Adam and Eve tasted the forbidden fruit and thus became separated from God, the author of life (Gen 3:6). To "taste" death means to experience its bitter reality. Jesus drank the cup of suffering and death to its dregs (see Mark 10:38; 14:36). But he did so "by the grace of God"—not by coercion or because of any merit on our part, but by God's free gift. Paul expresses the same truth in Romans: "God proves his love for us in that while we were still sinners Christ died for us" (Rom 5:8).

Reflection and Application (2:5–9)

Hebrews' confident assertion that "we do see Jesus" (2:9) is startling, especially when compared with Jesus' words to the apostle Thomas: "Have you come to believe because you have seen me? Blessed are those who have not seen and have believed" (John 20:29). It is true that we do not see Jesus physically as Thomas did. But Hebrews is accenting the fact that faith is truly a way of knowing. Through faith we can gaze upon Jesus, risen from the dead, and see in him the promise of our own future glory. The Church gives us several privileged ways of seeing Jesus: through reading Scripture, especially the Gospels; conversing with him in prayer; contemplating holy icons; gazing on him in Eucharistic adoration; and receiving him in the sacraments. As we look upon Jesus, we also become more like him: "All of us, gazing with unveiled face on the glory of the Lord, are being transformed into the same image from glory to glory, as from the Lord who is the Spirit" (2 Cor 3:18).

The Son's Solidarity with Humanity (2:10–18)

¹⁰For it was fitting that he, for whom and through whom all things exist, in bringing many children to glory, should make the leader to their salvation perfect through suffering. ¹¹He who consecrates and those who are being consecrated all have one origin. Therefore, he is not ashamed to call them "brothers," ¹²saying:

> "I will proclaim your name to my brothers,
> in the midst of the assembly I will praise you";

¹³and again:

> "I will put my trust in him";

and again:

> "Behold, I and the children God has given me."

¹⁴Now since the children share in blood and flesh, he likewise shared in them, that through death he might destroy the one who has the power of death, that is, the devil, ¹⁵and free those who through fear of death had been subject to slavery all their life. ¹⁶Surely he did not help angels but rather the descendants of Abraham; ¹⁷therefore, he had to become like his brothers in every way, that he might be a merciful and faithful high priest before God to expiate the sins of the people. ¹⁸Because he himself was tested through what he suffered, he is able to help those who are being tested.

OT: 2 Sam 22:3; Ps 22:23; Isa 8:17–18; 41:8–9
NT: Rom 11:36; 1 Cor 8:6
Catechism: Satan's power, 407; Jesus' love for us, 609; Jesus' atoning death, 615, 1992
Lectionary: 2:14–18: Feast of the Presentation of the Lord

The previous section showed that Jesus, the exalted firstborn Son of God, humbled himself to a status lower than that of the angels. Now Hebrews has to explain *why* he did so. To answer this question, the preacher makes one of the most astounding theological claims in the New Testament: *God made his Son perfect through suffering.* This statement would have startled the early Christians as much as it does us. In what sense could God's Son possibly need to be "made perfect"? And why did it have to be through suffering?

It was fitting (see also 7:26) means that what may seem inappropriate to   2:10
us—a crucified Messiah—is actually fully appropriate within God's perfect

plan (see 1 Cor 1:22–25). God is the one **for whom and through whom all things exist**, both the creator who made all things (Neh 9:6) and the end for whose sake all things exist (Rom 11:36; 1 Cor 8:6). It would have been supremely *unfitting* for him to let his creation fall into death and destruction.[18] Since his goal from the beginning was to bring **many children to glory**, he made his firstborn Son the **leader** who leads the way for his younger brothers and sisters. The Greek word for "leader" can also be translated "pioneer" (RSV) or "author." It is used again of Jesus in Hebrews 12:2 (see also Acts 3:15; 5:31). Jesus is not only the cause of our **salvation** but also the pioneer, the one who blazed before us the difficult trail from human fallenness to divine glory. We experience nothing on the path to salvation that he did not endure before us.

What does Hebrews mean by saying that Jesus had to be made **perfect**? The author seems to be using this verb in three senses.[19] First, "make perfect" (*teleioō*) is related to the adjective "perfect" (*teleios*), used in the †Septuagint for human beings who are morally blameless and upright (Gen 6:9; 1 Kings 15:3) and for animals that are whole and unblemished, worthy to be offered in sacrifice to God.[20] That Jesus had to be "made perfect" does not mean that he was ever morally flawed; rather, he freely chose to take on human nature in its fallen state, with the weakness, pain, and death that are intrinsic to it, and **through suffering** to perfect it in holiness.[21] It is easy to be virtuous when all goes well and people treat you kindly, as Jesus himself noted (Luke 6:32–34). But human virtue comes to perfection only when it is tried and tested by suffering. In enduring his passion, Jesus allowed all the evil unleashed upon him to bring forth the most perfect act of love, trust, and obedience to God that could ever come from a human heart. In the furnace of suffering his human nature was refined to limitless perfection. He was thus qualified to be offered in sacrifice as the perfect, unblemished Lamb (1 Pet 1:19).

Second, Christ was "made perfect" in that his human nature was transformed by his entrance into divine glory (v. 9); or to use a patristic term, he was "divinized." By becoming man he assumed our nature, which was subject to weakness and deprived of the heavenly glory for which it was made (see Rom 3:23). As Jesus affirmed in the Gospels, his passion was therefore necessary as

18. Hughes, *Hebrews*, 98.
19. I owe this insight to a short course on Hebrews taught by Father Francis Martin.
20. In Greek *teleios* can mean mature or complete (1 Cor 14:20; Phil 3:15; Col 1:28; Heb 5:14) as well as perfect (Matt 19:21; Rom 12:2; 1 Cor 13:10).
21. It is noteworthy that God's injunction in Leviticus, "Be holy, for I, the Lord your God, am holy" (Lev 19:2), is parallel to Jesus' injunction in the Gospel, "Be perfect, just as your heavenly Father is perfect" (Matt 5:48).

the God-appointed means for him to ascend to divine glory (Mark 8:31; Luke 24:26). So too for his followers, the path to glory is usually through suffering (2 Cor 4:17; Phil 3:10–11; Heb 12:10–11).

Finally, there is a further significance to *teleioō*. In the Septuagint this verb is used to translate the Hebrew expression meaning to "ordain" a priest (Exod 29:9; Lev 8:33; Num 3:3). As Hebrews will proceed to show, Jesus is the great high priest (4:14), and his rite of ordination is the cross.

By his †paschal mystery Jesus **consecrates** (or better, "sanctifies") God's **2:11** people. "To sanctify" means to set apart from all that is †profane and make worthy to enter the presence of the †holy God. In the Old Testament God revealed that his plan is to form a holy people, set apart for himself (Exod 19:6; Lev 11:45). As Hebrews will later explain, it is the one perfect †sacrifice of Jesus on the cross that makes us holy once and for all (10:10; 13:12).

But in order to make human beings holy, Jesus had to be one with them (see v. 17). He saves us not by a simple divine decree but rather by lowering himself to share our very **origin**. This could refer to the Jews' descent from Abraham (see v. 16) or, more likely, our common descent from Adam and Eve. But Jesus in turn brought us into his own family, making us sons and daughters of the heavenly Father (Matt 23:9; John 20:17; Rom 8:29). So he is **not ashamed** but rather is overjoyed to **call us brothers** and sisters.[22] The reference to his not being "ashamed" may also be a gentle reproach to some of the original readers of Hebrews who had for their part become "ashamed" of Jesus, who under persecution were reluctant to publicly acknowledge their identity as Christians (10:32–39; see Luke 9:26).

To support the point, Hebrews quotes three Old Testament verses, inter- **2:12** preting each as spoken by Jesus. The first is from Psalm 22:23: **I will proclaim your name to my brothers, / in the midst of the assembly I will praise you**. This is the psalm whose opening words Jesus prayed from the cross: "My God, my God, why have you forsaken me?" (Mark 15:34). Psalm 22 is a psalm of lament in which the psalmist cries out to God in anguish, recounting his terrible afflictions and his innocence of wrongdoing. But halfway through, the lament turns into a hope-filled song of praise. The psalmist begins to rejoice in anticipation of God's deliverance and vows to recount to the assembly gathered for worship how God has delivered him from his enemies. The Gospels see this psalm as fulfilled at Jesus' resurrection, when he charges the women to "go tell my brothers" about his great victory over death (Matt 28:10; John 20:17). This psalm has a perennial Christian fulfillment, since the Greek word

---

22. This statement is an example of litotes—an understatement using a double negative.

Christer the Leader of Our Worship

According to the Gospels, Jesus interpreted the Psalms as referring to himself.[a] Hebrews 2:12 cites Psalm 22 in the same way: the
speaker in the psalm is Christ himself, praising God in the midst of
the Church for the glorious victory of his resurrection. Commenting
on this psalm, St. Augustine wrote,

> When we speak to God in prayer, we do not separate the Son from God;
> and when the body of the Son prays, it does not separate its head from
> itself. The one sole savior of his body is our Lord Jesus Christ, the Son of
> God, who prays *for* us, prays *in* us, and is prayed to *by* us. He prays for
> us as our priest, he prays in us as our head, and he is prayed to by us as our God.
> Accordingly we must recognize our voices in him, and his accents in ourselves.[b]

a. Mark 12:36–37; 15:34; Luke 24:44. The early Church took up the same †christological interpretation
of the Psalms (e.g., Acts 2:25–31; 13:33–37).

b. *On the Psalms* 85.1 (translation adapted from Augustine, *Expositions of the Psalms, 73–98*, trans.
Maria Boulding, OSB, ed. John E. Rotelle, Works of Saint Augustine III/18 [Hyde Park, NY: New City
Press, 2002], 220).

for "assembly" (*ekklēsia*) also means "church." Every time Christians gather
for the †liturgy, Jesus declares the greatness of God to his brothers and sisters
in the midst of the assembly.

2:13   The second quotation is from the Septuagint version of 2 Samuel 22:3, another
hymn in which David celebrates God's mighty act of deliverance: "**I will put my
trust in him**. He is my protector, and the horn of my salvation, my helper, and
my sure refuge." To apply this saying to Jesus means that in his human nature
he too experienced fear and weakness but trusted totally in the Father. The
wording is similar to Isaiah 8:17, "I will trust in the Lord," which probably is
what brought to mind the third quotation, from Isaiah 8:18: **Behold, I and the
children God has given me**. In the context of this last passage, God is warning Israel to rely on him and not on foreign political alliances when they are
threatened by their enemies. Isaiah points to himself and his children (perhaps
meaning his disciples) as a faithful remnant who trust in the Lord. Applied to
Jesus, this passage portrays him presenting his disciples as a faithful remnant
given to him by the Father (see John 10:29; 17:24).

2:14   Verse 14 affirms the reality of Christ's human nature in graphic terms. **Blood
and flesh** (or flesh and blood) is a Hebrew expression for human nature, accenting both its weakness and the physical kinship that human beings share by
common descent (Gen 29:14; Matt 16:17; Eph 6:12). Since **the children**—the

brothers and sisters whom Christ sanctifies—**share** a human nature that is subject to suffering and mortality, **he likewise shared** in it. The verb "shared" indicates a past event, the incarnation. The Son of God became one with us in the most radical way possible; he became our blood relative.[23] Christ shared our flesh and blood so that we could share his own flesh and blood, now glorified through his resurrection from the dead.

Hebrews is asserting here (as in v. 9) that the reason Christ became human was precisely so that he could die. As St. Athanasius put it, "The Word assumed a human body expressly so that he might offer it in sacrifice for other like bodies."[24] Hebrews describes what Jesus accomplished by his death in two ways.[25] First, on a cosmic level, he conquered **the one who has the power of death, that is, the devil**. Satan holds the "power of death" in that he tempted our first parents to the sin that led to death (Gen 3; Wis 2:24), and thereby gained a certain dominion over human beings (see Eph 2:1–3; 1 John 5:19). Jesus' crucifixion was the ultimate confrontation with Satan, in which Jesus defeated him once and for all.[26] The great paradox is that Jesus conquered death **through death**—not by escaping it but by experiencing it, destroying death from within.[27]

Second, on a human level, he freed **those who through fear of death had been subject to slavery all their life**. This statement conveys a profound psychological insight about the human condition. Most of us recognize that the fear of death can be a potent force in situations of physical danger or serious illness. But Hebrews is saying that the fear of death is an underlying force throughout *all* of human life. We instinctively resist and recoil from everything that reminds us of our mortality—pain, deprivation, weakness, criticism, failure. This paralyzing fear influences many human choices on a subconscious level, leads to various forms of escapism and addiction, induces us to grasp the false security nets proffered by Satan, and keeps us from pursuing the will of God with freedom, peace, and confidence. It is the slavery from which Jesus came to set us **free** (see John 8:34; Rom 8:15).

2:15

---

23. There is an interesting parallel to this language in Paul's words on the Eucharist: "The cup of blessing that we bless, is it not a sharing in the blood of Christ? The bread that we break, is it not a sharing in the body of Christ?" (1 Cor 10:16 NRSV).

24. *On the Incarnation* 10 (translation from Athanasius, *On the Incarnation: The Treatise De incarnatione Verbi Dei*, trans. and ed. a religious of CSMV [Crestwood, NY: St. Vladimir's Seminary Press, 1993], 36).

25. See Thomas Aquinas, *Commentary on the Epistle to the Hebrews*, trans. Chrysostom Baer (South Bend, IN: St. Augustine's Press, 2006), 68.

26. Matt 12:29; Luke 11:22; John 12:31; 14:30; Col 2:15; 1 John 3:8.

27. Luke Timothy Johnson, *Hebrews: A Commentary*, New Testament Library (Louisville: Westminster John Knox, 2006), 100.

St. Athanasius on God's Solution to the Fall

LIVING TRADITION

St. Athanasius, a fourth-century bishop of Alexandria, explains one reason why the incarnation is God's answer to the enslavement of humanity.

What was God to do in face of this dehumanizing of mankind, this universal hiding of the knowledge of himself by the wiles of evil spirits? Was he to keep silence before so great a wrong and let men go on being deceived and kept in ignorance of himself? . . . What then was God to do? Being God, what else could he possibly do but renew his image in mankind, so that through it men might once more come to know him? And how could this be done except by the coming of the very image himself, our Savior Jesus Christ? Men could not have done it, for they are only made after the image; nor could angels have done it, for they are not the images of God. The Word of God came in his own Person, because it was he alone, the Image of the Father, who could recreate man after the image.[a]

a. Athanasius, *On the Incarnation* 13 (translation adapted from Athanasius, *On the Incarnation: The Treatise De incarnatione Verbi Dei*, trans. and ed. a religious of CSMV [Crestwood, NY: St. Vladimir's Seminary Press, 1993], 40–41).

2:16–17   Verse 16 sums up the section by returning to the contrast between Christ and the angels that began in 1:4. The Son of God is high above the angels, yet he lowered himself beneath them (v. 9) because it is not **angels** who need to be freed from death but human beings. Angels are "spirits" (1:14), purely spiritual beings who cannot die. The Greek verb for **help** (here in the present tense) can also be translated "take hold of," as God took his people by the hand to free them from slavery in Egypt (Jer 31:32 †LXX). Jesus takes hold of **the descendants of Abraham** (literally, "seed of Abraham"). The early Church came to recognize that the seed of Abraham refers to both his physical descendants, the Jews, and all believers who through faith have been brought into his covenant family (see Gal 3:29).

The insight that is at the heart of the theology of Hebrews is now directly stated for the first time: Jesus is **high priest**.[28] With the hindsight of two millennia of Christian thought, it is difficult for us to appreciate the groundbreaking originality of this insight. Other New Testament writings hint at the themes of priesthood and sacrifice in relation to Christ's death,[29] but only Hebrews calls

28. Hebrews identifies Christ as "high priest" in 3:1; 4:14, 15; 5:5, 10; 6:20; 7:26; 8:1, 3; 9:11.

29. Mark 10:45; Luke 22:19–20; John 2:19–22; 4:21–23. See Brant Pitre, "Jesus, the New Temple, and the New Priesthood," *Letter & Spirit* 4 (2008): 47–83; Crispin H. T. Fletcher-Louis, "Jesus as the High Priestly Messiah" (2 parts), *Journal for the Study of the Historical Jesus* 4, no. 2 (2006): 155–75;

By What Authority?

The author of Hebrews makes statements that are unique among the writings of the New Testament. Only he speaks of Christ as high priest, as having been "made perfect," and as having fulfilled the †Yom Kippur sacrifices. What is the source of his authority to make these claims?

First, it is important to note that this author's work is in full continuity with what the early Church already understood. Other texts present Jesus' death as a †sacrifice (1 Cor 5:7; Eph 5:2), based on Jesus' own words and gestures at the Last Supper (Mark 14:22–24). The New Testament also makes clear that it was Christ himself who offered this sacrifice (John 10:18; Eph 5:2). Jesus spoke in veiled terms of his priestly authority (Matt 12:3–6). The Gospel of Luke opens with a priest of the old covenant, Zechariah, entering the temple to offer incense, and ends with Jesus giving his apostles a priestly blessing (Luke 24:50)—a hint that the old covenant priesthood is fulfilled in him.

Second, the author of Hebrews has reflected deeply on the mystery of Christ in light of God's word in the Old Testament. His teaching shows how Christ has fulfilled the hidden meaning of the Scriptures, unraveling perplexities like that of Melchizedek and Psalm 110.

Finally, the early Church came to recognize this author's work as inspired by the Holy Spirit, including it in the canon of Scripture. The words of the apostle Paul can well be applied to the author of Hebrews: "When you read this you can understand my insight into the mystery of Christ, which was not made known to human beings in other generations as it has now been revealed to his holy apostles and prophets by the Spirit" (Eph 3:4–5). His deeper insight into Christ's paschal mystery was part of the process of the Holy Spirit leading the Church into all the truth, as Christ promised (John 16:13).

Jesus a "priest." Even more, Hebrews views Christ's priesthood as the interpretive key for explaining the whole mystery of how we are saved.

Verse 17 describes Jesus' priesthood in terms directly taken from the Old Testament: his task was **to expiate the sins of the people**. To "expiate" (*hilaskomai*) means to "atone for" or "remove" sin. It recalls the rite of the †Day of Atonement (Yom Kippur), when the high priest would enter the †Holy of Holies and sprinkle the blood of a sacrificed animal on the cover of the †ark of the covenant, the †mercy seat (*hilastērion*), making †atonement for the people's sins (Lev 16:15;

Journal for the Study of the Historical Jesus 5, no. 1 (2007): 57–79; Albert Vanhoye, *Old Testament Priests and the New Priest: According to the New Testament*, trans. Bernard Orchard, rev. ed. (Leominster: Gracewing, 2009).

Fig. 3. Stone carving of the ark of the covenant from the fourth- or fifth-century AD synagogue in Capernaum

© Baker Publishing Group

see sidebar, "The Day of Atonement," p. 168). How Jesus fulfills this rite will be explained in chapter 9.

In describing how Christ became a priest, Hebrews has a strikingly different emphasis from the Old Testament. The law of Moses underscores the need for a priest to be *set apart from* the people so he can approach the holy God (Lev 8–10). But for Christ to become a priest, Hebrews does not say he had to be separated from others. Rather, he had to be made **like his brothers in every way**; that is, he had to become incarnate (see sidebar, "Priestly Separation in the Old Covenant," p. 104). He had to experience temptation, suffering, and death, so **that he might be a merciful and faithful** high priest. This phrase alludes to God's promise in 1 Samuel 2:35: "I will choose a faithful priest who will do what I have in heart and mind." Significantly, Hebrews adds the quality "merciful." Mercy and faithfulness (sometimes translated as "steadfast love" and "fidelity") are two of the central attributes of God (Exod 34:6; Ps 25:10; 57:4; 61:8),[30] which Jesus now incarnates as man. Hebrews will elaborate in 3:1–6 on how Jesus is *faithful* to God, and in 4:14–5:10 on how he is *merciful* to his people.

2:18 Jesus has proven faithful precisely because his faithfulness was **tested** by his arduous sufferings. The verb for "tested" (*peirazomai*) also means to be "tempted"—to be put through a difficult trial that entices one toward sin. Jesus was tempted by Satan in the desert at the beginning of his ministry (Matt 4:1; Luke 4:2), by the Pharisees and even Peter in the middle of his ministry (Matt 16:1, 23), and by scoffers who goaded him to come down from the cross at the end of his ministry (Mark 15:29–32). **Because he himself** had the experience of having to resist temptation, **he is able to help those who are being tested**. In the Old Testament God is often said to "help" his people (Ps 37:40; Isa 41:10). But now there is a new and unexpected dimension to God's help. The Son of God can fully identify with us. He comes to us in times of trial as one who understands our human experience from the inside.

This densely packed section (2:10–18) has explained why it was "fitting" (v. 10) for God's Son to be made lower than the angels. At the same time, it has introduced the major themes that will be developed later in the letter: Jesus'

---

30. In these texts the Septuagint translates *emet*, the Hebrew word for "fidelity," with *alētheia* ("truth") or *alēthinos* ("truthful").

high priesthood (3:1–10:39), his atoning death on the cross (9:26), his role as "leader" of our salvation (12:2), and his solidarity as firstborn Son with us, his younger brothers and sisters (4:15).

Reflection and Application (2:10–18)

Hebrews 2:15 is a sober assessment of the human condition: we are "those who through fear of death had been subject to slavery all their life." Death is the one absolutely certain and inescapable reality of human existence. Ever since the fall, human beings have been gripped by a primordial fear not only of physical death but of every form of diminishment that is a sign of approaching death—bodily ailments, loss of youthful attractiveness, career disappointments and failures, being treated unjustly or rudely, getting bested by others. The compulsion to avoid these little deaths at all costs is a hidden cause of much destructive behavior, a genuine "slavery." But the core of the Christian good news is that Christ has defeated death. "Christ is risen from the dead. By death he trampled death and to those in the tomb he granted life."[31] Death has lost its "sting" (1 Cor 15:55) and become a doorway to a new and glorious life. Our life as Christians is meant to exhibit the freedom that comes from having this deep-seated fear progressively lifted from us.

St. Francis of Assisi was a striking example of such liberation. As his contemporaries recount, it was impossible to harm Francis. If you insulted him, he would thank you for reminding him of his sinfulness. If you threatened him, he would rejoice at the persecution. If you took his cloak, he would try to give you his robe as well. In his very vulnerability, he was invincible! Such joy and freedom even in the face of death was a major cause of the exponential spread of Christianity in the ancient world and plays a no less crucial role in the new evangelization today.

---

31. Easter Troparion, a liturgical hymn sung in the Eastern churches.

Pilgrims and Partakers

Hebrews 3:1–19

Among all the writings of the New Testament, Hebrews is unique in attributing to Jesus the title "priest." This was a brilliant insight, a deeper revelation arrived at only after years of reflection on the meaning of Christ's passion under the inspiration of the Holy Spirit (see sidebar, "By What Authority?," p. 67). For first-century Jews, recognizing Christ as a priest required a revolution in thought. For over a millennium they had related to God through the †levitical priesthood instituted during the exodus, whose function was to offer animal †sacrifices in the Jerusalem temple. In order to see Christ's death as a priestly act, the whole meaning of the priesthood had to be transposed to a new level and understood in a new way. Hebrews first announced the theme of Christ's priesthood in 2:17, and this insight will unfold throughout chapters 3–10. Chapters 3–5 begin by elaborating on the two qualities that described Christ's priesthood in 2:17: he is *faithful* (3:1–6) and *merciful* (4:14–5:10).

As noted above, Hebrews alternates between doctrine (teaching about God and what he has done for us) and exhortation (how we are to respond). The first exhortation was in 2:1–4. The second, in the form of a lengthy meditation on Psalm 95, runs all the way through chapters 3–4. The author uses this psalm to give Christians a vision of our identity as God's people, the Church.[1] Surprisingly, given his emphasis on the fulfillment of God's promises, he calls us to identify

1. Albert Vanhoye points out that 3:1–5:10 is the first of two great ecclesial sections in Hebrews, the second being 11:1–12:13 (*La structure littéraire de l'Épître aux Hébreux*, Studia neotestamentica 1 [Paris: Desclée de Brouwer, 1963], 240–42). The first is about how the Church must avoid faithlessness; the second is about how the Church must imitate faithfulness.

with the generation of Israelites who wandered for forty years in the desert. Like them, we are *pilgrims* traveling on the way to a promised homeland. Like them, we are being tested: In the face of trials and dangers will we cling to God in trust and obedience, or will we harden our hearts in unbelief? But there is also a crucial difference. Unlike the ancient Israelites, we are already *partakers* in Christ (3:14). Even now we share in the heavenly blessings promised by God, although not fully until we reach the city "that is to come" (13:14).

Greater than Moses (3:1–6)

¹Therefore, holy "brothers," sharing in a heavenly calling, reflect on Jesus, the apostle and high priest of our confession, ²who was faithful to the one who appointed him, just as Moses was "faithful in [all] his house." ³But he is worthy of more "glory" than Moses, as the founder of a house has more "honor" than the house itself. ⁴Every house is founded by someone, but the founder of all is God. ⁵Moses was "faithful in all his house" as a "servant" to testify to what would be spoken, ⁶but Christ was faithful as a son placed over his house. We are his house, if [only] we hold fast to our confidence and pride in our hope.

OT: Num 12:1–8; 2 Sam 7:12–13
NT: John 5:39, 46; Heb 3:14; 6:11, 18; 10:23
Catechism: the Church as household of God, 756; Israel and the Church, 761–62

No figure in Israel's history looms larger than Moses, the great lawgiver who led the people out of slavery in Egypt, parted the Rea Sea, and mediated God's covenant with Israel at Mount Sinai (Exod 19–24; see Sir 45:1–5). The law of Moses was the foundation of Israel's faith, and the levitical priesthood set up by Moses was the foundation of Israel's worship. Sirach even affirms that Moses was "equal in glory to the holy ones," the angels (Sir 45:2 RSV). Yet just as chapter 1 of Hebrews showed that Jesus is far superior to the angels who transmitted the law, so chapter 3 will explain that he is far superior to Moses the lawgiver. In fact, all that God did for his people in and through Moses has found its fulfillment in Jesus.

The author addresses his hearers solemnly but affectionately as **holy** **3:1** **"brothers."**[2] Christians are the brothers and sisters of whom Jesus is not ashamed, and to whom he proclaims God's name (2:11–12). Throughout the New

2. The NAB puts "brothers" in quotation marks to signal that Ps 22, quoted above at 2:12, is still being echoed.

zeevveez/Wikimedia Commons

Fig. 4. Mosaic of Moses holding a scroll of the Torah, located in the Jewish Quarter of Jerusalem

Testament Christians are called "holy" not because of a moral excellence we have achieved but because of what God has done for us (see Acts 9:13; 2 Cor 1:1). The holiness to which we are called is always a living out of the holiness already given to us through faith and baptism. We share in **a heavenly calling**, an invitation that comes from heaven and that draws us toward heaven, our true homeland (11:16; 13:14; Phil 3:20). Because of this calling we are like pilgrims on a journey, never completely at home in this life (see 11:13–16).

Jesus' solidarity with us, described above (2:10–18), ought to lead us to **reflect on**, "fix [our] thoughts on" (NIV), or "turn [our] minds to" (NJB) **Jesus**—an exhortation that will be repeated in 12:2. The original audience of Hebrews probably had to be reminded not to gaze backward toward Moses, the great leader of old, but forward to Jesus, who leads us to our heavenly destiny. Jesus is called **apostle** ("one who is sent," an emissary) only here in the New Testament, though in the Gospels he identifies himself as the one "sent" into the world by the Father (Mark 9:37; Luke 10:16; John 12:44). He is both the apostle sent to us by God and the **high priest** who responds to God on our behalf.

Jesus is also the substance of **our confession**, the faith we profess openly to the world. The idea that faith could be a private matter, "between me and God," is foreign to Hebrews, as it is to the entire New Testament. Christian faith is something to be boldly confessed, even at great cost to ourselves (see 10:32–34; Mark 8:38; Rom 10:10).

3:2–3   Before contrasting Jesus with Moses, Hebrews describes what they have in common. Jesus was faithful **to the one who appointed him, just as Moses was "faithful in [all] his house."** This phrase recalls the story in Numbers where Aaron and Miriam, in a fit of jealousy, challenged the authority of their younger brother, Moses. God, in response, rebuked them and reaffirmed Moses' unique status as his servant who had been entrusted with his whole household, the people of Israel (Num 12:7–8). Moses faithfully carried out his commission as a leader of God's wayward people. In this sense, Jesus is like Moses. Yet Jesus **is worthy of more "glory" than Moses, as the founder** (or "builder") **of a house has more "honor" than the house itself.**[3] Moses was an honored servant in God's household, but Jesus is the builder who created the household in the first place.

Jesus' role as builder of God's house was foreshadowed in the great promise that God made to David. David had wanted to build a temple for God, but God responded through the prophet Nathan, "I will raise up your offspring after you. . . . He it is who shall build a house for my name, and I will establish his royal throne forever" (2 Sam 7:12–13; see Zech 6:13). David's son Solomon built the temple, but it is Jesus who builds the Church, the true and lasting house for God's name, as he himself prophesied: "Destroy this temple and in three days I will raise it up" (John 2:19; see Mark 14:58).

It is self-evident that **every house is founded** (or "built") **by someone. But**   3:4 **the founder of all is God.** Hebrews is playing on the rich multivalence in the biblical meaning of "house." God's house can refer to the Jerusalem *temple* or to the household or family of God's people, *Israel*, and now to the *Church* (Eph 2:21; 1 Pet 2:5). God is the true architect and builder of the house in all these senses. But in verse 3 Hebrews identified Jesus too as the "founder" or builder, the divine craftsman of both the old creation and the new, redeemed creation (1:2, 10; 2:5; see Rev 21:1).

Emphasizing the contrast, Hebrews again states that **Moses was "faithful in**   3:5 **all his house" as a "servant,"** quoting Numbers 12:7. To be counted a servant of God was a high honor in the Old Testament.[4] During his lifetime Moses was chief servant, or steward, over the other servants in God's household. But his primary task was **to testify to what would be spoken** later. God gave the law and worked miracles through Moses, yet Moses was called to point beyond himself to the far greater revelation that these prefigured, the final word that God would speak through his Son (1:1–2). Like other saints of the old covenant, Moses "did not receive what had been promised but saw it and greeted it from afar" (11:13).

This understanding that the Old Testament bears witness to Christ, though in a hidden way, was foundational to the preaching of the early Church (see

---

3. The NAB puts "glory" and "honor" in quotation marks to signal that Hebrews is still echoing the quotation from Ps 8 above (2:6–8). "Glory" also implies another Jesus-Moses contrast based on the same passage in Num 12: whereas Moses had the privilege of seeing God's glory (Num 12:8 LXX), Jesus *is* the radiance of God's glory (Heb 1:3). See Luke Timothy Johnson, *Hebrews: A Commentary*, New Testament Library (Louisville: Westminster John Knox, 2006), 109.

4. The Old Testament accords this title to figures such as Abraham, Isaac, Jacob, Job, Moses, David, Elijah, Isaiah, and the whole people Israel (Isa 41:8).

Acts 10:43; Rom 3:21; 1 Pet 1:10–11). In the Gospel of John, Jesus asserts that the law of Moses testifies to him: "The scriptures . . . testify on my behalf. . . . If you had believed Moses, you would have believed me, because he wrote about me" (John 5:39, 46; see Luke 24:27, 44).

3:6   **Christ** was, like Moses, God's servant (Mark 10:45; Acts 3:13)—indeed the servant par excellence, in whom Isaiah's prophecies of the Suffering Servant are perfectly fulfilled.[5] Jesus' *attitude* was that of a servant, as Paul indicates: "He emptied himself, / taking the form of a slave, . . . he humbled himself, / becoming obedient to death" (Phil 2:7–8). But his *authority* is that of a **son placed over** God's **house**, the master to whom all the household servants are ultimately accountable (see Matt 25:19; Luke 12:37).

Hebrews ends the section by declaring that **we are his house** (literally, "whose house we are"); that is, we are both God's household or family and his temple, as Paul says in a similar way: "God's temple is holy, and that temple you are" (1 Cor 3:17 RSV). This statement affirms the continuity between God's people of the old covenant and the new. The same household in which Moses faithfully served is the one over which Christ rules as Son and heir, and to which all Christians, whether Jews or Gentiles, now belong. And it follows that everything written about God's people of old pertains to us as well, as will be seen in the next section.

But there is a proviso: **if [only] we hold fast to our confidence and pride in our hope**. The privilege of belonging to God's household calls for an ongoing faithful response: we must "hold fast" rather than "drift away" (see 2:1). What we are to have confidence in is not our own resources but the power of Christ's redemption. The Greek term for "confidence" (*parrēsia*) can mean "†boldness" or "fearlessness," as in the preaching of the apostles after Pentecost (Acts 4:13, 29, 31). It is a key theme in Hebrews, describing how we who have been cleansed by the blood of Jesus are now to approach God's throne: not timidly or fearfully but confidently (4:16; 10:19). Similarly, the Greek word for "pride" is literally "boast," and it refers not to the act of boasting but to the ground for our boasting, which is the glorious kingdom that we will one day receive in Christ (see 10:25; 12:28).

By speaking of our "hope," the passage returns full circle to the "heavenly calling" mentioned in 3:1. It began by looking ahead to the goal of our pilgrimage, then glanced backward at the old covenant household of God, now fulfilled in the Church, and ends by looking forward again to the consummation of God's

---

5. Isa 42:1–9; 49:1–7; 50:4–11; 52:12–53:13. See Philip Edgcumbe Hughes, *A Commentary on the Epistle to the Hebrews* (Grand Rapids: Eerdmans, 1977), 135.

plan. The same exhortation to hold on to hope will be repeated in 3:14; 6:11, 18; 10:23. We can sense the author's deep concern that his listeners—like many Christians today—are at risk of giving in to discouragement and so need to be rekindled in hope of their heavenly inheritance.

Harden Not Your Hearts (3:7–11)

⁷Therefore, as the holy Spirit says:

> "Oh, that today you would hear his voice,
>   ⁸"Harden not your hearts as at the rebellion
>   in the day of testing in the desert,
>   ⁹where your ancestors tested and tried me
>   and saw my works ¹⁰for forty years.
> Because of this I was provoked with that generation
>   and I said, "They have always been of erring heart,
>   and they do not know my ways."
>   ¹¹As I swore in my wrath,
>   "They shall not enter into my rest.""

OT: Ps 95; Num 14:28–35; Neh 9:15–16
NT: Matt 13:15; Acts 7:36–42, 51; 1 Cor 10:1–13
Catechism: "today" of the liturgy, 1165

Having shown that Jesus is infinitely greater than Moses, Hebrews now delivers a solemn warning to readers: do not follow the example of the exodus generation led by Moses! The admonition is in the form of a lengthy meditation on Psalm 95, running from 3:7 all the way to the end of chapter 4. The whole section is sprinkled with verbs of exhortation: "Hear . . . harden not . . . take care . . . encourage . . . hold firm . . . be on guard . . . strive . . . hold fast . . . confidently approach."

Psalm 95 is familiar to many Catholics as the invitatory psalm prayed daily at the beginning of the Liturgy of the Hours. This psalm recalls the great event of the exodus and urges God's people in the present not to rebel against God as the Israelites did in the past, for God speaks to us today just as he did then: "Oh, that today you would hear his voice!" Hebrews' use of the psalm implies that we, as Christians, are spiritually reliving the Israelites' pilgrimage in the desert. Like our ancient ancestors in faith, we have experienced God's mighty work of deliverance—they from slavery in Egypt, we from slavery to sin and death—and are called to enter into the inheritance that God has promised us. Faced with

Psalm 95 in Christian Tradition

LIVING TRADITION

Psalm 95 has held a special place of honor in Christian tradition ever since St. Benedict (c. 480–c. 547), the father of Western monasticism, mandated that it be the first psalm of the day, sung by monks in the hours long before dawn. Benedict knew that this psalm would dispose the one who prays it to listen attentively to God's voice throughout the day. He exhorts the just-awakened monk,

> Let us open our eyes to the deifying light, let us hear with awestruck ears the warning which the divine voice cries daily to us, "Today if you hear His voice, harden not your hearts" (Ps 95:8). And again, "Whoever has ears to hear, hear what the Spirit says to the churches" (Rev 2:7). And what does he say? "Come, my children, listen to me; I will teach you the fear of the Lord" (Ps 34:12). "Run while you have the light of life, lest the darkness of death overtake you" (John 12:35).[a]

a. *Rule of St. Benedict*, prologue.

fears, trials, and obstacles, we, like them, have a choice: either to trust that God will complete the mighty work he has begun or to grumble and rebel against him. The consequences for us are just as momentous as for our ancient forebears, who because of their disobedience were barred from entering the promised land (Num 14:22–23, 29–35). Then what difference is there between us and them? If they failed, what is to keep us from failing? The key to the admonition is in verse 14: we are partakers in Christ. No matter how weak we are in ourselves, we can share in Jesus' own faithfulness, if only we hold firm to the end.

3:7 Just as at 2:1, this exhortation begins with **therefore**, showing that it directly follows from the truths just presented (vv. 1–6). Before quoting Psalm 95, Hebrews reminds us that this psalm—and by implication, all Scripture—is not a dead letter remaining in the past. It is what **the holy Spirit says** to us today. This implies that the psalm finds its ultimate reference point, its fullest meaning, in Christ and his Church.[6] In a similar way, Paul says of the exodus generation, "These things happened to them as an example, and they have been written down as a warning to us, upon whom the end of the ages has come" (1 Cor 10:11).

Psalm 95 begins with a jubilant call to worship: "Come, let us sing joyfully to the LORD; / cry out to the rock of our salvation. / Let us come before him with a song of praise, / joyfully sing out our psalms." The psalm celebrates the

6. Donald Hagner, *Encountering the Book of Hebrews: An Exposition*, Encountering Biblical Studies (Grand Rapids: Baker Academic, 2002), 67.

How First-Century Jews Interpreted Scripture

BIBLICAL BACKGROUND

The author of Hebrews was, like St. Paul, deeply familiar with the Scriptures and was a master of ancient Jewish methods of interpretation. Much of Hebrews is in the form of midrash, a kind of interpretation that quotes a portion of Scripture and then draws out its meaning for the present generation. Hebrews 3–4 is a classic example of a midrash on Psalm 95 (for other examples, see Heb 2:5–9; 10:5–14; 12:5–11). After quoting a long portion of the psalm in 3:7–11, our author repeatedly picks up key phrases such as "today," "provoked for forty years," and "they shall not enter into my rest," showing how this psalm is God's "living and effective" word to present-day readers (see 4:12).

Hebrews also uses the form of argument known as *a fortiori* or, in Hebrew, [†]*qal wahomer* (see comments on 2:2). Hebrews 9:13–14, for instance, argues that if the blood of sacrificed animals could cleanse people ritually, how much more does the blood of Christ cleanse us truly and interiorly. Paul uses this device in his letters (Rom 5:15; 1 Cor 12:22; 2 Cor 3:11), as does Jesus in his preaching (Matt 6:30; 7:11).

Another technique, known as [†]*gezerah shawa*, draws a connection between two seemingly unrelated Scripture passages by means of a catchword that appears in both. Hebrews 4:3–4, for instance, connects Psalm 95:7–11 with Genesis 2:2 (in their Septuagint versions) based on the words "rest," "work," and "day."

The early Christians were formed by and wrote from within the Jewish tradition of biblical interpretation. But there was also an essential difference. The Christian conviction, rooted in the teaching of Jesus himself,[a] is that Jesus Christ is the key that opens up the meaning of all Scripture and all history.[b] God ordered all salvation history according to a plan that mysteriously pointed forward to Christ and reached its culmination in him. The entire thrust of the Letter to the Hebrews is to demonstrate this [†]christological fulfillment in an original and compelling way.

a. During his public ministry Jesus continually preached from biblical texts and interpreted them as referring to himself. For a representative sampling, see Matt 11:4–5; 21:42; 26:24, 31, 54; Mark 14:21, 49; Luke 4:18–21; 22:37; 24:27, 44–45; John 5:39, 46.

b. In Rev 5:1–7 this is illustrated by the image of the Lamb (Jesus) who alone can take the sealed scroll and break open its seals.

Lord, the "great king over all gods" and creator of all things, who shepherds his people like a flock. Hebrews surely has all this context in mind, but it begins the quotation at verse 7, where the psalm's mood suddenly changes to urgent exhortation: **Oh, that today you would hear his voice**. This phrase expresses God's longing that his people would listen to him, as in Psalm 81:14: "O that my people would listen to me, / that Israel would walk in my ways." It recalls the †Great Shema, Israel's central confession of faith: "Hear, O Israel . . ." (Deut 6:4). God's people are summoned not only to heed his past words but also to hear his living voice addressing us in the present.

3:8   The psalm continues: **Harden not your hearts as at the rebellion in the day of testing in the desert**. The original Hebrew version of the psalm names Massah and Meribah, the place where the Israelites grumbled that God had brought them out of Egypt only to let them die of thirst (Exod 17:1–7). But our author is quoting the †Septuagint, which translates the meaning of Massah and Meribah ("rebellion" and "testing") in order to refer to such misconduct in general. Verse 11 of the psalm refers to another key moment in Israel's desert journey: the rebellion at Kadesh (Num 14). There the Israelites, just when they arrived at the border of the promised land, gave in to panic when they heard about the gigantic, warlike Canaanite inhabitants and refused to enter the land. They groused, "If only we had died in the land of Egypt. . . . Why is the Lord bringing us into this land only to have us fall by the sword?" (Num 14:2–3). This was the generation that had witnessed the plagues visited on Egypt, had crossed the Red Sea on dry land, had fed on miraculous manna, and had seen water flow from the rock Moses struck. Yet when God invited them to enter the land he had promised them, they got cold feet and refused to trust him.

3:9–10   The psalm continues: **where your ancestors tested and tried me and saw my works for forty years**. It was because of the unbelief at Kadesh that God sentenced the Israelites to wander in the wilderness for forty years, "forty" being a number that in the Bible often signifies a time of testing.[7] During that period they continued to test God's patience with numerous acts of disobedience, as vividly depicted in Numbers 15–25. But in reality, it was God who was testing *them* (Deut 8:2), showing them countless proofs of his love, inviting them to trust him more deeply. Yet they "saw" those works without really seeing (Deut 29:1–3). Psalm 95 declares God's indictment of that wilderness generation: **They have always been of erring heart** (literally, "are always led astray in heart"), **and they do not know my ways**. An erring heart is one that wanders away from God, failing to believe him wholeheartedly, and is therefore prone to rely on human thinking and human resources.

Hebrews is inviting readers to see the parallels with their own situation: the temptation to abandon Christ and the unshakable kingdom he promises (12:28)

---

7. See Num 14:34; Deut 8:2; Jonah 3:4; Matt 4:2.

because of their fears, hardships, and persecutions. There may be a special significance in the mention of forty years. If Hebrews was written shortly before the destruction of the temple in AD 70 (see "Date" in the introduction), then it had been almost forty years since Jesus had accomplished his "exodus" in Jerusalem—his death and resurrection (see Luke 9:31). It was a new time of testing. The end of the old covenant worship—the whole †levitical system with its animal sacrifices—was imminent, and the Jewish Christian readers of Hebrews were being urgently called to leave behind their reliance on the old law and cling steadfastly to Christ.

Because the Israelites refused to enter the land (Num 14:2–4), God granted **3:11** their wish. In fact, he swore an oath that none of that generation, except Joshua and Caleb, who had trusted him, would set foot in the land (Num 14:28–35). **As I swore in my wrath, / "They shall not enter into my rest."** The "rest" from which the rebellious Israelites were barred was the land of Canaan, with its fertile pastureland, lush vineyards and orchards, and fortified cities providing security from enemies (see Neh 9:25). But as Hebrews will explain in chapter 4, the land points beyond itself to a far more glorious reality: the eternal rest of God himself. Hebrews is urgently exhorting Christians not to forfeit our right of entrance into that blessed inheritance.

A Call to Faithfulness (3:12–19)

---

¹²**Take care, brothers, that none of you may have an evil and unfaithful heart, so as to forsake the living God. ¹³Encourage yourselves daily while it is still "today," so that none of you may grow hardened by the deceit of sin. ¹⁴We have become partners of Christ if only we hold the beginning of the reality firm until the end, ¹⁵for it is said:**

> **"Oh, that today you would hear his voice:**
> **'Harden not your hearts as at the rebellion.'"**

¹⁶**Who were those who rebelled when they heard? Was it not all those who came out of Egypt under Moses? ¹⁷With whom was he "provoked for forty years"? Was it not those who had sinned, whose corpses fell in the desert? ¹⁸And to whom did he "swear that they should not enter into his rest," if not to those who were disobedient? ¹⁹And we see that they could not enter for lack of faith.**

OT: Ps 95; Num 14:21–35; Deut 1:34–35; Ps 78:17–22; Jer 7:23–24
NT: Acts 7:36–42, 51; 1 Cor 10:1–13; 1 Thess 5:11; Heb 6:11; 10:24; Jude 5
Catechism: "today" of the liturgy, 1165; hardened heart, 1432; faith and obedience, 144–49

3:12   Following the quotation from Psalm 95, Hebrews now applies it to present-day readers. The psalm prompts an urgent warning: **Take care, brothers, that none of you may have an evil and unfaithful heart** (literally, "an evil heart of unbelief"). A heart of unbelief is not that of a person who has never known Christ but rather of one who loses faith and falls away from him in time of trial, like the seed sown on rocky ground (Mark 4:16–17). As Hebrews will emphasize repeatedly, to abandon faith in Christ is far worse than never to have had faith in the first place (6:4–6; 10:26–27; see 2 Pet 2:20–21). Unfaithfulness is closely connected with evil because it is usually a willful attachment to sin that leads a person to **forsake the living God.** To forsake God is inevitably to fall into idolatry, to adore false and lifeless gods, whether the wood and stone idols that the ancients worshiped or the gods of material security, success, and pleasure that tempt people today.

3:13   Therefore, **encourage yourselves daily** (a better translation would be "encourage one another daily"). The Greek word for "encourage" (*parakaleō*) is related to Paraclete (meaning "comforter," "counselor," or "advocate"), the title Jesus gives the Holy Spirit in John 14:26. Our responsibility as Christians is to comfort, counsel, encourage, and exhort each other so that when one person falters in faith, he or she is upheld by others. **While it is still "today"** is a warning that a day will come, *the* day of the Lord (Heb 10:25), when God's plan will come to its culmination and no more decisions will be possible. Until then, we must be vigilant that none of us **grow hardened by the deceit of sin.** The "deceit of sin" alludes to the fall, when Satan deceived Eve into disobeying God through illusory promises of knowledge and immortality (Gen 3:1–6). The same psychology of sin prevails in every generation: Satan deludes us into thinking that God is the adversary of our happiness, and so we grasp for happiness on our own terms (see Eph 4:22). If a person persists in sin, that self-will can harden into active resistance to God.

3:14   The analogy between Christians and the rebellious exodus generation could lead to discouragement, unless we keep in mind a fundamental difference between us and them: **We have become partners of Christ** (or "we share in Christ," RSV; "we are made partakers of Christ," KJV). The Greek word for "partners" (*metochoi*) can mean "companions" as in 1:9, but here it probably refers on a deeper level to our union with Christ through faith and baptism. We have come to share in his own divine life and thus in his heavenly kingdom (see Luke 12:32; Rom 8:17). Later Hebrews will add that we have also become sharers (*metochoi*) in the Holy Spirit (6:4).

But this gift is conditional (as in v. 6): **if only we hold the beginning of the reality firm until the end** (or "if only we hold our first confidence firm to

Why We Need to Encourage One Another Daily

St. John Chrysostom, commenting on Hebrews 3:13, explained why we should always encourage sinners to have hope:

> He said "today," that they might never be without hope. "Exhort one another daily," he says. That is, even if persons have sinned, as long as it is "today" they have hope; let them not then despair so long as they live. Above all things indeed, he says, "Let there not be an evil, unbelieving heart." But even if there should be, let no one despair, but let that one recover; for as long as we are in this world, the "today" is in season.[a]

In more recent times a similar message of encouragement was given through St. Faustina Kowalska, the apostle of Divine Mercy:

> [Let] the greatest sinners place their trust in My mercy. They have the right before others to trust in the abyss of My mercy. . . . Souls that make an appeal to My mercy delight Me. To such souls I grant even more graces than they ask. I cannot punish even the greatest sinner if he makes an appeal to My compassion, but on the contrary, I justify him in My unfathomable and inscrutable mercy. Write: before I come as a just Judge, I first open wide the door of My mercy. He who refuses to pass through the door of My mercy must pass through the door of My justice.[b]

a. *Homilies on the Epistle to the Hebrews* 6.8 (translation adapted from *NPNF* I, vol. 14).
b. *Diary* 1146 (translation from *Diary: Divine Mercy in My Soul* [Stockbridge, MA: Marian Press, 2003]).

the end," RSV). We must not be presumptuous about our share in Christ, as Hebrews will say even more emphatically in chapter 6. In a similar way, Jesus urgently warned his disciples in the final days before his passion: "Be watchful! Be alert! . . . you do not know when the lord of the house is coming. . . . May he not come suddenly and find you sleeping" (Mark 13:33–36). The danger to be avoided at all costs is that of becoming complacent and slacking off from the radical commitment to Christ that we had at first, at the time of conversion or when we fully and consciously embraced our baptismal call.

The quote from Psalm 95 continues: **Oh, that today you would hear his** 3:15 **voice: / "Harden not your hearts as at the rebellion."** The speech of God that we are called to hear "today" is specifically the gospel, spoken through his Son (1:2; 2:3; 4:2). Christians need to hear God's living voice on a daily basis, speaking to us through prayer and Scripture, through the beauty of creation and the events of life, and through faith-building conversations with others.

Otherwise, Hebrews warns, the bumps and bruises of life can lead us imperceptibly to harden our hearts—to doubt God's love, presence, and care for us and to begin to close ourselves off from him.

3:16   The contemporary relevance of the psalm becomes even more evident in verses 16–17 with a series of rhetorical questions. **Who were those who rebelled when they heard? Was it not all those who came out of Egypt under Moses?** The sobering truth is that those who rebelled were not pagans who had no knowledge of God. They were God's chosen people who had experienced the most stupendous act of salvation ever seen up to that time—the plagues visited on Egypt, miraculous rescue from Pharaoh's army, and divine guidance in the desert. If such rebellion can occur in them, the implication is, do not think it cannot happen to you, for Christians have experienced an even greater act of salvation. In a similar way, Paul warned the early Christians to learn from the errors of our ancestors in faith: "Our ancestors were all . . . baptized into Moses in the cloud and in the sea. . . . Yet God was not pleased with most of them, for they were struck down in the desert. These things happened as examples for us" (1 Cor 10:1–6; see Jude 5).

3:17   **With whom was he "provoked for forty years"? Was it not those who had sinned, whose corpses fell in the desert?**[8] With the exception of Joshua and Caleb, all the Israelites who had been rescued from Egypt caved in to fear and refused God's invitation to enter the promised land. This was the sin that led to God's judgment: "Your bodies shall fall here in the wilderness, while your children will wander for forty years, suffering for your infidelity, till the last of you lies dead in the wilderness" (Num 14:32–33). A journey that could have taken only a few weeks lasted an entire generation (in Hebrew reckoning, a generation spans forty years). Only those who had been children during the exodus and were untainted by their parents' sin saw the fulfillment of the promise.

3:18–19   **And to whom did he "swear that they should not enter into his rest," if not to those who were disobedient?** The "rest" that the Israelites failed to enter was the land of Canaan, the land flowing with milk and honey (Num 14:8) where God wanted them to enjoy peace, security, and covenant fellowship with himself. In verse 18 Hebrews notes that it was because of disobedience that God barred them from entering it (see Num 14:22), but verse 19 seems to give a different reason: **they could not enter for lack of faith** (or "unbelief," RSV). What was the problem: disobedience or unbelief? In reality, Hebrews is showing that faith

---

8. The author has slightly varied the quotation: at 3:9–10 above, the people saw God's works for forty years; here God was provoked for the same forty years. Both are legitimate ways of reading Ps 95:9–10 LXX.

and obedience are two sides of a coin (see John 3:36; Rom 1:5; 16:26). There is no such thing as faith in God without obedience, nor obedience without faith. Faith is expressed in action. To obey God is to make an act of trust in him; to disobey is to fail to trust him. By their unbelief, the Israelites chose to rely on themselves and thus made themselves incapable of enjoying God's rest, because God's rest depends by its very nature on a relationship of trust in him. The readers of Hebrews are in danger of following precisely this pattern.

Reflection and Application (3:12–19)

Hebrews issues a stern warning of the kind we do not often hear today: it is possible for believers, even devout believers, to become hard of heart, "fall away from the living God," and forfeit our inheritance in Christ. Statistics documenting the vast numbers of Catholics and other Christians who have abandoned the faith bear out the contemporary relevance of this warning. What can cause a person's heart to become hard? Hebrews, by using verbs like "drift away" and "fall away," implies that it can occur without a deliberate choice, simply by letting oneself passively absorb influences that weaken faith. It can also occur through the "deceitfulness of sin," by choosing what we know is wrong, then finding subtle ways of justifying it and thereby distancing ourselves from God. Or it can occur through disappointments or hurtful experiences that discourage us or perhaps cause us to build a protective wall around our heart, shutting out God and others. How do we prevent such spiritual heart disease? The remedy that Hebrews prescribes here is to "exhort one another," to live the Christian life not on our own but in close fellowship with others who can challenge and encourage us (see also 10:25). One of the best ways to do so is to find, or found, a small group of committed believers (a Bible study, prayer group, or faith-sharing group) who meet on a regular basis to pray together, share their joys and sorrows, encourage one another in difficult times, and support one another in living as committed disciples of Jesus.[9]

---

9. Parish renewal and evangelization programs that take this approach include ChristLife, Alpha for Catholics, Christ Renews His Parish, and ACTS Missions. Bible studies that can serve as excellent faith-sharing opportunities include the Great Adventure Catholic Bible Study, Catholic Scripture Study International, and Catholic Way Bible Study.

Rest for the People of God

Hebrews 4:1–16

If there is one thing that characterizes the world of the twenty-first century, it is nonstop activity. From elementary school on, young people learn to pass their days in a hectic sequence of one organized activity after another; any spare moments in between (or during!) are caught up in communication or entertainment via wireless technology. Adults struggle to juggle the demands of jobs, family responsibilities, and numerous volunteer activities. Unless families take deliberate steps, they rarely find time for the "rest" of common meals or simply spending relaxed time together.

In the face of these cultural pressures, Hebrews 4 presents us with a challenging message: our goal and task as God's people is to enter his rest. It is not obvious at first glance what Hebrews means by "God's rest." This chapter, in fact, contains some of the most difficult and complex lines of reasoning in the entire letter. But once unpacked, it is both a sober warning and a profound encouragement. Not only in the life to come but even in this life, God invites us to enter into the peace, security, and well-being that can come from him alone.

The Rest That God Promised (4:1–11)

¹Therefore, let us be on our guard while the promise of entering into his rest remains, that none of you seem to have failed. ²For in fact we have received the good news just as they did. But the word that they heard did

not profit them, for they were not united in faith with those who listened. [3]For we who believed enter into [that] rest, just as he has said:

> "As I swore in my wrath,
>   'They shall not enter into my rest,'"

and yet his works were accomplished at the foundation of the world. [4]For he has spoken somewhere about the seventh day in this manner, "And God rested on the seventh day from all his works"; [5]and again, in the previously mentioned place, "They shall not enter into my rest." [6]Therefore, since it remains that some will enter into it, and those who formerly received the good news did not enter because of disobedience, [7]he once more set a day, "today," when long afterwards he spoke through David, as already quoted:

> "Oh, that today you would hear his voice:
>   'Harden not your hearts.'"

[8]Now if Joshua had given them rest, he would not have spoken afterwards of another day. [9]Therefore, a sabbath rest still remains for the people of God. [10]And whoever enters into God's rest, rests from his own works as God did from his. [11]Therefore, let us strive to enter into that rest, so that no one may fall after the same example of disobedience.

OT: Gen 2:2; Deut 12:9; Josh 23:1; Ps 95; Jer 6:16
NT: Matt 11:28–29; Luke 13:24; Acts 7:36–42, 51; 1 Cor 10:1–13; Rev 14:13
Catechism: "today" of the liturgy, 1165; the sabbath, 345–49, 2168–72; the Lord's day, 1166–67; God's rest, 1720; faith and obedience, 144–49

Chapter 4 continues the long meditation on Psalm 95 that began in 3:7, but now the focus shifts from *hearing God's voice* to *entering God's rest*. Hebrews is suggesting that reflection on this psalm gives us a profound clue to the meaning of the Christian life. Our life, like that of the ancient Israelites, is a pilgrimage through a desert toward a better land. But the "rest" promised to them, settlement in the land of Canaan, was only a foreshadowing of the far more wonderful rest that is now available to us—the eternal "rest" of God's own divine life. As Hebrews later says, we have "better promises" (8:6) and look forward to "a better homeland, a heavenly one" (11:16). For that reason, the warning sounded in this chapter is all the more urgent: God's offer of rest will not benefit us at all unless we embrace it through steadfast faith.

4:1   **Therefore** indicates a strong logical connection to the previous verses (3:16–19). Some of the Israelites forfeited their access to God's rest; so, **let us be on our guard** (literally, "let us fear"), lest the same thing happen to us. By using

Fig. 5. The lush farmlands of northern Israel

the first-person "us," the author shows that he himself is not exempt from this constant vigilance. The fear that he urges on us is not a frantic, panicky fear but rather a sober consideration of the consequences of our actions that leads us to make good choices. It is the opposite of spiritual complacency. The Old Testament teaches that this kind of fear is the foundation for spiritual growth: "The fear of the LORD is the beginning of wisdom" (Ps 111:10; see Prov 9:10; Sir 1:9–29). Similarly, Paul advises, "Work out your salvation with fear and trembling" (Phil 2:12), and "Let anyone who thinks that he stands take heed lest he fall" (1 Cor 10:12 RSV).

The Israelites did eventually end their desert wanderings and attain "rest" in the land of Canaan. Yet the exhortation of Psalm 95 shows that **the promise of entering into his rest remains**; that is, it is not yet truly fulfilled, as verses 7–8 will explain. We are still in the "today" of Psalm 95, both a time of grace while the door to God's rest remains open and a time of weighty responsibility in which it is possible for us to forfeit this privilege. During this time our concern should be that we, or any of our fellow Christians, should **seem to have failed** (or "be found to have fallen short," NIV)—that is, that any should deprive themselves of the joy of experiencing the true rest that God has in store for us. We are to have this concern not only for ourselves individually, but for one another as well.

4:2   Surprisingly, Hebrews says that **we have received the good news just as they did** (literally, "we have been evangelized just as they were"). This accents the profound continuity between Israel and the Church. The ancient Israelites never heard the gospel (*euangelion*) of Christ, yet they were "evangelized" in the sense that they experienced the foreshadowing of the gospel, God's mighty work of redemption through their deliverance from Egypt. Paul says in a similar way, "Scripture . . . foretold the good news to Abraham" (Gal 3:8). What the ancients received in "shadow" (Heb 10:1) and anticipation is the same good news that has been fully revealed to us in Christ.

But the sobering reality is that **the word that they heard did not profit them** (or "did them no good," NJB). The good news is good news only insofar as it is accepted in faith. The Israelites who refused to believe God's word **were not united in faith with those who listened**—that is, with those who did believe, probably referring to Joshua and Caleb (Num 14:24, 30).[1]

In contrast to the unfaithful Israelites, **we who believed enter into [that] rest.**   **4:3–5** The Greek verb "believed" indicates a past event, the time of conversion to Christ. The Church is by definition the community of believers or "the faithful"—those who have believed the good news of salvation in Jesus Christ and been joined to him in baptism (see Acts 8:13; 18:8). The present tense of "enter," on the other hand, indicates that we enter into God's rest not just in the future after we die, but we already begin to enter into it in this life (see 12:22). Yet the fearsome possibility remains that some who once believed will fail to persevere in that faith (see 3:13–14). The stern warning of Psalm 95 will apply to them just as to the ancients: **As I swore in my wrath, / "They shall not enter into my rest."**

Verses 3–4 use a form of argument that was common among the ancient rabbis, called †*gezerah shawa* (see sidebar, "How First-Century Jews Interpreted Scripture," p. 77). This method draws a connection between two seemingly unrelated Scripture passages through a key word that appears in both. The author has been focusing intensely on Psalm 95, but now he links it to another passage where the same key words "works," "rest," and "day" appear: God's rest on the seventh day of creation (Gen 2:2). The vague phrase **he has spoken somewhere** is a wry way of recalling a scripture that is very well known (as in 2:6). "He" probably refers to the Holy Spirit, inspirer of the sacred writings (see 3:7).

Genesis 2:2 tells us that **God rested on the seventh day from all his works.** This passage, according to Hebrews, gives the clue to what God's rest really means: God set apart the seventh day, the sabbath, as a sign of the covenant that he would establish with his people (see Exod 20:11; 31:16–17). God called his people to observe the weekly sabbath rest as a reminder that the deepest

---

1. Some ancient manuscripts have a slightly different reading, which is the basis for the RSV translation: the word "did not meet with faith in the hearers."

The Sabbath as a Window in Eternity

LIVING TRADITION

Abraham Joshua Heschel, a leading twentieth-century American rabbi, wrote these reflections on the sabbath in biblical and Jewish tradition:

> Six days a week we wrestle with the world, wringing profit from the earth; on the Sabbath we especially care for the seed of eternity planted in the soul. The world has our hands, but our soul belongs to Someone Else. Six days a week we seek to dominate the world, on the seventh day we try to dominate the self. . . .
>
> The Sabbath is not for the sake of the weekdays; the weekdays are for the sake of Sabbath. It is not an interlude but the climax of living. . . .
>
> The art of keeping the seventh day is the art of painting on the canvas of time the mysterious grandeur of the climax of creation: as He sanctified the seventh day, so shall we. The love of the Sabbath is the love of man for what he and God have in common. Our keeping the Sabbath day is a paraphrase of His sanctification of the seventh day.
>
> What would be a world without Sabbath? It would be a world that knew only itself or God distorted as a thing or the abyss separating Him from the world; a world without the vision of a window in eternity that opens into time.[a]

a. Abraham Joshua Heschel, *The Sabbath: Its Meaning for Modern Man* (New York: Farrar, Straus & Giroux, 1951), 13–16.

meaning of life is found not in work but in living in communion with him. Moreover, the creation story mentions an end to each of the six days ("evening came, and morning") but not to the seventh day, hinting that in some sense the seventh day is everlasting. Hebrews concludes that when God says in Psalm 95 **they shall not enter into my rest**, he is referring not only to the land of Canaan but also to the eternal rest of communion with God that it prefigures.

4:6–7   The point becomes clearer in verses 6–8. The exodus generation **who formerly received the good news** (literally, "who were evangelized," as in v. 2) **did not enter** the promised land **because of disobedience**. Disobedience is equated with unbelief (as in 3:18–19): they disobeyed God because they refused to believe in him. But the rest they forfeited was only an earthly territory. God's ultimate plan to give his people rest was not yet fulfilled. This is proven, Hebrews argues, by the fact that centuries after the exodus generation, when the Israelites were now residing in the promised land, the Holy Spirit **spoke through David** in Psalm 95, still urging God's people not to forfeit his rest. How could he do so unless there is a further rest that is still available to God's people—God's own eternal sabbath rest?

Hebrews quotes Psalm 95 for the fifth time: **Oh, that today you would hear his voice: / "Harden not your hearts."** This negative expression actually has a positive implication: it is not too late to let our hearts be softened so that we might receive the gift God has for us. God has **once more set a day** for his people to hear and obey his summons. It is the †eschatological **today** of the coming of Christ—a today that continues every day in the age of the Church. As Paul writes, "Behold, now is a very acceptable time; behold, now is the day of salvation" (2 Cor 6:2).

The Israelites did finally enter the land, yet that attainment of the promise **4:8** turned out not to be a perfect "rest." They were plagued by enemy invasions, droughts, famines, and eventually even exile from the land. **Now if Joshua had given them rest**, God **would not have spoken afterwards**, in Psalm 95, **of another day.** Here for the first time Hebrews mentions Joshua, the successor of Moses whose job it was to lead the Israelites across the Jordan into the promised land. Jesus' name in Hebrew (*Yeshua*) is a shortened form of Joshua (*Yehoshua*); in Greek they are spelled exactly the same: *Iēsous*. What Joshua of old could not do, Jesus, the new and greater Joshua, will accomplish: he will lead God's people into the fulfillment of God's promise of rest.

Verses 9–11 sum up the entire argument from Psalm 95 and conclude with a **4:9** final word of exhortation. **Therefore, a sabbath rest still remains for the people of God.** Like the land of Canaan, the sabbath—the weekly day of repose when God's people cease from work and gather to worship him—is an earthly reality that points forward to something far greater: the peace, happiness, and intimate communion that we will enjoy with God forever (see 12:26–28).

And whoever enters into God's rest, rests from his own works as God did **4:10** **from his.** How can God be said to "rest" when he continues to speak and act and sustain the world in existence? God's rest is his own divine life. "The 'rest' that is God's very being (God's glory) is not disturbed by God's 'working' in the world because all that God does . . . is an outpouring of infinitely rich life rather than an effort to redress a lack."[2]

How then do we enter God's rest? On one level, Hebrews is probably referring to the future heavenly kingdom, when we will finally be free from all the toils, trials, and troubles of this life. The book of Revelation declares, "Blessed are the dead who die in the Lord from now on. . . . Let them find rest from their labors, for their works accompany them" (Rev 14:13). But this does not at all mean that heaven will be eternal inactivity. What will end are the labors

---

2. Luke Timothy Johnson, *Hebrews: A Commentary*, New Testament Library (Louisville: Westminster John Knox, 2006), 130.

and hard strivings; what will remain is celebration and the fullness of life (Heb 12:22–24; Rev 21:1–4).

On another level, God's rest is a present reality that we are invited to enter— sharing in his divine life, experiencing the "peace of God that surpasses all understanding" (Phil 4:7), the peace the world cannot give (John 14:27). Five times in chapters 3–4 Hebrews repeats the word "today," emphasizing the present availability of that rest. We "rest from our works" not in the sense that we cease human effort (see v. 11), but in the sense that our works "are no longer a striving to fill a need, but share in an outpouring of abundant life."[3] The "good works" we do (10:24) are then in fact God acting in us by his own divine power (see Eph 2:10; Phil 2:13).

The imagery of rest thus symbolizes the whole reality of salvation, which is both personal and communal: it is entering into God's presence (4:16), the heavenly homeland (11:16), and the unshakable kingdom (12:28); it begins at baptism (10:22) and is fulfilled in the life to come.[4]

4:11   We are to **strive** (or "make every effort," NIV) **to enter into that rest**. A saying of Jesus uses similar words: "Strive to enter through the narrow door" (Luke 13:24). And Paul says, "One thing I do, forgetting what lies behind and straining forward to what lies ahead, I press on toward the goal for the prize of the upward call of God in Christ Jesus" (Phil 3:13–14 RSV). It is the exact opposite of the spiritual lethargy of some of the original readers of Hebrews, who are in danger of "drifting away" (2:1 RSV) and becoming "sluggish" (5:11) in their commitment to Christ.

The warning of verse 11 echoes the warning of verse 1, forming a frame around the passage. In both cases the author of Hebrews includes himself in the admonition: "Let *us* be on our guard" and "Let *us* strive." In both it is clear that we are to be vigilant not only for our own salvation but also for that of our fellow Christians, taking care **that no one may fall**. And both verses urgently warn us not to follow the **example of disobedience** of the wilderness generation, with its catastrophic results.

Reflection and Application (4:1–11)

Entering God's rest. Hebrews 4:1–11 brings to mind Jesus' consoling words to his followers: "Come to me, all who labor and are heavy laden, and I will

3. Ibid.
4. Harold W. Attridge, *The Epistle to the Hebrews: A Commentary on the Epistle to the Hebrews*, ed. Helmut Koester, Hermeneia (Philadelphia: Fortress, 1989), 128.

Four Different Rests

Like so many biblical words, "rest" (Greek *katapausis*, related to "pause" in English) has a richness of meaning that the author of Hebrews exploits to show how old covenant realities signify in a hidden way the transcendent realities of the new covenant in Christ.

First, "rest" in Genesis 2:2 refers to God ceasing from his works of creation on the seventh day, which is the foundation of the sabbath (Exod 20:11), the sacred day of rest that is the perpetual reminder of our †covenant relationship with him.

Second, "rest" in Psalm 95 refers to the Israelites ending their desert wanderings to settle in Canaan, the fertile land that God had promised to Abraham and his descendants (Gen 15:18–21).

Third, the original audience of Hebrews was probably aware that "rest" elsewhere in the †Septuagint refers to the Jerusalem temple, which God declared that he chose as his "resting place" (*katapausis*) forever (2 Chron 6:41; Ps 132:14). This declaration expresses God's unbreakable commitment to dwell in the midst of his people and be present to them as their God.

Finally, all these "rests" are images that symbolize the infinitely more glorious rest into which we are invited: the unending joy, fulfillment, and peace of God's own divine life. That rest is already available now, but it is ultimately fulfilled in the heavenly homeland at the end of the desert pilgrimage of this life, the consummation of our covenant relationship with God, and the new and living temple of all the redeemed united with Christ forever.

give you rest. Take my yoke upon you, and learn from me; for I am gentle and lowly in heart, and you will find rest for your souls. For my yoke is easy, and my burden is light" (Matt 11:28–30 RSV). The rest that Jesus offers is ultimately a share in God's own divine life. But Scripture nowhere indicates that we ought to think of this rest only in terms of life after death. To enter God's rest is to rest in his love, free from anxiety about the past or future or about our own inadequacies. Many of the saints exemplify this rest. Though they were among the busiest people on earth, they were always at rest in the present moment.

The day of rest. The third commandment, to keep the sabbath holy (Exod 20:8), is God's practical way of teaching his people how to keep the right priorities in life. For Christians, the day of rest has become Sunday, the day of Christ's resurrection. Although work is a privilege and a way of collaborating in God's creative activity, ceasing from work every seventh day reminds us that the ultimate goal of our life is fellowship with God. To observe this day of rest

St. Augustine on God's Rest

LIVING TRADITION

Augustine wrote of God's rest on the seventh day:

O Lord God, grant us your peace . . . the peace of quietness, the peace of the sabbath, the peace without an evening. All this most beautiful array of things, all so very good, will pass away when all their courses are finished—for in them there is both morning and evening. But the seventh day is without an evening, and it has no setting, for you have sanctified it with an everlasting duration. After all your works of creation, which were very good, you rested on the seventh day, although you had created them all in unbroken rest—and this so that the voice of your Book might speak to us with the prior assurance that after our works . . . we may find our rest in you in the sabbath of life eternal.[a]

a. Augustine, *Confessions* 13.35–26 (translation adapted from Augustine, *Confessions and Enchiridion*, trans. and ed. Albert C. Outler [Philadelphia: Westminster, 1954]).

is to trust God to provide for our needs and to avoid becoming a slave to work. As the Catechism teaches (2184–85),

> The institution of the Lord's Day helps everyone enjoy adequate rest and leisure to cultivate their familial, cultural, social, and religious lives (cf. *Gaudium et Spes* 67.3).
>
> On Sundays and other holy days of obligation, the faithful are to refrain from engaging in work or activities that hinder the worship owed to God, the joy proper to the Lord's Day, the performance of the works of mercy, and the appropriate relaxation of mind and body (cf. *Code of Canon Law*, canon 1247). Family needs or important social service can legitimately excuse from the obligation of Sunday rest.

The Two-Edged Sword (4:12–13)

> [12]Indeed, the word of God is living and effective, sharper than any two-edged sword, penetrating even between soul and spirit, joints and marrow, and able to discern reflections and thoughts of the heart. [13]No creature is concealed from him, but everything is naked and exposed to the eyes of him to whom we must render an account.

OT: 1 Sam 16:7; Ps 139:1–8; 149:6; Wis 18:14–16; Isa 49:2; 55:10–11; Jer 17:10
NT: Luke 12:2; John 12:47–48; Eph 6:17; Rev 1:16
Catechism: power of God's word, 124, 131; rendering an account to God, 678–79, 1039, 1059
Lectionary: 28th Sunday in Ordinary Time (Year B); Institution of Readers

Verse 12 is a brief but potent reflection on **the word of God**—the word that   **4:12**
fell on deaf ears in the exodus generation and which through Psalm 95 rings
out again "today," and which we dare not trifle with or neglect. God's "word"
(*logos*) is his revelation of himself and his will that comes to us in all Scripture,
now revealed in its deepest meaning by Christ and proclaimed in the apostolic
preaching (see 13:7). But "word of God" may also refer to the person of the
Son, as in John's Gospel (John 1:1–18)—the eternal word through whom God
created the world (Heb 1:2; 11:3).[5]

As Hebrews continually emphasizes, God's word is no mere written record
from the past. It is a **living** word, his "voice" (3:7, 15; 4:7), through which he
continues to speak to his children today. Unlike a human word, it is unfailingly
effective (Greek *energēs*, "energetic, active, powerful"). It never fails to accomplish that which it declares. When God speaks, things happen: "God said: Let
there be light, and there was light" (Gen 1:3; see Ps 33:9). A well-known passage
in Isaiah (55:10–11) expresses the dynamism of God's word:

> Just as from the heavens
>   the rain and snow come down
> And do not return there
>   till they have watered the earth,
>   making it fertile and fruitful,
> Giving seed to the one who sows
>   and bread to the one who eats,
> So shall my word be
>   that goes forth from my mouth;
> It shall not return to me empty,
>   but shall do what pleases me,
>   achieving the end for which I sent it.

That God's word is **sharper than any two-edged sword** draws on a common
biblical theme. In the book of Wisdom, God's word is personified as a "fierce
warrior bearing the sharp sword of your inexorable decree" (Wis 18:16; see
Isa 49:2). John has a vision of the risen Jesus with a sharp two-edged sword
coming from his mouth (Rev 1:16; 19:15), symbolizing his all-powerful word
that conquers evil. Paul speaks of God's word as a sword that Christians wield
against demonic powers (Eph 6:17; see Ps 149:6). And in Acts, the result of

---

5. See James Swetnam, *Hebrews—An Interpretation*, 83–84, published online at http://www.james
swetnamsclosereadings.com. However, there is no explicit *logos* †Christology in Hebrews as there is in
John, and it is noteworthy that Christ is nowhere in the New Testament said to *be* a sword, but rather
to wield the sword of the word (Rev 1:16; 2:12; 19:15).

Peter's Spirit-inspired preaching of the gospel is that the listeners were "cut to the heart" (Acts 2:37); they experienced profound conviction of sin and conversion to Christ.

Hebrews takes up this theme to emphasize that God's word has power to pierce to the very core of the human person, **penetrating even between soul and spirit, joints and marrow**. "Soul" often refers to natural human life, whereas "spirit" is our capacity to relate to God.[6] God's word is able to cut between even these most hidden dimensions of the person, separating what is merely human from what comes from God, just as only the sharpest sword could separate "joints" and "marrow," the most deeply hidden parts of the body. The image of the sword evokes God's promise that he would "circumcise the hearts" of his people (Deut 30:6; see Rom 2:28–29),[7] enabling them to relate to him with not only outward observance but also sincere and undivided love.

God's word is **able to discern** (literally, "judge") **reflections and thoughts of the heart**. God alone is able to probe the tortuous depths of the human heart (1 Sam 16:7; Jer 17:9–10), and his judgment is always perfectly just. The point here is that God's word, communicating as it does his infinite love and grace, is able to unmask what is truly going on in our hearts, which so often resist, ignore, and try to escape from that love. It is able to penetrate any armor we can devise and to expose all the motives and intentions that we seek to hide even from ourselves.

This judging capacity of the sword helps explain why Hebrews describes it as "two-edged." Some Church Fathers held that the double edge signifies the Old and New Testaments.[8] But more likely it symbolizes the twofold result of God's word: the same word will either save or condemn, depending on the disposition of the hearer (see John 5:24; 12:48). For those who reject it, God's word is a sword of judgment. But for those who receive it in faith, it is a sword that cuts away the gangrene in our hearts; it purifies and heals.

4:13   Verse 13 continues the theme of the penetrating knowledge of God. **No creature**—that is, nothing in the entire created universe—**is concealed from** the creator. The psalmist marvels (139:1–2, 7–8),

---

6. See 1 Cor 2:14–15; 15:44–46; Jude 19, where what is of the soul (*psychikos*) or merely "natural" is contrasted with what is of the Spirit (*pneumatikos*) or "spiritual."

7. See Swetnam, *Hebrews*, 93. The word as "sword" (*machaira*) recalls the knife (*machaira*) by which Joshua (mentioned in Heb 4:8) circumcised the Israelites before leading them into the promised land. That ineffectual circumcision is implicitly contrasted with the effective circumcision of heart accomplished by the word of God.

8. Tertullian, *Against the Jews* 9; Augustine, *The City of God* 20.21.

The Sword of the Word

LIVING TRADITION

An anonymous ancient author, reflecting on Hebrews 4:12, offered this fervent prayer:

> O you elect blade and sharpest sword . . . who are able powerfully to penetrate the hard shell of the human heart, transfix my heart with the shaft of your love. . . . Pierce, O Lord, pierce, I beseech you, this most obstinate mind of mine with the holy and powerful blade of your grace.[a]

a. *Liber Meditationum* 38 (Patrologia Latina 40.935; translation adapted from Philip Edgcumbe Hughes, *A Commentary on the Epistle to the Hebrews* [Grand Rapids: Eerdmans, 1977], 166).

LORD, you have probed me, you know me:
> you know when I sit and stand;
> you understand my thoughts from afar. . . .
Where can I go from your spirit?
> From your presence, where can I flee?
If I ascend to the heavens, you are there;
> if I lie down in Sheol, there you are.

Before the all-seeing **eyes** of the Lord, **everything is naked and exposed** (or "laid bare," RSV). Everyone will one day have to **render an account** to God, and all the excuses will melt away. Every human pretext, every façade by which we can ignore God's word or put off obeying it, will be stripped off. Jesus gives similar warnings in the Gospels: "There is nothing concealed that will not be revealed, nor secret that will not be known" (Luke 12:2; see Matt 12:36; Luke 8:17).

This allusion to the judgment of God, with its alarming yet salutary consequences for us, is a fitting conclusion to the meditation on Psalm 95 in Hebrews 3:7–4:11. Those who stand under the penetrating judgment of God's word begin to be aware of their desperate need for mercy. And this mercy, freely given us through Christ's sacrifice, is the heart of what the author wants to communicate in the next major part of the letter.

Reflection and Application (4:12–13)

The word of God is first and foremost Christ, the eternal Word. On another level, the word is God's revelation, given through the prophets in Israel and the preaching of the apostles. Finally, the word is sacred Scripture, God's revelation as it has been consigned to writing. Since Vatican Council II, the Church has been sounding an insistent call for all Catholics to "learn the surpassing knowledge of Jesus Christ by frequent reading of the divine Scriptures" (*Dei Verbum* 25). In his apostolic exhortation *Verbum Domini*, Pope Benedict XVI invited Catholics to rediscover the ancient practice of *lectio divina*, reading the Scriptures in prayerful conversation with God. He emphasized that there is nothing more powerful than the word of God to transform the human heart at the deepest level. If we are to fulfill Christ's mandate to bring the good news to the ends of the earth (Acts 1:8), we must begin with our own hearts by immersing ourselves in the word of God, becoming familiar with its contents, praying it every day. As the word of God renews our own minds and hearts, it will equip us to evangelize the culture.

Pope Benedict quoted these words of St. Jerome, exemplifying the early Church's profound reverence for the word of God:

> For me, the Gospel is the Body of Christ; for me, the holy Scriptures are his teaching. And when he says: *whoever does not eat my flesh and drink my blood* (John 6:53), even though these words can also be understood of the [Eucharistic] Mystery, Christ's body and blood are truly the word of Scripture, God's teaching. When we approach the [Eucharistic] Mystery, if a crumb falls to the ground we are troubled. Yet when we are listening to the word of God, and God's Word and Christ's flesh and blood are being poured into our ears yet we pay no heed, what great peril should we not feel?[9]

Jesus the Compassionate High Priest (4:14–16)

[14]Therefore, since we have a great high priest who has passed through the heavens, Jesus, the Son of God, let us hold fast to our confession. [15]For we do not have a high priest who is unable to sympathize with our weaknesses, but one who has similarly been tested in every way, yet without sin. [16]So let us confidently approach the throne of grace to receive mercy and to find grace for timely help.

OT: Lev 16:2

NT: Mark 16:19; Luke 4:2; Eph 3:12; Phil 2:7–8; Heb 3:1; 5:2; 6:20; 7:26; 10:19; 1 John 3:5

Catechism: Christ the high priest, 662, 1137, 1544–45; Christ as truly man, 467–70; Jesus' temptations, 538–40; Jesus' sinlessness, 612; Jesus' sympathy for us, 2602; confidence before God, 2777–78

Lectionary: 29th Sunday in Ordinary Time (Year B); Anointing of the Sick; Good Friday of the Lord's Passion

9. Jerome, *In Psalmum* 147, quoted in Pope Benedict XVI, *Verbum Domini* 56.

If readers feel a bit unsettled by the image of God's word as a piercing sword, laying bare our inmost thoughts and motives (vv. 12–13), that is exactly how the author of Hebrews wants us to feel. It is only when we become aware of our true spiritual condition that we recognize our radical need for a high priest to stand before God on our behalf. And the good news proclaimed by Hebrews is that we have such a high priest. Aware of this truth, readers are able to receive the encouraging words of verse 16 in the right spirit. We can approach the throne of the Father confidently, not out of presumption but because of the gracious mercy of Jesus our high priest.

Hebrews already introduced the idea that Jesus is our high priest (2:17; 3:1), but now it says he is our **great high priest**,[10] the one whose priestly ministry far surpasses all others in power and efficacy. The †levitical high priest could enter the inner †sanctuary of the earthly temple, but Jesus **has passed through the heavens**; he has ascended to the true, heavenly dwelling place of God (9:24; see Mark 16:19; Acts 1:9). Jewish tradition recognized various levels in the heavens (see 1 Kings 8:27; 2 Cor 12:2), and the implication is that Jesus has been exalted above them all. A human being, one of us, has entered into God's presence, leading the way for us (see 2:10). The name **Jesus** and title **Son of God** underscore that he is both truly man and truly God, and thus he alone is capable of overcoming the abyss between the holy God and sinful humanity **4:14**

This consoling fact gives us strong motivation to **hold fast to our confession**, as Hebrews constantly exhorts (3:6, 14; 10:23, 35). Christian faith is a "confession" because by its very nature it is not just something to be believed privately but something to be professed publicly before others (Matt 10:32–33; Rom 10:9–10).

Many Christians mistakenly assume that now that Jesus is exalted to the heavens, he is no longer human. Not so, says Hebrews. **For we do not have a high priest who is unable to sympathize with our weaknesses, but one who has similarly been tested in every way** (a point already emphasized in 2:18). The perfect tense "has been tested" signifies a past action that has continuing effects in the present. Jesus is and remains fully human. In assuming our nature, the Son of God placed himself in total solidarity with us. He understands all our weaknesses from within—our physical infirmities, our psychological limitations, our struggles against temptation. For that reason he is able to "sympathize" (literally, "co-suffer") with us. But Hebrews adds the crucial point that he was **without sin** (see 2 Cor 5:21; 1 Pet 2:22; 1 John 3:5). Otherwise he himself would **4:15**

---

10. The Old Testament term for the high priest is literally "great priest," so in effect Hebrews is calling Jesus the "great great priest," the priest par excellence.

Christ's Solidarity with the Weak

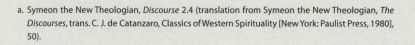

LIVING TRADITION

St. Symeon the New Theologian, a Byzantine monk of the eleventh century, wrote of Christ's empathy for human weakness:

> How great are God's gifts! He has left behind the wisdom, the power, and the wealth of the world, and has chosen its weakness, foolishness, and poverty (1 Cor 1:27).... For this alone who is capable of giving him worthy thanks? Nearly all men reject the weak and the poor ... an earthly king cannot bear the sight of them, rulers turn away from them, while the rich ignore them and pass them by when they meet them as though they did not exist; nobody thinks it desirable to associate with them. But God, who is served by myriads of powers without number, who "upholds the universe by his word of power," whose majesty is beyond anyone's endurance, has not disdained to become the father, the friend, the brother of those rejected ones. He willed to become incarnate so that he might become "like unto us in all things except for sin" and make us to share in his glory and his kingdom. What stupendous riches of his great goodness! What an ineffable condescension on the part of our master and our God![a]

a. Symeon the New Theologian, *Discourse* 2.4 (translation from Symeon the New Theologian, *The Discourses*, trans. C. J. de Catanzaro, Classics of Western Spirituality [New York: Paulist Press, 1980], 50).

have needed †atonement and would have been incapable of offering the perfect sacrifice for our redemption.

The question sometimes arises: How could Jesus truly be tempted if he had no sin? In fact, human experience shows that giving in to a temptation, even a little, lessens its intensity (even though giving in will lead to further temptation in the long run). Jesus' temptations were all the more intense precisely because he did not yield to them in the least. The Gospels present Jesus' whole ministry as a battle against temptation—in his forty days in the desert, in the challenges and threats of the religious authorities, and in the taunts thrown at him on the cross (Matt 4:1; 16:1; 27:39–44). His victory was not in the *absence* of temptations but in *resisting* them out of love for the Father and for us.

4:16 Jesus' high priesthood has placed us in an entirely new position before God. In the old covenant God's purpose in establishing the priesthood and temple was to enable his people to draw near to himself. Yet Scripture accents the unbridgeable divide between the holy God and sinful humanity. This divide was symbolized by the veil curtaining off the †Holy of Holies, which only the high priest could pass through (Lev 16:2). But the Gospels recount that at Christ's death, the veil was "torn in two from top to bottom" (Mark 15:38), signifying

The Suffering God

The teaching of Hebrews 4:14–16 may not strike us as surprising, but for the ancient world it was part of the astounding newness of Christianity.[a] The idea that God could actually enter into human experience and share personally in our suffering was totally unlike any previous conception of God.

Ancient Greek philosophy regarded God as an impersonal force. In the fourth century BC Aristotle defined God as the Unmoved Mover, who sets the whole universe in motion but cannot be involved in or even aware of anything in the universe because this would imply a lack of perfection. For Stoicism, a philosophical movement popular in the first century AD, the primary attribute of God (which Stoics identified as the universe itself) was *apatheia*, the total inability to suffer or feel anything. For God to feel emotions such as sorrow or joy would imply his being influenced by something outside himself, which is impossible. For Epicureanism, another philosophy contemporary with the writing of Hebrews, the gods were blissful immortal beings made of atoms who lived in space and were totally unconcerned with human affairs.

The Old Testament already reveals a God radically different from pagan notions, a God who initiates a relationship with the human beings he has created and who is deeply invested in them—a "jealous" God (Deut 4:24). As one who loves intensely, God is depicted as grieving over human violence and injustice (Gen 6:5–6) and over his people's ingratitude and unfaithfulness to him (Hosea 1–2). God is merciful and tender toward his people (Isa 54:5–8; Hosea 2:21–22), yet there remains a profound separation between God and man (Exod 19:21–24; Isa 59:2). God's dealings with Israel aroused a hope and longing for a restoration of the intimacy that prevailed in the garden of Eden, where God used to walk with Adam and Eve "in the cool of the day" (Gen 3:8 RSV). But this longing remains unfulfilled in the old covenant.

The Christian revelation that God's Son became human in order to suffer and "taste death" for us, as eloquently expressed by Hebrews (2:9; 4:15), brought a revolution in the understanding of God that is difficult for us to comprehend even today. God can no longer be seen as an impersonal force or a distant, detached judge. *He has become one of us.* There is no human emotion, temptation, or suffering that he does not know by personal experience. His compassion for us is rooted in this absolute solidarity. It is impossible to imagine a greater love (see John 15:13; 1 John 4:10).

a. This sidebar is partly indebted to William Barclay, *The Letter to the Hebrews*, rev. ed., Daily Study Bible Series (Philadelphia: Westminster, 1976), 42–43.

that the way is now opened for God's people to enter into his holy presence. Hebrews likewise, in striking contrast to the old covenant, exhorts us to **confidently approach the throne of grace**. Now that Christ has opened the way, confidence, or †boldness, in approaching God is a characteristic disposition of Christians (3:6; 10:19, 35; Eph 3:12). We draw near to the throne to **receive mercy** (forgiveness of sins already committed) and **find grace for timely help** (God's help for all our needs, especially to resist future sins and endure trials victoriously).

Jesus Our Great High Priest

Hebrews 5:1–10

Whoever reads the †Pentateuch, the first five books of the Bible, cannot help but notice that long, minutely detailed sections of it are devoted to the priesthood.[1] Matters that may seem inconsequential to us—details about priestly vestments, rites of ordination, the construction and furnishing of the sacred †tabernacle, the offering of †sacrifices—are prescribed with elaborate care. The priesthood was God's gracious provision for his people, making it possible for him to dwell in their midst and bestow his forgiveness and his blessings (Exod 29:44–46; Lev 16:30; Num 6:22–27). Yet the priestly legislation in the Old Testament also strongly accents the separation between priest and people. Since a priest was one who approached the holy God on behalf of the people, he had to be set apart from all that is †profane.[2]

Only in light of the Old Testament background is it possible to appreciate the transformation in the priesthood that takes place in Christ (see 7:12). When an ordinary man was made a priest, he required *separation* from others in order to relate to God. But when the Son of God through whom the universe was created (1:2) becomes a priest, it is his *solidarity* with human beings that must be assured. Thus Hebrews does not say that in order for Christ to become a high priest he had to be separated from others; rather, "he had to be made like his brethren in every respect, so that he might become a merciful and faithful high priest" (2:17 RSV).[3]

1. See especially Exodus through Numbers; there is also a significant focus on the priesthood in Ezra, 1–2 Samuel, 1–2 Chronicles, Jeremiah, Ezekiel, and to a lesser degree in other Old Testament books.
2. The root meaning of †holy in most ancient languages is "set apart" for God. The opposite of holy is profane, which refers to all that belongs to this world and is not set apart for God.
3. See Albert Vanhoye, *Our Priest Is Christ: The Doctrine of the Epistle to the Hebrews*, trans. M. Innocentia Richards (Rome: Pontificium Institutum Biblicum, 1977), 28.

Hebrews 5 begins to explain this transformation of priesthood. As with every aspect of Christian faith, the relation between the old †covenant and the new involves both continuity and discontinuity. On the one hand, Christ is the perfect realization of all that priesthood stood for in the Old Testament; on the other hand, he realizes it in an unexpected way, not fully conforming to the old pattern but elevating it to a new level.

The Order of Melchizedek (5:1–6)

[1]Every high priest is taken from among men and made their representative before God, to offer gifts and sacrifices for sins. [2]He is able to deal patiently with the ignorant and erring, for he himself is beset by weakness [3]and so, for this reason, must make sin offerings for himself as well as for the people. [4]No one takes this honor upon himself but only when called by God, just as Aaron was. [5]In the same way, it was not Christ who glorified himself in becoming high priest, but rather the one who said to him:

> "You are my son;
>   this day I have begotten you";

[6]just as he says in another place:

> "You are a priest forever
>   according to the order of Melchizedek."

OT: Gen 14:18–20; Exod 28:1; Lev 9:7; 16:11, 15; Num 15:22; Ps 2:7; 110:4
NT: John 7:18; 8:54; Acts 13:33; 2 Cor 5:21; 12:10
Catechism: priesthood of the old covenant, 1539–43; priesthood of Christ, 1544–45; ministerial and common priesthood, 901, 1545–47
Lectionary: 30th Sunday in Ordinary Time (Year B); 5:1–10: Mass for the Conferral of Holy Orders; for the Election of a Pope or Bishop; for Vocations to Holy Orders or Religious Life

Chapter 5 opens with an elegantly succinct definition of priesthood as it was understood in the Old Testament (v. 1). For the next five chapters (5:1–10:18), Hebrews will apply this definition to Christ to show how it describes him in a preeminent way.

5:1   Hebrews defines the priesthood with four essential characteristics. First, a priest is **taken from among men**.[4] In order to act on behalf of human beings, a

---

4. The Greek term used here (appearing twice in v. 1) is *anthrōpos* ("human being") rather than the gender-specific *anēr* ("male").

Fig. 6. The Garden of Gethsemane

priest must be one of them; he must be a genuine representative. An angel, for example, is not qualified to serve as a priest. Second, a priest is **made** (literally, "appointed") by God. One does not decide to enter the priesthood as a career, or even out of an altruistic desire to serve others. Appointment to this office is entirely at God's initiative. Third, a priest serves as the people's **representative before God**. This presupposes that there is a divide between God and man that must be overcome (see Isa 59:2), a fellowship that must be restored. God himself sets up priestly mediators to bridge that gulf. Finally, the way a priest carries out his mediation is by offering **gifts and sacrifices for sins** (see 8:3). Israel's worship included many different kinds of †sacrifices, such as those offered in thanksgiving for a favor or to fulfill a vow.[5] Hebrews, however, is focusing on sacrifices offered in †atonement for sin—those that prefigure in a special way the once-for-all sacrifice of Christ (see 10:12).

In verses 2–3 Hebrews elaborates on the first qualification: in order to rep-   **5:2–3** resent people before God, a priest must be one with them. **He is able to deal patiently with the ignorant and erring, for he himself is beset by weakness**. This was true, at least in principle, of the †levitical priests, who were in no position to be haughty or harsh toward wayward Israelites since they themselves were prone to the very same sins. Aaron himself had even played a lead role in

5. The †Septuagint uses the terms "gift" and "sacrifice" interchangeably to refer to blood sacrifices of animals, libations of wine, and offerings of grain, oil, or incense (Lev 1–7; Num 15:24).

Priestly Separation in the Old Covenant

BIBLICAL BACKGROUND

For ancient Israelites, the fact that a priest was "taken from among men" (5:1) was obvious, in that the priests were chosen from among their brethren of the tribe of Levi. However, the accent in the Old Testament is not on the commonality between priest and people but on how the priest has to be set apart from the people. The account of the ordination of Aaron and his sons (Lev 8–9; see Exod 29) expresses the extreme necessity of this separation. They are distinguished from others by their sacred vestments, their ceremonial bath that washes away the residue of any contact with the profane, their anointing with oil, and their sprinkling with sacrificial blood. They are subject to strict regulations to maintain ritual purity. They must be free of all blemishes and physical defects (Lev 21:17–23), and they must never approach a corpse or mourn for the dead except for their nearest kin (Lev 21:1–4).

In the case of the high priest, the rules are stricter still: he can never leave the †sanctuary,[a] and he may not even mourn for his parents (Lev 21:11–12). Only the priests may enter the sanctuary, and only the high priest may enter the inmost chamber, the †Holy of Holies, and only once a year, on the †Day of Atonement (Lev 16). Outside, the sanctuary is surrounded by a sacred zone in which the Levites stand guard to ensure that no layperson even inadvertently stray too near the sanctuary and bring down the wrath of God (Num 1:51–53; 3:10). All this had the effect of instilling an awareness of the immense gulf between the holy God and sinful humanity.

In light of this background, the priesthood of Christ as described in Hebrews, in which the accent is on his solidarity with and closeness to human beings, is a striking innovation.

a. Scholars debate the actual meaning of this requirement, since it could not have been fulfilled literally: for one thing, priests were expected to marry and have children, which involved actions resulting in ritual impurity (Lev 15:16–18), yet to remain in the sanctuary necessitated ritual purity.

---

the "original sin" of Israel: the disastrous idolatry of the golden calf (Exod 32). Hebrews mentions here only "ignorant" and "erring" offenders—those who sin through ignorance of God's law or by inadvertently straying away from it (Num 15:27–29). For sins committed willfully (Num 15:30–31), the old covenant provided no means of ritual atonement.[6]

6. Although the †Yom Kippur sacrifices provided collective atonement for Israel as a nation (Lev 16:30–34), Num 15:30–31 and Deut 17:12 mandate that an individual who sins defiantly is to be "cut off from among his people," or put to death. See comments on 9:7.

Because of the priest's own sinfulness, he **must make sin offerings for himself as well as for the people**. Both the rite of priestly ordination and the rite of the annual †Day of Atonement specify that the priest must offer sacrifice for his own sins first, then for the sins of the people (Lev 9:6–7; 16:11–15). As Hebrews will show, this requirement does not apply to Christ, who shared our weak nature but not our sin (2:18; 4:15), so he had no need to offer sacrifice for himself (7:27).

The second characteristic of a priest is that **no one takes this honor upon himself but only when called by God, just as Aaron was**. God had designated the family of Aaron within the tribe of Levi to serve as priests (Exod 28:1), and no other priesthood was allowed to function on behalf of God's people (Num 18:1–7). This divine mandate was impressively confirmed in the story of the revolt of Korah, Dathan, and Abiram, who accused Aaron of having promoted himself to the priesthood and who harbored ambitions of attaining it themselves (Num 16:1–10). So egregious was their sin of pride and jealousy that God caused the ground to open up and swallow them alive (Num 16:28–33). A further miraculous proof took place when Aaron's rod, placed among the rods of all the Israelite leaders, miraculously blossomed and put forth ripe almonds (Num 17:17–23).

5:4

Hebrews now applies this quality to Jesus: **In the same way, it was not Christ who glorified himself in becoming high priest**. As the New Testament often affirms, Jesus did not embark on his saving mission at his own initiative; he did so in obedience to the Father. Far from glorifying himself, he accepted his mission knowing it meant precisely the opposite: humiliation, rejection, agony, and death.[7] Jesus' sayings in the Gospel of John express his self-emptying disposition: "If I glorify myself, my glory is nothing; it is my Father who glorifies me" (John 8:54; see John 5:30; 6:38; 14:31).

5:5

The early Christians readily understood that it was God who appointed Jesus for his mission. But it was not at all obvious that God appointed him a *priest*. According to the law of Moses, a priest was a descendant of Aaron who offered animal sacrifices in the temple. Clearly, Jesus did not fit this description (7:14). How then can he be a priest? In order to demonstrate this central insight our author turns again to Psalm 2 and Psalm 110 (already quoted in chapter 1), the pillars on which his entire argument concerning Jesus' priesthood rests. Both are royal psalms referring to the Davidic Messiah-King who rules over God's

---

7. Matt 26:39; Mark 10:45; Rom 15:3; Phil 2:8. See Philip Edgcumbe Hughes, *A Commentary on the Epistle to the Hebrews* (Grand Rapids: Eerdmans, 1977), 180.

people. The early Christians knew these psalms well as prophecies of Jesus, the promised Messiah and son of David.[8]

Psalm 2:7 designates the king as God's son: **You are my son; / this day I have begotten you.** In its original context, this meant that the king was adopted by God in a figurative sense and given special divine honor and protection. But as Hebrews showed in chapter 1, "son" applies in a unique and transcendent way to Jesus, the eternal Son through whom God created the world. As the Son, he has the most intimate possible relationship with God, which is necessary for priesthood. But this does not yet explain how Christ was appointed a priest. So Hebrews now takes a crucial step forward by turning to Psalm 110:4.

5:6   Hebrews previously quoted Psalm 110:1, where God invites the king to sit at his right hand (1:13). Now Hebrews turns to verse 4 of the same psalm, which makes the surprising claim—unique in the Old Testament—that the Davidic king is a *priest*: "The LORD has sworn and will not change his mind, '**You are a priest forever / according to the order of Melchizedek.**'" The king belonged to the royal tribe of Judah, not the priestly tribe of Levi. Yet the psalm asserts that the king is a priest, implying that there is a valid priesthood other than the levitical priesthood established at Mount Sinai. The psalmist calls it the "order of Melchizedek," referring to the mysterious priest-king of Salem who blessed Abraham and offered bread and wine (Gen 14:18–20). The psalm suggests that such a priestly office belongs by right to the Davidic king; it is a royal priesthood. The Old Testament in fact records David and Solomon offering sacrifice, a function normally reserved to priests, apparently with God's approval.[9] Why would the king have such a privilege? Probably because he reigns in Jeru*salem*, which is another name for Salem, the city where Melchizedek reigned (see Ps 76:3); thus the Davidic king is the heir of the priest-king Melchizedek.[10] The fact that Melchizedek was a Gentile also suggests that this is a universal priesthood not limited to the Israelite people.

Psalm 110, as Hebrews interprets it, thus serves as a powerful argument that a royal and universal priesthood, superior to the levitical priesthood, has been reestablished in Christ, the son of David. This point will be spelled out in detail in Hebrews 7.

---

8. Both psalms appear prominently in the Gospels: Psalm 2 is alluded to in God the Father's declaration at Jesus' baptism and transfiguration (Matt 3:17; 17:5); Psalm 110 is quoted by Jesus in reference to himself (Matt 22:42–45).

9. 2 Sam 6:17–18; 24:25; 1 Kings 3:15; 8:62–64; 9:25. It is noteworthy that Saul, who did not reign in Jerusalem, was rebuked and punished for offering sacrifice (1 Sam 13:9–14); see also the case of King Uzziah illicitly burning incense (2 Chron 26:16–21).

10. See Joseph A. Fitzmyer, "'Now This Melchizedek . . .' (Heb. 7:1)," *Catholic Biblical Quarterly* 25 (1963): 307–8.

Obedience through Suffering (5:7–10)

⁷In the days when he was in the flesh, he offered prayers and supplications with loud cries and tears to the one who was able to save him from death, and he was heard because of his reverence. ⁸Son though he was, he learned obedience from what he suffered; ⁹and when he was made perfect, he became the source of eternal salvation for all who obey him, ¹⁰declared by God high priest according to the order of Melchizedek.

OT: Gen 14:18–20; Ps 88:2; 110:4

NT: Mark 14:33–36; 15:34, 37; John 12:27–28; Rom 8:3; Phil 2:7–8

Catechism: agony in the garden, 612; Jesus' suffering in love, 609, 616–17; Jesus' obedience, 1009, 2825; Jesus' prayer for us, 2606, 2741; order of Melchizedek, 1544

Lectionary: Heb 5:7–9: 5th Sunday of Lent (Year B); Our Lady of Sorrows; Mystery of the Holy Cross; Heb 4:14–16; 5:7–9: Good Friday of the Lord's Passion

Verses 7–10 reflect on the priestly meaning of Christ's passion and resurrection as recounted in the Gospels. This passage alludes to the agony in the garden, where Jesus prayed with anguish and dread as he faced his imminent passion (Mark 14:32–42), and to the crucifixion itself, where he forgave his persecutors (Luke 23:34) and cried out with a "loud cry" as he breathed his last (Mark 15:37).

5:7   **The days when he was in the flesh** are the time of Christ's life on earth, when "the Word became flesh / and made his dwelling among us" (John 1:14). Throughout that time, but particularly on the eve of his passion, Jesus **offered prayers and supplications** to the Father for those he came to save.[11] The Greek word for "offer" is the same term used for offering sacrifice (5:1, 3; 8:3–4) and suggests that Jesus' prayer was an essential part of his sacrifice. He also wept with sorrow for the fate of those who refused to believe in him (Matt 23:37; Luke 13:34; 19:41–44) and shed tears of compassion for human suffering (John 11:33–35). His prayer with **loud cries and tears** evokes the agony in Gethsemane, when he experienced the natural human dread of the prospect of unbearable suffering and death. He cried out **to the one who was able to save him from death**: "Abba, Father, all things are possible to you. Take this cup away from me, but not what I will but what you will" (Mark 14:36). In that garden Jesus reversed the original decision made in a garden: Adam and Eve's decision to disobey God (Gen 3:6). He freely accepted his mission to bear the full weight of human sin and its consequence of alienation from God—the "cup" of divine

11. Examples of the Gospels portraying Jesus praying are Luke 3:21; 5:16; 6:12; 9:18, 28–29; 11:1; 22:41–44; John 17.

The Ministerial Priesthood and the Priesthood of the Faithful

LIVING TRADITION

Hebrews speaks of Christ as the one priest of the new covenant, who offers the one perfect †sacrifice for sin in fulfillment of the former priesthood. Elsewhere the New Testament emphasizes the priestly identity of all Christians: "you are 'a chosen race, a royal priesthood, a holy nation'" (1 Pet 2:9; see Exod 19:6). By his passion Christ "has made us into a kingdom, priests for his God and Father" (Rev 1:6; see Rev 5:10; 20:6). All Christians are now empowered to offer our prayers, labors, and every small deed of love and service as a pleasing sacrifice to God (Heb 13:16). Thus Paul exhorts, "Offer your bodies as a living sacrifice, holy and pleasing to God, your spiritual worship" (Rom 12:1).

Although the New Testament does not use the term "priests" for the apostles whom Christ appointed, the Gospels contain subtle hints that Christ intended the Twelve to serve as a new priestly leadership for a renewed Israel.[a] The Letters of Paul likewise display Paul's awareness of his apostolic ministry as priestly (see Rom 15:16; 1 Cor 9:13–14; Phil 2:17).[b] From early on the Church's tradition, reflecting on Scripture, maintained that the apostles and their successors are priests in a special sense by participation in Christ's priesthood.[c] Around the end of the first century, for instance, Clement of Rome uses priestly terminology to describe bishops: they are those who have "offered the gifts."[d] Ignatius of Antioch likewise speaks of "one altar, one bishop" in reference to the Eucharist.[e] In the early third century Cyprian calls the bishop a "priest" (*sacerdos*) because in offering the Eucharist for the people he represents Christ.[f] Hebrews hints at this ordained priesthood by asserting that "We have an altar from which those who serve the tent have no right to eat" (Heb 13:10), likewise alluding to the Eucharist.

wrath (see Isa 51:17; 2 Cor 5:21). Thus his decision in the garden set in motion the events of his passion, culminating in his cry of desolation on the cross: "My God, my God, why have you forsaken me?" (Mark 15:34).

Jesus **was heard because of his reverence**. On the surface, this seems to contradict the facts, since he did not escape death. But as St. Thomas Aquinas observes, God did indeed "save him from death," not by sparing him the experience of dying but by raising him from death to indestructible life.[12] Moreover, Jesus' deepest prayer was that the Father's will might be done—that his death might become our salvation (7:25; 10:9–10). His prayer was heard because of

12. Thomas Aquinas, *Commentary on the Epistle to the Hebrews*, trans. Chrysostom Baer (South Bend, IN: St. Augustine's Press, 2006), 115.

The Catechism (1546–47) explains these two distinct ways of participating in Christ's priesthood, that of the whole people of God and that of the clergy:

> Christ, high priest and unique mediator, has made of the Church "a kingdom, priests for his God and Father" (Rev 1:6; cf. Rev 5:9–10; 1 Pet 2:5, 9). The whole community of believers is, as such, priestly. The faithful exercise their baptismal priesthood through their participation, each according to his own vocation, in Christ's mission as priest, prophet, and king.
>
> The ministerial or hierarchical priesthood of bishops and priests, and the common priesthood of all the faithful participate, "each in its own proper way, in the one priesthood of Christ." While being "ordered one to another," they differ essentially (*Lumen Gentium* 10.2). In what sense? While the common priesthood of the faithful is exercised by the unfolding of baptismal grace—a life of faith, hope, and charity, a life according to the Spirit—, the ministerial priesthood is at the service of the common priesthood. It is directed at the unfolding of the baptismal grace of all Christians. The ministerial priesthood is a *means* by which Christ unceasingly builds up and leads his Church. For this reason it is transmitted by its own sacrament, the sacrament of Holy Orders.

a. See, e.g., Matt 12:1–6; Luke 9:13; 22:19, 29–30. For a brief summary of these allusions and their significance, see Brant Pitre, "Jesus, the New Temple, and the New Priesthood," *Letter & Spirit* 4 (2008): 47–83.

b. Albert Vanhoye, *Old Testament Priests and the New Priest: According to the New Testament*, trans. Bernard Orchard, rev. ed. (Leominster: Gracewing, 2009), 267–69.

c. The New Testament terms for church leaders are *episkopos*, "overseer" or "bishop" (Phil 1:1; 1 Tim 3:2; Titus 1:7), and *presbyteros*, "elder" (Acts 14:23; 1 Tim 5:17; Titus 1:5; James 5:14). The word for "priest," or one who offers sacrifice (Greek *hiereus*, Latin *sacerdos*), gradually came to be used of bishops, and later of the presbyters who shared their ministry. By the Middle Ages, "priest" (*sacerdos*) became synonymous with "elder." The English term "priest" is derived from *presbyteros*.

d. *1 Clement* 44.4.

e. Ignatius, *Letter to the Philadelphians* 4.

f. Cyprian, *Epistle* 63.12; see also Hippolytus, *Philosophumena*, Proemium 6; Tertullian, *Exhortation to Chastity* 7.11.

his "reverence," his absolute commitment to honor and obey the Father. As the psalm declares, God "fulfills the desire of those who fear him; / he hears their cry and saves them" (Ps 145:19).

The bold claim already made in 2:10 is reiterated: **Son though he was, he** **5:8** **learned obedience from what he suffered**. The statement is an elegant rhyme in Greek: he "learned" (*emathen*) from what he "suffered" (*epathen*). It expresses a principle that was well known in the ancient world, even among pagans: there is a wisdom that can be gained in no other way than in the crucible of suffering.[13] But Hebrews means more than this. As the eternal Son of God, Jesus was sinless

13. See, for instance, Aeschylus, *Agamemnon* 177; Sophocles, *Trachiniae* 143; Herodotus, *Histories* 1.207; Aesop, *Fables* 134.1–3; 223.2–3; Philo, *Life of Moses* 2.55, 280.

(4:15); he could never have been disobedient. Yet in his human nature, frail like ours, he experienced how difficult and costly it can be to obey God.[14] Obedience, like all virtue, comes to perfection only by being tested in difficult circumstances.

5:9–10   Like a coal that is crushed under enormous pressure until it becomes a diamond, Jesus' human nature, crushed under the weight of his passion, was brought to infinite perfection. As in 2:10, that he **was made perfect** (*teleioō*) means that his human nature was perfected in virtue and made worthy of divine glory, but also it alludes to the fact that his passion was the moment he was ordained, **declared by God high priest**.[15] The related verb *teleō* appears in Jesus' declaration on the cross, "It is finished" (John 19:30). Having victoriously resisted sin in the most extreme test of suffering and temptation, he was perfected and his work of redemption completed.

His perfect obedience reversed the whole history of human rebellion, and thus **he became the source** (or "cause") **of eternal salvation for all who obey him**. This is another way of saying he was ordained high priest and, simultaneously, his mission was perfectly accomplished. His salvation is "eternal" because it consists in an everlasting communion of life with God. The condition of salvation is to obey him—to place one's life entirely under his lordship. For Hebrews, as for Paul (Rom 1:5; 16:26), faith in Christ is inseparable from obedience to him (3:18–19). As Jesus teaches in the Gospel, not everyone who says, "Lord, Lord," will enter the kingdom, but only those who do the will of the Father (Matt 7:21). But to obey him is no longer an impossible hurdle, because our obedience has been made possible by his.

Through his passion Jesus was ordained priest **according to the order of Melchizedek**, the perfect fulfillment of all that the old covenant priesthood aspired to. Our author wants to explain the mystery further, but first he interrupts the argument with another exhortation to his readers (5:11–6:20). They are spiritually immature and need to grow up in order to understand the advanced teaching he wants to set forth.

---

14. Aquinas, *Hebrews*, 117.

15. The verb *teleioō* is used in the †Septuagint to translate the Hebrew term for "ordain" a priest (Exod 29:9; Lev 8:33; Num 3:3); see comments on 2:10.

A Call to Maturity

Hebrews 5:11–6:20

Even the best of teachers know what it is like to be in the midst of explaining an important point, only to look out and see eyes glazing over and heads drooping. A good teacher knows how to gauge when students need a pause or digression to refresh their minds and help them turn back to the subject with renewed attention. The author of Hebrews seems to have arrived at such a point in 5:11. After gradually leading up to the central argument of the whole letter—concerning the high priesthood of Jesus—he pauses to interject another long pastoral exhortation (5:11–6:20). His primary concern, however, is not his audience's mental alertness but rather the maturity and stability of their Christian faith. So in this section he first gives a tough message: a call to grow up spiritually (5:11–14) and a sharp warning of the danger of falling away from Christ (6:1–8). Then he balances it with a consoling message: an encouragement to keep up the good work (6:9–12) and a reminder of the absolute trustworthiness of God's promises (6:13–20). After this interlude, 7:1 will pick up where 5:10 left off: Jesus' priesthood according to the order of Melchizedek.

Spiritual Babyhood (5:11–14)

---

[11]**About this we have much to say, and it is difficult to explain, for you have become sluggish in hearing. [12]Although you should be teachers by this time, you need to have someone teach you again the basic elements of the utterances of God. You need milk, [and] not solid food. [13]Everyone**

who lives on milk lacks experience of the word of righteousness, for he is a child. [14]But solid food is for the mature, for those whose faculties are trained by practice to discern good and evil.

OT: Isa 6:9–10; Jer 5:21; Ezek 12:2; Zech 7:11
NT: Matt 5:48; 1 Cor 3:1–3; 14:20; Eph 4:13–14; Phil 3:12
Catechism: growth toward spiritual maturity, 1248, 1253, 1466, 1709

5:11 Just as the preacher was about to arrive at the high point of his whole homily, the explanation of Jesus' high priesthood (see 5:10), he delivers a reprimand that must have felt like a splash of cold water. Although he still has **much to say** about Jesus' priesthood (and he will say it in chapters 7–10), **it is difficult to explain, for they have become sluggish in hearing.** The Greek word for "sluggish" (*nōthros*) could also be translated "lethargic, lazy, dull." It suggests a certain passive resistance to God's word, an unwillingness to listen to its challenging message. God's people are susceptible to such self-imposed deafness, as Scripture often warns.[1] In the Gospels Jesus tells his listeners that Isaiah's indictment applies to them: "This people's heart has grown dull, and their ears are heavy of hearing, and their eyes they have closed" (Matt 13:15 RSV; Isa 6:9–10). Jesus' (and Hebrews') constant exhortation is for people to *hear*—to listen to the word of God, appropriate it, allow it to sink into their hearts and change their whole lives.

5:12–13 Dullness of hearing is closely related to spiritual immaturity. **By this time—** which we can reasonably assume is some years or even decades since their conversion (see 10:32)—the audience of Hebrews **should be teachers.** This does not necessarily mean that all of them should be formally appointed as catechists, but all should be familiar enough with the faith to be able to instruct beginners by word and example. Yet they themselves need to be taught **again the basic elements of the utterances of God.** The "basic elements" are the ABCs, the rudiments of Christian doctrine that form the foundation for further growth. That the listeners need them "again" suggests that they have not only failed to grow up but have backslidden.

You need milk, [and] not solid food. In the ancient world, drinking milk was a common image for those who were capable of only elementary teaching.[2] There is nothing wrong with milk per se; in fact, drinking milk, or being

---

1. See Isa 6:9–10; Jer 5:21; Ezek 12:2; Zech 7:11; Mark 4:12; 8:17–18; Luke 8:10; John 8:43; 12:40; Acts 7:57; 28:26–27; Rom 11:8.

2. The Stoic philosopher Epictetus asks his students, "Are you like babes still unwilling to be weaned from mother's milk and partake of stronger food?" (*Discourses* 2.16.39). The Jewish philosopher Philo comments, "Milk is food for babes but wheaten cakes are for the mature" (*On Agriculture* 9).

nursed, is perfectly appropriate for people newly reborn in Christ (see 1 Thess 2:7; 1 Pet 2:2). The problem is that after years have passed, they should be able to receive more advanced teaching. Their inability to digest solid food is a sign of arrested development. **Everyone who lives on milk lacks experience of the word of righteousness, for he is a child**. The Greek word for "child" (*nēpios*) is in this context better translated "baby," one not yet weaned. Such a person is inexperienced in "the word of righteousness," which probably means the ability to discern and practice right conduct based on the truth of the gospel. As Hebrews constantly emphasizes, doctrine is inseparable from life. Paul gives a similar reprimand to the Corinthians: "Brothers, I could not talk to you as spiritual people, but as fleshly people, as infants in Christ. I fed you milk, not solid food, because you were unable to take it. . . . While there is jealousy and rivalry among you, are you not of the flesh, and behaving in an ordinary human way?" (1 Cor 3:1–3).

Readers may wonder how this reprimand squares with the teaching of Jesus, who exhorted his followers to be like children (Matt 18:3). But there is a world of difference between being child*like* (having an open, trusting, and receptive heart toward God) and being child*ish* (behaving like a child who lacks understanding and self-control).

Solid food, such as what our author is about to serve in chapters 7–10, **is for the mature**. The Greek word for "mature" (*teleios*) can also mean "perfect"; it is a form of the same word used for Jesus being "made perfect" (*teleioō*) in verse 9 above. With this statement Hebrews emphasizes, once again, that Christians are meant to grow into a state of spiritual maturity (as Paul too insists in 1 Cor 14:20; Eph 4:13–14; Phil 3:12). Although we never reach absolute perfection in this life, it is the high standard to which Jesus calls his disciples: "Be perfect [*teleios*], just as your heavenly Father is perfect" (Matt 5:48). | 5:14

The mature or perfect are **those whose faculties are trained** (Greek *gymnazō*, root of the English words "gym" and "gymnast") **by practice to discern good and evil**. Hebrews, like Paul, is comparing Christians to athletes (1 Cor 9:24–26). Those who consistently train and practice are in fit condition to run the race (see Heb 12:1). By diligently studying the word of God and living in accord with it, Christians train their faculties—their mind, will, and emotions—to discern between good and evil conduct and between true and false doctrine (see 1 Cor 2:14–15). They are no longer "infants, tossed by waves and swept along by every wind of teaching arising from human trickery" (Eph 4:14); they have learned to "discern what is the will of God, what is good and pleasing and

Spiritual Health Food and Junk Food

St. John Chrysostom, a fourth-century doctor of the Church, explains how our "faculties" need to be "trained" to discern between true and false doctrine:

> A baby does not know how to distinguish bad and good food. Often it even puts dirt into its mouth and takes what is harmful, and it does all things without judgment. But not so the full-grown person. Such babies are they who lightly listen to everything and yield their ears indiscriminately ... which he also hinted near the end [of Hebrews], saying, "Do not be carried away by all kinds of strange teaching" (Heb 13:9). ... But how do our "faculties" become "trained"? By continual hearing and by experience of the Scriptures.[a]

a. *Homilies on the Epistle to the Hebrews* 8.7 (translation adapted from *NPNF* I, vol. 14).

perfect" (Rom 12:2). All Christians are capable of—and are called to—such spiritual proficiency.

Reflection and Application (5:11–14)

Today in health care, education, engineering, business, and virtually every secular career, continuing education and professional development are considered essential for success. But ironically, many Catholics seem satisfied with an eighth-grade or lower level of understanding of their faith, the most important dimension of their lives. How many are diligent to keep well-informed about current events but are surprisingly ignorant of Scripture, of what Jesus really said and did, and of Catholic teaching on faith and morals? A 2010 survey found that Catholics in the United States scored lower in religious knowledge—including knowledge of the Bible and Christianity—than Protestants, Mormons, Jews, agnostics, and even atheists.[3]

St. John Paul II, recognizing the spiritually numbing effects of today's culture, sounded a call to maturity similar to that of Hebrews:

> Often in today's world, which is dominated by a secular culture that proposes models of life without God, the faith of many is greatly tested and often suffocated and put out. Therefore there is an urgent need for a strong testimony and

3. Pew Research Center, "U.S. Religious Knowledge Survey: Executive Summary," http://www.pewforum.org/2010/09/28/u-s-religious-knowledge-survey/.

a Christian formation that is solid and deep. What a great need there is today for mature Christian personalities who are aware of their baptismal identity, of their call and mission in the Church and in the world![4]

One can make good progress toward such a "solid and deep" Christian formation by spending time with the word of God every day. By reading Scripture for only fifteen minutes a day, one can read through the entire Bible in a couple of years. It is also vital to read the Catechism (or the shorter *United States Catholic Catechism for Adults*), which distills two millennia of Church teaching and reflection on the word of God.

The Danger of Apostasy (6:1–8)

[1]Therefore, let us leave behind the basic teaching about Christ and advance to maturity, without laying the foundation all over again: repentance from dead works and faith in God, [2]instruction about baptisms and laying on of hands, resurrection of the dead and eternal judgment. [3]And we shall do this, if only God permits. [4]For it is impossible in the case of those who have once been enlightened and tasted the heavenly gift and shared in the holy Spirit [5]and tasted the good word of God and the powers of the age to come, [6]and then have fallen away, to bring them to repentance again, since they are recrucifying the Son of God for themselves and holding him up to contempt. [7]Ground that has absorbed the rain falling upon it repeatedly and brings forth crops useful to those for whom it is cultivated receives a blessing from God. [8]But if it produces thorns and thistles, it is rejected; it will soon be cursed and finally burned.

OT: Gen 3:18; Ps 34:9; Isa 5:1–7; Dan 12:2
NT: Matt 25:41; Mark 1:15; Acts 2:38; 8:16–17; 1 Cor 14:20; Titus 3:5–7; 1 Pet 2:3
Catechism: repentance and faith, 537, 981; baptism, 1213–16; laying on of hands, 699, 1288; resurrection, 651–55; judgment, 678–79; crucifying Christ again, 598

Like an expedition guide rallying his weary companions, the author sounds **6:1** a call to press on: Let's get going! **Let us leave behind the basic teaching about Christ and advance to maturity.**[5] The Christian life is a journey, a progress from infancy to adulthood (5:13–14), and whoever stops moving forward is

4. Address to members of ecclesial movements and new communities, *L'Osservatore Romano*, June 5, 1998.
5. The word for "basic" (*archē*) is literally "beginning"; the word for "maturity" (*teleiotēs*) is related to the "end" (*telos*).

likely to drift backward (see 2:1). To "leave behind" the basics does not mean to abandon them but rather to build on them, just as a teacher of algebra, for instance, takes for granted that students have the basics of arithmetic under their belts. To have to lay **the foundation all over again** would be a frustrating waste of time.

Hebrews summarizes this basic Christian catechesis in six headings, arranged in pairs: repentance and faith, baptisms and laying on of hands, resurrection and judgment. All of these elements are featured in the earliest preaching of the apostles as recorded in Acts.[6] Interestingly, all are beliefs that Christianity shares with Judaism, though understood in a very different way (see below). It may be that what the Jewish Christian readers of Hebrews have forgotten, or never fully understood, is precisely the radical newness of the Christian understanding of these realities.

The first two items have to do with initial conversion: **repentance from dead works and faith in God**. These are two sides of the same act of conversion: turning *away from* sin in repentance and *toward* God in faith. The Greek word for "repentance" (*metanoia*) literally means a "change of mind," a sincere repudiation of sin and return to God and his ways. The call for God's people to turn back to him with all their hearts is a constant theme in the Old Testament (see Neh 1:9; Isa 44:22; Hosea 14:2) and was at the center of John the Baptist's preaching (Matt 3:2; Mark 1:4). "Dead works" may refer to sins, since sin leads to death (Rom 6:23). Or it may mean reliance on empty religious rites while having an unconverted heart—the sin of presumption, for which the prophets often indicted the Israelites (see Isa 58:1–7; Jer 7:1–11; Amos 5:21) and of which Jesus warns his disciples (Matt 6:1; 23:1–7). Or finally, in the context of Hebrews "dead works" may also refer to the temple sacrifices on which the original readers were tempted to rely. They are "dead" in that they are powerless to give life (see 10:4, 8) and have been made superfluous by the all-sufficient †sacrifice of Christ.

Jesus himself called for repentance and faith as the basic human response to his preaching of the kingdom: "Repent, and believe in the gospel" (Mark 1:15). Now that he has come, "faith in God" specifically means faith in him, the incarnate Son who makes the Father known (Heb 1:2).

6:2   The second two items are sacramental signs through which grace is given: **instruction about baptisms and laying on of hands**. The word translated "baptisms" (*baptismos*) is slightly different from the usual word for Christian

6. See Acts 2:38 (repentance and baptism); 4:4; 9:42; 16:31 (faith); 6:6; 8:17; 13:3 (laying on of hands); 4:2; 26:23 (resurrection); 10:42; 17:31 (judgment).

baptism (*baptisma*); also it is in the plural, whereas the latter never is. It may refer to Jewish ceremonial washings (as in Mark 7:4; Heb 9:10); thus the RSV translation "ablutions." Or it may refer to Christian baptism[7] or, for that matter, the baptism of John. What Hebrews may mean is precisely that the readers, like other early Christians (Acts 18:25; 19:3–5), were fuzzy on the distinction between these. Jewish ritual washings and John's baptism only foreshadowed the infinitely greater reality of baptism into Christ, which brings forgiveness of sins, the gift of the Holy Spirit, and eternal life (Acts 2:38; Titus 3:5–7).

Laying on of hands was also an important gesture in ancient Judaism, used to impart blessings (Gen 48:14; Mark 10:13) or to ordain or commission a person for a task (Num 8:10; Deut 34:9). The early Church took over this practice for healing, ordaining, or commissioning (Acts 6:6; 9:12; 13:3; 28:8), and also for completing Christian initiation by imparting the Holy Spirit and his gifts (Acts 8:16–17; 9:17; 19:6).

The final two items have to do with †eschatology, or the last things: **resurrection of the dead and eternal judgment**. In the first century many Jews, though not all, believed in a resurrection of the dead and final judgment (Acts 23:8; see Dan 12:2). But now these must be understood in relation to Christ. His resurrection is the sign and pledge of ours (1 Cor 15:20–22), and he is the judge to whom everyone will render an account (2 Cor 5:10; 2 Tim 4:1). The curious phrase "eternal judgment" may be intended to emphasize that the consequences of that judgment are eternal and irrevocable (Matt 25:41, 46; 2 Thess 1:9).

It may seem surprising that this list of catechetical basics makes no mention of the Eucharist, often referred to by early Christians as the "breaking of bread" (see Luke 24:35; Acts 2:42). A possible reason is that for the early Church, teaching about the Eucharistic mystery belonged not to prebaptismal catechesis but to more advanced instruction for the baptized—what was later called mystagogy.[8] That the Messiah would give his disciples his body to eat was such a radically new idea (see John 6:52) that it had to be introduced to new converts only after they were well grounded in the faith.

Despite the spiritual immaturity of his addressees (5:12–14), the preacher is **6:3** confident that **we shall do this**—that is, "advance to maturity" (6:1). The proviso **if only God permits** is a reminder that our lives are entirely in God's hands

---

7. The same word, but in the singular, appears in Col 2:12 in reference to Christian baptism.

8. St. Cyril of Jerusalem, for instance, instructs those about to be baptized, "If a catechumen asks you what the teachers have said, tell nothing to one who is outside. For we deliver to you a mystery, and a hope of the life to come. Guard the mystery for Him who gives the reward" (*Catechetical Lectures*, prologue 12).

(see James 4:13–15) and that it is God who is at work in us, giving us both the desire and the grace to grow toward perfection (see Phil 2:13).

6:4   At this point the preacher interjects a solemn warning of the danger of †apostasy (which will be repeated in 10:26–31; 12:25–29). He wants to express his grave pastoral concern for the spiritual condition of his audience, who seem to be flagging in their Christian commitment and even tempted to drop out.

He begins by describing the privileges of the Christian life, in five phrases. This description is remarkable for its experiential emphasis: Christian faith is not merely a set of beliefs but a vivid experience of new things.

Christians are, first, those **who have once been enlightened**; that is, their minds, formerly mired in the darkness of ignorance and sin (Rom 1:21; Eph 4:17–18), have been illumined by the radiant light of Christ, who reveals the truth about God's love and about the meaning of human life (see John 1:9). Paul expressed the same idea: "God who said, 'Let light shine out of darkness,' has shone in our hearts to bring to light the knowledge of the glory of God on the face of [Jesus] Christ" (2 Cor 4:6; see Eph 5:14; 1 Pet 2:9). The phrase may allude specifically to baptism, which in the early Church was often called "enlightenment."[9]

Second, Christians have **tasted the heavenly gift**. This phrase refers, as St. Thomas Aquinas noted, to all the grace freely bestowed on us by God, "who has blessed us in Christ with every spiritual blessing in the heavens" (Eph 1:3).[10] It probably also alludes to the Eucharist, in which we taste in a most literal way the heavenly gift, God himself, who became for us "living bread . . . from heaven" (John 6:51). "Tasted" conveys a very real and experiential knowledge of something (as Christ tasted death, Heb 2:9). Christians not only *know about* the heavenly grace that God lavishes on his children but *experience* it. In a similar way, 1 Peter tells newly baptized Christians, "You have tasted that the Lord is good" (1 Pet 2:3; see Ps 34:9).

Third, Christians have **shared in the holy Spirit** just as they have shared in Christ (the same term is used in 3:14). In the old covenant many prophets and chosen leaders were granted the Spirit's inspiration and power,[11] but the New Testament affirms that only those redeemed by Christ have the Holy Spirit *dwelling* within them.[12] The Holy Spirit is the love of God poured into our

9. See, e.g., Justin Martyr, *First Apology* 1.61.12; Clement of Alexandria, *Christ the Teacher* 1.6.26; Gregory Nazianzen, *Orations* 40.3–4.

10. Thomas Aquinas, *Commentary on the Epistle to the Hebrews*, trans. Chrysostom Baer (South Bend, IN: St. Augustine's Press, 2006), 127.

11. See, for instance, Exod 31:3; Judg 3:10; 11:29; 1 Sam 10:10; 16:13; Ezek 11:5.

12. John 7:39; 16:7; Acts 1:4–5; 2:38; Rom 8:11.

hearts (Rom 5:5), the power that enables us to grow in holiness (Rom 15:16; Eph 3:16–17), and the "seal" or pledge that gives us assurance of eternal life (2 Cor 1:22; Eph 1:14). Hebrews may also be alluding to the charisms distributed by the Spirit for building up the Church (2:4; see Rom 12:6–8; 1 Cor 12:4–11).

Fourth, Christians have **tasted the good word of God** (or "tasted the good- **6:5** ness of the word of God," RSV). The verb "taste" conveys that we savor by personal experience the sweetness and life-giving effect of God's word, whether it is preached, taught, proclaimed in the †liturgy, or read in private devotion. As the psalmist sings, "The statutes of the LORD are true, / . . . More desirable than gold, / than a hoard of purest gold, / Sweeter also than honey / or drippings from the comb" (Ps 19:10–11). The supreme goodness of that word is fully revealed in the gospel.

Finally, Christians have tasted **the powers of the age to come**. The Greek word for "powers" (*dynameis*) could also be translated "miracles" (the same word is translated "acts of power" in 2:4). It probably refers both to the power to put off sin and live a holy life (Rom 8:2–4) and to the healings, exorcisms, and other miracles that are visible evidence of the Spirit's activity in Christians.[13] In the life of Jesus and in the early Church such miracles were a sign that "the age to come" had arrived (see Acts 2:17)—the time promised by the prophets, when God would decisively intervene in history to destroy the power of evil and bring about a new creation. The Christian good news is that in Christ the age to come *has come* (see Heb 1:2; 1 Cor 10:11), even though, for now, the old age endures in the midst of the new.

The listing of these five sublime gifts makes the subsequent warning stand **6:6** out all the more starkly: it is impossible in the case of those who have received such gifts, **and then have fallen away, to bring them to repentance again**. The verb "fallen away" refers not to specific sins but to apostasy, turning away from faith in Christ. But it is difficult to know how to interpret this seemingly absolute statement, since it is a historical fact that some Christians have fallen away but then repented and come back. In the patristic era some Christian sects such as the Novatians claimed, on the basis of this text, that those who had denied the faith under persecution could never be readmitted to the Church. But the Church rejected this rigorist stance. After all, even Peter, the leader of the apostles, had denied Christ and had been restored. Alternatively, many patristic authors interpreted "bring to repentance again" to refer to the rebaptism of believers who have lapsed and want to be reinstated. As the Church later explicitly taught, such people can be forgiven but should not be rebaptized because baptism is

---

13. See Mark 16:17–18; Acts 2:22, 43; 5:12; Rom 15:19; Gal 3:5.

a once-for-all act that imparts an indelible character (see Catechism 1121). Hebrews, however, is more likely referring to a person who persists in sin and out of hardness of heart rejects the very ground of repentance, God's offer of salvation in Christ (see 2:3).[14] Perhaps the point is that there is nothing one can do for people who are in such a condition. As long as they maintain their present attitude, they are beyond the reach of any pastoral efforts. Although there is the danger that they will not come to repentance, and they are ground that "will soon be cursed" (v. 8), it is not impossible that they will turn back. But unless and until they decide to do so, there is no way to reach them.

Shockingly, such people are **recrucifying the Son of God for themselves and holding him up to contempt**.[15] By turning their backs on Christ, they are despising the gift of salvation, paid for by his blood on the cross. They are in effect—and sometimes in reality—joining forces with those who hold up Christ and the Church to derision.

The preacher is cautioning his audience in the strongest possible terms not to naively assume they can abandon the faith for the time being, while the social situation is unsafe or uncomfortable for Christians, and take it up again later. They may well find that before they decide it is safe to come back, it is already too late (see 12:16–17; Matt 25:10). This grave warning should, however, be read in the context of Jesus' declaration, "For human beings it is impossible, but not for God. All things are possible for God" (Mark 10:27).

6:7–8   The preacher drives home his point with a short parable. God's people are to be like fertile **ground that has absorbed the rain falling upon it repeatedly and brings forth crops**. This is a common biblical image for God's people, who are his field (1 Cor 3:9), his vineyard (Isa 5:1–7) that ought to bring forth the rich produce of faith, love, and good deeds (see Mark 4:20; 12:1–2). The "rain falling upon it" may allude to the Holy Spirit, who is often compared to life-giving water poured out on God's people (Isa 44:3; Joel 3:1; Acts 2:17). Such land, if fruitful, **receives a blessing from God**.

But if, on the other hand, such well-cultivated land **produces thorns and thistles, it is rejected; it will soon be cursed** (or "is near to being cursed," RSV) **and finally burned**. The image of thorns and thistles recalls God's declaration about the consequences of Adam's sin: "Cursed is the ground because of you! / In toil you shall eat its yield / all the days of your life. / Thorns and thistles it

---

14. See Luke Timothy Johnson, *Hebrews: A Commentary*, New Testament Library (Louisville: Westminster John Knox, 2006), 163–64.

15. Harold W. Attridge points out that the Greek verb that the NAB translates as "recrucify" more likely means simply "crucify" (*The Epistle to the Hebrews: A Commentary on the Epistle to the Hebrews*, ed. Helmut Koester, Hermeneia [Philadelphia: Fortress, 1989], 171).

shall bear for you" (Gen 3:17–18). Later God declared that his beloved vineyard, Israel, which had failed to bring forth good fruit, would be "overgrown with thorns and briers" (Isa 5:6). Jesus gave similar sharp warnings about those who receive his saving grace yet fail to let it produce good fruit in their lives: "Every tree that does not bear good fruit will be cut down and thrown into the fire" (Matt 7:19; see John 15:6). But the future tense indicates that there is still time for repentance, while life remains.

Reflection and Application (6:1–8)

Experience in the Christian life. The strongly experiential description of the Christian life in Hebrews 6:4–5 may seem surprising to readers today, since in the modern era we have come to think of the faith in a highly cognitive-moral way while downplaying the experiential. But this was not the case in earlier Christian tradition. St. Augustine, for example, taught his congregation that God "has awakened in us a great longing for that sweet experience of His presence within; it is by daily growth that we acquire it." St. Bernard of Clairvaux urged, "Let those without experience [of God] burn with desire so that they will not so much know as experience." And St. Thomas Aquinas, commenting on the Psalms, exclaimed that "the love of the Holy Spirit . . . causes a force in the soul like a torrent. . . . And it is a torrent of delight because it causes pleasure and sweetness in the soul."[16] Spiritual writers today often warn against the danger of seeking spiritual experience—rightly so, if experience is taken in a subjective, individualistic sense, as in seeking for a spiritual high. But as Hebrews suggests, authentic Christian experience is a tasting of the objective divine realities given to us in the liturgy, the sacraments, prayer, and daily life: the love of the Father poured into our hearts (see Rom 5:5), liberation from sin through the power of Christ's death and resurrection, the presence of the Holy Spirit dwelling within us and imparting his gifts.

The danger of falling away. Although there are examples of Christians who abandon the faith and then return, pastoral experience suggests that the vast majority of those who drift away after knowing all the blessings of life in Christ do not return. Whatever led them to make that choice against Christ is psychologically and spiritually very difficult to reverse. Thus the author of Hebrews warns his readers that if they allow themselves to fall away, there is a good chance they will never return for salvation. We might say the same to

16. Augustine, *Tractates in the Gospel of John* 54.12.8; Bernard, *Sermons on the Song of Songs* 1.11; Thomas Aquinas, *Commentary on the Psalms of David* 36:9 (35:9 LXX).

people who rationalize, "I can commit a serious sin today and go to confession tomorrow, and all will be okay." When we make choices, either to sin against Christ or to hold steadfastly to him in faith, those decisions shape who we become.

Endurance for the Long Haul (6:9–12)

⁹But we are sure in your regard, beloved, of better things related to salvation, even though we speak in this way. ¹⁰For God is not unjust so as to overlook your work and the love you have demonstrated for his name by having served and continuing to serve the holy ones. ¹¹We earnestly desire each of you to demonstrate the same eagerness for the fulfillment of hope until the end, ¹²so that you may not become sluggish, but imitators of those who, through faith and patience, are inheriting the promises.

OT: Gen 19:29; Neh 5:19; Dan 14:38
NT: Matt 10:22; Luke 8:15; 1 Cor 11:1; Phil 3:17; Rev 2:26
Catechism: imitating the saints, 957; merit of good works, 2008; perseverance to the end, 1821

6:9 As is typical in Hebrews, words of stern admonition are followed by words of loving encouragement, similar to the letters to the seven churches in Revelation (Rev 2–3). For the only time in the sermon, the preacher addresses his audience with the affectionate term **beloved**, perhaps thinking of what he will say later: "whom the Lord loves, he disciplines" (12:6). The warning of the very real danger of spiritual stagnation and apostasy (5:11–6:8) was just that—a warning, not a condemnation of something that has already happened. In their case he is **sure** (or "confident") **of better things related to salvation**.[17] The very fact that he cautions them is a sign of his—and God's—love for them.

6:10 The basis of his confidence is the clear evidence that God's grace is operative among them: their **work and the love** they **have demonstrated for his name by having served and continuing to serve the holy ones**.[18] The genuineness of their love has been shown by their works. We learn later what some of these works were: they had willingly endured public insult, abuse, and the confiscation of their property; they had put themselves at risk by ministering to fellow

17. The phrase is literally "*the* better things of salvation." The "better things" brought by Christ, in comparison with the lesser realities of the old covenant, is a constant theme in Hebrews (7:19, 22; 8:6; 9:23; 10:1, 34; 11:16, 35, 40).
18. "Holy ones," or "saints," is the New Testament appellation for all Christians, made holy by faith and baptism.

Christians imprisoned for their faith; and they had shown hospitality, probably to missionaries or itinerant prophets (10:33–34; 13:2). Though they may be flagging in faith, these struggling believers continued to express their love for God by serving their fellow Christians (see 1 John 4:21). If they are slow to mature (5:12), they are nevertheless bearing some good fruit and not only "thorns and thistles" (6:8).

That **God is not unjust so as to overlook** these good deeds is meant as a deliberate understatement.[19] A strong biblical theme is that God, who is justice itself, always remembers and rewards the deeds of those who have served him (Gen 19:29; Neh 5:19; Dan 14:38; Acts 10:31). These good deeds are in fact possible only because of God's grace at work in us (1 Cor 15:10; Eph 2:10; Phil 2:13).

6:11 The verb **earnestly desire** expresses strong emotion,[20] revealing the heart of a pastor who cares deeply for his flock, like Paul, who wrote to the Philippians, "God is my witness, how I long for all of you with the affection of Christ Jesus" (Phil 1:8). The author is concerned not only for the well-being of the community as a whole but for every member individually: **each of you**. What he desires is that they **demonstrate the same eagerness** or "diligence" in advancing toward the finish line as they have in their past good works. Evidently, this is a community of believers who have passed beyond the honeymoon phase of devotion to Christ and need encouragement to persevere for the long haul. As in a good marriage, what counts is not only the initial surge of romantic feelings but the faithful love that endures through hard times and periods of dryness and becomes, for that very reason, immeasurably deeper and richer. As Hebrews emphasized in the pilgrimage exhortation of 3:7–4:11, the Christian life is not a static state but a dynamic journey **until the end** (see Matt 10:22; Luke 8:15; Phil 3:13–14; Rev 2:26). The end is **the fulfillment of hope**,[21] or full realization of all that we hope for. But the way we get there is not by slogging it out on our own but steadfastly holding on to hope in God, as verses 13–20 will go on to explain (see 3:6, 14; 6:18).

6:12 The exact opposite of the "eagerness" of verse 11 is being **sluggish**, the vice to which this community is prone (see 5:11). One way they can stir up their wilting zeal is to consider the inspiring example of others **who, through faith and patience, are inheriting the promises**. This probably refers to the †patriarchs

---

19. Johnson, *Hebrews*, 165.

20. The force of the Greek verb (*epithymeō*) is not adequately expressed by the RSV translation ("we desire"), nor by the NSRV and NIV ("we want").

21. Other translations render this phrase in a more subjective sense: "full assurance of hope" (RSV, NRSV).

and heroes of the old covenant, whose stirring example will be praised in detail in chapter 11 (the same qualities of *faith* and *patience* are ascribed to Abraham in 11:8; 6:15). Even though these ancestors in faith did not see the fulfillment of God's promises in their lifetime, they will one day see it (11:39–40). The author may also have in mind saints of the new covenant who have fought the good fight and "finished the race" (see 2 Tim 4:7). The mention of *faith* in verse 12, together with *love* in verse 10 and *hope* in verse 11, completes the triad of theological virtues (as in 10:22–24; see 1 Cor 13:13).

This verse implies that as important as systematic catechesis is, it cannot substitute for seeing concretely what holiness looks like in a holy person's life. Thus an important part of spiritual growth is to look around for models of holiness, including faithful church leaders (13:7), and be **imitators** of them. So Paul often urges his disciples, not out of pride but out of awareness of the transformative effect of grace in his own life, "Be imitators of me, as I am of Christ" (1 Cor 11:1; see 1 Cor 4:16; Phil 3:17; 2 Thess 3:7–9).

God Takes the Stand (6:13–20)

[13]When God made the promise to Abraham, since he had no one greater by whom to swear, "he swore by himself," [14]and said, "I will indeed bless you and multiply" you. [15]And so, after patient waiting, he obtained the promise. [16]Human beings swear by someone greater than themselves; for them an oath serves as a guarantee and puts an end to all argument. [17]So when God wanted to give the heirs of his promise an even clearer demonstration of the immutability of his purpose, he intervened with an oath, [18]so that by two immutable things, in which it was impossible for God to lie, we who have taken refuge might be strongly encouraged to hold fast to the hope that lies before us. [19]This we have as an anchor of the soul, sure and firm, which reaches into the interior behind the veil, [20]where Jesus has entered on our behalf as forerunner, becoming high priest forever according to the order of Melchizedek.

OT: Gen 12:1–3; 22:16–17; Ps 33:11
NT: John 17:17; Rom 4:18–19; Phil 1:6; 2:12; Titus 1:2; Heb 10:19–20
Catechism: God's oath to Abraham, 2810; Christian hope, 1817–21, 2090–92; Jesus' high priest-hood, 1544–45

Life can sometimes seem like a boat ride in a turbulent, storm-tossed sea. Such it must have seemed to the Jewish Christian readers of Hebrews, who lived at a time of cataclysmic change, when the ancient Jewish institutions of temple, priesthood, and sacrifice were on the verge of collapse[22] and Christians too were subject to harsh persecution (see 10:32–34). At times like this, Hebrews says, we need to know that we have a sure and firm anchor that will hold us safely through the storm (v. 19). That anchor is the absolutely reliable promise of God—a promise made nearly four thousand years ago to Abraham, but one that belongs by right to us too, as Abraham's children.

Verse 12 mentioned "the promises" that Christians will inherit if we persevere in faith and patience. Now Hebrews explains what those promises are by turning our attention to Abraham, the great biblical example of faith and patience. It was to **Abraham** that God first made his great **promise**, declaring that through Abraham he would bless all nations (Gen 12:1–3). But the key point, Hebrews notes, is that God not only gave his promise but also later reinforced it by swearing an oath (Gen 22:16–18). To promise is to give assurance of something that one will do or not do. But an oath is much more solemn: it is to invoke God as witness to a promise, asking for his help to keep it and, in effect, making one liable to his penalty if one does not.[23] Even today, oaths of public office or oaths in court are made by saying "so help me God" or a similar phrase, and the failure to keep such oaths is considered a serious offense.

6:13–14

But God has no need to swear an oath! His word is already absolute truth and completely trustworthy (John 17:17; Titus 1:2). The fact that he did so shows his amazing consideration for human frailty. God knows that human beings find it hard to trust because of our all-too-common experience of broken promises and failed commitments. So, **since he had no one greater by whom to swear, "he swore by himself," and said, "I will indeed bless you and multiply" you** (Gen 22:16–17). The wording of this oath is an idiom that could be rendered literally, "If I do not absolutely bless you and multiply you . . ." It is an unfinished sentence that implies unnamed dire consequences if one should break the oath.

It was not by chance that God's oath in Genesis 22 was given after he had put Abraham's faith to the most extreme test by asking him to sacrifice his beloved son Isaac, the very one in whom the promise had begun to come true (see Heb 11:17–19). Although God intervened to rescue Isaac, that event was a foreshadowing of the ultimate act of love: God's giving up of his own Son, who was not rescued but sacrificed for our salvation. In response to the extraordinarily faithful obedience that Abraham showed on that occasion, God swore,

---

22. This collapse would have been evident to many observers at the time, even if Hebrews was written before the destruction of the Jerusalem temple in AD 70.

23. See the Catechism 2150–51. On the biblical significance of oaths, see Scott Hahn, *Swear to God: The Promise and Power of the Sacraments* (New York: Doubleday, 2004), especially 61–72.

"Because you acted as you did in not withholding from me your son, your only one, I will bless you and make your descendants as countless as the stars of the sky and the sands of the seashore" (Gen 22:16–17).

6:15 **And so, after patient waiting** (or "longsuffering"), Abraham **obtained the promise**. The patriarch had indeed already waited a long time. When God first promised him descendants, Abraham was already a venerable seventy-five years old, and Sarah his wife was sixty-five and barren (Gen 11:30; 12:4); and it would be another twenty-five years before their son Isaac was born (Gen 21:5). During that time, to all external appearances God's promise was impossible—laughable! (see Gen 17:17; 18:12). Yet as Paul says, Abraham "believed, hoping against hope. . . . He did not weaken in faith when he considered his own body as [already] dead (for he was almost a hundred years old) and the dead womb of Sarah" (Rom 4:18–19). Part of God's plan was, and is, the testing of faith through long years of patient endurance. Having finally "obtained" the promised son by birth, Abraham "obtained" him again after being willing to give him up (Gen 22:13).

6:16 When human beings want to buttress their words, they **swear by someone greater than themselves; for them an oath serves as a guarantee and puts an end to all argument**. A similar principle is expressed in Exodus 22:9–11, which legislates that someone in a dispute who is suspected of fraud can take an oath that serves as a guarantee of innocence. Oaths were taken extremely seriously in the ancient world, both in Israel and in pagan nations, because of the strong belief that God (or the gods) would not let a perjurer go unpunished.[24]

6:17–18 It is all the more astounding that God, the supreme authority whom human beings invoke to guarantee our own words, himself **intervened with an oath**. This shows the lengths to which God will go to assure his people of the trustworthiness of his promise. The **heirs** who inherit this **promise** are all of Abraham's children, both by physical descent (Jews) and by faith (Christians).[25] **God wanted to give** all these heirs of Abraham **an even clearer demonstration of the immutability of his purpose**. That is, he wanted to prove to them that his plan to bless them, and bless the whole world through them, will be accomplished without fail: "The plan of the LORD stands forever" (Ps 33:11). Because

24. In Matt 5:33–37 Jesus forbids oaths, precisely because through his grace we are empowered to be truthful in all our words without having to resort to oaths. The Catechism (2154) notes, "Following St. Paul (2 Cor 1:23; Gal 1:20) the tradition of the Church has understood Jesus' words as not excluding oaths made for grave and right reasons (for example, in court)."

25. A common New Testament theme is that all those who believe in Christ have become children of Abraham by faith (see Heb 2:16; Rom 4:9–13; Gal 3:6–29).

Fig. 7. Ancient anchors on display at Caesarea Maritima, Israel

it is so easy for human beings to distrust God, he gave us **two immutable** (or "unchangeable") **things**—the promise and the oath—**in which it was impossible for God to lie.**[26]

Abraham's children by faith are **we who have taken refuge**, or "have fled," perhaps alluding to Old Testament prophecies that "many nations shall flee for refuge to the Lord in that day" (Zech 2:15 †LXX; see Isa 55:5). Like Abraham, Christians are pilgrims and aliens in this world, seeking security not in earthly resources but in God, "For here we have no lasting city, but we seek the one that is to come" (Heb 13:14). The language is emphatic: God wants us to be **strongly encouraged to hold fast to** (or "seize") **the hope that lies before us**—that is, our hope of one day sharing in God's glory (2:10), entering into his rest (4:10), and experiencing the joy of eternal communion with Christ and all those redeemed by him (12:22–24).

"Hope" in the New Testament is something very different from earthly hope, **6:19** which is a vague optimism that things will turn out okay: "I hope the weather will be nice tomorrow." Biblical hope is confident assurance and expectancy based on the absolute trustworthiness of God. Hebrews describes this hope with a threefold metaphor that is not easy to integrate, relating to a ship, the

---

26. Alternatively, the "two immutable things" could be interpreted as God's oaths in Gen 22 (discussed here) and in Ps 110 (discussed in the next chapter). See Albert Vanhoye, *A Different Priest: The Letter to the Hebrews*, trans. Leo Arnold, Colección Rhetorica Semitica (Miami: Convivium, 2011), 193.

temple, and a race. First, our hope is **an anchor of the soul, sure and firm**. As an anchor keeps a ship stable in storms or rising tides and prevents it from either running aground or drifting away, so our hope keeps us from drifting away from Christ, as the original readers were in danger of doing (see 2:1), or from being spiritually unstable, "tossed by waves and swept along by every wind of teaching arising from human trickery" (Eph 4:14).

A ship's anchor is set on the shore or lowered to the bottom of the sea; our anchor, in contrast, is fixed above in God's heavenly temple. It **reaches into the interior behind the veil**, the inmost chamber of the †sanctuary, the †Holy of Holies. In the old covenant, the Holy of Holies was the most sacred place on earth, which only the high priest could enter and only once a year (see 9:7). But as Hebrews will later tell us, the earthly temple was only a symbol or shadow of God's true temple in heaven (8:5; 9:11), and now in Christ we have been given access to that inmost throne room of God (4:16; 10:19–20). As we struggle with the ups and downs of this life, we are to hold tightly the cable to an anchor that reaches all the way into the presence of God.

6:20 The Christian life is also a race—one that is measured not by speed but by endurance (12:1). The race is a favorite metaphor of St. Paul, who urges Christians, "Run so as to win" (1 Cor 9:24; see Gal 5:7; Phil 2:16; 2 Tim 4:7). **Jesus has entered** that heavenly sanctuary toward which we are running **on our behalf as forerunner** (the Greek word, *prodromos*, literally means "one who runs before"). This is strikingly different from the †levitical high priests, who were not in any sense forerunners, since they alone entered "behind the veil" and all other Israelites were strictly forbidden to do so.[27] But Jesus is "the leader" to our salvation (2:10), "the leader and perfecter of faith" (12:2), whose whole purpose in entering God's heavenly throne room was to open the way for his brothers and sisters to follow. It was for this purpose that he became **high priest forever according to the order of Melchizedek**.[28]

With this statement the writer brings the long exhortation of 5:11–6:20 full circle and deftly resumes the topic that he introduced in 5:10. Having given a strong warning against complacency and presumption (5:11–6:12), he has balanced it with even stronger reasons for hope and confidence (6:13–20). Now readers are ready for the "solid food" (5:12) of the next four chapters, which will explain the mystery of Jesus' high priesthood according to the order of Melchizedek.

27. Philip Edgcumbe Hughes, *A Commentary on the Epistle to the Hebrews* (Grand Rapids: Eerdmans, 1977), 236.
28. The Greek word for "order," *taxis*, refers to a post, rank, or position.

Reflection and Application (6:13–20)

On the one hand, Hebrews seems to be instilling uncertainty about whether we will be saved or not (2:3; 3:6, 14; 6:4–8; 10:26–31); on the other hand, it seems to advocate confident security (4:16; 6:9, 17–20; 10:23). There is a similar paradox in Paul telling the Philippians: "work out your salvation with fear and trembling" (Phil 2:12) and yet trust that "the one who began a good work in you will continue to complete it until the day of Christ Jesus" (Phil 1:6). How are we to reconcile the two? Some Christians have embraced the misguided doctrine of "eternal security," which is sometimes expressed as "once saved, always saved." However, this view is inconsistent with many New Testament texts that warn Christians of the possibility of forfeiting our eternal salvation.[29] The key to resolving the paradox is to recognize the distinction between *presumption* and *hope* (see Catechism 2090–92). Presumption is human self-reliance; it takes for granted that we will attain a heavenly reward based on our own goodness or on a false idea of God's mercy. Paul warns, "Do you presume upon the riches of his kindness and forbearance and patience? Do you not know that God's kindness is meant to lead you to repentance?" (Rom 2:4 RSV). Instead we need a sober self-knowledge, recognizing that we are always capable of turning away from God and will need ongoing conversion until the day we die. Hope, on the other hand, is a confident, trusting reliance on God, who desires our salvation infinitely more than we do and will give us every powerful grace we need to attain it. Jesus has prepared a place for us in his Father's house (John 14:2–3). He is faithful, and he will bring his promises to fulfillment in us, "if only we hold our first confidence firm to the end" (Heb 3:14 RSV; see 1 Cor 1:8; 1 Thess 5:23–24).

---

29. Matt 7:21; 24:10; Luke 8:13; Rom 11:22; 1 Cor 6:9–10; 9:24–27; 10:1–12; Gal 5:4; 1 Tim 1:19; Rev 22:19; see Catechism 837.

The Priesthood of Melchizedek

Hebrews 7:1–28

Reflecting on Scripture in the light of Christ's passion, the author of Hebrews probes biblical texts in a way that no one before him ever had. The priest-king Melchizedek was an obscure figure, mentioned in only two brief passages of the Old Testament (Gen 14:18–20; Ps 110:4).[1] But Hebrews recognizes him as one of the great foreshadowings of the new covenant hidden in the old. The aim of chapter 7 is to show how this Gentile priest, who lived centuries before the †levitical priesthood was instituted, is a †type of the new and eternal high priesthood of Jesus Christ.

The discourse on Melchizedek began in chapter 5 but was interrupted for the long exhortation of 5:11–6:20. The preacher has "much to say" on this advanced subject but was concerned that his hearers were not ready for it, since they had "become sluggish in hearing" and were still in need of milk rather than solid food (5:11–12). He now seems confident that the warnings and encouragements of chapters 5–6 have sufficiently prepared them for the deep waters into which chapter 7 will dive. This chapter contains matters that seem strange or puzzling to modern readers, since they depend on assumptions that were common among first-century Jews but are unfamiliar to us. But the effort required to understand them is more than worthwhile, since it will help unlock the meaning not only of Hebrews but also of the Old Testament passages on which the author draws.

---

1. Melchizedek did, however, become an important figure in some Jewish literature contemporary with or postdating Hebrews, for instance, the Qumran fragment *11QMelchizedek*; Philo, *Allegorical Laws* 3.79–82; Josephus, *Antiquities* 1.179–81; *Targum Neofiti* and *Targum Yerushalmi*. See Luke Timothy Johnson, *Hebrews: A Commentary*, New Testament Library (Louisville: Westminster John Knox, 2006), 181–83.

Melchizedek, King and Priest (7:1–10)

[1]This "Melchizedek, king of Salem and priest of God Most High," "met Abraham as he returned from his defeat of the kings" and "blessed him." [2]And Abraham apportioned to him "a tenth of everything." His name first means righteous king, and he was also "king of Salem," that is, king of peace. [3]Without father, mother, or ancestry, without beginning of days or end of life, thus made to resemble the Son of God, he remains a priest forever.

[4]See how great he is to whom the patriarch "Abraham [indeed] gave a tenth" of his spoils. [5]The descendants of Levi who receive the office of priesthood have a commandment according to the law to exact tithes from the people, that is, from their brothers, although they also have come from the loins of Abraham. [6]But he who was not of their ancestry received tithes from Abraham and blessed him who had received the promises. [7]Unquestionably, a lesser person is blessed by a greater. [8]In the one case, mortal men receive tithes; in the other, a man of whom it is testified that he lives on. [9]One might even say that Levi himself, who receives tithes, was tithed through Abraham, [10]for he was still in his father's loins when Melchizedek met him.

OT: Gen 14:18–20; Num 18:21–28; Ps 76:3; 85:10 RSV; 110:4
NT: Gal 3:29; Rev 1:18
Catechism: Melchizedek a figure of Christ, 58

Psalm 110:1 was well known to the early Christians, who regarded it as a key prophecy of Jesus, the Messiah who is exalted at God's "right hand."[2] But the unique contribution of Hebrews is to unpack the significance of verse 4 of the same psalm, where God declares the Messiah "a priest forever, according to the order of Melchizedek." If Jesus is the Messiah seated at God's right hand, then he is also the eternal priest! But who is Melchizedek, and what is his "order"? Even before the time of Christ, this line of the psalm was puzzling, since the Messiah was to be from the royal line of David, of the tribe of Judah, but priests were from the line of Aaron, of the tribe of Levi. How could the son of David be a priest? It is in answering this question that Hebrews finds a clue to understanding the whole mystery of Jesus' passion. Our author has led up to this point by quoting the line about Melchizedek three times already (5:6, 10; 6:20). Now he finally begins to delve into its meaning by looking at the only other biblical passage where Melchizedek is mentioned: Genesis 14:18–20.

2. Jesus himself applies Ps 110:1 to himself obliquely in Matt 22:42–45; 26:64; Mark 12:35–37; 14:62; Luke 20:41–44; 22:69; other allusions to the verse can be found in Mark 16:19; Acts 2:33–35; 5:31; 7:55–56; Rom 8:34; Eph 1:20; Col 3:1; 1 Pet 3:22.

Fig. 8. Thirteenth-century mosaic depicting the meeting of Abraham and Melchizedek, St. Mark's Basilica, Venice

7:1–2   Genesis 14 tells the story of a battle in which **Abraham**, with a band of only 318 men, defeats a coalition of four **kings** and rescues his nephew Lot and others from captivity. Upon Abraham's return, **Melchizedek, king of Salem**, appears on the scene to bless him and bless the Lord who gave him victory. Melchizedek is the first person in the Bible to be called a priest. Genesis makes clear that he is no idol-worshiping pagan but is a **priest of God Most High**, the one true God, the creator of heaven and earth (see Gen 14:19). **Abraham**, in thanksgiving to God for his victory, apportions to Melchizedek the priest **a tenth** of the spoils of battle. A tenth part, or tithe, was the standard portion of one's earnings to be returned to God, acknowledging that all we have comes from him.[3] After his interaction with Abraham, Melchizedek disappears from the scene and is never mentioned again in Genesis.

But there is hidden significance in his name, as Hebrews points out. The name Melchizedek means **righteous king**,[4] and his title **king of Salem** can be interpreted to mean **king of peace** (Hebrew *shalom*). Melchizedek thus exemplifies

---

3. See Gen 28:22; Lev 27:30; Deut 14:22–23.

4. As scholars point out, the original meaning probably was "Zedek is my king" or "my king is righteous."

the two great qualities of the promised Messiah: righteousness and peace (see Ps 72:7 RSV; 85:11; Isa 9:6). Genesis also tells us that he brought forth bread and wine (Gen 14:18), presumably as a thank offering for Abraham's victory, which Christian readers recognize as a foreshadowing of Jesus' self-offering in the Eucharist.[5] According to later biblical tradition, the city of Salem is none other than Jeru*salem* (Ps 76:3), making the link with Jesus even stronger.

Verse 3 is often misunderstood. That Melchizedek is **without father, mother,**   **7:3** **or ancestry** (literally, "genealogy"), **without beginning of days or end of life**, does not mean that Hebrews views him as some kind of supernatural being.[6] Rather, the fact that Genesis, a book full of genealogies, says nothing about his parentage is striking. It means he lacks the essential qualification for priest-hood according to the law of Moses: priestly lineage (see Num 18:7; Ezra 2:62).[7] And the silence about his lifespan, in a book that carefully records years of life, gives the impression that his priesthood, unlike that of the †levitical priests, is continuous and unending.[8] In this sense, he **remains a priest forever**[9] and thus resembles **the Son of God**, who is "the same yesterday, today, and forever" (Heb 13:8). That Jesus' priesthood is of the "order" of Melchizedek means that his priesthood is similar—or to put it more accurately, that Melchizedek is similar to Jesus. As one scholar points out, Hebrews looks back upon the fig-ure of Melchizedek as a "shadow, a signpost pointing to someone greater than himself. He is like a primeval John the Baptist who testifies in effect, 'After me comes one who ranks before me, for he was before me' (Jn. 1:30)."[10]

Verses 4–10 use two arguments to explain Melchizedek's superiority to **the**   **7:4–10** **patriarch** Abraham and therefore also to Abraham's great-grandson Levi. First, Abraham paid a **tenth of his spoils** (i.e., a tithe) to Melchizedek—a standard way of giving honor and financial support to a priest. According to the law of Moses, the levitical priests **exact tithes from the people** of Israel, **that is, from**

5. See, for instance, Eucharistic Prayer 1 of the Roman Rite liturgy, which includes the prayer that God accept these offerings "as once you were pleased to accept . . . the offering of your high priest Melchizedek."

6. Some Jews of the period did seem to view him as such—for instance, the author of the Qumran fragment *11QMelchizedek*.

7. Albert Vanhoye, *A Different Priest: The Letter to the Hebrews*, trans. Leo Arnold, Series Rhetorica Semitica (Miami: Convivium, 2011), 207.

8. An interesting parallel to Melchizedek in several respects is Jethro (sometimes called "Reuel"), the father-in-law of Moses (Exod 3:1; 18:9–12). Like Melchizedek, he is a Gentile priest yet worships the one true God; there is no mention of his ancestry or lifespan; and he blesses God for Moses' victory over an enemy nation (Egypt).

9. A better translation of the Greek phrase used here would be "perpetually," since it is weaker than the word for "forever" that describes Jesus' priesthood in 5:6; 6:20; 7:17, 21, 24, 28 and Jesus' throne in 1:8.

10. Philip Edgcumbe Hughes, *A Commentary on the Epistle to the Hebrews* (Grand Rapids: Eerd-mans, 1977), 264.

their brothers. This statement combines what were actually two layers of tith-ing: the Levites, who cared for the †sanctuary and all its vessels, received tithes from the other tribes of Israel (Num 18:21–24); the priests, in turn, received a tithe of the tithes from their fellow Levites (Num 18:25–28). In this way the priests were honored and supported by lay Israelites, **although** the laypeople **also have come from the loins of Abraham**.

Yet Melchizedek, **who was not of their ancestry**—not a member of the priestly tribe of Levi—**received tithes from Abraham**! Not only that, but **one might even say that Levi himself, who receives tithes** from Israel, paid tithes to Melchizedek **through Abraham**, since **he was still in his father's loins when Melchizedek met him**. At this point the logic of Hebrews may seem extremely foreign to us. How can one speak of Levi paying tithes through Abraham when Levi would not even be born until more than a century later? This claim depends on the biblical understanding of human beings not as isolated individuals but as members of a people, profoundly linked through both genealogy and tradition (see sidebar, "Levi 'in the Loins' of Abraham?"). Through their founding father Abraham, all Israel, so to speak, paid homage to the priest Melchizedek.[11]

In sum, the first argument is that **in the one case, mortal men** (literally, "dying men") **receive tithes; in the other, a man of whom it is testified that he lives on** (literally, "he lives"). As Hebrews will emphasize later, the fact that the levitical priests die proves the limited and imperfect nature of their priesthood (7:23–24). In the case of Melchizedek, on the other hand, Scrip-ture simply presents him as a living person; that is, it contains no record of his death. Again the point is not that Melchizedek was literally immortal but that his depiction in Scripture prefigures Christ, whose priesthood is eternal because he lives forever.

The second proof that Melchizedek outranks Abraham is that he **blessed him**. Abraham was the great patriarch, founder of the chosen people and original recipient of God's **promises** of land, blessing, and countless descendants (Gen 12:1–4). The Jews' great boast was that they were descendants of Abraham (see Matt 3:9; John 8:33, 39).[12] Yet, as Hebrews points out, the striking fact is that Scripture implies an even higher status for Melchizedek, since an undisputed biblical premise was that **a lesser person is blessed by a greater**. The underly-ing logic is this: If Melchizedek, the shadow and †type, is greater than Abraham

---

11. In a similar way, Paul argues that through Adam's disobedience many were made sinners (Rom 5:19).

12. Hughes, *Hebrews*, 251.

Levi "in the Loins" of Abraham?

In biblical thought each nation, and in a broader sense the whole of humanity, extending into both the past and the future, is not a collection of disparate individuals but rather a single, organic reality. This biblical principle is crucial to understanding the thought of Hebrews, particularly the argument based on Levi being "in his father's loins" when Abraham met Melchizedek (7:10). It is also crucial to Paul's teaching on how we inherit original sin based on our common descent from Adam (Rom 5:12–19). C. S. Lewis gives an illuminating explanation:

> They [human beings] look separate because you see them walking about separately. But then, we are so made that we can see only the present moment. If we could see the past, then of course it would look different. For there was a time when every man was part of his mother, and (earlier still) part of his father as well: and when they were part of his grandparents. If you could see humanity spread out in time, as God sees it, it would not look like a lot of separate things dotted about. It would look like one single growing thing—rather like a very complicated tree. Every individual would appear connected with every other. And not only that. Individuals are not really separate from God any more than from one another. . . . Consequently, when Christ becomes man . . . it is as if something which is always affecting the whole human mass begins, at one point, to affect the whole human mass in a new way. From that point the effect spreads through all mankind.[a]

a. C. S. Lewis, *Mere Christianity* (New York: Macmillan, 1943), 155–56.

and his descendants the levitical priests, how much greater yet is Christ, the reality to whom the shadow points?

Both of these biblical arguments would have been startling, but compelling, to Hebrews' first-century Jewish Christian readers.

A New Priest from the Tribe of Judah (7:11–19)

[11]If, then, perfection came through the levitical priesthood, on the basis of which the people received the law, what need would there still have been for another priest to arise according to the order of Melchizedek, and not reckoned according to the order of Aaron? [12]When there is a change of priesthood, there is necessarily a change of law as well. [13]Now he of whom these things are said belonged to a different tribe, of which no member ever officiated at the altar. [14]It is clear that our Lord arose from

Judah, and in regard to that tribe Moses said nothing about priests. [15]It
is even more obvious if another priest is raised up after the likeness of
Melchizedek, [16]who has become so, not by a law expressed in a commandment concerning physical descent but by the power of a life that cannot be
destroyed. [17]For it is testified:

> "You are a priest forever
>   according to the order of Melchizedek."

[18]On the one hand, a former commandment is annulled because of its
weakness and uselessness, [19]for the law brought nothing to perfection; on
the other hand, a better hope is introduced, through which we draw near
to God.

OT: Num 17:5; 1 Sam 2:35; Ps 110:4
NT: Rom 3:20; 8:3; Gal 2:21; Eph 3:12; Rev 1:18; 5:5
Catechism: priestly orders, 1537–38; Jesus' indestructible life, 646, 648

Now that Melchizedek's superiority to Levi has been established (vv. 1–10),
Hebrews can take the next logical step: Scripture itself points forward to something greater and more lasting than the †levitical priesthood. The line of reasoning here is very similar to that of chapters 3–4. There, the exhortation to enter
God's rest in Psalm 95 implied that the land of Israel is not the ultimate "rest"
that God has for his people. Here, the declaration that the messiah belongs
to the priestly "order of Melchizedek" in Psalm 110 implies that the levitical
priesthood is not the ultimate priesthood that God has for his people.[13] In both
cases, the forward-looking hope expressed in the Psalms proves that the law
of Moses does not contain the fullness of all that God destined for his people.
Only in the risen Jesus is that fullness attained.

7:11–12   Verse 11 neatly lays out the argument: if the **levitical priesthood** were
permanent and sufficient—as the original readers of Hebrews may have been
inclined to think—why would the psalm have spoken of the Messiah as **another priest** belonging to a different order, **the order of Melchizedek?** The
psalm bears eloquent witness to the inadequacy of **the order of Aaron.** The
preacher is telling his Jewish Christian audience that their vision needs to be
expanded: God's purpose in appointing a priesthood for his people is nothing
less than **perfection.** "Perfection" (Greek *teleiōsis*) is a key word in Hebrews,
along with the related verb "to make perfect" (see comments on 2:10). It means
not so much flawlessness as *completeness*, the full realization of God's plan for

13. See Heb 8:9–13, which will make a similar argument about the "new covenant" promise in
Jeremiah as revealing the inadequacy of the former covenant.

human beings—something that is impossible through the levitical priesthood.

The imperfection of the old system is why another priest had **to arise**. Hebrews is very deliberate in using the verb "arise" (*anistēmi*). On one level, "arise" simply means "to appear in history"; but on another level it also points toward Jesus' resurrection: he "arose" from the dead.[14] As Hebrews will explain below, it is precisely by rising to eternal life that Jesus has become a "priest forever according to the order of Melchizedek."

Fig. 9. Reproduction of an eighth-century BC horned altar for animal sacrifice found at Beer-sheba, Israel

That there is a new priesthood has revolutionary implications for **the law** since priesthood and law were inextricably linked in God's †covenant with Israel (as in many world religions). The law governs how the priesthood operates, and the priesthood upholds the law by providing a means of †atonement when it is violated. Both the priesthood and the law had been established by God through Moses on Mount Sinai (Exod 20–31). So it follows that **when there is a change of priesthood, there is necessarily a change of law as well**. All the detailed rules in the †Torah concerning the levitical priesthood and animal sacrifices are rendered obsolete, since their true purpose—to point to a greater fulfillment in Christ—has been attained. Even more, as Hebrews will explain later, the "change of law" means that God's law will no longer be written on stone but on human hearts, bringing about an inner transformation (8:7–13).

How do we know there has been a "change of priesthood"? Because **he of whom these things are said**—Jesus, the priest-king foretold in Psalm 110—**belonged to a different tribe, of which no member ever officiated at the altar**. In the law of Moses the primary qualification for priesthood was physical descent from Aaron within the tribe of Levi (Num 18:1–7). Yet Psalm 110 speaks of a priest-king of the royal line of David, from the tribe of **Judah**, a tribe in regard to which **Moses said nothing about priests**. 7:13–14

For the early Christians it was a **clear**, undisputed fact that Jesus was from the line of David.[15] Hebrews refers to him as **our Lord**, a title expressing both

---

14. The word "arise" (Greek *anistēmi*) is a common New Testament verb for Jesus' resurrection (e.g., Mark 16:9; Luke 24:7; John 20:9).

15. See the genealogies in Matt 1 and Luke 3 and the title "son of David" often used during Jesus' public ministry (Matt 9:27; 15:22; 20:30–31; 21:9, 15) as well as affirmations of Jesus' Davidic ancestry in Acts 2:29–32; Rom 1:3; Rev 5:5.

reverence and affection. As in verse 11, instead of saying Jesus "descended" from Judah, Hebrews again uses a word that evokes his resurrection: he **arose**. In this case the verb for "arose" (*anatellō*) is one often used for the rising of the sun (Mal 3:20 †LXX; Matt 4:16) or the stars (2 Pet 1:19). It recalls Balaam's famous prophecy of the coming king (Num 24:17):

> I see him, though not now;
> > I observe him, though not near:
> A star shall advance from Jacob,
> > and a scepter shall rise from Israel.

7:15   It is **even more obvious**—obvious, that is, that the law is being changed (v. 12)—**if another priest is raised up after the likeness of Melchizedek**. For the third time (see vv. 11, 14) Hebrews deliberately uses a resurrection verb, "raised up" (*anistēmi*), driving home the point that the whole basis of Jesus' priesthood is his death and resurrection.

7:16   Verse 16 expresses the contrast between old and new in the strongest terms possible. Whereas the levitical priesthood was **by a law expressed in a commandment concerning physical descent** (literally, "by a law of fleshly commandment"), Jesus' priesthood is **by the power of a life that cannot be destroyed** (literally, "by the power of an indestructible life"). The two phrases are perfectly balanced, with three contrasting terms:[16]

law	power
fleshly	indestructible
commandment	life

The old priesthood was established by "law"—that is, by a legal requirement concerning levitical lineage. It was part of the whole Mosaic system of externally imposed "commandments." And the law was "fleshly" in that it had to do with physical descent, and also in that it was weakened by human sin and therefore incapable of attaining its true goal.[17]

Jesus' priesthood, in contrast, is established by the "power" of his exaltation to God's own "life," which is "indestructible." Having been raised from the dead, Jesus is alive forever. And because he shares God's life and power, he can also

---

16. See Johnson, *Hebrews*, 188.

17. The adjective "fleshly" (*sarkinos* or its synonym *sarkikos*) and the noun "flesh" (*sarkos*) are often used in the New Testament to mean what is merely human and is therefore weak and subject to sinful inclinations, in contrast to what is of God (cf. Rom 7:14; 8:3; 1 Cor 3:1, 3; 2 Cor 1:12; 10:4; 1 Pet 2:11).

Does Hebrews Contradict the Words of Jesus?

Alert readers may wonder how the statement in Hebrews 7:18, "a former commandment is annulled because of its weakness and uselessness," can be squared with Jesus' words in the Sermon on the Mount: "Do not think that I have come to abolish the law or the prophets. I have come not to abolish but to fulfill. Amen, I say to you, until heaven and earth pass away, not the smallest letter or the smallest part of a letter will pass from the law, until all things have taken place" (Matt 5:17–18). Is Hebrews contradicting the words of Jesus?

This question should be approached in the same way we approach other apparent inconsistencies in Scripture. Because God is its primary author, Scripture is a single work that is consistent with itself. At the same time, the Bible is a library, a collection of books written by various authors in different time periods. These diverse voices should not be artificially harmonized; each author is speaking from his own unique perspective to a distinct audience with distinct needs. When we encounter a tension between one statement and another, it forces us to think more deeply to grasp what God is saying through each author's unique perspective on the truth.

In this case, the thought of Hebrews is similar to that of Paul, who wrote that Jesus "has abolished the law with its commandments and ordinances" (Eph 2:15 NRSV). Both Paul and Hebrews are declaring that in Christ's death and resurrection the true aim of the Torah—a lasting, unbreakable covenant relationship with the Lord—has been perfectly accomplished. The †cultic prescriptions of the old law (all the rules having to do with priesthood, sacrifice, and ritual purity) have therefore been rendered obsolete. Their purpose was to prepare for and point to the great high priest, the perfect sacrifice, and the cleansing of the heart that it provides. Now that their purpose is accomplished, these cultic laws are no longer needed. When the sun has risen, why continue to hold a candle?

Jesus' statement in Matthew, on the other hand, refers primarily to the moral law. By saying that that he came not to destroy the law but to fulfill it, he emphasizes that his teaching supremely accomplishes the intention of the law: to direct people toward true righteousness. As Paul explains, that righteousness is made possible by the power of the Holy Spirit, who imparts to us the grace of Christ's cross and resurrection: "The just requirement of the law [is] fulfilled in us, who walk not according to the flesh but according to the Spirit" (Rom 8:4 RSV; see Rom 8:29). At the same time, Jesus' statement emphasizes the prophetic role of the law: what the Torah prophesied is fulfilled in his own life, death, and resurrection. Thus at the deepest level the thought of Hebrews and Paul is consistent with Jesus' declaration in the Gospel of Matthew.

share it with others;[18] he can raise up our fallen nature to his own divine glory. This is the true goal of priesthood, with which all the aspirations of the levitical priesthood pale in comparison.

7:17   Hebrews supports this point by quoting Psalm 110:4 for the fifth time, this time as if putting the word "forever" in bold capital letters: **You are a priest forever / according to the order of Melchizedek.** Jesus' priesthood is never-ending because he is alive forever.

7:18–19   Hebrews does not shrink from asserting the radical implications: **a former commandment is annulled because of its weakness and uselessness.** The Greek word for "annulled" is a legal term that means "cancelled," "set aside" (NIV, RSV), or "abolished" (NJB). All the Mosaic legislation concerning the priest-hood, temple, and animal sacrifices has been cancelled in view of the infinitely more efficacious redemptive work of Christ. It was a temporary, provisional arrangement whose purpose was to prepare for the greater things to come. Now that the fulfillment has come, the old law is outmoded. It was "weak" and "useless" in the sense that it **brought nothing to perfection.** Here, as in verse 11, "perfection" expresses God's true purpose for human beings—nothing less than a participation in his own divine glory (see 2:10; 12:23). The old law and priesthood were incapable of accomplishing such a lofty goal. As Paul often emphasizes, the problem was not in the law itself, which was a gift from God, but rather in fallen human nature with its deep-rooted inclination to sin (see Rom 3:20; 8:3; Gal 3:21). The law could make people keenly aware of their sins, but it was powerless to keep them from sinning, much less give them a share in God's own life.

While the old law is abrogated, **a better hope is introduced**—introduced prophetically in Psalm 110 and actually in the coming of Christ. "Hope" here refers to the *content* of the hope: the fact that in Christ **we** can now **draw near to God.** It is a "better" hope because what God's people in the old covenant had only in promise (as chapter 11 will show), we have in fulfillment. The very purpose of the levitical priesthood was to enable the people to draw near to God, yet a great separation remained. The people were forbidden to approach the †sanctuary, or even the court of the sanctuary; to do so was to incur a death sentence (Num 18:22).[19] In striking contrast, Christ has qualified us to draw near and enter God's presence with the confidence of sons and daughters ap-proaching their heavenly Father (see 10:19–22).

18. Johnson, *Hebrews*, 188.
19. See also Exod 19:12–13; 24:2; Num 3:10; 17:5; Deut 18:16–17.

The Dead Sea Scrolls: Hope for Two Messiahs

BIBLICAL
BACKGROUND

One of the greatest modern archaeological finds is the Dead Sea Scrolls, a collection of nearly a thousand manuscripts and manuscript fragments that were hidden in jars in caves near the Dead Sea and discovered accidentally by a Bedouin shepherd in 1947. Most scholars believe the scrolls were written and collected by the Essenes, a Jewish sect that had a large community in nearby Qumran. These scrolls date from about 200 BC to AD 80 and thus have immensely enriched our knowledge of Judaism at the time of Christ.

There is evidence in the scrolls and other ancient documents that some Jews expected two different messiahs or "anointed ones": a messiah of Israel (probably a king descended from David) and a messiah of Aaron (a priest descended from Aaron). These two messiahs would exhibit perfect righteousness and together would preside over God's restored people—a belief based in part on Zechariah's vision of "two anointed ones who stand by the Lord of the whole earth" (Zech 4:14; see Zech 6:13).

In Hebrews these two currents of messianic hope converge and are fulfilled perfectly in one person, Christ, the royal son of David and great high priest.

Reflection and Application (7:11–19)

One of the characteristics of Hebrews is its profound gratitude for God's gifts in the old covenant, coupled with a clear affirmation that what we now possess in Christ is unimaginably greater. Every year in the Passover †liturgy Jews pray this prayer of exuberant thanksgiving:

How many are the claims of the Almighty upon our thankfulness! Had he taken us out of Egypt, but not executed judgments on our oppressors, it would have been enough! Had he executed judgments on them, but not torn apart the sea for us, it would have been enough! Had he torn apart the sea for us, but not fed us manna in the desert, it would have been enough! Had he fed us manna in the desert, but not brought us into the Promised Land, it would have been enough!

Christians could add a prayer of praise for what God has done for us in the new covenant, along these lines:

Had he brought us into the Promised Land, but not given us a Messiah, Jesus his only Son, it would have been enough! Had he given us his Son, but not perpetuated his perfect sacrifice for us in the Eucharist, it would have been enough! Had he given us the Eucharist, but not poured out his Holy Spirit on us to write the law on our hearts, it would have been enough! Had he poured out his Holy Spirit but not prepared a kingdom for us to dwell in forever, it would have been enough! Then how much more, doubled and redoubled, is the claim the Almighty has upon our thankfulness! For all these things and more he has done for us.

Jesus' Oath of Office (7:20–28)

20And to the degree that this happened not without the taking of an oath—for others became priests without an oath, 21but he with an oath, through the one who said to him:

> "The Lord has sworn, and he will not repent:
> 'You are a priest forever'"—

22to that same degree has Jesus [also] become the guarantee of an [even] better covenant. 23Those priests were many because they were prevented by death from remaining in office, 24but he, because he remains forever, has a priesthood that does not pass away. 25Therefore, he is always able to save those who approach God through him, since he lives forever to make intercession for them.

26It was fitting that we should have such a high priest: holy, innocent, undefiled, separated from sinners, higher than the heavens. 27He has no need, as did the high priests, to offer sacrifice day after day, first for his own sins and then for those of the people; he did that once for all when he offered himself. 28For the law appoints men subject to weakness to be high priests, but the word of the oath, which was taken after the law, appoints a son, who has been made perfect forever.

OT: Exod 29:36; Lev 16:6; Deut 32:50; 1 Sam 2:35; Ps 110:4
NT: Matt 26:28; Luke 23:47; Rom 6:9; 8:27; Eph 2:18; 3:12; 4:10; 5:2; 1 Pet 2:22; Rev 1:18
Catechism: Jesus' once-for-all sacrifice made present in the liturgy, 1084–85, 1364–68; Jesus' intercession for us, 519, 662, 2634, 2741; priesthood of the old covenant, 1539–43

Hebrews has one more surprising implication to draw out from Psalm 110: unlike the †levitical priesthood, the priesthood of the Messiah was established by God's oath and is therefore unchangeable. This is the third of three solemn divine oaths that Hebrews focuses on. The first oath was punitive: God swore that the rebellious exodus generation would never enter his rest (3:11; Ps 95:11). The other two are oaths of promise, resolving the crisis caused by the first: God's oath to bless and multiply Abraham (6:13–14; Gen 22:16–18) and his oath that the son of David would be a priest forever (7:21; Ps 110:4). In chapter 6 Hebrews explained the extraordinary significance of these divine declarations: God, who is truth itself, has no need to swear an oath, yet he does so out of compassion for human weakness, so that we might be absolutely assured of his purposes and "strongly encouraged to hold fast to the hope that lies before us" (6:17–18).

That God established the priestly order of Melchizedek **not without the taking of an oath** highlights the contrast with the levitical priests, who **became priests without an oath**.[20] This biblical observation must have startled the original readers of Hebrews, who would have realized its truth immediately. God did not swear any oath when he instituted the levitical priesthood. He simply instructed Moses, "Have your brother Aaron, and with him his sons, brought to you . . . that they may be my priests" (Exod 28:1). The absence of an oath by God implies that that priesthood can be changed or revoked. Jesus, on the other hand, took office **with an oath**. His "oath of office," so to speak, was God's own solemn guarantee: **The Lord has sworn, and he will not repent: / "You are a priest forever."** That God will not "repent" means that he will not change his mind, regret, or retract his decision, as he did, for instance, in regard to making Saul king over Israel (1 Sam 15:35) and of a threatened punishment (1 Chron 21:15). Not all of God's plans and decrees are intended to be permanent. But if God has confirmed by oath that Jesus' priesthood is "forever," it can never pass away.

7:20–21

Since Jesus' priesthood replaces the priesthood of the old covenant, it follows that he has also **become the guarantee of an [even] better covenant**. This is the first time Hebrews has mentioned the †covenant, but it will become a central focus in chapters 8–10. The covenant was the enduring bond that God established with his people through Moses at Mount Sinai.[21] Part of the purpose of the priesthood was to uphold the covenant by providing †atonement whenever the people violated its provisions. But if Jesus has become a high priest forever, that means there is a "better" covenant not subject to the failures of the old. The Greek word for "guarantee" (*engyos*) refers to a pledge or surety that someone puts up to ensure that a contract or promise will be honored.

7:22

20. The verb in Greek is literally "having become" (a perfect participle), which implies a past action that continues in the present. This is evidence that the levitical priesthood was still in operation when Hebrews was written, and thus that Hebrews predates the destruction of the temple in AD 70.

21. In the prophets this bond is understood as a spousal relationship: Isa 54:5; Jer 2:1–2; Hosea 2:20–22. For an illuminating study of the meaning of the covenant throughout Scripture, see Scott Hahn, *Kinship by Covenant: A Canonical Approach to the Fulfillment of God's Promises*, Anchor Yale Bible Reference Library (New Haven: Yale University Press, 2009).

In the book of Genesis, Judah offered himself to his father as a guarantee that his brother Benjamin would come back from Egypt safely; or if not, Judah would pay the price (Gen 43:8–9). Sirach admonishes, "A good man will be surety for his neighbor. . . . Do not forget all the kindness of your surety, for he has given his life for you" (Sir 29:14–15 RSV). This is exactly what Jesus does for us.[22] He guarantees, at the cost of his life, that God's covenant with us will remain forever.

7:23   By the simple fact of human mortality, the old covenant **priests were many because they were prevented by death from remaining in office**.[23] There is irony in this observation, for as the original readers of Hebrews knew well, the rules of the levitical priesthood were designed to keep priests as far away as possible from anything connected with death. Because they served in the †sanctuary of the living God, priests were forbidden to touch corpses (Lev 21:1–4). Yet they themselves would eventually *become* corpses through physical death. Their priestly consecration did not change their mortal human condition.

7:24   Christ, on the other hand, **remains forever**. Many first-century Jews expected a messiah who would remain forever, but they could not imagine how that could be compatible with a crucified messiah. In the Gospel of John, Jesus' opponents challenged him on just this point: "We have heard from the law that the Messiah remains forever. Then how can you say that the Son of Man must be lifted up [on a cross]?" (John 12:34). Jesus was indeed "lifted up" on the cross, but having been raised from the dead, he now lives forever. As Paul says, "Christ, raised from the dead, dies no more; death no longer has power over him" (Rom 6:9; see Rev 1:17–18). There is no longer any need for a continual succession in priestly office as one generation dies and is replaced by another. Jesus, victorious over death, is the one and only priest, who has **a priesthood that does not pass away** (literally, is "permanent, unalterable").

7:25   **Therefore, he is always able to save those who approach God through him**. The first phrase could be translated "he is able to save completely" (NIV) or "his power to save . . . is absolute" (NJB).[24] The levitical priests were able to "save" people only in the sense of providing temporary ritual cleansing from impurities and sins. But Jesus, because he is alive with God's own life, is able to save in the fullest sense by doing away with sin in the human heart (see 10:14–18) and giving that same divine life to others.

22. Johnson, *Hebrews*, 193.
23. The verb in Greek is actually present tense: the levitical priests "are many," again implying that the temple still stood at the time Hebrews was written (see note on 7:20–21 above).
24. The same Greek phrase (*to panteles*) is used in Luke 13:11, where it describes the woman who was "completely" unable to stand erect.

Enthroned at God's right hand, Christ is not just basking in his own divine glory; rather, he **lives forever to make intercession for them**.[25] This does *not* imply that God is ill-disposed toward sinners and Christ's role is to try to change God's mind. Such a notion is totally foreign to Scripture. On the contrary, God himself calls forth intercessors to plead before him on behalf of sinners. In Ezekiel, for instance, God says, "I have searched among them for someone who would build a wall or stand in the breach before me to keep me from destroying the land; but I found no one" (Ezek 22:30).[26] By making his own Son high priest, God has established the most efficacious intercessor possible. As Paul says in Romans, "Who will bring a charge against God's chosen ones? It is God who acquits us. Who will condemn?" The implied answer is "No one!" because it is God's own Son "who died, rather, was raised, who also is at the right hand of God, who indeed intercedes for us" (Rom 8:33–34). Paul also affirms that the Holy Spirit "intercedes for the holy ones according to God's will" (Rom 8:27). All these statements are meant to instill an unshakable confidence that absolutely no sin is beyond Christ's power to forgive; nothing can stand in the way of his power to bring us to eternal life in God's presence.

Hebrews lists five qualities that make Jesus unique as high priest. He is **holy** (Greek *hosios*, "godly, devout"). He is **innocent** in that he is totally without sin (see 4:15). Even Pontius Pilate and the centurion affirmed Christ's innocence during his passion (Luke 23:4, 47), though without realizing its full extent. He is **undefiled**, free from any moral or spiritual defect, just as the lambs offered in the temple had to be free of any physical defect. He is **separated from sinners**, not in the sense that he segregates himself from sinners—indeed, during his public ministry he positively favored the company of sinners (Matt 9:10; 11:19)—but in the sense that his human nature, totally transformed by divine life, can no longer be affected by sinners as it was during his passion. Finally, he is **higher than the heavens**—at God's right hand, as Psalm 110:1 says—so his priestly intercession is carried out in the very place where God dwells. That **it was fitting** means that it was God's will **that we should have such a high priest**. God wants only the best for his children. **7:26**

Jesus **has no need, as did the high priests, to offer sacrifice day after day, first for his own sins and then for those of the people**.[27] This statement fuses **7:27**

---

25. Christ's role as intercessor is mentioned in Rom 8:34, and it may be implied in Stephen's vision of Christ "standing" at God's right hand (Acts 7:56).

26. See also Gen 18:17–33; 20:6–7, 17; Job 42:8–9.

27. The past-tense verb "did" in this sentence is misleading, since it implies that the levitical priesthood is defunct at the time Hebrews was written; however, the translator has to supply the verb since there is no verb in the Greek. The RSV translates more literally: "He has no need, like those high priests, to offer sacrifices daily."

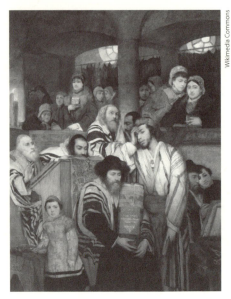

Fig. 10. Jews praying in a synagogue on Yom Kippur, by Maurycy Gottlieb

two distinct activities of the levitical priesthood, perhaps to emphasize that Jesus fulfills both. Every morning and evening, the priests offered the *daily* burnt offering of a lamb together with flour and wine, as prescribed in Exodus 29:38–42 (this was known as the †*tamid*, or perpetual sacrifice).[28] But once a year, on the †Day of Atonement, the high priest offered the *annual* sacrifice of atonement, first a bull for his own sins and then a goat for the sins of the people (Lev 16:11–19).

In contrast to these continually repeated †sacrifices, Jesus atoned for sin **once for all**—an all-important point that Hebrews will repeat four more times (9:12, 26, 28; 10:10). Jesus' one sacrifice is absolutely complete, all-sufficient, and eternally efficacious, needing no repetition. The reason is that **he offered himself**. Here Hebrews arrives at the heart of a mystery that could not have been foreseen in the old covenant: in Christ, priest and sacrifice are one and the same. No longer is the sacrifice a brute beast that had no choice in the matter and could never repair the breach in a personal relationship with the personal God. Now the gift is the giver himself, who freely chooses to offer his life in solidarity with sinners, as Jesus said at the Last Supper: "This is *my* blood of the covenant, which will be shed on behalf of many for the forgiveness of sins" (Matt 26:28, emphasis added).

7:28   Verse 28 summarizes the argument of the whole section (vv. 20–27). **The law of Moses appoints men subject to weakness to be high priests**. The "weakness" of the former priests was the same twofold flaw that afflicts all the descendants of Adam and Eve: they were sinners, and they were mortal. They were therefore just as in need of atonement as the people they served, and they were incapable of offering a sacrifice of infinite and lasting value. Jesus too was subject to "weakness"—the human weaknesses of temptation, weariness, and suffering that he assumed in his incarnation, so that he can "sympathize with our weakness" (4:15). But he triumphed over those weaknesses by his absolute fidelity to God even to death.

28. See also Num 28:1–8; 2 Kings 16:15; 2 Chron 13:11; Neh 10:34; Ezek 46:13–15.

In contrast to the old law, **the word of the oath**, which was given **after the law, appoints a son**. Hebrews is alluding once more to God's oath in Psalm 110:4, "You are a priest forever," read in light of Psalm 2:7, "You are my son." God's oath given in the time of David proves that what the law of Moses provided was inadequate and temporary. In contrast to many imperfect priests, God promised one perfect Son, who shares his own divine glory (1:2, 5, 8). This Son **has been made perfect forever**. Through his passion and resurrection, Jesus' human nature has been brought to the fullness of divine glory and he has been consecrated a priest (see comments on 2:10).

Here there is an interesting parallel with the reasoning of Paul in Galatians 3:17–18. Paul reasons that God's promise to Abraham, given centuries *before* the law, cannot be nullified by the law. Hebrews reasons that God's oath to David, made centuries *after* the law, supersedes the †cultic law with its imperfections. From opposite directions, Paul and Hebrews arrive at essentially the same conclusion: the law in its Old Testament form was temporary. All along God had planned for something far better for his people.

Reflection and Application (7:20–28)

One priest or many? Since Hebrews teaches that there is but one priest of the new covenant, Jesus Christ, in contrast to the many priests of the old covenant, why is it that there is a multiplicity of priests who serve in the Church? The Catechism (1545) explains,

> The redemptive sacrifice of Christ is unique, accomplished once for all; yet it is made present in the Eucharistic sacrifice of the Church. The same is true of the one priesthood of Christ; it is made present through the ministerial priesthood without diminishing the uniqueness of Christ's priesthood: "Only Christ is the true priest, the others being only his ministers" (Thomas Aquinas, *Commentary on Hebrews* 8:4).

Those ordained to the priesthood are priests not in their own right but by participation in the one priesthood of Christ. In all their ministry they remain entirely dependent on him. By their ministry of preaching, sanctifying, and governing, and by their example of a holy life, they make the one priesthood of Christ visible and available to God's people in every generation.

Are you saved? A complete answer to this question must take into account the teaching of Hebrews, and the entire New Testament, that Christ's work of salvation takes place in three phases: Jesus already accomplished the defeat of

Priest and Offering Are One

LIVING TRADITION

Herveus, a medieval commentator, wrote that "four things are to be taken into account in every sacrifice, namely, what is offered, to whom it is offered, by whom it is offered, and for whom it is offered." In the old covenant, these four would be animals (or agricultural produce), God, the priests, and the people. But "he who is our one true Mediator, reconciling us to God by a sacrifice of peace, remained one with him to whom he offered, became one with those for whom he offered, and as the person who offered was one and the same with what was offered. . . . So great is this sacrifice that, although it is one and once offered, it suffices to eternity."[a]

a. Herveus, *In Epistolam ad Hebraeos* (Patrologia Latina 181.1591; translation from Philip Edgcumbe Hughes, *A Commentary on the Epistle to the Hebrews* [Grand Rapids: Eerdmans, 1977], 178).

sin, Satan, and death with his first coming and sacrifice on Calvary (9:28); his work of salvation is continuing day by day in the lives of those who believe in him (7:25); and he will one day return in glory to complete the work of salvation and bring his people to eternal life in the "unshakable kingdom" (12:28). The Christian life on earth thus includes an "already" and a "not yet": we *have been saved* in that we have been reconciled with God and liberated from the bondage of sin (Eph 2:5–8; Titus 3:5); we *are being saved* as we gradually appropriate that gift, through faith, and allow grace to transform our lives (1 Cor 1:18; 15:2); and we *will be saved* on the last day when we are fully and finally united with God and all the redeemed in the heavenly Jerusalem (Heb 12:22).

The True Tabernacle and the New Covenant

Hebrews 8:1–13

Hebrews 8:1 is the midpoint of the whole homily, and it is precisely here that the preacher tells us his central thesis, "the main point of what has been said." The main point is that "we have such a high priest"—Jesus, the Son seated at God's right hand, who fulfills all that was promised and prophesied in the old covenant. This announcement begins a long section, running all the way to 10:18, that unfolds the implications of Jesus' priesthood according to the order of Melchizedek. His priesthood means he ministers in the *true heavenly sanctuary* (8:1–6; 9:23–28), and mediates a *new and everlasting covenant* (8:7–13; 9:15–22), and offers a *once-for-all sacrifice* that has infinite power to sanctify those who believe in him (9:1–14; 10:1–18). This section is the heart of Hebrews; it is the meatiest part of the "solid food" (5:12, 14) that the preacher began to provide at 7:1. After 10:18, the rest of the homily will largely consist of applying these truths to Christian life.

The Earthly Tabernacle and the True Tabernacle in Heaven (8:1–6)

¹The main point of what has been said is this: we have such a high priest, who has taken his seat at the right hand of the throne of the Majesty in heaven, ²a minister of the sanctuary and of the true tabernacle that the Lord, not man, set up. ³Now every high priest is appointed to offer gifts and sacrifices; thus the necessity for this one also to have something to offer. ⁴If then he were on earth, he would not be a priest, since there

are those who offer gifts according to the law. ⁵They worship in a copy
and shadow of the heavenly sanctuary, as Moses was warned when he was
about to erect the tabernacle. For he says, "See that you make everything
according to the pattern shown you on the mountain." ⁶Now he has obtained so much more excellent a ministry as he is mediator of a better covenant, enacted on better promises.

OT: Exod 25:9, 40; 28:1; Num 17:5

NT: Acts 7:48; Gal 3:21; Eph 5:2; Col 2:17

Catechism: Jesus as celebrant of the heavenly liturgy, 662, 1090; the Church shares in Christ's
priesthood, 1070; meaning of the liturgy, 1066–75

In this section the preacher takes a bold new step. Previously he has noted
that what we have in Christ is "better" and "more" than what came before.
But now he says that the Jerusalem temple—the holiest place on earth, in
which the Jews had worshiped God for centuries—is only a "copy," an earthly,
shadowy replica of the true sanctuary in heaven, where Jesus ministers as
high priest. He goes on to show how this surprising statement is actually
rooted in Scripture.

8:1   Chapter 7 unpacked Psalm 110 to describe the exalted qualities of the "high
priest according to the order of Melchizedek." This priest must be a priest forever,
without beginning or end (7:3), superior to Abraham (7:4–7), qualified not by
tribal lineage but by his own greatness and the power of his indestructible life
(7:16). His priesthood is established by God's unbreakable oath (7:20–21) and

Fig. 11. Wall painting from a third-century AD synagogue in Dura Europos, Syria, depicting the consecration of the tabernacle

is totally efficacious in enabling people to draw near to God (7:19). He is invulnerable to death (7:23–24), exalted above the highest heavens, utterly without sin (7:26), and his †sacrifice never needs to be repeated (7:27). Now Hebrews sums up **the main point of what has been said** in chapter 7 and in the entire homily: **we have such a high priest**. The good news is that Jesus has all these qualities, and we have Jesus![1]

Jesus **has taken his seat at the right hand of the throne of the Majesty in heaven**—a phrase that once more quotes Psalm 110:1 (see 1:3, 13). The "right hand" is the place of highest honor and authority. Unlike the earthbound priests of the old covenant, Jesus exercises his priesthood in the place of heavenly glory where God dwells.

Jesus is the **minister** of the †liturgy that takes place in the heavenly **sanctuary** and **the true tabernacle that the Lord, not man, set up**.[2] This implies that the earthly tabernacle was a sign pointing both *forward* in time to Christ and *upward* to heavenly realities, just as the "rest" of the land of Canaan pointed both forward in time and upward to God's eternal rest (Heb 3–4).[3]

The Greek word for "minister," *leitourgos*, originally referred to someone who performed a public service (*leitourgia*), such as building a monument or sponsoring a festival. The †Septuagint uses *leitourgia* for the "public service" of Israel's worship (Num 8:22; 16:9)—that is, its liturgy. Jesus is the celebrant of the eternal, heavenly liturgy, in which every earthly liturgy participates.[4]

A priest is, by definition, one who is **appointed to offer gifts and sacrifices**, as Hebrews already explained in 5:1. It is by such offerings that a priest carries out his ministry of atoning for sin and bringing reconciliation between God and man. **Thus** if Jesus is truly a priest, then he too must **have something to offer**. Hebrews already told us that what Christ offers is nothing less than *himself* (7:27). The implication here is that Christ assumed human nature—our fragile frame that can suffer, be wounded, and die—precisely so that he would have something to offer the Father.

Christ does not carry out his priestly ministry on earth, in the perishable temple of Jerusalem (which did in fact perish in AD 70). If **he were on earth, he would not be a priest** at all, since **those who offer gifts according to the law** of Moses are the †levitical priests. As mentioned in 7:14, Jesus belonged

8:2

8:3

8:4

---

1. See Luke Timothy Johnson, *Hebrews: A Commentary*, New Testament Library (Louisville: Westminster John Knox, 2006), 197.
2. See sidebar, "What Is the True Tabernacle?," p. 174.
3. See Harold W. Attridge, "'Let Us Strive to Enter That Rest': The Logic of Hebrews 4:1–11," *Harvard Theological Review* 73 (1980): 279–88.
4. See Vatican Council II, *Sacrosanctum Concilium* (Constitution on the Sacred Liturgy), 8.

How Jesus Fulfills the Sacrifices of the Old Covenant

BIBLICAL BACKGROUND

The law of Moses provided detailed instructions for five main types of †sacrifice in ancient Israel: the burnt offering, grain offering, peace offering, purification offering, and reparation offering (Lev 1–7). Although the New Testament does not mention each of these explicitly, in the light of the New Testament each can be recognized as prefiguring Christ in a unique way; each brings out a distinct aspect of his †paschal mystery.

The first three types are freewill sacrifices, offered voluntarily to express one's love and devotion to the Lord. In the *burnt offering*, or †holocaust (Lev 1), the animal was entirely burnt on the altar, going up to the Lord in the form of smoke (the Hebrew word for "holocaust," *olah*, is from the verb "ascend"). It was a powerful symbol of offering oneself totally to God, holding nothing back. On a national level, Israel offered the †*tamid*, or daily burnt offering, of a lamb every morning and evening. Jesus' death on the cross was a "holocaust" in that he was entirely consumed by his self-offering; he gave himself so completely that he had nothing left to give. As the Gospel of John puts it, "he loved them to the end" (13:1)—that is, to an unlimited extent. And he ascended back to God having been "made perfect" (Heb 2:10; 5:9), transformed in his human nature, by the fire of the Holy Spirit (see comments on 9:14).

The *grain offering* (Lev 2; 6:7–16) consisted of raw flour, cooked cakes, or roast grain, part of which would be burned on the altar and the rest eaten by the priests. It may have been intended as a form of burnt offering that the poor could afford. Grain, along with wine and oil, was also offered with the daily *tamid*. Jesus' passion was a "grain offering" in that through it he becomes the bread of life for us (John 6:35; see John 12:24). By partaking of this bread in the Eucharist (see Heb 13:10), we share in his own divine life.

The *peace offering*, or communion sacrifice (Lev 3; 7:11–36), the only sacrifice in which some of the meat was eaten by the worshiper and his household,

not to the priestly tribe of Levi but the royal tribe of Judah, "and in regard to that tribe Moses said nothing about priests."

8:5   The next sentence seems to demote the status of the Jerusalem temple in a way that would have been startling to first-century Jews, even though it is suggested by the Old Testament itself (see 1 Kings 8:27; Isa 66:1). The temple (and its forerunner, the desert tabernacle) where the Jews **worship** is only **a copy and shadow of the heavenly sanctuary**. Stephen's similar statements to the Sanhedrin probably helped precipitate his martyrdom (Acts 7:48–50). The was a festive sacrifice offered to fulfill a vow, celebrate a special occasion, or thank God for a particular favor such as saving one from death. In the latter case it was called the "thanksgiving sacrifice" (see Ps 107:21–22; 116:17). The sacred banquet in the vicinity of the temple, accompanied by songs of praise, was an expression of joyous communion with the Lord and with one another (see Deut 12:7). The annual Passover sacrifice was Israel's great national peace offering. The New Testament reveals that Jesus' passion, and the sacred banquet by which it would be signified and made present for all time, are the fulfillment of Passover and the peace offering that establishes the ultimate communion between God and man (see Luke 22:17–19).[a] Thus the Christian name for the celebration of the Lord's Supper is "Eucharist" (*eucharistia*), meaning "thanksgiving."

The last two types were expiatory sacrifices, offered to atone for wrongdoing. The *purification offering*, or sin offering (Lev 4:1–5:13; 6:17–23), was for the purpose of cleansing the †sanctuary from contamination due to sins. The victim's blood was sprinkled before the veil of the †Holy of Holies and smeared on the altar of incense, after which the animal was burned outside the camp. The annual †Yom Kippur sacrifices were Israel's great national purification offering. Hebrews 13:11–12 suggests that Jesus' passion was a purification offering, since he "suffered outside the gate to sanctify the people with his own blood" (NJB). His blood purifies the living temple, the Church, of all sin for all time (see 1:3; 10:10).

The *reparation offering*, or guilt offering (Lev 5:14–26; 7:1–10), was the sacrifice of a ram in †atonement for acts of sacrilege or offenses against one's neighbor such as theft or perjury. Besides bringing the ram, the worshiper confessed his guilt and made restitution plus one fifth. Isaiah foretells that the Suffering Servant of the Lord, in accord with God's will, would give *himself* as a "reparation offering" (Isa 53:10)—a prophecy fulfilled by Christ, whose sacrifice was the all-sufficient restitution to God of the human love, trust, and obedience that had been withheld due to sin.

a. See Hartmut Gese, "The Origins of the Lord's Supper," in *Essays on Biblical Theology*, trans. Keith Crim (Minneapolis: Augsburg, 1981), 117–40; Joseph Ratzinger, *The Feast of Faith: Approaches to a Theology of the Liturgy*, trans. Graham Harrison (San Francisco: Ignatius Press, 1986), 51–60.

Greek word for "copy" (*hypodeigma*) can indicate a sketch, replica, or diagram and suggests that the earthly temple corresponds to the heavenly sanctuary, but in a limited way, just as a sketch of a building may accurately represent it but is a far cry from the building itself. Likewise, a shadow cast by an object may resemble its shape but has no substance in itself.

Hebrews immediately supports this point by referring to the very place in the Torah where God commanded Moses to **erect the tabernacle**. God **warned** or "instructed" Moses, **See that you make everything according to the pattern**

shown you on the mountain (Exod 25:40).[5] This implies that there is a heavenly sanctuary after which the earthly one is patterned, and Moses was in some mysterious way privileged to see it.

8:6   Verse 6 both wraps up the present section and transitions to a new section (8:7–13) that will begin to focus on the covenant. Christ **has obtained** his priestly **ministry** (*leitourgia*, related to the word for "minister" in v. 2)—that is, he has become a priest—by the act of offering himself on the cross (see comments on 2:10). And this ministry is **much more excellent** than that of the levitical priests as **he is mediator of a better covenant**. The Greek word for "mediator" (*mesitēs*) comes from "middle" (*mesos*) and refers to a go-between, someone who stands in the middle between two parties and seeks to unite them. Moses was the mediator of the old covenant forged at Mount Sinai, yet that covenant was incapable of bringing about perfect union between God and man. In a poignant passage of the book of Job (9:32–33), Job cries out in the midst of his suffering and bewilderment,

> [God] is not a man like myself, that I should answer him,
>   that we should come together in judgment.
> Would that there were an arbiter [LXX *mesitēs*] between us,
>   who could lay his hand upon us both.

Job expresses the human longing for a perfect mediator, someone who can bridge the immense gulf between man and God. Hebrews proclaims that that longing is now fulfilled in Christ. He is the "one mediator between God and the human race" (1 Tim 2:5)—the only one perfectly qualified to mediate, not by merely negotiating between two parties but by *uniting in his own person* both parties, God and man.

Christ's ministry is superior because his covenant is **enacted** (or "legislated") **on better promises** than those of the old law. The "better promises" are God's solemn oath in Psalm 110:4, "You are a priest forever," but also the great promise given through the prophet Jeremiah, that God would establish a "new covenant" with his people, written on their hearts (Jer 31:31). So Hebrews now turns to a lengthy citation of that passage.

The New Covenant Written on the Heart (8:7–13)

[7]For if that first covenant had been faultless, no place would have been sought for a second one. [8]But he finds fault with them and says:

5. See also Exod 25:9; 26:30; 27:8; Num 8:4; Acts 7:44.

"Behold, the days are coming, says the Lord,
     when I will conclude a new covenant with the house of Israel
          and the house of Judah.
⁹It will not be like the covenant I made with their fathers
     the day I took them by the hand to lead them forth from the
          land of Egypt;
for they did not stand by my covenant
     and I ignored them, says the Lord.
¹⁰But this is the covenant I will establish with the house of Israel
     after those days, says the Lord:
I will put my laws in their minds
     and I will write them upon their hearts.
I will be their God,
     and they shall be my people.
¹¹And they shall not teach, each one his fellow citizen
     and kinsman, saying, 'Know the Lord,'
for all shall know me,
     from least to greatest.
¹²For I will forgive their evildoing
     and remember their sins no more."

¹³When he speaks of a "new" covenant, he declares the first one obsolete.
And what has become obsolete and has grown old is close to disappearing.

OT: 2 Kings 17:15; Jer 22:9; 31:31–34; Ezek 36:26
NT: Luke 22:20; Rom 11:27; 1 Cor 11:25; 2 Cor 3:3–6
Catechism: the new law, 1965–74; the new covenant, 66, 613, 1365; Jesus did not abolish but
     fulfilled the law, 592

Hebrews 7:22 gave a preview of this next step in the argument by mentioning the "covenant" for the first time. Since Psalm 110 foretells a new, nonlevitical priest, there must be a new law (7:12), which implies a new covenant. Here the preacher picks up the thread: a new covenant is precisely what God promised through the prophet Jeremiah.

Hebrews quotes the prophecy here in full in order to explain what it is that the priesthood of Jesus accomplishes. This quotation from Jeremiah 31:31–34 is the longest Old Testament quotation in the entire New Testament. Its length gives an indication of its exceptional importance to the author of Hebrews.

Hebrews prefaces the quotation with another statement that, like 8:1–2, **8:7–8** would have been disconcerting, yet indisputable, to first-century Jews: **For if that first covenant had been faultless, no place would have been sought for a second one**. The very fact that Scripture speaks of a "*new* covenant" implies that

The New Covenant Written on the Heart

Jeremiah 31:31–34 is the only Old Testament passage that mentions a "new covenant"[a]—the phrase that for Christians sums up the entire redemptive work of Christ, surpassing and fulfilling the old covenant. In ancient times the same phrase was translated into Latin as *novum testamentum*, which is why "New Testament" is the term still used today for the biblical writings of the new covenant.

Jeremiah's prophecy was delivered at the lowest of low points in Israel's history. After centuries of warnings by the prophets, the people's continual idolatry and infidelity had finally led to the judgment that God had threatened: a devastating invasion and conquest by their enemy, the Babylonian Empire, in 586 BC. Jerusalem was burned to the ground, the temple was razed, the king and people were taken into exile into Babylon. For all practical purposes, it seemed that God's wonderful promises to the descendants of Abraham had been permanently forfeited. At that gloomy time, as Jeremiah reflected on Israel's failure to keep the covenant, God gave him an immensely significant revelation: in order for the covenant to succeed, God would have to do still more than he had already done. It was not a matter of the people trying harder. God would have to change the human heart from within, impressing on it a supernatural ability to respond faithfully to him.[b] He would have to uphold the covenant not only on his side but also on ours. And this is precisely what God promised to do: he would write the "new covenant" not on mere tablets of stone but on the human heart.

The next time the phrase "new covenant" appears in Scripture is on the lips of Jesus, at a climactic moment in his mission: on the night before he died. He took the cup after supper, saying, "This cup is the new covenant in my blood. Do this, as often as you drink it, in remembrance of me" (1 Cor 11:25; see Luke 22:20).[c] Jesus was announcing that Jeremiah's prophecy was about to be fulfilled. Through his imminent death and resurrection, sins would be forgiven, the law would be written on the hearts of God's people, and a new and everlasting covenant would be established. This new covenant would be made permanently present to God's people in the Eucharist.

a. Similar ideas, however, are developed by the prophets, who speak of "something new" (Isa 43:19; see Isa 42:9; 48:6; Jer 31:22); "a new name" (Isa 62:2; see Isa 65:15); and "a new heart and a new spirit" (Ezek 18:31; 36:26).

b. See Francis Martin, *Sacred Scripture: The Disclosure of the Word* (Naples, FL: Sapientia Press, 2006), 8–9.

c. The accounts of the Last Supper in Matthew and Mark have a different emphasis: Jesus says, "This is my blood of the covenant" (Matt 26:28; Mark 14:24), alluding to the ratification of the Sinai covenant in Exod 24:8. By referring to "*my* blood of the covenant," Jesus indicates that his death is a covenant-ratifying sacrifice.

there was something wrong with the first. But how could a covenant instituted by God be defective? Hebrews immediately clarifies that the problem was not with the covenant itself but with the people, who were incapable of keeping it:[6] God **finds fault with them**. The covenant could not expel sin from the human heart. In fact, the covenant had hardly been ratified when the high priest Aaron himself led the people into worshiping the golden calf—a kind of "original sin" of Israel. The very fact that the people were incapable of keeping the covenant meant that it would never achieve its true purpose, which was to establish a perfect and lasting bond of communion between the holy God and his people.

As usual, Hebrews introduces a biblical passage with **he . . . says**. The Scriptures are not inert words on a page; they are God's living voice speaking to us today. **Behold, the days are coming, says the Lord, / when I will conclude a new covenant**.[7] "The days are coming" is a standard biblical way of referring to the future age when God would decisively intervene in history to bring his plan to completion. It is the same as "these last days" (1:2) in which we are living. The Lord announces that he will bring about the new covenant entirely at his own gracious initiative.

This covenant will be with both **the house of Israel and the house of Judah**, the two kingdoms that had been divided since the tenth century BC (1 Kings 12). God thus promises not only a new relationship with himself but also the healing of human divisions. The reconciliation of Israel and Judah symbolizes the reconciliation of all people and nations in Christ (see John 11:52; Eph 2:14).[8] In human terms, however, this promise seemed impossible. The ten tribes of the northern kingdom, or "house of Israel," had been deported by the Assyrians in 722 BC and irretrievably assimilated among the nations. Nevertheless, God promises that the new covenant will restore and reunite his whole people (see Ezek 37:16–28).

The new covenant **will not be like the covenant I made with their fathers**.   8:9 It will differ in that it will transform the human heart at the deepest level and will therefore be unbreakable. The defective covenant "with their fathers" is not the one with Abraham (Gen 15) but the one established through Moses at Mount Sinai (Exod 24). That covenant was founded on God's great act of deliverance in the exodus, when he **took them by the hand to lead them forth from the land of Egypt**. Yet God's people **did not stand by my covenant**; that

---

6. See Paul's similar argument about the law in Rom 7:7–14.

7. The verb for "I will conclude" (*synteleō*) could also be translated "I will perfect"; it has the same root as the verb for "make perfect" in, e.g., 2:10; 5:9; 7:28.

8. Philip Edgcumbe Hughes, *A Commentary on the Epistle to the Hebrews* (Grand Rapids: Eerdmans, 1977), 300.

is, they broke it continually (as Heb 3–4 emphasized). The new covenant will be founded on a far greater act of deliverance: God's deliverance of his people from sin and death through the blood of Christ.

And I ignored them, says the Lord. This last phrase follows the †Septuagint wording, which differs from the original Hebrew: "though I was their husband, says the LORD" (Jer 31:32).[9] The Hebrew version conveys the idea that the covenant was no mere contractual arrangement: it was a spousal bond, the breach of which wounds the heart of God. The Septuagint version conveys the idea that God's response to the breach of the covenant was to temporarily ignore or abandon his people, although he promised, "with great tenderness I will take you back" (Isa 54:6–7).

8:10   Jeremiah explains the decisive difference between the old covenant and the new: **this is the covenant I will establish with the house of Israel / after those days, says the Lord: / I will put my laws in their minds / and I will write them upon their hearts.**[10] God's law—his gracious teaching on how to live in communion with himself and with one another—will no longer be a legal obligation imposed from without; it will be engraved on the heart, which in biblical terms means the hidden center of the person, the deepest source of our thoughts and decisions. God's people will be empowered to love, trust, and wholly obey him by his own divine work within them (see 2 Cor 3:3).

It is not that the old covenant was purely external; it too was meant to be a matter of the heart. Moses had directed, "These words, all that I command you this day, shall be in your heart and in your soul" (Deut 6:6 †LXX). But that goal could never be fully achieved; as Paul says, the law could command righteousness but it could not bring about righteousness (Rom 7:12–23; 8:3). It could make people keenly aware of their sin, but it could not cure sin. The difference between the old and the new is not the goal but the divine power to accomplish that goal.[11] As St. Augustine expressed it, "The law was given so that grace might be sought; grace was given so the law might be fulfilled."[12]

The essence of the covenant was summed up in the expression of mutual belonging, **I will be their God, / and they shall be my people.** This promise, declared by God at Mount Sinai (Exod 6:7), reappears throughout the Old Testament. If his people keep all his commandments, God pledges, "I will walk among you, and

---

9. The NAB translates it "and I had to show myself their master, says the LORD." The same Hebrew verb can mean either "be the husband of" or "rule over."

10. The Septuagint version quoted here again differs slightly from the Hebrew, which reads, "I will place my law within them" rather than "I will put my laws in their minds" (Jer 31:33).

11. Johnson, *Hebrews*, 207.

12. Augustine, *The Spirit and the Letter* 19.34.

will be your God, and you shall be my people" (Lev 26:12 RSV).[13] This statement evokes the friendship with God that existed in the garden of Eden, before the fall (Gen 3:8). By their constant infidelities, God's people had cut themselves off from that blessed intimacy. Now, however, it is available once and for all in Christ.

The new covenant brings about a direct and immediate relationship with God that is not possible under the old. **And they shall not teach, each one his fellow citizen and / kinsman, saying, "Know the Lord," / for all shall know me, from least to greatest.** In the biblical view, knowledge is not primarily informational, but relational. The verb "to know" can even express spousal union: "Adam knew Eve his wife, and she conceived" (Gen 4:1 RSV). To know the Lord is to be in personal relationship with him. The prophet Hosea pleaded with his fellow Israelites, "Let us know, let us strive to know the LORD" (Hosea 6:3), and announced God's promise: "I will betroth you to me forever: / I will betroth you to me with justice and with judgment, / with loyalty and with compassion; / I will betroth you to me with fidelity, / and you shall know the LORD" (Hosea 2:21–22).[14] What the old covenant sought, the new covenant accomplishes. God's people, even the simplest, will know him personally and not merely by hearing about him from others (see 1 John 2:14, 27). Of course, this does not preclude the need for catechesis, but such instruction is meant to supplement, not replace, a personal and direct knowledge of God.

8:11

This knowledge of God will come about, Jeremiah explains, by God's astounding act of mercy: **For I will forgive** (literally, "I will be merciful toward") **their evildoing / and remember their sins no more.** In the old covenant God often revealed himself as the God of mercy: "The LORD, the LORD, a God gracious and merciful, slow to anger and abounding in love and fidelity" (Exod 34:6; see Ps 103:8). It is by directly experiencing this mercy, by having their sins totally blotted out by the sacrifice of Christ, that God's people will truly come to know him. To say that God *will not remember* our sins (see Isa 43:25) is the same as saying that he *will remember* us (the opposite of "ignored" in v. 9). As Micah prophesied, "You will cast into the depths of the sea all our sins" (Mic 7:19).

8:12

Having completed the quotation, Hebrews closes this section by making the obvious point that when God **speaks of a "new" covenant, he declares the first one obsolete.** That is, the mention of a "new covenant" implies that the first covenant is "old" or "outmoded." However, this does not mean, as so many Christians over the centuries have tragically misinterpreted it, that God's

8:13

---

13. See Exod 29:45; Deut 26:17–19; 29:12; Jer 7:23; 11:4; Ezek 37:26–27.

14. The promise of knowledge of God is a common theme in the prophets: see Isa 19:21; Ezek 37:14; 39:22, 28; Joel 2:26–27.

The Old Covenant Has Never Been Revoked

LIVING TRADITION

Church teaching makes clear that Hebrews 8:13 cannot be understood to mean that God has revoked his covenant with the Jews. Overcoming centuries of misguided theological views among Christians, Vatican Council II taught that "God holds the Jews most dear for the sake of their Fathers; He does not repent of the gifts He makes or of the calls He issues—such is the witness of the Apostle (cf. Rom 11:28–29)."[a]

St. John Paul II further developed the implications of this declaration. During a 1980 visit to the synagogue of Mainz, Germany, he noted that "the Old Covenant . . . has never been abrogated by God (cf. Rom 11:29)." In a 1986 visit to the synagogue of Rome he said, "The Jewish religion is not 'extrinsic' to us, but in a certain manner, it is 'intrinsic' to our religion. We have therefore a relationship with it which we do not have with any other religion. You are our favored brothers and, in a certain sense, one can say our elder brothers." Finally, he noted in 1997 that the Jewish people "has been called and led by God, Creator of heaven and earth. Their existence then is not a mere natural or cultural happening. . . . It is a supernatural one. This people continues in spite of everything to be the people of the covenant and, despite human infidelity, the Lord is faithful to his covenant."[b]

a. *Nostra Aetate* (Declaration on the Relationship of the Church to Non-Christian Religions), 4.
b. For references to these papal addresses, see the Pontifical Biblical Commission, *The Jewish People and Their Sacred Scriptures in the Christian Bible* (Rome: Libreria Editrice Vaticana, 2001), 86. See also Catechism 121.

covenant with Israel is abrogated. As Paul says, referring to Israel, "The gifts and the call of God are irrevocable" (Rom 11:29). The former covenant remains, but it has been surpassed by a "better covenant" (Heb 7:22).

And what has become obsolete and has grown old is close to disappearing (or "is ready to vanish away," RSV). The author is probably referring specifically to the Mosaic form of worship with its †levitical priesthood and animal sacrifices, which was never intended to be the permanent way of relating to God. Although the covenant as a bond of love endures, these †cultic rites are now obsolete (see 10:8–9). This statement is one of the clearest indications that Hebrews was written before the temple was destroyed in AD 70, but when such a disaster was clearly on the horizon. Jesus himself had foretold that the temple would be demolished (Mark 13:2). There was no longer any place for the ineffective rituals of the old order, now that perfect and everlasting communion with God had been brought about by the sacrifice of Christ.

God's Answer to the Problem of Sin

Hebrews 9:1–28

All human cultures around the world and throughout history, diverse as they are, attempt in one way or another to deal with the problem of sin. There seems to be a near-universal recognition that sin—wrongdoing against God or others—requires some form of †atonement. The evil deeds that result from human selfishness, greed, lust, jealousy, or vengeance, and the harm they cause, cannot be adequately addressed by simply making an apology and moving on. The damage must be undone, the debt must be paid, the relationship must be healed. If this is true of offenses against human beings, all the more is it true of offenses against God.

Hebrews 9–10, continuing the central argument of the letter (chapters 8–10), presents God's answer to the problem of sin. Here the author summarizes the heart of the good news: in Christ, God has dealt with sin once and for all—not by a divine decree that simply wipes it off the ledger, but by providing the all-sufficient †sacrifice that atones for sin, purifies the human heart, and repairs the broken relationship between God and man.

Chapter 9 explains how the sacrificial system of Israel, temporary and imperfect as it was, was designed to point forward to that one perfect sacrifice of Christ. Those former rites impressed upon God's people profound truths about the gravity of sin and how God provides atonement for it. In biblical terms, the old covenant sacrifices are †types—signs that point in a veiled way toward the culmination of God's plan in Christ. Hebrews 9 shows, first, why those rites could never fully resolve the problem of sin (9:1–10). It then explains how Christ's blood, in contrast, is totally efficacious (9:11–14); how the covenant has been renewed and fulfilled (9:15–22); and how Christ's work of atonement has been accomplished in the true, heavenly sanctuary (9:23–28).

This part of Hebrews is theologically rich but far from easy reading, alluding as it does to Israelite rituals that may at first seem strange or irrelevant. But readers who patiently engage with the biblical text will be rewarded by a far deeper understanding of Christ's sacrifice for our redemption.

The Powerless Rites of the Old Covenant (9:1–10)

[1]Now [even] the first covenant had regulations for worship and an earthly sanctuary. [2]For a tabernacle was constructed, the outer one, in which were the lampstand, the table, and the bread of offering; this is called the Holy Place. [3]Behind the second veil was the tabernacle called the Holy of Holies, [4]in which were the gold altar of incense and the ark of the covenant entirely covered with gold. In it were the gold jar containing the manna, the staff of Aaron that had sprouted, and the tablets of the covenant. [5]Above it were the cherubim of glory overshadowing the place of expiation. Now is not the time to speak of these in detail.

[6]With these arrangements for worship, the priests, in performing their service, go into the outer tabernacle repeatedly, [7]but the high priest alone goes into the inner one once a year, not without blood that he offers for himself and for the sins of the people. [8]In this way the holy Spirit shows that the way into the sanctuary had not yet been revealed while the outer tabernacle still had its place. [9]This is a symbol of the present time, in which gifts and sacrifices are offered that cannot perfect the worshiper in conscience [10]but only in matters of food and drink and various ritual washings: regulations concerning the flesh, imposed until the time of the new order.

OT: Exod 16:33–34; 25–26; 30; Lev 16; Num 17:23; Mic 6:7
NT: Mark 7:3–4; Luke 1:8–11; Rom 3:25; Heb 10:19–20
Catechism: high priest of Israel and Holy of Holies, 433; Day of Atonement, 578; Jesus and the temple, 583–86; priests of the new covenant, 1564

Hebrews 9 returns to the theme of Israel's †sanctuary and worship, which was the topic of 8:1–6. The long quotation from Jeremiah about the new covenant (8:7–13) may have seemed a sidetrack, but it was not, since covenant and worship go hand in hand (see 7:12). One of the primary purposes of the covenant is to stipulate how, when, and where the people will celebrate the †liturgy, their public worship. And the liturgy, in turn, is the highest expression of the covenant relationship.[1] A new covenant, therefore, implies that there is a new liturgy.

To set the stage for the contrast with Christ, Hebrews first describes the old covenant sanctuary, its furnishings and rites. This description depicts neither the first temple, built by Solomon and destroyed by the Babylonians in 586 BC, nor the second temple, built in 515 BC and probably still standing at the time Hebrews was written.[2] Rather, it depicts the precursor to the temple, the †tabernacle or tent-sanctuary that was Israel's place of worship during the desert wanderings. This is probably because the Scripture passages that most fully set forth God's instructions for worship are the parts of Exodus that describe the tabernacle. During Israel's sojourn at Mount Sinai, God gave Moses elaborately detailed instructions for building the tabernacle (Exod 25–31), which Moses then carried out to the letter (Exod 35–40).

After briefly recalling these details (vv. 1–5), Hebrews notes that the very structure of the tabernacle hinted at its own incompleteness and pointed forward to something better (vv. 6–10).

Even **the first covenant had regulations for worship and an earthly sanc-** **9:1**
tuary. The Greek word for "earthly" (*kosmikos*) could be translated "worldly" or "of this world," and it implies that this sanctuary could never bring people into true communion with God, who dwells in heaven. But the sanctuary was also "worldly" or "cosmic" in another sense: in ancient Israel, the sanctuary was considered a microcosm of the whole created universe. The architecture and features of the tabernacle (and later, the temple) were designed to symbolize the cosmos—the heavens and the earth, the sea, the sun, moon, and stars—and to remind the worshipers that God intended all creation to be one great temple in which all creatures would glorify God.[3]

Although Hebrews seems to refer to two tabernacles (or tents), there was actu- **9:2**
ally one tent with two rooms: **the outer one, . . . called the Holy Place,**[4] and the inner room, the †Holy of Holies. The †Holy Place was entered through a veil, and the Holy of Holies was curtained off by a **second veil**, made of precious fabric and embroidered with images of cherubim (Exod 26:31–33). This arrangement,

1. See Scott Hahn, "From Old to New: 'Covenant' or 'Testament' in Hebrews 9?," *Letter & Spirit* 8 (2013): 13–33.
2. The word "temple" (*hieron*) and the usual word for the "sanctuary" (*naos*) in fact never appear in Hebrews. The term that Hebrews uses to refer to the sanctuary is literally "the holy" or "the holy things."
3. See G. K. Beale, *The Temple and the Church's Mission: A Biblical Theology of the Dwelling Place of God* (Downers Grove, IL: InterVarsity, 2004), 29–80.
4. As Albert Vanhoye argues, the Greek phrase for "Holy Place" in 9:2 can best be understood as a feminine singular, "holy," rather than a neuter plural, "holy things" (*A Different Priest: The Letter to the Hebrews*, trans. Leo Arnold, Series Rhetorica Semitica [Miami: Convivium, 2011], 236).

Fig. 12. Floor mosaic in the fourth-century AD synagogue in Hammat Tiberias, Israel. In the center is the curtained "ark" that held Torah scrolls. On either side are a seven-branched menorah, a shofar (ram's horn), an incense pan, and a palm frond and citron used during the Feast of Booths.

along with the courtyard that surrounded the tent, created zones of restricted access. The Levites served in the courtyard, but only the priests could enter the tent itself, and only the high priest could enter the Holy of Holies (Lev 16). Even the area immediately outside the court was off limits to ordinary Israelites (Num 1:51–53). Although the purpose of the tent was to serve as a meeting place between God and his people, at the same time these zones served to instill a profound awareness of the abyss that separated humanity from the transcendent, holy God.

In the Holy Place were three sacred objects. First was the seven-branched **lampstand**, or menorah, made of pure gold (Exod 25:31–40)—to this day a famous symbol of Judaism. Each branch held an oil lamp, with cups shaped like almond blossoms for holding the oil. The menorah was to be kept perpetually lit as a sign of the Lord's abiding presence with his people (Lev 24:2–4). With its blazing blossoms, the menorah was probably designed to evoke the burning bush where God had first spoken to Moses and revealed his holy name (Exod 3).

Second, there was **the table** made of acacia wood overlaid with gold (Exod 25:23–30), on which was placed **the bread of offering** (in Hebrew, "bread of the Presence," or translated more literally, "bread of the Face"). These were twelve loaves representing the twelve tribes of Israel, which were replaced with fresh loaves every sabbath (Exod 25:30; Lev 24:5–9). The table also held bowls and pitchers for libations of wine, perhaps to recall the sacred meal that concluded

The Bread of the Presence

BIBLICAL BACKGROUND

The †Talmud, the compilation of Jewish oral traditions that was put in writing between AD 200 and 600, records a striking custom that was carried out three times a year, on each of the three great annual pilgrimage feasts of Israel: Passover, Pentecost, and Tabernacles. The priests removed the table of the bread of the Presence from the sanctuary and brought it out into the temple courts so that the Jewish pilgrims could see it.

> They used to lift it up and exhibit the Bread of the Presence on it to those who came up for the festivals, saying to them, "Behold, God's love for you!"[a]

The bread of the Presence was a sign of God's love because it was a sign of the everlasting covenant that God had made with them (Lev 24:7–8). God's people, who traveled to the temple longing to "see the face of God" (Ps 42:3), saw in the "bread of the Face" a visible sign of his presence in their midst. All the more can Christians see in the true bread of the Face, the Eucharist, a visible sign of the enduring presence and love of Christ.

a. Babylonian Talmud, *Menahot* 29A; see Brant Pitre, *Jesus and the Jewish Roots of the Eucharist: Unlocking the Secrets of the Last Supper* (New York: Doubleday, 2011), 130–31.

the covenant on Mount Sinai, when Moses and the elders of Israel "beheld the God of Israel" and ate and drank in his presence (Exod 24:9–11). For the Christian readers of Hebrews, the items on the table even more strikingly evoke the sacred banquet of the new covenant, the Eucharist, in which Christ offers the cup of salvation and the true "bread of the Presence"—the bread that is in the most literal sense God's presence in the midst of his people.

The third object was **the gold altar of incense**, although for unexplained **9:3–4** reasons Hebrews depicts it in the Holy of Holies rather than in the Holy Place, where Exodus seems to place it (see Exod 30:1–6).[5] On this altar, also made of acacia wood overlaid with gold, fragrant incense was burned twice a day before the Lord (Exod 30:1–10). This is the sacred duty that the priest Zechariah was performing when the angel Gabriel appeared to him to announce the birth of John the Baptist (Luke 1:8–11).

5. There is an ambiguity in Exodus concerning the placement of the altar of incense. Although Exod 30:6 and 40:26 situate it in the Holy Place, where daily priestly duties were performed, in Exod 40:5 God tells Moses to place it "in front of the ark of the covenant," which could seem to imply a location inside the Holy of Holies (see also 1 Kings 6:22). See Harold W. Attridge, *The Epistle to the Hebrews: A Commentary on the Epistle to the Hebrews*, ed. Helmut Koester, Hermeneia (Philadelphia: Fortress, 1989), 234–35.

The word here translated as "altar of incense," however, could also be translated as "censer," a vessel for burning incense.[6] Each year during the liturgy of the †Day of Atonement, which Hebrews will mention in verse 25, the high priest brought the censer into the Holy of Holies (Lev 16:12). The fragrant cloud of incense may have symbolized the prayers of God's people continually ascending to him, as in Revelation: "Another angel came and stood at the altar, holding a gold censer. He was given a great quantity of incense to offer, along with the prayers of all the holy ones, on the gold altar that was before the throne" (Rev 8:3).

Behind the second veil, within **the Holy of Holies**, was the most sacred object in all Israel: **the ark of the covenant**. It too was made of acacia wood **entirely covered with gold** (Exod 25:10–22). Inside the †ark were three sacred objects: first, **the gold jar containing the manna**, a perpetual reminder of how God miraculously provided bread for his people in the desert (Exod 16:33–34); second, **the staff of Aaron that had sprouted**, a reminder of the priesthood of Aaron that God miraculously confirmed when Aaron's staff put forth shoots, blossoms, and even ripe almonds (Num 17:23);[7] third, **the tablets of the covenant**, the stone tablets on which God had inscribed the Ten Commandments (Exod 25:16, 21; 31:18; Deut 10:1–5). The tablets were often simply called "the testimony," because they testified to the terms of the covenant (Exod 24:3, 7).

9:5   The primary reason for the ark's sacredness, however, was its cover: a slab of pure gold upon which stood two **cherubim** made of hammered gold, facing each other with their wings outstretched, **overshadowing** the ark (Exod 25:17–22). Hebrews refers to them as the cherubim **of glory** because above them God revealed his presence in the cloud, the visible sign of his glory (Exod 40:34–35; Lev 16:2). The cover of the ark was called the †**place of expiation** (*hilastērion*, literally, "the expiation," or the wiping away of sins),[8] because there the high priest sprinkled the blood of sacrificed animals, making †atonement for sins (Lev 16:14–15, 34). Other translations call it the †**mercy seat** because

6. The same word *thymiatērion* is used to mean "censer" in 2 Chron 26:19; Ezek 8:11 †LXX, although the more common term was *pyreion*.

7. The Old Testament does not specifically mention the jar of manna and Aaron's staff as being in the ark, but Hebrews may be inferring this from the passages where God tells Moses to place the jar "before the Lord" (Exod 16:33) and the staff "in front of the covenant" (Num 17:25). According to 1 Kings 8:9, "There was nothing in the ark but the two stone tablets which Moses had put there at Horeb," but Hebrews may be ignoring this verse because it referred to the temple at the time of Solomon.

8. The †Septuagint uses *hilastērion* to translate the Hebrew word used for the cover of the ark, *kapporet*, which means "place of atonement" or "place of purging from sin." The same root appears in †Yom Kippur, the †Day of Atonement. *Hilastērion* appears in only one other passage in the New Testament, Rom 3:25, where Paul identifies Jesus himself as the *hilastērion* or expiation for our sins. The related noun *hilasmos* ("expiation") appears in 1 John 2:2; 4:10, and the verb *hilaskomai* ("expiate") in Luke 18:13; Heb 2:17.

Where Is the Ark of the Covenant?

The †ark of the covenant ranks among the most mysterious and sought-after objects in all religious history. Ever since the Babylonians burned Jerusalem and the temple to the ground in 586 BC (2 Kings 24:13; 25:9), the ark has been lost to history. However, 2 Maccabees recounts that the prophet Jeremiah, foreseeing the destruction of the temple, removed the ark and hid it in a cave on Mount Nebo, along with the tent and the altar of incense. Some Jews followed him, intending to mark the path, but they could not find it. Jeremiah admonished them, "The place is to remain unknown until God gathers his people together again and shows them mercy. Then the Lord will disclose these things, and the glory of the Lord and the cloud will be seen, just as they appeared in the time of Moses and of Solomon when he prayed that the place might be greatly sanctified" (2 Macc 2:7–8).

Because the ark was never found, during the time of the second temple (515 BC–AD 70), the Holy of Holies was completely empty. From a Christian perspective, the ark has been rendered obsolete now that its purpose has been fulfilled by an infinitely more efficacious "place of expiation," the crucified and risen Son of God.[a]

a. Moreover, as Luke's Gospel suggests, the ark of the *new* covenant is Mary, mother of Christ, the holy dwelling place in which God the Son became present in the flesh. See Edward Sri, *Walking with Mary: A Biblical Journey from Nazareth to the Cross* (New York: Image, 2013).

Scripture speaks of God "enthroned on the cherubim" that were over the ark (2 Kings 19:15; see Ps 80:2; 99:1), and it was the place where God manifested his mercy, as he had declared: "There I will meet you and there, from above the cover, between the two cherubim on the ark of the covenant, I will tell you all that I command you regarding the Israelites" (Exod 25:22).

But **now is not the time to speak of these in detail**, because the author is less concerned with the tabernacle itself than with the sacrificial rites carried out there, which he proceeds to describe in verses 6–10.

Most of the priestly rites were carried out in the **outer** room of the **tabernacle**, the Holy Place. In **performing their service**, or "worship," the priests entered the tabernacle **repeatedly**—this in marked contrast to Christ, who entered "once for all" (v. 12). Their service involved three regular duties: tending to the menorah every morning and evening so that the lamps were kept burning continually (Exod 27:20–21), burning fragrant incense before the Lord every morning and evening (Exod 30:7–8), and replacing the bread of the Presence with fresh loaves every sabbath (Lev 24:8–9).

9:6

The Day of Atonement

Yom Kippur, the Day of Atonement, was (and still is) the holiest day of the Jewish liturgical year, the day when atonement was made for the sins of the priests and the people and for any inadvertent defilement of the altar or tabernacle (Lev 16:33). It takes place in September, ten days after the beginning of the Jewish new year. On this day all Israel fasted in repentance for sin and gathered in solemn assembly.

Hebrews only briefly summarizes the complicated rites of that day, which are described in detail in Leviticus 16. First, the high priest ceremonially washed himself and donned his sacred linen garments and miter. He sacrificed a bull as a sin offering for himself and his household. He then took two goats and a ram from the people and cast lots over the goats to determine which one would be the scapegoat; the other he sacrificed as a sin offering to atone for the sins of the people.

He then entered the †Holy of Holies with burning incense and sprinkled the blood of the sacrificed bull seven times on the †mercy seat, making atonement for himself and his household. Leviticus specifies that the cloud of incense covered the mercy seat to prevent what would otherwise be the priest's sudden death in the presence of the holy God. The high priest then did the same with the goat's blood, making atonement for the sins of the people. He then smeared the blood of both the bull and the goat on the altar in the courtyard.

Next was the scapegoat ceremony: laying his hands on the goat's head, he confessed over it the sins of Israel, then sent the goat into the desert "to carry off all their iniquities" (Lev 16:22). Finally, he bathed and put on his usual priestly attire and offered two rams as whole burnt offerings for himself and for the people.

According to the Talmud, the priests had a custom of tying a scarlet cord to the scapegoat, and every year the cord was reported to have turned white as the goat was led away from the city, a miraculous sign that God had accepted the sacrifice (see Isa 1:18). The Talmud records that for the last forty years before the destruction of the temple in AD 70, the cord failed to change color, causing great consternation.[a] Moreover, during the same period, inexplicably the western light of the menorah kept going out and the doors of the temple kept opening of their own accord. The rabbis later interpreted these ominous phenomena as presaging the imminent destruction of the temple. Amazingly, they began to occur just at the time when Christ, the all-holy victim, offered the once-for-all sacrifice for sin. There was no longer a need for a scapegoat or for any of the rites of the old covenant.

a. Babylonian Talmud, *Yoma* 39b.

In contrast to this daily activity is the single most sacred rite of the Israelite　**9:7**
liturgical calendar: the Day of Atonement, when **the high priest alone goes
into the inner** room, the Holy of Holies (see sidebar, "The Day of Atonement").
He enters **not without blood that he offers for himself and for the sins of the
people**. The high priest needed atonement like everyone else; in fact, simply
entering the Holy of Holies, in such proximity to the all-holy God, put him in
danger of sudden death (Lev 16:13). For ancient Israel, as for many religions
of the world, it was axiomatic that only the shedding of blood could atone
for sin, since blood, as the seat of life, had supreme value (Heb 9:22; see Lev
17:11). Yet the rites of †Yom Kippur inevitably raise the question: How could
the blood of brute beasts ever make reparation for the sins of human beings?
The word translated here as "sins" (*agnoēmata*) is literally "ignorances" (or
"sins committed unintentionally," NRSV; "faults of inadvertence," NJB). According to Numbers 15:22–30, only such inadvertent faults can be expiated by
sacrifice.[9] Sins committed "with a high hand"—that is, deliberately and with
full knowledge—cannot be atoned for; they incur the death penalty (Num
15:30; Deut 17:12).

Through these ancient rites **the holy Spirit**, who inspired the Scriptures　**9:8**
that prescribe them, reveals hidden truths about God's plan. In this case the
restricted zones of access and the elaborate blood rituals show **that the way
into the sanctuary had not yet been revealed**; that is, God's people had no
chance of coming into his holy presence. **The outer tabernacle** (the Holy Place)
barred the way into the Holy of Holies, nor could the people enter the outer
tabernacle itself, nor even its courtyard or immediate environs. Nor was it
known how such access to God could ever come about. However, the qualify-
ing word "yet" hints that God's ultimate purpose was to open the way, to give
his people full and unrestricted access to his presence. Hebrews will complete
this thought at 10:19–20: "Therefore, brothers, . . . through the blood of Jesus
we have confidence of entrance into the sanctuary by the new and living way
he opened for us through the veil, that is, his flesh."

There is also a temporal symbolism in the arrangement of the wilderness　**9:9**
tabernacle. The outer room, the Holy Place, **is a symbol** (literally, a "parable") **of the present time**—the time when Hebrews was written, when the

---

9. Although Lev 16:16, 30 speaks of the Yom Kippur rites as cleansing "all sins," Hebrews applies
to these rites the limitation of Num 15, as Jewish tradition also seems to do (Mishnah, *Yoma* 8.9). See
Luke Timothy Johnson, *Hebrews: A Commentary*, New Testament Library (Louisville: Westminster John
Knox, 2006), 223. Numbers 15 uses the term "unwittingly" (*akousiōs*), which is similar in meaning to
"ignorances" in Heb 9:7. The sharp distinction between inadvertent and deliberate sins also exists in
the new covenant (see Heb 10:26).

old covenant system remained in place, the temple was still standing, and the †levitical rites were still being carried out. During the old covenant period, **gifts and sacrifices are offered that cannot perfect the worshiper in conscience**. This is one of the strongest statements in Hebrews of the radical inadequacy of the old system. It provided outward, ceremonial purity but was powerless to cleanse the conscience, the inner tribunal where we are aware of the rightness or wrongness of our actions (see Rom 2:15) and know that we have fallen short of the holiness that God demands (Rom 3:23).[10] The Old Testament itself acknowledges this insufficiency: "Will the LORD be pleased with thousands of rams, / with myriad streams of oil?" (Mic 6:7). As Hebrews has already stated, the goal of worship has always been nothing less than moral and spiritual perfection—that God's people would be made capable of sharing in his own glory (see 2:10; 7:19).

9:10   The rituals of the old covenant could purify people **only in matters of food and drink**—that is, in relation to the dietary laws that prohibited the eating of unclean animals and barred priests on duty from drinking wine (Lev 10:9; 11:1–47). The law also prescribed a variety of **ritual washings** (literally, "baptisms")—for instance, after touching unclean objects, after sexual relations, after healing from skin disease, and after performing certain priestly duties (Lev 11:40; 14:7–9; 15:5–18; 16:24). Jewish oral tradition added even more to these, as the Gospel of Mark observes: "For the Pharisees and, in fact, all Jews, do not eat without carefully washing their hands. . . . And on coming from the marketplace they do not eat without purifying themselves. And there are many other things that they have traditionally observed, the purification of cups and jugs and kettles [and beds]" (Mark 7:3–4). All these are **regulations concerning the flesh**. They provided an external purity and roused a hope for the true purity of heart that God would one day bring about. Thus they were a signpost, a provisional arrangement **imposed until the time of the new order**, or "until the time comes to set things right" (NRSV). Then the shadows would be replaced by the substance, and the signpost by "the good things that have come" (v. 11). The wording "food and drink and . . . baptisms" may be deliberately intended to evoke the two foundational sacraments of the new covenant, baptism and the Eucharist, which truly change the human person from within.

Now that Hebrews has briefly outlined the furnishings and activities of the old covenant system of atonement, the stage is set for the comparison with Christ that begins in verse 11.

---

10. God did, however, provide other means of provisional atonement in the old covenant. See sidebar, "Atonement through Almsgiving," p. 186.

Reflection and Application (9:1–10)

Part of the reason Hebrews is so challenging to read is that the author is thinking on so many levels at once. This is especially true of his description of the wilderness tabernacle in 9:1–10. On a literal level, he emphasizes the fact that the tabernacle had two rooms, the Holy Place and the Holy of Holies. On a symbolic level, this floor plan has not just one but three different dimensions. First, the outer and inner represent *the former age and the new age* (vv. 8–9a): the old covenant with its repeated, ineffective rites versus the new covenant with the perfect, once-for-all sacrifice of Christ. Second, the outer and inner stand for *the exterior and interior of the person* (vv. 9b–10): the outward ritual purity provided by the levitical rites versus the purity of conscience brought by Christ.[11] Finally, the outer and inner also symbolize *earth and heaven* (8:5; 9:11–12): the levitical rites are "a copy and shadow" of the eternal worship in God's true sanctuary of heaven.

These three symbolic levels roughly correspond to what Christian tradition calls the threefold spiritual sense of Scripture (see Catechism 117): the allegorical sense (signifying Christ and the new covenant), the moral sense (signifying our life in Christ), and the anagogical sense (signifying our heavenly destiny). These three spiritual senses are all based on the literal, the sense intended and expressed by the human author.

Reflection on the wilderness tabernacle also suggests further †typology beyond that which is explored by Hebrews. The three sacred objects in the ark—the jar of manna, the tablets of the law, and Aaron's rod—can all be seen as foreshadowing Christ. He is the "hidden manna" (Rev 2:17), the heavenly bread that nourishes Christians on their pilgrimage of faith. He is the giver of the new law, "the law of the spirit of life in Christ Jesus" that is written not on tablets of stone but on human hearts (Rom 8:2; see Heb 8:10). And he is the great high priest whose power to sanctify infinitely surpasses that of Aaron (Heb 4:14)—the same power that caused Aaron's wooden staff to blossom and that enables us to blossom and bear fruit for God (John 15:5, 8; Gal 5:22–23).[12]

The Power of Christ's Blood (9:11–14)

> **[11]But when Christ came as high priest of the good things that have come to be, passing through the greater and more perfect tabernacle not**

---

11. Strictly speaking, Christ's sacrifice brings both interior and exterior purity (see 10:22).
12. Philip Edgcumbe Hughes, *A Commentary on the Epistle to the Hebrews* (Grand Rapids: Eerdmans, 1977), 316.

made by hands, that is, not belonging to this creation, [12]he entered once for all into the sanctuary, not with the blood of goats and calves but with his own blood, thus obtaining eternal redemption. [13]For if the blood of goats and bulls and the sprinkling of a heifer's ashes can sanctify those who are defiled so that their flesh is cleansed, [14]how much more will the blood of Christ, who through the eternal spirit offered himself unblemished to God, cleanse our consciences from dead works to worship the living God.

OT: Exod 24:5; Lev 1:3; 16:15; Num 19:1–13

NT: Mark 14:58; Heb 6:1; 1 Pet 1:19; 1 John 1:7; Rev 7:14

Catechism: Jesus as celebrant of the heavenly liturgy, 662; Jesus' once-for-all sacrifice, 613–14, 1085, 2100; the mercy seat, 433

Lectionary: Heb 9:11–15: Solemnity of the Most Holy Body and Blood of Christ (Year B), the Most Holy Eucharist; Institution of Acolytes

By contemplating the old covenant rites just described (vv. 1–10), we are able to understand the far greater realities they foreshadowed. The goal of Hebrews 9:11–14 is to help readers recognize how inexpressibly good are the "good things that have come to be" in Christ. His sacrifice is better than the old sacrifices in three specific ways. First, Christ entered not an earthly tent but the true sanctuary, God's own dwelling place in heaven. Second, he offered not the blood of irrational animals but his own blood freely poured out in love. Finally, his blood brings not outward ritual purity but a cleansing that reaches the very depths of the person.

9:11   The phrase **but when Christ came** indicates a turning point—the turn of the ages, the change from the former preparatory stage to the time of fulfillment. The "new order" (v. 10), which so many prophets and kings longed to see (Luke 10:24), has arrived. Jesus came **as high priest of the good things that have come to be**, finally bestowing all the blessings that God had destined for his children. These good things, indeed all things, have become ours in Christ (see 1 Cor 3:21–23), although we do not yet experience them in their fullness (see Heb 13:14; 1 Pet 1:4). As Paul exclaims, "He who did not spare his own Son but gave him up for us all, will he not also give us all things with him?" (Rom 8:32 RSV).

The †tabernacle built by Moses foreshadowed **the greater and more perfect tabernacle**, or tent, through which Christ has entered into the heavenly sanctuary.[13] That greater tabernacle probably refers to Christ's own risen body (see sidebar, "What Is the True Tabernacle?," p. 174), which is **not made by hands,**

---

13. The NAB translators inserted the verb "passing through," but the Greek actually contains only the preposition "through" (*dia*).

that is, not belonging to this creation. His earthly body belonged to this passing world, since he shared our flesh and blood (2:14). But his risen body, now exalted at the Father's right hand (1:3), is the beginning of the *new creation*, the transformation of the whole cosmos by God's power. Instead of restricting access to God, as the earthly tabernacle did, it opens the way to God for all believers; even more, it is a temple made up of all believers (3:6; see 1 Cor 3:17).[14] The phrase "more perfect" recalls the theme that has been running throughout Hebrews: in his human nature Christ was "made perfect" by the act of love in which he suffered and died for us (2:10; 5:9; 7:28).

In contrast to the levitical high priest, who entered God's presence once a year (v. 7), Christ **entered once for all into the sanctuary**, the true dwelling place of God that is "heaven itself" (v. 24). As the eternal Son (1:2, 5) he was always there, but *as a human being* he had to enter by way of his passion and resurrection. And once he had accomplished perfect atonement, there was no need for continually repeated sacrifices as in the old covenant (10:1).   **9:12**

Again in contrast to the levitical high priest, Christ entered **not with the blood of goats and calves**. These are the two animals whose blood was sprinkled on the †mercy seat on the Day of Atonement, a bull calf for sins of the high priest and his family, a goat for sins of the people (Lev 16:11, 15). In ancient Israel these animal sacrifices provided a powerful visual sign for the worshipers—"the life of the sacrificial animal, symbolized by the blood, being poured out in death as a sign that, though our lives are indeed forfeit because of our wickedness and impurity, God will rescue us by providing a life-given-in-death instead of ours."[15] But in a startling departure from this pattern, Christ the high priest came into God's presence **with his own blood**, the blood that was shed violently on the cross. He is at one and the same time both priest and victim, the sacrifice offered and the one offering the sacrifice.

The shedding of an animal's blood is at best only a symbolic substitute for a human life offered to God. It can never pay the debt of human sin. But Christ entered God's presence having freely laid down his own infinitely valuable life, **thus obtaining** (or better, "having thus obtained") **eternal redemption**.[16] "Redemption" refers to the payment of a ransom to release someone or something that would otherwise be lost or enslaved (see Lev 25:48; Ps 49:8–9). Sometimes,

14. Vanhoye, *A Different Priest*, 278.

15. N. T. Wright, *Hebrews for Everyone*, New Testament for Everyone (Louisville: Westminster John Knox, 2004), 96.

16. The participle is in the †aorist, which indicates a completed event—that is, Christ's death on the cross. Just as the levitical high priest entered the Holy of Holies with blood only after having slain the animal in the courtyard of the tent, so Christ entered heaven itself after having laid down his life in the "courtyard" of this world. See Hughes, *Hebrews*, 328.

What Is the True Tabernacle?

BIBLICAL BACKGROUND

Scholars have long debated what Hebrews means by "the true tabernacle . . . the greater and more perfect tabernacle not made by hands" (8:2; 9:11).ª The Greek word for "tabernacle" (*skēnē*) is literally "tent"; in the †Septuagint it refers to the sacred tent that housed the †ark of the covenant during Israel's desert wanderings (Exod 25:9). One interpretation holds that the true tent is synonymous with the †*sanctuary* in verse 12, referring to God's dwelling place in heaven. However, verses 11–12 seem to differentiate between the tent and the sanctuary: "passing through the greater and more perfect tabernacle . . . he entered once for all into the sanctuary." Another view is that the true tent refers to the *outer heavens*, through which Jesus passed into the true †Holy of Holies, God's own presence (4:14; 9:11–12). But this seems to conflict with the way Hebrews also uses "tent" to refer to the Holy of Holies (9:3). A third interpretation is that the true tent is the *Church*, or alternatively, the *souls of individual Christians*. However, there is no direct indication that Hebrews has the Church in mind, and nowhere in Scripture are the people of God referred to as a tent.

A fourth opinion is that the true tent is *the human body that Christ assumed* in his incarnation. Scripture often refers to the human body as a tent (Isa 38:12; 2 Cor 5:1, 4; 2 Pet 1:13), and the Gospel of John says that in his incarnation the eternal Word "made his dwelling" (literally, "pitched his tent") among us (John 1:14). But this view runs into the difficulty that Hebrews says the tent is

---

however, the word is used more broadly to refer to liberation. In the Old Testament God shows that he himself is the redeemer of Israel, who liberates his people from slavery in Egypt (Exod 15:13; Isa 43:14). But only in the New Testament is it revealed that God redeems us from the far deeper slavery of sin, and that the ransom price is nothing less than the life of God's own Son (see Mark 10:45; 1 Tim 2:6). It is not that the price was paid *to* anyone; rather, sin itself held humanity captive, and now its hold is broken. Because this redemption never needs to be repeated (7:27), it is not temporary but eternal (5:9).

9:13   Besides the †Yom Kippur rites with **the blood of goats and bulls**, the law of Moses prescribed another †atonement ritual: **the sprinkling of a heifer's ashes**.[17] This peculiar rite, detailed in Numbers 19:1–3, called for an unblemished

---

17. The RSV interprets the verb "sprinkling" to go with the blood as well as the ashes: "the sprinkling of defiled persons with the blood of goats and bulls and with the ashes of a heifer." If this is correct, then Hebrews is alluding to the covenant at Mount Sinai (Exod 24:8), the only time that the people themselves were sprinkled with blood (although Aaron and his sons were sprinkled with blood as part of their ordination rites in Exod 29:21; Lev 8:30). But the blood of the covenant in Exod 24 had to do

"not belonging to this creation" (9:11). Jesus' human body did belong to this creation, for he shares our "blood and flesh" human nature (2:14).

Finally, the most plausible interpretation is that the true tent is indeed Christ's human body, but his *risen and glorified* body, which is indeed not of this creation since it is the beginning of the new creation.[b] Jesus prophesied that three days after his death he would raise up a "temple . . . not made with hands," referring to his own glorified body (Mark 14:58; see John 2:19–21), in wording very similar to the tent "not made with hands" in Hebrews 9:11.

This is not to say the true tent has no connection to the Church. The Church, the body of Christ, is the new, spiritual temple in which God dwells (1 Cor 3:16; Eph 2:21). Thus the Church is, in an extended sense, the true tent "that the Lord, not man, set up" and in which Christ now ministers as high priest (Heb 8:2). The risen Lord, in the midst of his people, continually celebrates the heavenly liturgy; that is, he presents to the Father his one eternal sacrifice for our sins and continually leads his people in the chorus of praise that ascends to God's throne (see 2:12).

a. For a helpful summary of the differing views, see Philip Edgcumbe Hughes, *A Commentary on the Epistle to the Hebrews* (Grand Rapids: Eerdmans, 1977), 283–90.
b. As noted in note 13 at 9:11, the Greek of that verse does not say "passing through" but contains only the preposition "through" (*dia*). This preposition can indicate not only direction in space but also instrument or agency, just as the English "through" can indicate not only direction in space ("she walked through the room") but also instrument or agency ("he communicated with her through letters"). The statement in 9:11, then, may mean that Jesus entered the sanctuary of heaven "by means of" the perfect tabernacle that is his risen body.

red heifer to be completely burned, together with cedar, hyssop, and a piece of scarlet cloth. The ashes were then mixed with water, which was kept for sprinkling on those who had become ritually defiled by touching the dead. Although burying the dead was considered a virtuous act and even a moral duty (see Tob 12:12–13), it still caused ritual defilement, which meant the individual was barred from public worship until he was cleansed. But Hebrews points out that the water for purification could do no more than **sanctify those who are defiled so that their flesh is cleansed**. Like the Yom Kippur rites, it could provide outward, ceremonial cleansing but could do nothing to change and renew the human heart.

Hebrews completes the thought with a lesser-to-greater argument ([†]*qal wa-homer*). If animal blood could provide ceremonial cleansing, **how much more efficacious is the blood of Christ**. The sacrificial animals had to be unblemished

9:14

with a kinship bond between God and his people, not a cleansing from defilement. It seems best to read the Greek of Heb 9:13 as the NAB does.

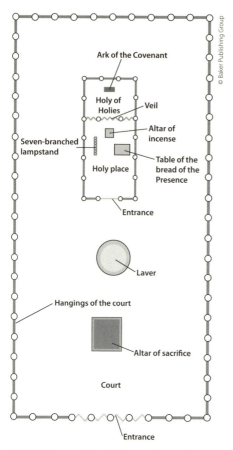

Fig. 13. Diagram of the wilderness tabernacle

in the sense of being free of physical defects, but Christ was **unblemished** to the very depths of his being, innocent of all sin (4:15; see 2 Cor 5:21) and thus able to offer God an act of unlimited love and obedience. The goats and calves were completely passive, incapable of any understanding or voluntary participation in their sacrifice, but Christ willingly **offered himself**: "I lay down my life in order to take it up again. No one takes it from me, but I lay it down on my own" (John 10:17–18). His self-offering was foreshadowed in Isaiah's song of the Suffering Servant, who "makes himself an offering for sin" (Isa 53:10 RSV), and earlier in Isaac's willingness to let himself be sacrificed by his father Abraham, even though that sacrifice was never carried out (Gen 22:1–10; Heb 11:17–18).[18]

What does Hebrews mean by the unusual phrase **through the eternal spirit**, which is found nowhere else in the Bible? As Albert Vanhoye points out, it may allude to the fire on the altar of sacrifice.[19]

This fire had been miraculously ignited by God when the priesthood was first instituted (Lev 9:24; 2 Chron 7:1), and the priests had to take care never to let it go out (Lev 6:5–6); thus it was called the "perpetual fire." The fire was what transformed the sacrifices and sent them up to God in the form of smoke. Only fire that came from God was capable of making the sacrifices holy and acceptable to him. Hebrews suggests, then, that the "perpetual fire" foreshadowed the eternal divine fire that engulfs Jesus' sacrifice: the Holy Spirit. Through Jesus' sufferings, the Holy Spirit set his human heart ablaze so that he could offer God the limitless self-gift that God had deserved but never received from humanity.

His blood is therefore able to **cleanse our consciences from dead works**. "Dead works" (mentioned in 6:1) may refer to sins in general, or to sacrifices

18. According to Jewish tradition, Isaac's submission to being bound by Abraham demonstrated his willing assent to the sacrifice (*Genesis Rabbah* 56.3).

19. Vanhoye, *A Different Priest*, 283–84. See *1 Esdras* 6:23.

Through the Eternal Spirit

Reflecting on Hebrews 9, Pope John Paul II wrote in his encyclical on the Holy Spirit,

The Old Testament on several occasions speaks of "fire from heaven" which burnt the oblations presented by men (cf. Lev 9:24; 1 Kg 18:38; 2 Chr 7:1). By analogy one can say that the Holy Spirit is the "fire from heaven" which works in the depth of the mystery of the Cross. . . . The Holy Spirit as Love and Gift comes down, in a certain sense, into the very heart of the sacrifice which is offered on the Cross. Referring here to the biblical tradition, we can say: He consumes this sacrifice with the fire of the love which unites the Son with the Father in the Trinitarian communion. And since the sacrifice of the Cross is an act proper to Christ, also in this sacrifice he "receives" the Holy Spirit. He receives the Holy Spirit in such a way that afterwards—and he alone with God the Father—can "give him" to the Apostles, to the Church, to humanity. He alone "sends" the Spirit from the Father.[a]

a. *On the Holy Spirit in the Life of the Church and the World* 41.

not accompanied by conversion of heart, which are incapable of making people acceptable to God. It may also allude to the water for purification mentioned just above. Whereas that water cleansed people who were contaminated by contact with the dead, Christ's blood cleanses us from the far more serious defilement of a sinful conscience. "The blood of his Son Jesus cleanses us from all sin" (1 John 1:7; see Rev 1:5). Freedom from dead works, in turn, enables us **to worship the living God**—to offer him joyful service and praise, free from the slightest burden of guilt or sin.

Reflection and Application (9:11–14)

Christians throughout history have venerated the blood of Christ and even formed confraternities whose purpose is to spread devotion to the precious blood. Many Catholics today are aware that we have been redeemed by Christ's blood but do not realize that the blood is a power we can draw upon daily to free us from sin and the effects of sin that arise within us and keep us from experiencing the kingdom in its fullness. We can call on the power of Christ's blood, for example, against temptation, against fears and insecurities, anger, moodiness, confusion, depression, tension, disunity, or a lingering sense of guilt for sins already confessed. We can invoke the blood over troubled situations among our families, at work, and in the world; against sickness and danger.

We have the privilege of drinking that same blood in holy Communion, which gives us eternal life (John 6:54). Regardless of whether or not we subjectively feel its effects, Christ's blood is powerful and effective. It frees us of sin (Rev 1:5), gives us victory over Satan (Rev 12:10–11), draws us near to God (Eph 2:13), and equips us to do his will (Heb 13:20–21).

The Covenant Renewed and Fulfilled (9:15–22)

---

[15]For this reason he is mediator of a new covenant: since a death has taken place for deliverance from transgressions under the first covenant, those who are called may receive the promised eternal inheritance. [16]Now where there is a will, the death of the testator must be established. [17]For a will takes effect only at death; it has no force while the testator is alive. [18]Thus not even the first covenant was inaugurated without blood. [19]When every commandment had been proclaimed by Moses to all the people according to the law, he took the blood of calves [and goats], together with water and crimson wool and hyssop, and sprinkled both the book itself and all the people, [20]saying, "This is 'the blood of the covenant which God has enjoined upon you.'" [21]In the same way, he sprinkled also the tabernacle and all the vessels of worship with blood. [22]According to the law almost everything is purified by blood, and without the shedding of blood there is no forgiveness.

OT: Gen 15:7–21; Exod 24:3–8; Lev 17:11; Num 19:6; Isa 53:11–12; Jer 31:31–32
NT: Matt 26:28; Luke 22:19–20, 29; Rom 3:25; Gal 3:15–17; 1 Pet 1:18–19; 1 John 1:7
Catechism: the first covenant as a preparation for Christ, 522; the curse of the law, 580; Jesus' blood the expiation for our sins, 601–18, 1851, 1992

This section is one of the most challenging in the Letter to the Hebrews, partly because it relies on Greek wordplay and partly because it revolves around ancient notions of †atonement that are foreign, even shocking, to modern readers. Yet these verses lead us into the very center of the mystery of God's redeeming love.

9:15   Verse 15 returns to the theme of chapter 8, that Christ is **mediator** of the **new covenant** promised in Jeremiah (8:6; see 7:22; 12:24). Here Hebrews finally begins to make the connection between that biblical passage and the overarching theme of chapters 8–10, Christ's death as the true †Yom Kippur. The phrase **for this reason** forms a strong link with the previous sections (9:1–14): it is because of the efficacy of his sacrifice, which interiorly cleanses the consciences of his people (v. 14), that Christ can establish a new and lasting covenant that has none of the limitations of the old.

Christ's **death** brings a twofold grace.[20] First, it has brought **deliverance from transgressions under the first covenant**—that is, explicit violations of the law of Moses. This grace applies specifically to the Jews, the people of the covenant. God's covenant with Israel at Mount Sinai was conditional on their keeping the law, and it pronounced judgment and severe penalties for breaking the law (Deut 28:15–68). Since the Israelites, fallen human beings that they were, were incapable of keeping the law, it was a broken covenant, a ruptured relationship (Jer 31:32). But Christ himself has borne the covenant penalties and has therefore brought deliverance, or "redemption," from those transgressions. Only by removing those faults committed under the first covenant could a new and universal covenant be established. In verses 17–22 Hebrews will explain further how that occurs. Here, a key point is that Christ's atonement is *retroactive*. The redeeming power of his death extends even to those who lived before him—Abraham and Sarah, Moses, Aaron, Miriam, Hannah, Samuel, David, and all the faithful people of the old covenant, who trusted in God's promise without seeing its fulfillment and will one day be "made perfect" along with us (11:39–40).

Second, since the sins committed under the old covenant have been wiped away, **those who are called**—the people of both the old covenant and the new—**may receive the promised eternal inheritance**. As the original readers of Hebrews may have noticed, "those who are called" (*keklēmenoi*) is another way of naming the Church (*ekklēsia*); both words are rooted in the same verb "to call" (*kaleō*).[21] At the same time, the mention of being "called" and of an "inheritance" recalls Abraham, the original recipient of God's call, to whom God promised the land of Canaan as an eternal inheritance (Gen 12:7; 13:15). That land, however, as Hebrews explained in chapter 4, was only a sign and foreshadowing of the greater inheritance God had in mind, the eternal rest of God himself.

As Paul notes in Galatians 3:17, God's covenant with Abraham was an unconditional promise and was never annulled. The Sinai covenant, which came 430 years later, was conditional on keeping the law, but it did not invalidate the earlier covenant with Abraham. Thus Paul and Hebrews proclaim, in different ways, that the new covenant in Christ renews that original covenant and fulfills God's promise that all nations of the earth would find blessing in Abraham (Gen 12:3).

---

20. The Greek conjunction *hopōs*, translated "since" in the NAB in verse 15, is better translated "so that" (expressing purpose, as in the RSV). The phrase then reads: "so that, a death having occurred . . ."

21. See also Heb 2:12; 3:1. *Ekklēsia* is the word usually used in the Septuagint to translate the Hebrew term for the "assembly" of Israel (e.g., Deut 31:30). Thus *ekklēsia* in the New Testament evokes both Israel and the New Testament Church.

God's Covenant with Abraham

BIBLICAL
BACKGROUND

Although Abraham is not directly mentioned in Hebrews 9:15, he is very much in the background, as he was the first to be "called" and promised an "inheritance." God's covenant with Abraham was established by means of a mysterious blood ritual, described in Genesis 15:9–18. God asked Abraham to take several animals typically used in sacrifice, cut them in two, and place the two halves opposite each other in rows. This was an ancient form of covenant-making (also mentioned in Jer 34:18) in which the two parties each passed between the slaughtered animals, saying in effect, "So let it be to me if I break the covenant." This ritual action was thus a kind of conditional self-curse, a powerful deterrent to breaking the covenant.

What is astounding about the covenant in Genesis 15 is that the only party to pass between the pieces is God, symbolized by a smoking fire pot and a flaming torch (see Deut 4:24). That is, God alone undertakes the conditional self-curse. God pledges himself unilaterally to the covenant; Abraham is required to do nothing at all. This scene is moving testimony to God's absolute determination to establish an unbreakable bond with his people. But its full meaning is revealed only in the New Testament. By passing between the pieces, God had committed himself to upholding the covenant not only from his side (where it was never in danger) but also from the side of man (where it was at risk of being broken from the start). God will uphold the covenant even at the highest possible cost to himself: the death of his beloved Son.

9:16   **Now where there is a will** (*diathēkē*), **the death of the testator must be established**. Most modern Bibles include a footnote here explaining that the Greek word used here, *diathēkē*, can mean either a "covenant" or a "will," depending on the context. In the †Septuagint it is regularly used to translate the Hebrew word for "covenant," and that is how it is almost always used in the New Testament (with the possible exception of Gal 3:15). But in secular Greek, *diathēkē* meant a "will" or "testament." Here in verses 16–17 Hebrews seems to suddenly shift from the biblical meaning to the secular meaning, then back to the biblical meaning in verse 18—a confusing move for translators, commentators, and readers alike! In order to grasp what is going on with this wordplay, it is important to realize that *diathēkē* was a flexible term and the two meanings were not entirely distinct.[22] They are alike in that both an ordinary

---

22. This is evident from the fact that we use "covenant" for Jesus' words of institution at the Last Supper—"the new covenant [*diathēkē*] in my blood" (Luke 22:20)—and "testament" for the written record of this covenant, the New Testament (*diathēkē*).

will and God's *covenant* involve a unilateral promise, established at the initiative of one party. The meanings are different, however, in that a will specifies how a person's property will be distributed after he or she dies; a covenant, in contrast, establishes a relationship between two parties. Hebrews is fully aware of and exploits this dual meaning, because the new *diathēkē* in Christ has elements of both a covenant and a will. Just moments after instituting the new covenant in his blood, Jesus told his disciples, "I confer [*diatithemai*] a kingdom on you, just as my Father has conferred one on me" (Luke 22:29), using the verbal form of the noun *diathēkē* in a way that suggests a last will and testament.[23] Through his passion and death Jesus bequeaths to his disciples the kingdom.

At first only the meaning "will" seems to apply in verse 17: **For a will takes**   **9:17–18** **effect only at death; it has no force while the testator is alive**. A covenant, in contrast, does not depend on the death of either party—or does it? In fact, God's covenant with Israel at Mount Sinai, and his earlier covenant with Abraham (see sidebar, "God's Covenant with Abraham"), did involve the death of sacrificial animals—a shedding of blood that had profound symbolic meaning. The animals stood in the place of the parties to the covenant, and the outpoured blood represented the total giving of their lives.[24] Moreover, violations of the covenant are atoned for by blood. At the root of this concept was a deep intuition that nothing could ever repay the damage done by covenant-breaking, except the forfeiting of one's life; yet God does not desire the death of anyone (Ezek 18:23), so he provides a substitute. As Hebrews notes, **Thus not even the first covenant was inaugurated without blood**.

Verses 19–21 describe how the Sinai covenant was inaugurated (Exod 24),   **9:19–21** but incorporate details from later cleansing rituals (Lev 8–9; 14; 16; Num 19) in a way that can be confusing. Probably the point is that the initial establishment of the covenant contained within itself all the later provisions for purification.[25] The covenant ceremony had a twofold structure—the same basic structure that the †liturgy of the new covenant, the Mass, still has today. First there was a liturgy of the word: **every commandment** given by God was **proclaimed by Moses to all the people** (Exod 24:3, 7). Then there was a liturgy of †sacrifice: bull **calves**[26] were sacrificed, and Moses **took** their **blood** and **sprinkled** it on the altar **and**

23. Paul plays on the same dual meaning of *diathēkē* as "covenant" and "will" in Gal 3:15–17.

24. The covenant rituals in Gen 15 and Exod 24 contain multiple levels of symbolism; thus the blood also consecrates the people to God, and the sharing of blood establishes kinship.

25. See Thomas Aquinas, *Commentary on the Epistle to the Hebrews*, trans. Chrysostom Baer (South Bend, IN: St. Augustine's Press, 2006), 193.

26. The phrase "and goats" is missing from some manuscripts of Hebrews and may have been added by scribal error, since there is no mention of goats in Exod 24. Or, if it was written by the author, he is

Christ's Death as a Sacrifice of Atonement   **BIBLICAL BACKGROUND**

For first-century Jews, Jesus' death on the cross would have in no way appeared as a ⁺sacrifice—in fact, the furthest thing from it. A sacrifice entailed the offering of a slaughtered animal to God by fire, carried out by the ⁺levitical priests in a sacred place, the ⁺tabernacle or the temple. Jesus' death, in contrast, was a criminal penalty carried out by Roman soldiers outside the city (see Heb 13:12). The temple sacrifices were solemn and often joyful events, bringing down God's blessings on his people. A crucifixion, in contrast, was a terrifying and gruesome event—a sign that the victim was accursed (Gal 3:13).

How, then, did Hebrews arrive at the understanding of Christ's death as a sacrifice, indeed, the one perfect sacrifice of which all previous sacrifices were only shadows and copies? The logical source of this insight is Christ's own words at the Last Supper.[a] There, according to the Synoptic Gospels and Paul, Jesus pronounced over the cup words that recalled the institution of the covenant at Sinai, linking "blood" with "covenant" (Matt 26:28; Mark 14:24; Luke 22:20; 1 Cor 11:25). Jesus also indicated that he would give his body and blood "for you," or "on behalf of many," indicating that he would suffer vicariously on our behalf "for the forgiveness of sins" (Matt 26:28). With these words, the Last Supper became a prophecy in gesture, interpreting his passion that was to occur the next day. Jesus' death, far from being a tragic misfortune or a heroic martyrdom for a cause, was an atoning sacrifice. It was the fulfillment of Isaiah's prophecy of the Suffering Servant, who "makes himself an offering for sin" (Isa 53:10 RSV). Reflecting on this theme, the author of Hebrews develops in depth the Christian understanding of the cross as the one infinitely efficacious sacrifice, in which Christ is both victim and priest.

a. Albert Vanhoye, *Old Testament Priests and the New Priest: According to the New Testament*, trans. Bernard Orchard, rev. ed. (Leominster: Gracewing, 2009), 50–51.

all the people (Exod 24:5–6, 8). Finally, the ceremony culminated with a sacred banquet in which Moses and the elders of Israel enjoyed table fellowship in the presence of God himself (Exod 24:9–11). Exodus does not mention sprinkling **the book itself**, but Hebrews probably assumes this was part of the rite, since at the heart of the covenant was the people's pledge to do the will of God, obeying all the commandments written in the book of the law. As Hebrews will show, this disposition of obedience is perfectly embodied in Christ (10:7).

---

combining the Sinai ceremony with the later Day of Atonement rites, which did use the blood of goats (see Heb 9:12–13).

With the sprinkling Moses pronounced the solemn covenant formula: **This is "the blood of the covenant which God has enjoined upon you."** Significantly, Hebrews tweaks the wording: instead of "Behold the blood" as in Exodus 24:8 †LXX, it says, "This is the blood," which is closer to the words used by Jesus at the Last Supper.[27] Hebrews may be intentionally pointing to Christ's fulfillment of the Sinai covenant in the Eucharist. At Sinai, the sprinkling of blood on both the altar (representing God) and the people signified the forging of a kinship bond: God and his people were now blood relatives, if only on a symbolic level. But when Christ, who shares our "blood and flesh" (Heb 2:14), gives us his blood in the Eucharist, the kinship bond is brought to a whole new level of realism. We are truly his blood brothers and sisters, one flesh with him in the family of God.

In the covenant ritual of Exodus 24 there is no mention of **water and crimson wool and hyssop**. These were prescribed later for purification rites, for the cleansing of lepers (Lev 14:4) and of those defiled by contact with corpses (Num 19:6, already alluded to at v. 13 above). Nor does Exodus indicate that Moses **sprinkled also the tabernacle and all the vessels of worship** (literally, "vessels of the liturgy") **with blood**. The tabernacle was later dedicated using oil (Exod 40:9–10), although blood was sprinkled on the altar at the ordination of Aaron (Lev 8:15, 19) and on the ark's cover as part of the †Day of Atonement rites (Lev 16:15–16). However, Hebrews mentions these rites here in the context of the Sinai covenant ceremony because from the beginning the covenant had to make provision for impurities, transgressions, and all that could separate the people from God.

Verse 22 sums up the principle underlying all the rites just mentioned: **According to the law almost everything is purified by blood, and without the shedding of blood there is no forgiveness**. Because of the damage in relationships caused by sin, †atonement for sin always involves a cost, and that cost can be met only by the offering of a life—that is, by blood, which as the bearer of life is supremely valuable. This rule is expressed in Leviticus 17:11: "It is the blood as life that makes atonement." The only exceptions to the rule of purification by blood were for minor ritual impurities that required only washing with water (Lev 15), though some of these also involved animal sacrifice; and the sin offering of fine flour instead of animals, which was allowed for the destitute poor (Lev 5:11).

9:22

27. Unfortunately, this tweak is not visible to readers in translation, since the NABRE, like many English translations, renders the Hebrew phrase in Exod 24:8 "This is," whereas the Septuagint renders it *idou* ("behold"). Mark 14:24 has *touto estin to haima* (see also Matt 26:28), a phrase nearly identical to *touto to haima* in Heb 9:20. In the Greek word order "my" follows "blood."

Reflection and Application (9:15–22)

The biblical principle that "without the shedding of blood there is no forgiveness" is one of the most difficult statements to accept in Hebrews, and even in the whole Bible. The very idea is repugnant to many modern readers. It seems to embody a primitive notion of retribution. It seems to presuppose a bloodthirsty God whose wrath can be satisfied only by a violent, bloody punishment.

This principle is indeed very easy to misunderstand. But understood rightly, it is part of the foundation of the whole plan of salvation. It can be traced to Genesis, where God tells Adam that if he eats from the forbidden tree, "in the day that you eat of it you shall surely die" (Gen 2:17 ESV). That is, death is an intrinsic consequence of sin. Sin separates human beings from the all-holy God, the source of life, and thereby leaves them subject to death and decay. It causes a fatal wound in the human heart that cannot simply be willed away. The damage done by sin must be borne, and sin itself must be undone or reversed.[28]

Forgiveness of sins therefore comes at a supremely high cost, as Isaiah's hymn of the Suffering Servant (Isa 53:5) attests:

> He was pierced for our sins,
>   crushed for our iniquity.
> He bore the punishment that makes us whole,
>   by his wounds we were healed.

Jesus, the innocent victim, freely and willingly took this cost upon himself, and his sacrifice alone reconciles us to God.[29] At the Last Supper he declared, "This is my blood of the covenant, which will be shed on behalf of many for the forgiveness of sins" (Matt 26:28). All the blood sacrifices of the old covenant, therefore, are signs leading us into the mystery of God's own self-giving love.

Christ's All-Sufficient Sacrifice in the True Tabernacle (9:23–28)

[23]Therefore, it was necessary for the copies of the heavenly things to be purified by these rites, but the heavenly things themselves by better sacrifices than these. [24]For Christ did not enter into a sanctuary made by

---

28. For a profound theological reflection on this theme, see Norbert Hoffmann, "Atonement and Ontological Coherence between the Trinity and the Cross," in *Towards a Civilization of Love: A Symposium on the Scriptural and Theological Foundations of the Devotion to the Heart of Jesus*, trans. Erasmo Leiva-Merikakis (San Francisco: Ignatius Press, 1985), 213–66.

29. See Rom 3:25; Col 1:22; 1 Pet 1:18–19; 1 John 1:7; Rev 1:5; 7:14.

hands, a copy of the true one, but heaven itself, that he might now appear before God on our behalf. ²⁵Not that he might offer himself repeatedly, as the high priest enters each year into the sanctuary with blood that is not his own; ²⁶if that were so, he would have had to suffer repeatedly from the foundation of the world. But now once for all he has appeared at the end of the ages to take away sin by his sacrifice. ²⁷Just as it is appointed that human beings die once, and after this the judgment, ²⁸so also Christ, offered once to take away the sins of many, will appear a second time, not to take away sin but to bring salvation to those who eagerly await him.

OT: Exod 28:29; Lev 16:11–16; 1 Kings 8:27; Sir 50:5; Isa 53:12

NT: John 1:29; Rom 6:9; 8:34; Titus 2:13; 1 Pet 1:20; 1 John 2:1

Catechism: Christ in God's presence on our behalf, 519, 662, 2741; Christ's death once for all, 571; reincarnation, 1013; judgment after death, 1021–22

Lectionary: 32nd Sunday in Ordinary Time (Year B); Ascension of the Lord (Year C)

We tend to think of earthly things as real, and of heaven as somehow unreal, ethereal, even imaginary. Hebrews affirms that just the opposite is true. Returning to the contrast made at the beginning of chapter 8, the author tells us that the desert tabernacle built by Moses, and all the old covenant rites, were only a copy or sketch of the heavenly realities. But Christ is a minister of the true sanctuary that is heaven itself.

It was necessary for the copies of the heavenly things to be purified by these rites—that is, the blood †sacrifices and sprinklings just described in verses 19–22. **But the heavenly things themselves** need to be purified **by better sacrifices than these**—that is, the sacrifice of Christ. "Sacrifices" is plural for the sake of the parallel with "these rites," but as Hebrews continually insists, Christ's sacrifice is not many but one: the single, once-for-all offering of himself on the cross (see 7:27; 9:12; 10:10, 12, 14).

9:23

But this verse raises another question: Why would the heavenly things themselves need to be purified? How could there possibly be any impurity in heaven? One solution is that "purified" here means consecrated for holy use, as "inaugurated" with blood in verse 18 is parallel to "purified" by blood in verse 22. But that still leaves the problem of why heavenly things would need to be consecrated. This question is best answered by considering the *earthly* things purified with blood (vv. 19–21) that are parallel with these "heavenly things": the book of the law, the people, the tabernacle, and the vessels for worship.[30] All these were "copies" in the sense that they were figures pointing forward to greater realities: the law written on the heart, the redeemed people

30. See Vanhoye, *A Different Priest*, 293–94.

Atonement through Almsgiving

A few Old Testament passages express a principle that seems to contradict Hebrews 9:22, namely, that generosity to the poor and other righteous acts can atone for sin. The book of Tobit, for example, declares that "almsgiving saves from death, and purges all sin" (Tob 12:9). Sirach states that "almsgiving atones for sins" (Sir 3:30) and "Those who honor their father atone for sins" (Sir 3:3; see 35:2). It is important to note that these passages were written at a time after the Babylonian exile, when many Jews were living in lands far from Israel and no longer had access to the temple and its sacrifices. For a few generations there had been no temple at all, before it was rebuilt in 515 BC. In this painful situation the Jews came to recognize that God would provide other means of †atonement than the blood sacrifices prescribed in the Torah.[a] This is clearly expressed in Daniel 3:38–40:

> We have in our day no prince, prophet, or leader,
> no burnt offering, sacrifice, oblation, or incense,
> no place to offer first fruits, to find favor with you.
> But with contrite heart and humble spirit
> let us be received;
> As though it were burnt offerings of rams and bulls,
> or tens of thousands of fat lambs,
> So let our sacrifice be in your presence today.

In light of the New Testament, however, we see that this was a partial and provisional atonement. Not even the highest human righteousness can heal the wound of sin and the broken relationship with God (Rom 3:20–26; Eph 2:8–10). Otherwise, some especially virtuous people could save themselves and would have no need of Christ, as the fourth-century heretic Pelagius taught. All human beings without exception are in need of redemption through the outpoured blood of Jesus Christ.[b]

a. For an illuminating study of the role of almsgiving in biblical religion, see Gary Anderson, *Charity: The Place of the Poor in Biblical Tradition* (New Haven: Yale University Press, 2014).
b. Catechism 616, 1851, 1992. The Catechism affirms that even Mary, who was immaculately conceived and free from all stain of sin, was redeemed by Christ—in her case, by a singular grace, from the first moment of her conception (490–93).

of God, the true tent that is Christ's glorified humanity, and the new covenant liturgy.[31] These are the "heavenly things" that Christ purifies. But how can realities that belong to the Church on earth be called "heavenly"? They have

31. As Harold Attridge puts it, "The heavenly or ideal realities cleansed by Christ's sacrifice are none other than the consciences of the members of the new covenant" (*Hebrews*, 262).

become heavenly by Christ's sacrifice in order to participate already in the "heavenly Jerusalem" (12:22).[32]

The perfection of Christ's sacrifice is highlighted by further contrasts with **9:24** the †Day of Atonement rites. First, **Christ did not enter into a sanctuary made by hands, a copy of the true one** (see 8:5). Already in the Old Testament it was recognized that God does not really dwell in a tent or a stone building made by human hands. At the dedication of the temple Solomon exclaimed, "Is God indeed to dwell on earth? If the heavens and the highest heavens cannot contain you, how much less this house which I have built!" (1 Kings 8:27; see Acts 7:48). The true sanctuary is **heaven itself**—not the heavens of this creation, which are the works of God's hands and will one day perish (Heb 1:10–12), but the invisible, transcendent dwelling place of God.

Christ, in his risen, glorified humanity, ascended there **that he might now appear before God** (literally, "before the face of God"). Throughout Scripture the ultimate human longing is to see God's face (Exod 33:18–20; Ps 4:7), yet to do so is also an awesome, overwhelming experience that puts one at risk of instant death (Gen 32:31; Judg 13:22; Isa 6:1–7). When the high priest entered the †Holy of Holies, he had to first hide himself by filling the room with a cloud of incense (Lev 16:13). Jesus, in contrast, has appeared before the face of God so that we too might see God's face (see 1 John 3:2). But there is a similarity: the high priest entered the Holy of Holies bearing the names of the twelve tribes of Israel on the breastplate over his heart, interceding for them (Exod 28:29); Jesus, likewise, is in heaven not for his own sake but **on our behalf**, as our advocate who "lives forever to make intercession" for us (7:25; see Rom 8:34; 1 John 2:1).

Second, Christ's sacrifice, once accomplished, has fully and forever achieved **9:25–26** its purpose. He did not need to **offer himself repeatedly, as the high priest enters each year into the sanctuary**. The annual repetition of the Day of Atonement ritual only proved that it had no lasting effect. The †levitical high priest brought **blood that is not his own**, the blood of unwitting animal victims. But Christ brought his own human blood, blood that is of infinite value because it was poured out in love by the incarnate Son. If his offering had had to be repeated—if it did not atone finally and definitively for all the sins ever committed in all human history, past and future—then **he would have had to suffer repeatedly from the foundation of the world**. But because he is the all-holy Son, his offering is all-sufficient to atone for the sins of the world.

---

32. This interpretation is confirmed by Hebrews' use of "heavenly" to describe the calling of Christians (3:1), the gift they have tasted, probably alluding to the Eucharist (6:4), and the homeland that they await (11:16).

Christ's Life and Death on Our Behalf

To be a mature human being is to be other-oriented, to be willing to give of oneself for the sake of others. The principle of self-giving appears in countless ways in ordinary life, especially in family relationships but also in professions like that of doctor, firefighter, soldier, or teacher, where people sacrificially give of themselves, thereby setting others free to be themselves. As Vatican Council II taught, "Man, who is the only creature on earth which God willed for itself, cannot fully find himself except through a sincere gift of himself."[a] The supreme example of self-giving for others is Christ, who, as the New Testament affirms in countless ways, offered his life on our behalf. He tasted death "for everyone" (Heb 2:9); he shed his blood "for many" (Mark 14:24); he died "for all" (2 Cor 5:14; 1 Tim 2:6), for the people (John 11:50; 18:14), for each person (Rom 14:15), "for me" (Gal 2:20), "for you" (Luke 22:19; 1 Cor 11:24), "for us" (Rom 5:8; 2 Cor 5:21; Gal 3:13; 1 Thess 5:10), for the Church (Eph 5:25), "for the sheep" (John 10:11–15). Other texts use wording that can be translated "in place of" (Mark 10:45), "for the sake of" (1 Cor 8:11), or "on behalf of" (Matt 26:28).

Christ's action on our behalf did not end with his cross and resurrection. Having laid down his life for us, he now continues to stand in the presence of God "on our behalf" (Heb 9:24), living to make intercession for us (7:25).

a. *Gaudium et Spes* (Joy and Hope) 22.

Christ's coming in the flesh and his †paschal mystery are the turning point of history: **now once for all he has appeared at the end of the ages**, or "the consummation of the ages," the conclusion to all that had gone before. The old era of waiting and longing is over; the final days have begun (1:2). The same idea is expressed in 1 Peter 1:20: Christ "was known before the foundation of the world but revealed in the final time for you." He came to deal with sin once and for all: **to take away sin by his sacrifice**. The Greek word for "take away" could also be translated "annul" or "do away with." Christ's sacrifice not only provided forgiveness for past sins but also abolished sin itself. As John the Baptist announced, Jesus is "the Lamb of God, who takes away the sin of the world" (John 1:29).

9:27   Having been born into the fallen race of Adam, Jesus shares fully in our humanity (2:14), including the most inescapable fact of human existence: death. His sacrificial death cannot be repeated for the simple reason that **human beings die once**, and with that the choices and actions that determine their destiny are concluded. After death comes **the judgment**: God's full evaluation

Christs Once-for-All Sacrifice

LIVING TRADITION

The Catechism explains how Christ's passion and resurrection is the once-for-all event that affects all human history.

> His Paschal mystery is a real event that occurred in our history, but it is unique: all other historical events happen once, and then they pass away, swallowed up in the past. The Paschal mystery of Christ, by contrast, cannot remain only in the past, because by his death he destroyed death, and all that Christ is—all that he did and suffered for all men—participates in the divine eternity, and so transcends all times while being made present in them all. The event of the Cross and Resurrection *abides* and draws everything toward life. (1085)

of all that a person has done in life, whether for good or evil.[33] Having been raised from the dead, Jesus cannot die again; he has risen to "a life that cannot be destroyed" (7:16; see Rom 6:9).

As human beings die once, **so also Christ** was **offered once to take away** **9:28** **the sins of many**. The verb "take away" could also be translated "bear," in the sense of carrying a burden: Christ "bore our sins in his body upon the cross" (1 Pet 2:24). This wording alludes to the Suffering Servant in Isaiah, who "surrendered himself to death" and "bore the sins of many" (Isa 53:12). "Many" does not imply a limitation, as if Christ died only for some people, but rather is a biblical way of expressing a vast number. The same Isaiah passage says, "the LORD laid upon him / the guilt of us *all*" (Isa 53:6, emphasis added).[34] As the New Testament repeatedly affirms, Christ died *for all* (Heb 2:9; 2 Cor 5:14–15; 1 Tim 2:6), though not all receive this gift (see Heb 2:3; 10:26–27).

The original readers of Hebrews probably noticed another parallel with the Day of Atonement in verse 28. After entering the Holy of Holies and sprinkling the blood on the †mercy seat, the high priest would reemerge before the eagerly waiting assembly of Israel to announce that atonement had once again been made. The book of Sirach (50:5, 14, 17) says of the high priest on this occasion,

> How splendid he was as he looked out from the tent,
>   as he came from within the veil! . . .
> Once he had completed the service at the altar
>   and arranged the sacrificial hearth for the Most High. . . .

33. Matt 25:31–46; John 5:25–29; Acts 17:31; Rom 2:16; 14:10–12; 1 Cor 3:13; 2 Cor 5:10; Rev 20:12.
34. In a similar way "many" and "all" are synonymous in Rom 5:12–18. See Catechism 605.

> All the people with one accord
>> would fall with face to the ground
> In adoration before the Most High,
>> before the Holy One of Israel.

So too, after entering God's heavenly sanctuary, Christ **will appear a second time**. This is the clearest reference in Hebrews to the †parousia, the coming of Christ in glory at the end of history. This passage has actually mentioned three appearances of Christ. He "appeared at the end of the ages" (v. 26) in his incarnation and earthly life, culminating in his sacrifice on the cross. As 1 Timothy 3:16 says, using the same verb, he "was manifested in the flesh." After rising from the dead, he appeared "before God on our behalf" in the heavenly sanctuary (v. 24). Finally, he will appear again on earth, **not to take away sin but to bring salvation to those who eagerly await him**. As we profess in the Nicene Creed, "He will come again in glory to judge the living and the dead." The Christian attitude toward Christ's coming is not fear and dread but eager longing "as we await the blessed hope, the appearance of the glory of the great God and of our savior Jesus Christ" (Titus 2:13), the day when we will finally see him face-to-face (1 Cor 13:12).[35]

Reflection and Application (9:23–28)

How does Christ's death on the cross two thousand years ago relate to us? How does *his* death save *me*? Christ's passion on our behalf is a mystery of such unfathomable depth and richness that every attempt to explain it will always fall short. It is like a brilliant white light too dazzling to behold directly; we need a prism refracting it into a spectrum of colors that we are able to see. This is what the New Testament provides by giving us a wealth of images that help illuminate the mystery, though without exhausting it: redemption, expiation, justification, sacrifice, reconciliation, liberation, ransom, salvation, and new creation, to name only a few.

Hebrews 9:23–28 offers a kind of tapestry of such images, each of which helps explain how Christ's death saves us. He is the sacrificial victim whose blood purifies the living temple, the Church, as the blood of animals purified the ancient tabernacle on †Yom Kippur (9:23). He is the high priest who appears before God in heaven on our behalf, forever interceding for us (9:24–26). He is the Suffering Servant, who, as Isaiah prophesied, offered himself to take away

35. See Rom 8:23; 1 Cor 1:7; 2 Cor 5:2; Col 3:4; 2 Tim 4:8; 2 Pet 3:12.

the sins of many (9:28). By reflecting on these images and others in Hebrews, we come to see that God did not deal with sin merely by divine fiat, cancelling the debt but leaving the sinner unchanged. Rather, in Christ he entered into the midst of the drama of human sin to annihilate sin and undo its damage from within, as Hebrews will explain further in chapter 10.

We Have Been Sanctified Once and for All

Hebrews 10:1–18

Hebrews 10:1–18 culminates the long section that began with chapter 7, explaining how Christ's work of redemption surpasses and fulfills all that preceded it in the old covenant. Chapter 7 contrasted the †levitical priests with Christ the great high priest. Chapters 8–9 contrasted the old covenant with the new, and the earthly sanctuary with God's true sanctuary in heaven. Finally, 10:1–18 contrasts the repeated animal sacrifices with the once-for-all †sacrifice that proceeded from the free decision of Christ's human will. But here Hebrews takes a further step by explaining the effect of Jesus' sacrifice on the worshipers. Through a meditation on Psalm 40, Hebrews shows that because Christ alone offered God a sacrifice that sprang from the perfect obedience of a human heart, he is able to change the human heart radically and permanently from within. Christ's passion has sanctified his sisters and brothers, whose flesh and blood he shares (see 2:14).

With 10:1–18, the main theological argument of Hebrews comes to its conclusion. The preacher has demonstrated his central insight regarding the priesthood and once-for-all sacrifice of Christ. But as is true throughout the Bible, doctrine is never of purely academic interest. In the remainder of the homily the preacher will show his listeners how to apply this saving truth to their lives.

The Imperfection of the Law (10:1–4)

¹Since the law has only a shadow of the good things to come, and
not the very image of them, it can never make perfect those who come

to worship by the same sacrifices that they offer continually each year. [2]Otherwise, would not the sacrifices have ceased to be offered, since the worshipers, once cleansed, would no longer have had any consciousness of sins? [3]But in those sacrifices there is only a yearly remembrance of sins, [4]for it is impossible that the blood of bulls and goats take away sins.

OT: Lev 16; 23:26–32; Ps 51:12
NT: Luke 22:19; 1 Cor 11:24–25; Col 2:17
Catechism: priesthood of the old covenant, 1539–43; the old covenant prefigures the new, 128–30

Chapter 10, like chapter 9, sets up a contrast with Christ by pointing out a fundamental weakness of the old covenant sacrifices. In 9:1–10 the main weakness was that the tent sanctuary (and later the temple) was only an earthly copy of God's true dwelling place in heaven. Here in 10:1–4 the weakness is that animal sacrifices could never really solve the problem of human sin. Therefore they can never provide the full, uninhibited access to God that is the real aim of worship.[1]

The previous contrast (9:1–10) was "vertical," between the earthly and heav-   **10:1**
enly realms; here Hebrews makes a "horizontal" contrast between stages in salvation history. The author seems to have three stages in view. First, there is the time between Moses and Jesus, the period of **the law**. As already indicated in 8:5 and 9:23–24, that former age with its mortal priests, earthly sanctuary, and multiple sacrifices provided only **a shadow**, or sketch, of the good things God destined for his people. Paul uses almost the same phrase to describe the ritual laws of the †Torah: "These are shadows of things to come; the reality belongs to Christ" (Col 2:17). Christ and the new covenant are the substantive reality; the former things were like silhouettes that dimly revealed the pattern of what was to come. Christ, at the center of history, cast his shadow backward, so to speak, so that God's people could get a glimpse of the future fulfillment, even if blurry and indistinct.

Second, there is the time of grace following the coming of Christ, in which we have **the very image** (Greek *eikōn*) of these good things that the law foreshadowed. "Image" here does not mean merely a copy or reproduction, but rather the "true form of these realities" (RSV), as Christ is the image of God (2 Cor 4:4). As Hebrews said earlier, we have "tasted the heavenly gift and shared in the holy Spirit and tasted the good word of God and the powers of the age to come" (Heb 6:4–5). That is, even now we possess the heavenly realities, though still in sign and symbol and not yet in their fullness.

1. Luke Timothy Johnson, *Hebrews: A Commentary*, New Testament Library (Louisville: Westminster John Knox, 2006), 246.

Finally there is the time of glory (see 2:10) when we will possess **the good things to come** in their fullness, when we are with Christ in the "city . . . that is to come" (13:14).

The old law had its purpose in God's plan, but the coming of Christ makes clear how limited and temporary that purpose was. The law **can never make perfect those who come to worship by the same sacrifices that they offer continually each year**. "Those who come to worship" is literally "those who come near." The goal of worship is to give people access to God, yet as Hebrews already pointed out, the levitical system was intrinsically unable to accomplish this aim. The people could come near—but not too near! "Any unauthorized person who comes near shall be put to death" (Num 3:10; see Heb 12:18–20). Hebrews implies that a sacrifice for sin has truly achieved its goal only if it "perfects" sinners—that is, permanently transforms them from within so they can enter into the holy presence of God. But the very fact that the levitical sacrifices are continually repeated proves that they were powerless to do so (echoing what Hebrews already said in 7:19 and 9:9).

10:2   Verse 2 elaborates this point with a rhetorical question: **Otherwise, would not the sacrifices have ceased to be offered, since the worshipers, once cleansed, would no longer have had any consciousness of sins?** This contrast implies the startling conclusion that the new covenant people of God, those who in fact have been cleansed by the once-for-all sacrifice of Christ, no longer have a consciousness of sins. The Greek word for "consciousness" (*syneidēsis*) is the same word usually translated "conscience" (9:9, 14; 10:22; 13:18). It refers to both the inner awareness of sin and the objective guilt that disqualifies us from drawing near to the holy God—the "evil conscience" mentioned in verse 22 below. To be truly effective, a sacrifice has to provide not just ritual purity but a true cleansing of conscience in both these senses. The implication is that Christ's sacrifice has done so in a way that is "permanently effective and therefore unrepeatable."[2] Jesus' words to Peter in John 13:10 express the same truth in a different way: "Whoever has bathed has no need except to have his feet washed, for he is clean all over."

10:3   **But in those sacrifices there is only a yearly remembrance of sins**.[3] The annual repetition of the †Day of Atonement with its blood rituals, confession of sins over the scapegoat (Lev 16), and fasting (Lev 23:26–32) only showed its ineffectiveness. It reminded the people of their sins without being able to remove those sins.

---

2. F. F. Bruce, *The Epistle to the Hebrews*, rev. ed., New International Commentary on the New Testament (Grand Rapids: Eerdmans, 2012), 236.

3. The NAB has added to this phrase the word "only," which is not present in the Greek.

Moreover, "remembrance" refers not just to human memory but to God's memory. At the heart of the new covenant prophecy in Jeremiah 31 is God's promise, "I will remember their sin no more" (Jer 31:34 RSV)—a promise that could not be fulfilled through the old covenant sacrifices. Hebrews is still reflecting on this prophecy, which was quoted in full at 8:8–12 and will be quoted again at 10:16–17.

In using the word "remembrance" (*anamnēsis*), the author may also be making an implicit comparison with Jesus' words at the Last Supper: "Do this in remembrance of me" (1 Cor 11:24–25; see Luke 22:19). The former sacrifices brought a remembrance of sin, but Jesus' sacrifice is a remembrance of the mercy of God that cleanses us from sin. "The gospel transforms *anamnēsis* from a remembrance of guilt to a remembrance of grace!"[4]

For it is impossible that the blood of bulls and goats take away sins. This   **10:4** is the strongest declaration in the entire letter of the futility of the old covenant sacrifices. It seems at first glance to contradict the law of Moses, which states that animal sacrifices do atone for sins (e.g., Lev 4:35; 5:10; 19:22). But as the Old Testament itself teaches, if read carefully, this was a provisional atonement that covered over sin and allowed God's covenant relationship with Israel to continue but did not change the sinner from within. In the next section Hebrews will provide scriptural proof of this assertion with a quotation from Psalm 40.

Christ's Perfect Fulfillment of God's Will (10:5–10)

---

[5]**For this reason, when he came into the world, he said:**

> **"Sacrifice and offering you did not desire,**
>   **but a body you prepared for me;**
> [6]**holocausts and sin offerings you took no delight in.**
> [7]**Then I said, 'As is written of me in the scroll,**
>   **Behold, I come to do your will, O God.'"**

[8]**First he says, "Sacrifices and offerings, holocausts and sin offerings, you neither desired nor delighted in." These are offered according to the law.** [9]**Then he says, "Behold, I come to do your will." He takes away the first to establish the second.** [10]**By this "will," we have been consecrated through the offering of the body of Jesus Christ once for all.**

OT: Exod 24:7; Ps 40:7–9; 50:9–13

---

4. Philip Edgcumbe Hughes, *A Commentary on the Epistle to the Hebrews* (Grand Rapids: Eerdmans, 1977), 394.

NT: Matt 26:24, 53–54; Mark 14:49; Luke 24:25–26, 44; John 1:9–11; 6:38
Catechism: Christ came to do God's will, 461–63, 606–7, 2824–25; Christ's once-for-all sacrifice, 613–14, 1085
Lectionary: Fourth Sunday of Advent (Year C); Solemnity of the Annunciation of the Lord

This section provides the positive side of the contrast that was set up in verses 1–4, explaining why Christ's †sacrifice *is* able to take away sins. Again, as in 4:1–11 and 7:11–19, the author calls on a psalm to show that the old covenant testifies to its own incompleteness, pointing beyond itself to the greater things God destined for his people. In this case, Psalm 40 provides the perfect capstone to what Hebrews has been saying about the superiority of Christ's sacrifice. It illuminates the deepest reason why Christ's death is efficacious, fulfilling the new covenant promise of Jeremiah 31. Along with Psalms 2, 8, 95, and 110, this psalm is one of the strategic pillars of the whole letter.

10:5   **For this reason**—that is, because of the inefficacy of the former sacrifices (v. 4)—Christ spoke the words of Psalm 40 **when he came into the world**, that is, when he became incarnate. What does the preacher mean by saying that Jesus spoke this psalm? He means that this psalm, traditionally ascribed to David—and inspired by the Holy Spirit (see 3:7; 10:15)—expresses what was in the heart of the Messiah, the son of David, in becoming man to fulfill the Father's plan of salvation. Christ himself speaks only twice in Hebrews, both times quoting the Psalms: in 2:12 declaring his total solidarity with human beings (quoting Ps 22:23), and here at 10:5–6 declaring his total submission to the will of the Father. Together they perfectly express his role as mediator between God and man.[5]

Hebrews quotes verses 7–9 of the psalm, which have an A-B-A-B pattern, with A expressing what God *does not* desire and B expressing what God *does* desire:

A Sacrifice and offering you did not desire
  B but a body you prepared for me;
A holocausts and sin offerings you took no delight in . . .
  B Behold, I come to do your will, O God.

God does not desire **sacrifice and offering**. This seems to contradict the †Torah (especially Lev 1–16 and Num 15; 28), where God prescribes numerous animal sacrifices, libations of wine, and offerings of grain, oil, and incense that his people are to offer. But a certain tension runs throughout the Old Testament. God does require sacrifices in †atonement for sin and as expressions of thanksgiving, yet apart from a disposition of love and obedience, these

5. See Johnson, *Hebrews*, 250; Harold W. Attridge, *Essays on John and Hebrews*, Wissenschaftliche Untersuchungen zum Neuen Testament 264 (Tübingen: Mohr Siebeck, 2010), 320–30.

sacrifices are worthless, even odious to God (see sidebar, "Obedience Is Better Than Sacrifice," p. 200). The sacrifices are meant to be a visible sign of what God truly desires: the people's covenant fidelity. When that is lacking, they are mere hypocrisy, an insult to God.

The next line of Psalm 40 says literally in Hebrew, "ears you dug for me," meaning, "you gave me the ability to hear and obey your voice." But our author quotes from the †Septuagint version: **but a body you prepared for me.**[6] The Septuagint translators may have had Genesis 2:7 in mind, where God forms Adam from the dust of the earth, and may have wished to emphasize that obedience to God is a matter of not only one's ears but one's whole bodily life. But Hebrews sees this translation as beautifully apt to allude to Christ's incarnation. On the lips of the eternal Son, "you prepared a body for me" means "you gave me a flesh-and-blood human existence, a presence within the world and human history, so that I would have something to offer to you." Christ assumed human flesh because the flesh can suffer; the flesh can die. His own human, bodily existence became the sacrifice laid on the altar out of love for the Father and for us.

The next lines of the psalm repeat the same thought in different words: **holocausts and sin offerings you took no delight in.** All these external rites were incapable of bringing about the relationship that God desires with his people. Instead, the next words reveal what God does delight in, the true expression of covenant love: **Then I said, "As is written of me in the scroll, / Behold, I come to do your will, O God."** For the psalmist, "the scroll" probably referred to the book of the law, given through Moses on Mount Sinai, which God's people pledged to obey (Exod 24:7).[7] But these words are perfectly suited to express the attitude of Christ, who "came" in his incarnation (see John 1:9–11) and whose whole life was centered on doing the will of the Father. "I came down from heaven not to do my own will but the will of the one who sent me" (John 6:38; see Heb 5:8). As Jesus often declares in the Gospels, he submitted to the Father's plan as it was written of him in the Scriptures (Matt 26:24, 53–54; Mark 14:49; Luke 24:25–26, 44), even though that plan included rejection, unbearable pain, and death. His passion would have had no saving value apart from this free decision of his human will.

Hebrews repeats the key lines of the psalm to comment on their meaning. **First** Christ **says,** in the words of the psalm, **Sacrifices and offerings, holocausts and sin offerings, you neither desired nor delighted in.** This combines the

10:6–7

10:8

---

6. Some later manuscripts of the †Septuagint have "ears" in Ps 40:7 (a more literal translation of the Hebrew), but the earliest manuscripts have "body."

7. The phrase in Heb 10:7, as in Ps 40:7 (both in the Hebrew and in the Septuagint), is literally "the scroll of the book." The same word for "book" (*biblion*) appears in Exod 24:7 LXX.

St. Athanasius on the Incarnation

St. Athanasius, a fourth-century bishop and father of the Church, explains why the Son of God assumed a human body:

> As the Word who is immortal and the Father's Son, it was impossible for him to die. For this reason, therefore, he assumed a body capable of dying, so that, belonging to the Word who is above all, in dying it might become a sufficient exchange for all, and . . . by the grace of the resurrection put an end to corruption for all. It was by surrendering to death the body he had taken, as an offering and sacrifice free from every stain, that he at once abolished death for his human brethren. . . . For the solidarity of mankind is such that, by virtue of the Word's indwelling in a single human body, the corruption that goes with death has lost its power over all.
>
> You know how it is when some great king enters a large city and dwells in one of its houses; because of his dwelling in that single house, the whole city is honored, and enemies and robbers cease to molest it. So it is with the King of all: he has come into our country and dwelt in one body amid the many, and as a result the plans of the enemy against mankind have been foiled and the corruption of death, which formerly held them in its power, has simply ceased to be. For the human race would have perished utterly had not the Lord and Savior of all, the Son of God, come among us to put an end to death.[a]

a. Athanasius, *On the Incarnation* 9 (translation adapted from Athanasius, *On the Incarnation: The Treatise De incarnatione Verbi Dei*, trans. and ed. a religious of CSMV [Crestwood, NY: St. Vladimir's Seminary Press, 1993], 35).

two A parts of the quotation: God does not want these offerings themselves, but rather what they stand for. **These are offered according to the law**. [†]Holocausts and sin offerings were two of the specific kinds of sacrifices prescribed in the Torah (Lev 1; 4). A holocaust was particularly costly because it was the only kind of sacrifice in which the animal was entirely burnt on the altar, going up to God in the form of smoke. But as Psalm 50:9–14 declares, the eternal creator God has no need for burnt animals.

> I will not take a bullock from your house,
>   or he-goats from your folds.
> For every animal of the forest is mine,
>   beasts by the thousands on my mountains. . . .
> Do I eat the flesh of bulls
>   or drink the blood of he-goats?
> Offer praise as your sacrifice to God;
>   fulfill your vows to the Most High.

The sacrifice that God desires is, rather, a human heart that is utterly devoted **10:9**
to him and expresses that devotion in concrete acts of obedience. Thus Christ
says (summing up the B parts of the psalm quotation), **Behold, I come to do
your will**. Christ came into the world to accomplish the Father's will: "I always
do what is pleasing to him" (John 8:29). The Gospels record that on the night
before he died Jesus freely embraced this will, even in the face of inconceiv-
able suffering: "Abba, Father, all things are possible to you. Take this cup away
from me, but not what I will but what you will" (Mark 14:36). God's will was
fulfilled by Jesus' laying down his life on the cross, an offering of infinitely
greater value than animal sacrifices because it was given freely in love. As Paul
writes, "Christ loved us and handed himself over for us as a sacrificial offering
to God for a fragrant aroma" (Eph 5:2). Thus God **takes away the first**—the
whole sacrificial system of the law of Moses, which is now obsolete—in order
to establish the second, the salvation of the human race through the one all-
sufficient sacrifice of Christ.

The concluding sentence sums up the insight of this section: **By this "will"** **10:10**
(God's will, mentioned in v. 9), **we have been consecrated through the offering of the body of Jesus Christ once for all**. The Greek word for "consecrated"
(*hagiazō*) would be better translated as "sanctified" or "made holy," since here it
connotes not only being "set apart" for God but coming to share in God's own
holiness.[8] The reason Jesus' sacrifice has power to sanctify is that he offered no
mere substitute but himself, his own human life wholly given over in love. His
sacrifice therefore transforms human nature from within; it heals the self-will,
pride, rebellion, and unbelief that have deeply wounded human nature ever
since the fall. Hebrews emphatically declares that this sanctification is already
an accomplished fact, "once for all." Christ's passion is the fulcrum of human
history, the act that has definitively reconciled humanity to God and given access to God's own holiness. Yet paradoxically, Hebrews will say in verse 14 that
we who believe in Christ "are being sanctified"; the accomplished fact must be
personally appropriated and lived by every believer (see also 12:10, 14).

Reflection and Application (10:1–10)

Doing the Father's will. The reflection on Psalm 40 in Hebrews 10:1–10 is not
only an inspired account of what was in Christ's heart as he laid down his life
for us but also an incentive for us to imitate him. To do the Father's will is far

8. The verb means "consecrate" or set apart for God in some texts (e.g., Exod 13:2, 12; 19:23; 28:38,
41 LXX), but in the New Testament it more often means "cause to share in God's holiness."

Obedience Is Better Than Sacrifice

BIBLICAL BACKGROUND

A constant theme throughout the Old Testament is that sacrifices, even those commanded by God, have no value apart from what they are meant to express: full obedience to God's will. The classic expression of this theme is in 1 Samuel 15, where King Saul flagrantly disobeyed God's command but thought that he could still buy God's favor with lavish sacrifices. The prophet Samuel rebuked him (1 Sam 15:22):

> Does the Lord delight in burnt offerings and sacrifices
>   as much as in obedience to the Lord's command?
> Obedience is better than sacrifice,
>   to listen, better than the fat of rams.

The point is not that sacrifices are, in themselves, displeasing to God (see Ps 50:8), but that no sacrifice can substitute for the loving submission of heart and will that God truly desires. David expresses this awareness in Psalm 51, a psalm of contrition:

> For you take no delight in sacrifice;
>   were I to give a burnt offering, you would not be pleased.
> The sacrifice acceptable to God is a broken spirit;
>   a broken and contrite heart, O God, you will not despise.
>   (Ps 51:18–19 RSV-CE)

The theme becomes even more pronounced in the writings of the prophets, in which God rails against the false piety of those who offer perfunctory sacrifices, all the while practicing injustice and corruption.

> I hate, I despise your feasts,
>   I take no pleasure in your solemnities.
> Even though you bring me your burnt offerings and grain offerings
>   I will not accept them;

more than keeping the commandments; it is a personal relationship in which we seek to hear the Father's voice and carry out his *specific* will for our life, day by day. To do so is to discover that the Father's will leads to profound peace and joy, whereas resisting his will and clinging to our own brings unhappiness, disorder, and even chaos. In the Our Father we pray, "Thy kingdom come, thy will be done on earth as it is in heaven." To do the Father's will, in union with Christ, is to live in his kingdom and make heaven present on earth.

The Sacrament of Reconciliation. We have been sanctified "through the offering of the body of Jesus Christ once for all" (Heb 10:10). For Catholics,

Your stall-fed communion offerings,
  I will not look upon them.
Take away from me
  your noisy songs;
The melodies of your harps,
  I will not listen to them.
Rather let justice surge like waters,
  and righteousness like an unfailing stream.
                    (Amos 5:21–24)

What do I care for the multitude of your sacrifices?
  says the LORD.
I have had enough of whole-burnt rams
  and fat of fatlings;
In the blood of calves, lambs, and goats
  I find no pleasure.
When you come to appear before me,
  who asks these things of you?
Trample my courts no more!
  To bring offerings is useless;
  incense is an abomination to me.
          (Isa 1:11–13; see Mic 6:6–8)

In the Gospels Jesus quotes Hosea's version of this theme (Matt 9:13; 12:7):

For it is loyalty that I desire, not sacrifice,
  and knowledge of God rather than burnt offerings.
                    (Hosea 6:6)

Hebrews expresses this theme by means of Psalm 40:7–9 to show how Christ's death on the cross, in a marvelously unexpected way, fulfills at one and the same time the requirement of blood sacrifice (Heb 9:22) and the free obedience of the human heart that God desires.

Hebrews' strong emphasis on the once-for-all sufficiency of Christ's sacrifice raises a question: What is the role of the Sacrament of Reconciliation, in which forgiveness is offered repeatedly?

A proper understanding of confession depends on first appreciating the full power of baptism. Through baptism, a believer is joined to Christ in his death and resurrection. Christ's once-for-all sacrifice is actualized in one's life. The human heart is radically changed: the old self is put to death, the person is born anew as a son or daughter of God, all sins are forgiven, and there is a new power within to live and act under the prompting of the Holy Spirit. Sin

---

The Moment of Christ's Immolation Is the Beginning of Our Own Lives

LIVING
TRADITION

An ancient Easter homily explains how we enter into the new life that Jesus has conferred on us through his sacrifice. We receive this divine life *objectively* in baptism, but *subjectively* when we become aware of it and begin to live by it.

> Christ, the sacrifice that was offered up for us, is the father of the world to come. He puts an end to our former life, and through the regenerating waters of baptism in which we imitate his death and resurrection, he gives us the beginning of a new life. Knowing that Christ is the Passover lamb who was sacrificed for us should make us regard the moment of his sacrifice as the beginning of our own lives. As far as we are concerned, Christ's sacrifice on our behalf takes place when we become aware of this grace and understand the life conferred on us by this sacrifice. Having once understood it, we should enter upon this new life with all eagerness and never return to the old one, which is now at an end. As Scripture says: We have died to sin—how then can we continue to live in it?[a]

a. Pseudo-Chrysostom, Easter homily (translation adapted from the Office of Readings for Monday of the second week of Easter).

---

no longer holds dominion. As the Catechism says, "One must appreciate the magnitude of the gift God has given us in the sacraments of Christian initiation in order to grasp the degree to which *sin is excluded for him who has 'put on Christ'* (Gal 3:27)" (Catechism 1425, emphasis added). Sin is no longer normal for the Christian (see 1 John 3:6, 9).

However, certain effects of the fall remain in the baptized, including the inclination to sin. The whole Christian life is a journey toward deeper conversion as we strive to put off sinful patterns and more fully appropriate the grace of baptism. Thus Christ has provided the Sacrament of Reconciliation so that whenever we sin, we can be forgiven and our broken communion with God and neighbor healed (see 1 John 1:7–9). St. Thomas Aquinas offers a helpful analogy: "In the life of the body a man is sometimes sick, and unless he takes medicine, he will die. Even so in the spiritual life a man is sick on account of sin. For that reason he needs medicine so that he may be restored to health; and this grace is bestowed in the Sacrament of Penance."[9] The sacraments are ways in which the unlimited grace and power flowing from Christ's sacrifice are imparted to

---

9. Thomas Aquinas, *Catechetical Lectures, The Apostles' Creed*, article 10.

us; thus they provide the true cleansing from sin that the †Day of Atonement sacrifices could only dimly foreshadow. As often as we become aware of our sins, then, we are to be even more aware of the unlimited cleansing power of the blood of Christ and avail ourselves of that power through faith, repentance, and the sacraments. The Christian life is meant to be characterized by the freedom and intimacy with God that comes from having a clean conscience.

God's People Made Perfect Forever (10:11–18)

¹¹Every priest stands daily at his ministry, offering frequently those same sacrifices that can never take away sins. ¹²But this one offered one sacrifice for sins, and took his seat forever at the right hand of God; ¹³now he waits until his enemies are made his footstool. ¹⁴For by one offering he has made perfect forever those who are being consecrated. ¹⁵The holy Spirit also testifies to us, for after saying:

¹⁶"This is the covenant I will establish with them after those days,
        says the Lord:
    'I will put my laws in their hearts,
    and I will write them upon their minds,'"

¹⁷he also says:

    "Their sins and their evildoing
    I will remember no more."

¹⁸Where there is forgiveness of these, there is no longer offering for sin.

OT: Num 28:3–8; Ps 110:1; Isa 43:25; Jer 31:33–34
NT: John 19:30; 1 Cor 15:26–27; 2 Cor 3:3
Catechism: priesthood of the old covenant, 1539–43; definitive sanctification in Christ, 1540

With this section the central argument of the letter, all about Jesus' priesthood and sacrifice (7:1–10:18), finally comes to a close. The preacher had warned, "About this we have much to say" (5:11), and indeed he did! Here he recapitulates one last time the contrast between Jesus and the old covenant priesthood, neatly weaving in his key themes from Psalm 110 and Jeremiah 31. Following this section he will return to a pastoral exhortation for the first time since chapter 6, once again helping his listeners make the passage from doctrine to life.

Verses 11–13 restate the contrast already made between the futile, endlessly **10:11–13** repeated †levitical sacrifices and the once-for-all sacrifice of Christ, but with two new accents. First, the focus here is on the **daily** duties of the ordinary levitical priests rather than on the yearly †Day of Atonement rite performed by the high priest alone. Besides their duties inside the tabernacle (see comments on 9:6), the priests had to offer the twice-daily sacrifice on the altar outdoors. As detailed in Numbers 28:3–8, this daily sacrifice, called the †*tamid*, or perpetual burnt offering, consisted of an unblemished lamb every morning and every evening, along with a drink offering of wine and a grain offering of flour mixed with oil (see sidebar, "How Jesus Fulfills the Sacrifices of the Old Covenant," p. 152). Like the Day of Atonement sacrifices, **those same sacrifices** offered twice daily **can never take away sins**. But for readers of Hebrews, the mention of the *tamid*—a sacrifice of a lamb with grain and wine—calls to mind what it prefigured: the true Lamb of God, Jesus, who does take away sins, and who gave us the memorial of his sacrifice in the form of bread and wine (John 1:29; Luke 22:19–20).

Second, Hebrews draws a striking contrast between the levitical priest, who **stands** at his ministry (see Deut 18:7), and Jesus, who **took his seat forever**. This echoes what was said in the prologue: "When he had accomplished purification from sins, / he took his seat at the right hand of the Majesty on high" (1:3). In the ancient world, standing was the ordinary posture for work. To sit down meant that one had finished one's labor and could rest. That Jesus "took his seat forever" is a vivid way of affirming that his work is finished (see John 19:30); his **one sacrifice for sins** is complete, its goal accomplished.[10] This does not mean, however, that the risen Jesus is inactive; rather, his being seated means he is enthroned and reigning as king. Moreover, as Hebrews already mentioned, he continues to communicate to his brothers and sisters the grace and power of his victory: he "lives forever to make intercession for them" and so is able to "help those who are being tested" (7:25; 2:18; see 4:16).

That Jesus is seated **at the right hand of God** alludes once more to the psalm that runs like a golden thread through Hebrews, Psalm 110. Hebrews quoted these opening words of the psalm at 1:13 and then gave an extended meditation on the priesthood according to the order of Melchizedek, from Psalm 110:4, in chapters 5–8. Here the words of the psalm affirm the awesome and triumphant power of the Messiah. His victory is complete; all that remains is for every hostile power in the universe to be made subject to him: **now he waits until his enemies are made his footstool**. Paul quotes this same line in 1 Corinthians 15:26–27, adding, "The last enemy to be destroyed is death."

---

10. Different passages in the New Testament depict the exalted Lord in various postures that express who he is and what he does. In Mark 16:20 the risen Lord is *working* with his disciples as they preach the gospel; in Acts 7:56 Stephen sees the Son of Man *standing* at the right hand of God; in Rev 3:21 Christ is *sitting* on the heavenly throne; in Rev 5:6 the Lamb is *standing* in the midst of the throne.

The Double Wall Removed

St. Nicholas Cabasilas, a fourteenth-century Orthodox mystic and spiritual writer, explains the twofold effect of Christ's incarnation and passion:

> Between us and the Spirit of God there was a double wall of separation: that of nature and that of the will corrupted by evil; the former was taken away by the Savior with his incarnation, and the latter with his crucifixion, since the cross destroyed sin. Both obstacles being removed, nothing further can impede the outpouring of the Holy Spirit on all flesh.[a]

In speaking of human nature as a "wall of separation," Cabasilas does not mean our nature is evil, but that it is finite and therefore, in itself, radically incapable of the divine life for which God created us. By becoming one of us, dying, and rising from the dead, Christ not only dealt with sin but also made human nature capable of sharing in God's own nature.

a. *The Life in Christ* 3.1.

The present age of the Church is thus the time of both the "already" and the "not yet." Jesus has definitively conquered Satan by his death and resurrection (John 16:11; Col 2:15), but as Hebrews said earlier, "At present we do not see 'all things subject to him'" (2:8).

10:14   Several times Hebrews has used the term "make perfect" (*teleioō*) to express how Jesus was transformed by his passion (2:10; 5:9; 7:28). Here the author reiterates what Christ's sacrifice has accomplished by using this term in a new way, now applied to his people! **For by one offering he has made perfect forever those who are being consecrated.**[11] This suggests that the same three senses of *teleioō* that applied to Jesus (see comments on 2:10) also apply to those "many children" he is bringing to glory: they are made holy and pleasing to God, they are made sharers in divine life, and they are ordained priests of the new covenant. This is confirmed in verse 19 below, where Hebrews declares that believers have a privilege surpassing that of the high priest of Israel: we can freely enter the sanctuary, the presence of the living God—and not only one day a year but always.[12]

11. The Gospel of John uses the same two verbs "sanctify" and "perfect" to express what Jesus' passion will accomplish: "For their sake I sanctify myself, so that they also may be sanctified in truth . . . that they may be perfected in unity" (John 17:19, 23, literal translation).

12. See Albert Vanhoye, *A Different Priest: The Letter to the Hebrews*, trans. Leo Arnold, Series Rhetorica Semitica (Miami: Convivium, 2011), 313.

Fig. 14. Fresco of the crucifixion from around 740–750 AD, in Santa Maria Antiqua, Rome

The whole life of Christians is now qualified to be a priestly life, in which all our actions and sufferings can be offered as "a sacrifice of praise" that is pleasing to God (13:15–16; see 12:28–29).

Hebrews refers to believers with the same term "consecrated" (or better, "made holy") as in verse 10, but now with a different verb tense. Whereas verse 10 said we *have been made holy* (an already existing state), verse 14 says we *are being made holy* (an ongoing action). Again there is the paradox of the "already" and the "not yet." The sacrifice of Christ truly has uprooted sin from the human heart and cleansed the conscience of all who believe in him. But believers must appropriate and live this new freedom. We are like a paralyzed person whose nervous system has been restored through surgery: the disability has been removed, but now the person must learn to use muscles unaccustomed to walking. In Christ, believers have a new ability to resist sin and obey God from the heart, which now has to be exercised. As Paul says, "You also must consider yourselves dead to sin and alive to God in Christ Jesus. Let not sin therefore reign in your mortal bodies" (Rom 6:11–12 RSV).

10:15   The section concludes with a reprise of the new covenant passage of Jeremiah 31, which was already quoted in full at 8:8–12. Here it is abbreviated and slightly rearranged. But first there is another reminder that Scripture ultimately comes from **the holy Spirit**, and therefore has divine authority (see 2 Tim 3:16; 2 Pet 1:21). Scripture is a living word that speaks to us in the present. In this case, the Spirit **testifies to us** that what the preacher has just said about the perfect †atonement accomplished by Christ is true.

10:16   Hebrews focuses on the two primary blessings of **the covenant** that **the Lord** said he would **establish** with his people in the final **days** (Jer 31:33–34): he would deal with both the *root of sin* in the human heart and the *guilt of sins* already committed. First, there is the law written on the heart: **I will put my**

laws in their hearts, / and I will write them upon their minds. God's law—the law that is summed up in love of God and neighbor (Matt 22:37–40)—is no longer something externally imposed, a limitation on our freedom against which we chafe and sometimes rebel. Instead it springs from the depths of the heart. Jesus, who was "made perfect" by his sufferings (5:9; see 2:10), has passed on that perfection to all those who belong to him (10:14). There is a new capacity in the human mind to understand God's ways (see 1 Cor 2:12–16) and in the human heart to respond to God with filial love, trust, and obedience.

Second, God promises, **Their sins and their evildoing / I will remember no more**. For God to "remember" sins means to punish them, to let people bear their destructive consequences (see Hosea 9:9). Conversely, for God to "forget" sins means to blot them out forever (Ps 25:7; Isa 43:25). And if God has forgotten them, they are no longer to burden and condemn the human conscience, which has been fully cleansed by the blood of Christ "from dead works to worship the living God" (Heb 9:14).

10:17

The last sentence of the central section of Hebrews (7:1–10:18) has a tone of ringing finality: **Where there is forgiveness of these, there is no longer offering for sin**. To attempt to add to Christ's †atonement by reverting to the ineffectual animal sacrifices of the temple (2:1–3; 3:12), as the original readers of Hebrews may have been tempted to do, would be an insult to God.[13] Paul speaks in a similarly strong way: "You are separated from Christ, you who are trying to be justified by law; you have fallen from grace" (Gal 5:4). God has provided the all-sufficient remedy for sin and the means of access to himself. All that remains is for us to lay hold of those blessings, which the author of Hebrews will now ardently exhort us to do.

10:18

Reflection and Application (10:11–18)

Ever since Christ's death, "there is no longer offering for sin" (Heb 10:18). The letter's emphatic insistence on the absolute finality of Christ's sacrifice (see also 7:27; 9:12, 26; 10:10, 12, 14, 18) raises a question similar to the one on the Sacrament of Reconciliation discussed at 10:5–10 above: If Christ's sacrifice has accomplished our redemption "once for all," why do we continue to offer this sacrifice at every Mass? Is this a return to the old covenant pattern of futile, endlessly repeated sacrifices?

13. See Thomas Aquinas, *Commentary on the Epistle to the Hebrews*, trans. Chrysostom Baer (South Bend, IN: St. Augustine's Press, 2006), 209.

The Catechism explains that when Jesus instructed his apostles, "Do this in memory of me" (Luke 22:19; 1 Cor 11:24), he established the Eucharist as the memorial of his †paschal mystery. And a memorial in the biblical sense is not just to remember what God has accomplished.

> The Eucharist is thus a sacrifice because it *re-presents* (makes present) the sacrifice of the cross, because it is its *memorial* and because it *applies* its fruit. . . .
>
> The sacrifice of Christ and the sacrifice of the Eucharist are *one single sacrifice*: "The victim is one and the same: the same now offers through the ministry of priests, who then offered himself on the cross; only the manner of offering is different." "And since in this divine sacrifice which is celebrated in the Mass, the same Christ who offered himself once in a bloody manner on the altar of the cross is contained and is offered in an unbloody manner . . . this sacrifice is truly propitiatory."[14]

Thus it is not that Jesus is sacrificed again and again, but rather in every †liturgy his once-for-all sacrifice on the cross is made present to us; or better, we are made present to the cross and receive the unlimited grace and power that flow from it.

---

14. Catechism 1366–67, quoting the Council of Trent, *Doctrina de ss. Missae sacrificio*, c. 2; cf. Heb 9:14, 27.

Confidence to Enter God's Presence

Hebrews 10:19–39

The preacher has now completed the heart of the homily, his brilliant demonstration of Christ's high priesthood and once-for-all †sacrifice for our salvation. As we have come to expect, he now returns to exhortation, showing listeners how to apply that truth to life. For Hebrews, as for the whole New Testament, doctrine (teaching about who God is and what he has done for us) always has priority over exhortation (an appeal to good conduct). God's gift is first; the moral life is second. Living as disciples of Christ is possible only because of and in response to God's prior grace.

Here the exhortation is in three parts: two messages of strong encouragement (vv. 19–25 and 32–39) and, sandwiched between them, a severe warning (vv. 26–31). Christians are to take advantage of the stupendous privilege we have been given: access to the very throne of God! At the same time we must remain steadfast in our fidelity to Christ and avoid the very real danger of †apostasy.

Confidence to Approach God (10:19–25)

[19]Therefore, brothers, since through the blood of Jesus we have confidence of entrance into the sanctuary [20]by the new and living way he opened for us through the veil, that is, his flesh, [21]and since we have "a great priest over the house of God," [22]let us approach with a sincere heart and in absolute trust, with our hearts sprinkled clean from an evil conscience and our bodies washed in pure water. [23]Let us hold unwaveringly to our confession that gives us hope, for he who made the promise

is trustworthy. [24]We must consider how to rouse one another to love and good works. [25]We should not stay away from our assembly, as is the custom of some, but encourage one another, and this all the more as you see the day drawing near.

OT: Exod 29:4, 21; Num 3:10; Lev 16:2; Ezek 36:25–27
NT: Mark 15:38; John 14:6; Acts 2:20; 20:7; 22:16; Eph 3:12; 1 Pet 2:5
Catechism: confidence, 2778; faith, hope, and love, 1812–29; baptism as washing, 1215; the Sunday liturgy, 1166–67, 2177–79

The first message of encouragement is a single long sentence, calling the hearers to a threefold response to Christ's work of redemption: "let us approach . . . ," "let us hold fast . . . ," "let us consider . . ." (vv. 22, 23, 24, literal translation).[1] This response is rooted in the three theological virtues so often found together in Paul's Letters: faith (translated as "trust" in v. 22), hope (v. 23), and love (v. 24).[2] Hebrews is not speaking only of individual Christian living. The whole section is also a call to worship—to join our brothers and sisters in the †liturgy of the new covenant, the fulfillment of the old, in which we enter confidently into the very throne room of God, cleansed by the blood of Christ.

10:19–20   Addressing his readers affectionately as **brothers** (a term inclusive of women and men), the author briefly recaps all the benefits of Christ's sacrifice explained in chapters 7–10 above. First, **through the blood of Jesus we have confidence of entrance into the sanctuary**. Paul makes a similar declaration: in Christ "we have boldness and confidence of access through our faith in him" (Eph 3:12 RSV; see 1 John 3:21; 5:14). The Greek word for "confidence" (*parrēsia*) means an attitude of †boldness or fearless freedom. The Catechism calls it "straightforward simplicity, filial trust, joyous assurance, humble boldness, the certainty of being loved" (2778).[3] This confidence of entrance, a result of being purified by the blood of Jesus (Heb 9:14), is in striking contrast to the restricted access to God's sanctuary in the old covenant. We have a doubly greater privilege than even the high priest had: we can freely enter not the earthly †Holy of Holies—a mere copy and shadow—but God's true presence in heaven (9:24), and not only once a year but at all times.

We enter God's presence not on our own but **by the new and living way** Christ **opened for us** through his passion and resurrection. The "way" is nothing other than himself. As Jesus declares in the Gospel of John: "I am the way and the

---

1. The NAB obscures the parallelism by changing the verb tense and mood. In Greek the verbs "approach," "hold," and "consider" in verses 22–24 are hortatory subjunctives; the verbs in verse 25 are participles (literally, "not staying away . . . encouraging one another").

2. For other instances of the triad, see 1 Cor 13:13; Col 1:4–5; 1 Thess 1:3; 5:8; Heb 6:10–12.

3. Cf. Eph 3:12; Heb 3:6; 4:16; 1 John 2:28; 3:21; 5:14.

truth and the life. No one comes to the Father except through me" (John 14:6). Having been perfected in his own human nature, he has become the pioneer who leads all humanity into the very life of the Trinity (Heb 2:10). The "new and living way" is thus equivalent to the "greater and more perfect tabernacle" (9:11), which is his own risen body.[4] It is "new" because until Christ came no one had ever gone into God's presence: "the way into the sanctuary had not yet been revealed" (9:8; see John 3:13). It is "living" because Jesus is alive forever: "death no longer has power over him" (Rom 6:9; see Heb 7:16).

As the high priest entered the Holy of Holies through the veil, so believers enter into God's presence **through the veil, that is**, the **flesh** of Christ. What does Hebrews mean by equating the veil with Christ's flesh? The sense may be that, as God was present but hidden behind the veil of the †tabernacle, so in Christ God is present but veiled by his human nature. But in Jesus' death on the cross—paradoxically, at the moment of greatest hiddenness—God's innermost mystery is finally and fully revealed. The Synoptic Gospels report that at that moment "the veil of the sanctuary was torn in two from top to bottom" (Matt 27:51; Mark 15:38; Luke 23:45). Christ's humanity, torn and crushed by human sin, opened the way into the very heart of God. We enter "through the veil of his flesh" in the sense that from now on, we have access to the Father through him, the crucified one who is exalted at God's right hand.

The mention of Jesus' blood and flesh in verses 19–20 is probably an allusion to the Eucharist, especially as verse 22 will allude to baptism. These sacraments are the way believers become united with Christ in his †paschal mystery. As mentioned above, the whole section is an invitation to join the Christian community in worship, which takes place supremely in the Eucharistic liturgy.

10:21 The next phrase succinctly sums up everything Hebrews has said about Christ's priesthood: **we have "a great priest over the house of God."**[5] As God's Son and our brother, he is the *great* priest who alone can unite us with God (see 4:14). The "house of God" is the community of God's people, the Church, over whom Jesus is "faithful as a son" (3:6).

10:22 Verses 22–25 present a threefold summons to respond to what God has done for us.

First, **let us approach** God. This was already said in 4:16, but now that Hebrews has fully explained Christ's priesthood and atoning sacrifice, we have all the more reason to approach confidently. In Scripture the verb "approach" is

4. Albert Vanhoye, *A Different Priest: The Letter to the Hebrews*, trans. Leo Arnold, Series Rhetorica Semitica (Miami: Convivium, 2011), 327.

5. It is unclear why the NAB puts this phrase in quotation marks, since it is not a direct quote from Scripture, although it may be alluding to Zech 6:11–12 †LXX.

an idiom for "come to worship" (as in Lev 9:5; Heb 12:22); thus we are invited to draw near to God not only in personal faith but also in the public worship of the Christian community. Again there is a dramatic contrast with the old covenant tabernacle, approach to which was forbidden on pain of death: "Any unauthorized person who comes near shall be put to death" (Num 3:10; see Lev 16:2). It is not that God has changed, but that God's people, having been made holy by Christ's blood, are now capable of being in his holy presence. So we are to approach **with a sincere heart and in absolute trust**. A "sincere heart" (literally, a "true heart") is a heart that unreservedly embraces God's will, as in Jeremiah's new covenant promise quoted above (8:10; Jer 31:33). It is the opposite of the "evil and unfaithful heart" of the exodus generation (3:12). The Greek for "absolute trust" could be translated as "full assurance of faith" (RSV)—that is, unwavering faith in Christ and his all-sufficient work of redemption.

That disposition flows from the transformation that takes place in baptism. Through that sacrament **our bodies** are **washed in pure water** as an outward sign and instrument of the inner cleansing accomplished by Christ (see 9:14): **our hearts** are **sprinkled clean from an evil conscience**. Other New Testament passages similarly speak of baptism as a washing (Acts 22:16; Eph 5:26; Titus 3:5). In the old covenant, priests were *washed* with water and *sprinkled* with blood as part of the ordination rite (Exod 29:4, 21). By saying here that believers are washed and sprinkled, Hebrews is again implying that Christ's sacrifice has qualified the whole people of God to be a holy priesthood, to offer sacrifices pleasing to him (13:15–16; 1 Pet 2:5).[6] The mention of "pure water" and "sprinkling" also brings to mind God's promise in Ezekiel, building on the new covenant promise in Jeremiah 31: "I will sprinkle clean water over you to make you clean; from all your impurities . . . I will cleanse you. . . . I will give you a new heart, and a new spirit I will put within you. . . . I will put my spirit within you so that you walk in my statutes, observe my ordinances, and keep them" (Ezek 36:25–27).

10:23   Second, **Let us hold unwaveringly to our confession that gives us hope** (literally, "the confession of our hope"). As in 4:14, Hebrews reminds us that Christianity is not just a matter of believing in the heart, but of confessing with the lips—that is, publicly bearing witness to Christ (see Matt 10:32–33; Rom 10:9–10). This may be another allusion to adult baptism, in which new believers publicly confess their faith in Christ (see 1 Tim 6:12). Here Hebrews speaks of hope. Whereas *faith* looks to present unseen realities, *hope* looks forward

---

6. See Peter J. Leithart, "Womb of the World: Baptism and the Priesthood of the New Covenant in Hebrews 10.19–22," *Journal for the Study of the New Testament* 78 (2000): 49–65.

to future realities, the full enjoyment of all the blessings promised by God. Yet hope can be severely tested, battered by the unbelief, mockery, and cynicism of the surrounding culture, or by painful events or simply the busyness of life. The original readers of Hebrews were, like many Christians today, wavering in their commitment to Christ and at risk of drifting away (2:1). So the preacher reiterates again and again that the Christian life is about holding fast to the hope that arises from faith, all the way to the finish line (3:6, 14; 6:11, 18). If our hope were in ourselves, it would be precarious to say the least, but the ground for our hope is God, and **he who made the promise is trustworthy**, as Abraham and Sarah discovered (11:11).[7]

Finally, the third appeal is to **consider how to rouse** (or "stir up," RSV; "spur," NIV; "provoke," NRSV) **one another to love and good works**. Faith and hope give birth to love, and love is expressed concretely in good works (see Gal 5:13–14; 6:10; Titus 3:8). As the whole New Testament insists, the Christian life is inescapably communal. There is no such thing as a private Christian. Every member is responsible for supporting, building up, encouraging, consoling, and calling others to holiness (see Rom 15:1–2; Gal 6:1–2; 1 Thess 5:11). Nor is it enough to do good works for others; love also includes stirring up others, by word and example, to do good works themselves. The real source of these good deeds, as Paul declares, is not ourselves but God, who has prepared these good works "in advance, that we should live in them" (Eph 2:10). **10:24**

So then, **we should not stay away from our assembly, as is the custom of some**. This appeal probably refers especially to the Eucharistic liturgy, which from apostolic times was celebrated every Sunday: "On the first day of the week . . . we gathered to break bread" (Acts 20:7). But it also refers to Christian fellowship in general: meeting together for prayer (Acts 12:12; 1 Tim 2:8), for hearing the word of God (1 Tim 4:13), for meals (Acts 2:46), and for service (1 Pet 4:10). That the author has to insist on Christian fellowship is evidence that some of the original readers were tending toward an individualistic Christianity, seeing no need to gather with others. They may have had what seemed a good reason: not just indifference, but the threat of persecution (see vv. 32–34), which made showing up at liturgies risky. But such neglect of Christian fellowship is a symptom of selfishness and lack of love, since it is only by meeting together that we are able to **encourage one another**. If some church members start absenting themselves in tough times, others can easily become discouraged. One's claimed love for God is an illusion if it is not expressed concretely in love for others (1 John 4:7–21), especially other members of the local church (Gal **10:25**

7. See also 1 Cor 1:9; 10:13; 2 Cor 1:18; 1 Thess 5:24; 2 Tim 2:13.

The Early Christian Liturgy

BIBLICAL
BACKGROUND

A fascinating piece of historical evidence regarding the early Christian liturgy is a letter written around AD 110 by Pliny the Younger, the pagan governor of Bithynia (what is today northwest Turkey), to the emperor Trajan, asking for advice on how to deal with a new sect known as the Christians. He writes,

> They regularly assembled on a certain day before daybreak. They sang in alternate verses a hymn to Christ, as to a god, and bound themselves by a solemn oath not to do any wicked deeds but to abstain from theft, robbery, adultery, breach of faith, and embezzlement of property entrusted to them. After this it was their custom to separate, and then to come together again to partake of a meal, but an ordinary and innocent one.[a]

Pliny's report provides indirect evidence of the radical moral transformation that many Christians underwent following their conversion from paganism.

a. Pliny the Younger, *Letters* 10.96–97.

6:10). Moreover, failing to gather with other believers for worship and fellowship is the surest way to weaken one's own faith, and even to court the danger of apostasy, as the next section warns (vv. 26–31).

The need for such mutual encouragement is **all the more as you see the day drawing near**. "The day" is the day of the Lord promised by the prophets, the day of judgment, when God would act decisively to reward the righteous and punish the wicked (Isa 13:6–9; Ezek 30:3; Joel 1:15). In the New Testament it is also called "the great and splendid day of the Lord" (Acts 2:20), when Christ will return in glory to bring about his everlasting kingdom.[8] Jesus taught that his followers must live in vigilant readiness for that day (Mark 13:32–37).

Reflection and Application (10:19–25)

A large number of people today identify themselves as "spiritual but not religious." Or in a variation of this claim, "I'm a follower of Jesus, just not the church." Such statements are often a form of protest against organized religion with its doctrines, authority structures, and rules governing moral behavior and church attendance. Spirituality, it is claimed, has to do instead with compassion, tolerance, and authenticity to oneself. One problem with these claims, however,

8. See Matt 7:22; 10:15; 1 Cor 3:13; 1 Thess 5:2; 2 Thess 2:2; Heb 9:28; 12:26–28; 2 Pet 3:10, 12.

is that they do not at all square with God's word. From the beginning to the end of the Bible, God reveals that his plan is to form a *people* who relate to him in and through their relationships with one another. In the New Testament God further reveals that that people is a family, united with one another in bonds of love as brothers and sisters, children of one heavenly Father. As Hebrews teaches, this family of God includes specific doctrines (13:9); structures of leadership (13:17); a moral code (13:4–5); and obligations regarding church attendance (10:25), prayer (13:15, 18–19), and works of charity (13:16).

Besides being unbiblical, the idea of religionless spirituality conflicts with our embodied and social nature as human beings. Ultimately, we are not satisfied by spiritual ideas alone; we instinctively join with others to *act on* our beliefs and build a way of life based on them. Human experience confirms what Scripture teaches: "It is not good for the man to be alone" (Gen 2:18). God created us as intrinsically communal beings who cannot find fulfillment except in making a gift of self to others.[9] It is by living in communion with others, both in individual families and in the great family of the Church, that we learn to receive and give love and so prepare to share in God's own life and love forever. In contrast, the impulse toward spirituality without religion, which is rooted in the individualistic mentality of contemporary Western culture, has contributed to profound alienation and a breakdown of relationships in families, communities, and nations.

For those who are acutely aware of faults and failings in the Church and are tempted to absent themselves, Hebrews offers a challenge: Show up. Exhort and encourage your brothers and sisters. Be an example of faith and steadfast endurance. Pray fervently for others, especially leaders. Draw near to the throne of God with confident trust, asking for grace and mercy in time of need. If the family of God has problems, be a part of the solution.

A Call to Endurance (10:26–31)

---

²⁶**If we sin deliberately after receiving knowledge of the truth, there no longer remains sacrifice for sins** ²⁷**but a fearful prospect of judgment and a flaming fire that is going to consume the adversaries.** ²⁸**Anyone who rejects the law of Moses is put to death without pity on the testimony of two or three witnesses.** ²⁹**Do you not think that a much worse punishment is due the one who has contempt for the Son of God, considers unclean**

9. See Vatican Council II, *Gaudium et Spes* 24.

the covenant-blood by which he was consecrated, and insults the spirit of grace? [30]We know the one who said:

"Vengeance is mine; I will repay,"

and again:

"The Lord will judge his people."

[31]It is a fearful thing to fall into the hands of the living God.

OT: Deut 13:9; 17:6; 32:35–36; Isa 26:11
NT: Matt 25:41; Mark 3:29; John 3:18–19; 1 Cor 11:27–29; 2 Pet 2:20–21
Catechism: final judgment, 678–79, 1038–41; hell, 1033–37

The exhortation not to skip meetings of the church in verse 25 leads into a much more severe warning against what could follow from such negligence (similar to 6:4–8). This section is, along with some sayings of Jesus himself (e.g., Matt 13:41–42; 25:41; Luke 19:27), among the sternest passages in the entire New Testament. It is a warning not against sin in general but against the grave sin of †apostasy—turning away from faith in Christ (see 3:12). Hebrews has just spent several chapters unveiling the all-sufficient †atonement won by Christ on the cross, the unlimited grace and mercy available to us, the unfathomable privilege we have of entering into God's very presence. The point is this: If you reject that offer of mercy, what do you have left?

10:26   Verse 26 brings up the danger already mentioned repeatedly (2:1–3; 3:12; 4:1–11; 6:4–8): that of abandoning Christian faith and the holy way of life that goes with it. To receive **knowledge of the truth** is to come to know the true God and his gracious offer of salvation—that is, to become a Christian (1 Tim 2:4; 2 Tim 2:25; 3:7). To **sin deliberately** is to turn away from that truth. Often the reason for apostasy is that a person does not like the constraints that God's law puts on his or her conduct. As Paul's letter to Timothy puts it, "The time is coming when people will not endure sound teaching, but having itching ears they will accumulate for themselves teachers to suit their own likings, and will turn away from listening to the truth" (2 Tim 4:3–4 RSV; see Prov 2:13).

Hebrews refers to those who "sin deliberately," in contrast to those who are merely "ignorant and erring" (5:2). This distinction is rooted in the law of Moses, which specified that only sins committed "inadvertently" (i.e., unwittingly or unwillingly) could be atoned for by sacrifice (Lev 4:2–3; Num 15:22–31).[10] Anyone who sinned "defiantly," with full knowledge and will, was to be "cut off from

---

10. See comments on 9:7.

among the people" (Num 15:30). The once-for-all sacrifice of Jesus, in contrast, atones for *all* sins (Heb 8:12; 9:26; see 1 John 1:7; 2:1). But if a person deliberately rejects that sacrifice, **there no longer remains sacrifice for sins**. To refuse what God has provided for our salvation is to be left with no means of salvation at all. The qualifier "deliberately" indicates that Hebrews is referring not to those who go astray out of ignorance but rather to those who freely choose to return to unbelief, whether by slow drift or by a onetime decision (see 3:12; 4:11; 6:6; 12:15). The Second Letter of Peter expresses an equally sober warning: "If [believers], having escaped the defilements of the world through the knowledge of [our] Lord and savior Jesus Christ, again become entangled and overcome by them, their last condition is worse than their first. For it would have been better for them not to have known the way of righteousness than after knowing it to turn back" (2 Pet 2:20–21).

To deny Christ is to choose judgment. If we spurn the prospect of salvation **10:27** that God has offered, all we have is **a fearful** (or "dreadful," NJB) **prospect of judgment**. The New Testament writings, like the Old, teach that every human being is faced with a stark choice. For those who choose good, God promises life and salvation; for those who choose evil, severe judgment is in store.[11] Although things may look murky or ambiguous in this life, there is no middle ground between these two ultimate destinies. Hebrews describes the judgment as **a flaming fire that is going to consume the adversaries**, alluding to Isaiah 26:11: "Let the fire prepared for your enemies consume them." Scripture often uses the imagery of fire to describe the end-time judgment of the wicked. In the Gospel of Matthew Jesus teaches, "Every tree that does not bear good fruit will be cut down and thrown into the fire" (Matt 7:19); evildoers will be thrown "into the fiery furnace, where there will be wailing and grinding of teeth" (Matt 13:42; see Matt 25:41).[12] Hebrews calls those who have abandoned the faith "adversaries," implying they have joined the ranks of Christ's "enemies," who will be placed under his feet (10:13). History bears out the fact that those who were once believers but later reject the faith sometimes do become Christ's most implacable enemies.

Hebrews underlines the gravity of the warning with an argument that reasons **10:28** from the lesser to the greater (†*qal wahomer*), similar to the one used in 2:1–4. The law of Moses meted out the extreme penalty for the gravest sin, that of breaking the covenant with God by worshiping idols. **Anyone who rejects the law of**

---

11. See Deut 30:15–20; Ps 145:20; Matt 13:40–43; 16:27; 25:31–46; Mark 16:16; John 3:16–19; Rom 2:5–8; Gal 6:8; Rev 22:12.

12. See also Matt 3:10–12; 5:22; John 15:6; 2 Thess 1:8; James 5:3; 2 Pet 3:7; Rev 17:16; 18:8; 20:15; 21:8.

The Catechism on Hell

LIVING TRADITION

Concerning the "prospect of judgment," the Catechism teaches (1036–37),

> The affirmations of Sacred Scripture and the teachings of the Church on the subject of hell are a *call to the responsibility* incumbent upon man to make use of his freedom in view of his eternal destiny. They are at the same time an urgent *call to conversion*: "Enter by the narrow gate; for the gate is wide and the way is easy, that leads to destruction, and those who enter by it are many. For the gate is narrow and the way is hard, that leads to life, and those who find it are few" (Matt 7:13–14). . . .
>
> God predestines no one to go to hell (Council of Orange II; Council of Trent); for this, a willful turning away from God (a mortal sin) is necessary, and persistence in it until the end. In the Eucharistic liturgy and in the daily prayers of her faithful, the Church implores the mercy of God, who does not want "any to perish, but all to come to repentance" (2 Pet 3:9).

Moses is put to death without pity on the testimony of two or three witnesses. Deuteronomy 17:6 stipulates that such capital punishment can be carried out only when the facts are confirmed by two or three witnesses; Deuteronomy 13:9 directs that the offender must not be spared out of pity.[13] The Greek word for "rejects" is a strong word that can mean "violate" or "nullify." The New Testament often uses it for those who refuse to listen to Christ's teaching and thereby reject "the plan of God for themselves" (Luke 7:30) as well as rejecting Christ, the Father who sent him, and the Holy Spirit (Luke 10:16; John 12:48; 1 Thess 4:8).

10:29   Hebrews reasons from that severe punishment in the old covenant, where God's people had only the promises and not their fulfillment (11:39), to the far higher stakes involved in the new covenant, now that God has provided the all-sufficient remedy for sin. The argument is in the form of a rhetorical question: **Do you not think that a much worse punishment is due . . . ?** The offenders are described in three ways that make it clear that Hebrews has in mind not repentant sinners but those who are obstinate and unrepentant in their apostasy.[14]

First, such a person **has contempt for** (literally, "tramples underfoot") **the Son of God,** treating with disdain the one who is most worthy of honor, the

13. Biblical passages that mandate capital punishment, like this one, need to be interpreted in light of the whole canon of Scripture and subsequent Tradition, keeping in mind the fact that God's revelation was given progressively over many centuries; thus the Old Testament books "contain matters imperfect and provisional" (Catechism 122; *Dei Verbum* 15). For Catholic teaching on capital punishment, see Catechism 2267.

14. See Vanhoye, *A Different Priest*, 328.

one who sustains the whole universe and who, after giving up his life for us, was exalted at God's right hand (1:3).

Second, such a person also dishonors Christ's work of redemption: he **considers unclean the covenant-blood by which he was consecrated** (or "sanctified"). This phrase has some shock value. The covenant-blood is Christ's blood shed on the cross in love for us, which unites us to God in the new and eternal covenant, and which we receive in the Eucharist (see Luke 22:20). To consider it "unclean" (literally, "profane") is to count it worthless.

Third, such a person **insults the spirit of grace**, the Holy Spirit, who applies to our lives the divine grace poured out through Christ's passion and resurrection. The meaning is close to Jesus' admonition, "Whoever blasphemes against the holy Spirit will never have forgiveness, but is guilty of an everlasting sin" (Mark 3:29). To "insult" (or "outrage," NRSV) the Holy Spirit is to refuse the Holy Spirit's inner summons to conversion, willfully rejecting the mercy and grace that are available from "the throne of grace" (4:16). It is to choose darkness rather than light, a lie rather than the truth revealed by God, condemnation rather than eternal life (John 3:18–19; Rom 1:25; Acts 13:46).

10:30 The solemn warning is given even more weight with two quotations from Deuteronomy, recalling the unfaithful exodus generation that was the topic of Hebrews 3–4. Since **we know** the God whose word this is, no one can claim ignorance as an excuse. The quotations are from Moses' farewell address, in which he reminds the Israelites of God's kindness and fidelity and warns them of the horrific consequences of apostasy. First God says, **Vengeance is mine; I will repay**;[15] then in the next verse, **The Lord will judge his people** (Deut 32:35–36). In context, both statements are an assurance that no one will ultimately get away with evil, whether oppressive foreign powers or Israelites who break faith with the Lord. The Greek word for "judge," like the Hebrew word that lies behind it, could also be translated "vindicate" (as in Ps 135:14 RSV), since the act of judgment by which God requites his enemies is at the same time his vindication of his faithful people.

10:31 The final statement is stark: **It is a fearful thing to fall into the hands of the living God**. This does not mean that God is unmerciful. As David affirms, it is better to fall into God's hands than into human hands: "Let us fall into the hand of God, whose mercy is great, rather than into human hands" (2 Sam

---

15. The wording is slightly different from both the Hebrew and Septuagint versions of Deut 32:35, but is nearly identical to Paul's citation of this passage in Rom 12:19. The wording may be based on an alternative Hebrew text.

24:14; see Sir 2:18). In order to receive an abundance of mercy and forgiveness from him, all one needs to do is ask with a sincere heart (Heb 4:16). But with the Lord, one cannot play games, make up excuses, or hide behind masks. "The living God" is a biblical phrase that emphasizes the abyss of difference between the true God and inert, man-made idols (see Jer 10:1–16). The living God sees into the depths of the human heart and holds his creatures accountable (Heb 4:12).

Reflection and Application (10:26–31)

Hebrews teaches, as does the whole New Testament, that on the last day every person will stand before the Lord Christ to be judged according to his or her deeds. The judgment will bring to light what each person has chosen and done in this life. C. S. Lewis, in the last book of the Chronicles of Narnia series, gives an imaginative description of the judgment. As the world ends, each creature approaches the lion Aslan, a figure of Christ:

> The creatures came rushing on, their eyes brighter and brighter as they drew nearer and nearer. . . . But as they came right up to Aslan one or other of two things happened to each of them. They all looked straight in his face, I don't think they had any choice about that. And when some looked, the expression of their faces changed terribly—it was fear and hatred. . . . And all the creatures who looked at Aslan in that way swerved to their right, his left, and disappeared into his huge black shadow. . . . I don't know what became of them. But the others looked in the face of Aslan and loved him, though some of them were very frightened at the same time. And all these came in at the Door, in on Aslan's right.[16]

Remember Your Early Fervor (10:32–39)

[32]Remember the days past when, after you had been enlightened, you endured a great contest of suffering. [33]At times you were publicly exposed to abuse and affliction; at other times you associated yourselves with those so treated. [34]You even joined in the sufferings of those in prison and joyfully accepted the confiscation of your property, knowing that you had a better and lasting possession. [35]Therefore, do not throw away your confidence; it will have great recompense. [36]You need endurance to do the will of God and receive what he has promised.

16. C. S. Lewis, *The Last Battle* (New York: HarperCollins, 1982), 751.

³⁷"For, after just a brief moment,
    he who is to come shall come;
    he shall not delay.
³⁸But my just one shall live by faith,
    and if he draws back I take no pleasure in him."

³⁹We are not among those who draw back and perish, but among those who have faith and will possess life.

OT: Isa 26:20; Hab 2:3–4

NT: Matt 25:36; Luke 17:33; 21:19; 1 Cor 12:26; 2 Cor 4:17; Rev 2:4–5

Catechism: baptism as enlightenment, 1216; persecution for faith, 769, 1808, 1816; the second coming, 673–77

Lectionary: Heb 10:32–36: Common of Martyrs

Skilled pastor that he is, the author of Hebrews knows that after the dire warnings of verses 26–31 it is time to return to words of encouragement and consolation. This third part of the exhortation (following vv. 19–25, 26–31) is in the form of praise for their fervor in the early days of their Christian conversion and a call to return to that fervor.

Like other books of the New Testament (Gal 3:1–4; 1 Thess 1:5–6; Rev **10:32** 2:4–5; 3:3), Hebrews exhorts readers to **remember** the grace-filled time when they first came to faith in Christ. Calling to mind that original experience of grace can be a powerful source of encouragement and spiritual strength as the years take their toll. The term **enlightened** is probably a specific reference to baptism, when Christ illumined their minds with the truth of the gospel (6:4; see John 1:9; Eph 5:14).[17] For many in those early generations—as for many today—becoming a Christian led predictably to social ostracism, antipathy, and ridicule. So too the addressees of this letter **endured a great contest of suffering**. The Greek word for "contest" (*athlēsis*, root of the English word "athlete") suggests the idea of the Christian life as an athletic competition, a favorite metaphor of Paul (see 1 Cor 9:25–27; 1 Tim 4:7–8; 2 Tim 2:5) that Hebrews will also develop in 12:1–13. One of the essential qualities of an athlete is endurance (see v. 36), and in fact these early believers did stay the course, despite their suffering.

Their hardships took various forms. **At times** they **were publicly exposed to** **10:33** **abuse and affliction**. That they were "publicly exposed" (Greek *theatrizō*, related to the English word "theater") suggests that they were subjected to public shaming in a culture that was extremely sensitive to matters of honor and shame. Paul

---

17. In the early Church baptism was often described as "enlightenment." See Catechism 1216.

uses a form of the same word to describe his own apostolic sufferings: "God has exhibited us apostles as the last of all, like people sentenced to death, since we have become a spectacle [*theatron*] to the world" (1 Cor 4:9). The Greek word for "abuse" could be translated "insult" or "reproach" and can refer to any kind of verbal abuse, like that which Christ bore (13:13). "Afflictions" may refer to physical abuse, like the thirty-nine lashes that Paul endured five times (2 Cor 11:24), or other forms of persecution (see Acts 14:19–22).

Even in times of relative reprieve, they **associated** themselves **with those so treated**. That is, they were willing to publicly identify with other Christians who were being targeted, even at risk to their own safety.

10:34   They **even joined in the sufferings of those in prison**. For the early Church, bearing witness to Christ often meant getting thrown into prison. Peter and other apostles were repeatedly imprisoned in Jerusalem (Acts 4:3; 5:18; 12:4); Paul, prior to his conversion, imprisoned many Christians (Acts 8:3), and then after his conversion he himself was jailed in Philippi, Jerusalem, Caesarea, Rome, and other cities. The NAB aptly translates the Greek verb *sympatheō* as "joined in the sufferings" because it means much more than "sympathize" as in "feel sorry for." It is not just a sentiment, but rather an active sharing in the afflictions of others, just as Jesus "sympathizes with our weaknesses" by experiencing them himself (4:15). Paul taught that if one member of the body of Christ suffers, all members "suffer with it" (*sympaschō*, 1 Cor 12:26). One concrete way to express this solidarity with incarcerated Christians is to visit them and minister to their needs, as Jesus taught: "I was . . . in prison and you visited me" (Matt 25:35–36). For Paul, such prison visits from his fellow Christians were a source of great consolation (Phil 2:25–30; Philem 13).

They also **joyfully accepted the confiscation of** their **property**. The Greek word for "confiscation" suggests violent seizure or plundering, perhaps by hostile neighbors with tacit approval from public authorities, or perhaps by the authorities themselves. The seized property may have included their homes, financial assets, and personal possessions. Yet amazingly, they bore such outrageous violations of their rights with joy—the paradoxical Christian response to suffering for the name of Jesus (see sidebar, "Joy in Suffering for the Name of Jesus"). Their joy was founded on the secure knowledge that comes from faith: **knowing that you had a better and lasting possession**. Their confidence in the heavenly homeland promised by God (11:16) was so secure that they did not become dispirited by the loss of earthly treasure (see Matt 6:20). They knew that "this momentary light affliction is producing for us an eternal weight of glory beyond all comparison" (2 Cor 4:17).

Joy in Suffering for the Name of Jesus

BIBLICAL BACKGROUND

One of the most remarkable and countercultural qualities of the early Christians—one that astounded observers and drew many to faith in Christ—was their joyful response to persecution. The early Christians took seriously Jesus' beatitude: "Blessed are you when people hate you, / and when they exclude and insult you, / and denounce your name as evil / on account of the Son of Man. / Rejoice and leap for joy on that day! Behold, your reward will be great in heaven" (Luke 6:22–23). When the apostles were publicly flogged by the Sanhedrin, they left "rejoicing that they had been found worthy to suffer dishonor for the sake of the name" (Acts 5:41). When Paul and Silas were beaten and thrown into jail, they spent the night "praying and singing hymns to God" (Acts 16:25). Paul rejoiced in his sufferings "for the sake of" and for the "glory" of his fellow Christians (Col 1:24; Eph 3:13).

The many New Testament exhortations to rejoice in persecution show that joy is not just an emotion that comes and goes depending on circumstances; it is a grace given by the Holy Spirit (Acts 13:52; Rom 14:17; Gal 5:22; 1 Thess 1:6) and, at the same time, a disposition that we *choose*. "Consider it all joy, my brothers, when you encounter various trials" (James 1:2). "Rejoice to the extent that you share in the sufferings of Christ. . . . If you are insulted for the name of Christ, blessed are you, for the Spirit of glory and of God rests upon you" (1 Pet 4:13–14). "Rejoice in the Lord always. I shall say it again: rejoice!" (Phil 4:4).

10:35

The addressees of the letter, perhaps some twenty or thirty years after their conversion to Christ, are now facing renewed external pressures as well as internal demoralization. **Therefore** they need to be reminded: **do not throw away your confidence**, which is precisely what they are in danger of doing (2:1; 4:1; 10:25). The Greek word for "confidence" (*parrēsia*) can also be translated "†boldness." It is the unbounded trust in God's love that enables us to "draw near to the throne of grace" (4:16 RSV) and enter the sanctuary by the blood of Jesus (10:19). To throw away that confidence would be to drop out of the race within a few yards of the finish line, just as the Israelites lost heart on the very threshold of the promised land and complained, "Would it not be better for us to return to Egypt?" (Num 14:3; see Heb 3:16–18).[18] Nothing could be more foolish, since this confidence **will have great recompense**. The recompense is not an earned reward; it is the incomparably great gift that God has in store for

18. Philip Edgcumbe Hughes, *A Commentary on the Epistle to the Hebrews* (Grand Rapids: Eerdmans, 1977), 432.

his children, which will more than make up for their earthly sufferings. Scripture elsewhere calls it "the riches of his glorious inheritance in the saints" (Eph 1:18 RSV), "the unfading crown of glory" (1 Pet 5:4), and "what has not entered the human heart, / what God has prepared for those who love him" (1 Cor 2:9).

10:36   The virtue they most **need** at the present time is **endurance** (or "persever-ance," NJB). Jesus taught that "whoever endures to the end will be saved" (Matt 10:22) and "by your endurance you will gain your lives" (Luke 21:19 RSV).[19] Christian endurance is not a grim, passive submission to hard circumstances but rather a cheerful steadfastness that turns adversity into a victory for Christ (see Col 1:11, 24; 1 John 5:4). Paul exemplified this endurance: "I have learned, in whatever state I am, to be content. I know how to be abased, and I know how to abound; in any and all circumstances I have learned the secret of fac-ing plenty and hunger, abundance and want" (Phil 4:11–12 RSV). Endurance implies steadfast determination to **do the will of God**, as Jesus did the will of God in undergoing his passion (Heb 10:7, 9). Doing God's will is not a sprint but a marathon, all the way to our last breath (see Rev 2:10). But it will seem short when we finally **receive what he has promised**, the unshakable kingdom (12:28) and the joy of sharing in God's life forever (4:10).

10:37–38   The exhortation concludes with a combined quotation from Isaiah and Ha-bakkuk, two prophets who, like the original readers of Hebrews, lived in times of foreboding and distress.[20] The first phrase, **after just a brief moment**, is from Isaiah 26, a passage already alluded to in verse 27 above. In its context, it was part of a call to endurance in a time of brief but severe calamity: "Go, my people, enter your chambers, / and close the doors behind you; / Hide yourselves for a brief moment, / until the wrath is past" (Isa 26:20).

God similarly called Habakkuk to patient endurance as he awaited a savior whom God would send: "Though he should tarry, wait for him; for he will surely come, and will not delay" (Hab 2:3 †LXX).[21] Hebrews slightly rephrases the quote to point more clearly to Jesus: **he who is to come shall come; / he shall not delay**. "He who is to come" was a Jewish title for the Messiah, as in John the Baptist's question: "Are you the one who is to come, or should we look for another?" (Luke 7:19).[22] God's promise to Habakkuk was initially fulfilled

19. See Luke 8:15; Rom 5:3–4; 8:25; 15:4–5; 1 Thess 1:3; 2 Thess 1:4; 3:5; James 1:3–4; 2 Pet 1:6.

20. Isaiah lived during the Assyrian invasion of the eighth century BC; Habakkuk wrote just before the Babylonian invasion and destruction of the first temple in 586 BC. Hebrews was probably written just before the Roman destruction of the second temple in AD 70.

21. Hebrews 10:37–38 is a free rendering of the Septuagint version of Hab 2:3–4, which itself freely renders the Hebrew. The Hebrew reads, "It will surely come, it will not be late. See, the rash have no integrity; but the just one who is righteous because of faith shall live."

22. See Matt 3:11; 11:3; John 1:9; 3:31; 6:14; 11:27.

in the incarnation of Christ, and it will be fulfilled again for those who eagerly await Christ's second coming (see Heb 9:28). Of course, the two millennia since the first coming might well seem to be a delay, but 2 Peter 3:8–9 reminds us that "with the Lord one day is like a thousand years and a thousand years like one day. The Lord does not delay his promise, as some regard 'delay,' but he is patient with you, not wishing that any should perish but that all should come to repentance."

The age of the Church is a time of waiting, longing, and holding on to God's promises by faith. So the quotation continues, **my just one shall live by faith, / and if he draws back I take no pleasure in him** (Hab 2:4 LXX).[23] For Hebrews, "my just one" is whoever belongs to God and has been justified by the grace of Christ (see Titus 3:7). The foundation of such a person's life must be faith—the virtue that chapter 11 will illustrate at length—in the sense of both *having faith in* God and *being faithful to* God. On the other hand, God is displeased with those who "draw back"—that is, withdraw from faith in Christ or communion with his Church (see vv. 25–26).

Finally, the author again puts himself in solidarity with his readers with a   **10:39** word of encouragement using "we." **We are not among those who draw back and perish**. To "draw back" (*hypostolē*) from faith in Christ is the opposite of the "endurance" (*hypomonē*) called for in verse 36.[24] Retreating from faith in Christ, that is, †apostasy, has the gravest of consequences: it is to put oneself on a path toward destruction (see Phil 3:18–19; 2 Pet 3:7). But as in chapter 6, the author's severe language is not a condemnation of something that has already occurred but rather a warning of danger, since for them he is sure of better things (6:9). He is convinced that they are **among those who have faith and will possess life**. The Greek word for "life" (*psychē*) can also be translated "soul," as in Jesus' paradoxical saying, "Whoever seeks to preserve his life [*psychē*] will lose it, but whoever loses it will save it" (Luke 17:33). Those who remain faithful, even to the point of losing their lives, will keep their lives eternally. The next chapter will elaborate on this point at length with a roll call of biblical heroes of faith.

23. Hebrews has inverted the clauses of Hab 2:4. This verse is a key text for Paul in Rom 1:17; Gal 3:11; he too translates it somewhat freely.

24. Vanhoye, *A Different Priest*, 331.

In Praise of Faith

Hebrews 11:1–40

Faith is the starting point and bedrock of any relationship with God. Yet most of us can easily identify with the distraught father of the epileptic boy in the Gospel, who cried out, "I do believe, help my unbelief!" (Mark 9:24). Faith can falter in times of trial, and it can be feeble even in times of ease. How easy it is to doubt God's love for us, his sovereignty over every circumstance, his ability to work all things for our good (see Rom 8:28). How often Jesus said to his disciples, "You of little faith!"[1]

Hebrews 11 is the Bible's great chapter on faith. It celebrates the blessings that accrue to faith through a long list of faithful men and women of the old covenant who clung to God in all manner of difficult circumstances. Just before this chapter, Hebrews quoted from the prophet Habakkuk: "My just one shall live by faith" (10:38). But what does it mean to live by faith? How does one do so? The answer is chapter 11. Here the preacher shows what faith looks like by providing real-life examples for imitation (see 6:12). Each example illustrates the dynamic quality of faith—faith not as passive belief but as an active, obedient reliance on God, especially in times of trial.

This chapter is a kind of counterpart to Hebrews 3–4, which spoke of the rebellious exodus generation. One might expect that generation, which had seen miracles the world had never seen before, to have the greatest faith. Yet at the very brink of the promised land they became fearful and chose not to trust God; in consequence, they perished in the wilderness. Their example was a warning:

---

1. Matt 6:30; 8:26; 14:31; see 16:8; 17:20.

do not be like them! But that generation was by no means representative of all Israelites. Hebrews 11 balances Hebrews 3–4 by celebrating the great saints and martyrs of the Old Testament.

What Faith Is (11:1–3)

[1]Faith is the realization of what is hoped for and evidence of things not seen. [2]Because of it the ancients were well attested. [3]By faith we understand that the universe was ordered by the word of God, so that what is visible came into being through the invisible.

OT: Gen 1; 2 Macc 7:28; Ps 33:6; Wis 9:1; Sir 42:15
NT: Rom 8:24–25; 2 Cor 5:7; 2 Pet 3:5
Catechism: faith in God the creator, 279–89; Old Testament models of faith, 145–47

At the beginning of the roll call of heroes of faith Hebrews provides a definition of faith that explains what all these biblical saints had in common, so that we can imitate them.

11:1 **Faith is the realization of what is hoped for and evidence of things not seen**. This apparently simple statement has been a perennial challenge to translators (see sidebar, "Defining Faith," p. 228). But it is closely related to the exhortation made so often in Hebrews to "hold fast" our confidence and hope in Christ (3:6, 14; 6:18; 10:23, 35). Faith holds on to both *future* realities ("what is hoped for," the full consummation of God's promises in the heavenly kingdom) and *present invisible* realities ("things not seen," such as Christ reigning in majesty at the Father's right hand). Those who live by faith are so convinced of God's truthfulness that they stake their whole lives on his promises, showing that these promises are real. Thus, in a sense, faith makes future realities present and unseen realities visible.[2]

11:2 **Because of** their faith **the ancients were well attested**. The "ancients" (*presbyteroi*, literally, "elders") are all God's faithful people of the past, including those who predated Israel. God "attested" to these women and men of faith either by having Scripture speak approvingly of them (for instance, in the case of Abel and Enoch), or by doing mighty deeds through them (Samson and David), or by saving them from death (Isaac and Rahab). This declaration of God's approval reappears in verse 39, framing the whole chapter.[3]

---

2. Donald Hagner, *Encountering the Book of Hebrews: An Exposition*, Encountering Biblical Studies (Grand Rapids: Baker Academic, 2002), 142.
3. The NAB translates the same verb *martyreō* as "attested" in verses 2, 4–5 and as "approved" in verse 39.

Defining Faith

The meaning of the famous definition of faith in Hebrews 11:1 depends on how we interpret the key words that the NAB renders "realization" (*hypostasis*) and "evidence" (*elenchos*). The main question is, Should these be understood in a more objective sense, as the *ground* of faith, or in a more subjective sense, as *our inner assurance* of faith? Translators are divided. The KJV, for example, has the objective meaning ("faith is the substance of things hoped for, the evidence of things not seen"), whereas the NIV (1984) opts for the subjective meaning ("faith is being sure of what we hope for and certain of what we do not see").

The literal meaning of *hypostasis* is something that "stands under"—that is, a foundation or substructure. But it had several other connotations in ancient Greek: (1) the real nature or essence of something, such as God's "being" in Hebrews 1:3; (2) a title deed to property, or guarantee of ownership; and (3) confident assurance or conviction, as in Hebrews 3:14 and as Paul seems to use it in 2 Corinthians 9:4; 11:17.[a] All these meanings may be in the background, but the second and third are especially relevant. Faith is our guarantee of ownership of what God has promised, and our confident assurance of those future blessings.

The word *elenchos* appears only here in the New Testament, but in secular Greek it could refer to (1) a reproof, reprimand, or conviction of sin, as the related verb *elenchō* is used in 1 Corinthians 14:24 and 1 Timothy 5:20; (2) a proof or compelling argument; or (3) evidence used in a proof. Here too, the second and third meanings are both possible. Faith provides evidence that what God has said is true, even if it is not yet seen.

The best clue to the meaning is the examples of faith given throughout chapter 11. The biblical saints were utterly convinced of God's faithfulness. Although they did not yet possess what God had promised, they "saw it and greeted it from afar" (11:13). Thus the subjective meaning is appropriate. At the same time, the biblical saints displayed more than simply a subjective feeling of certainty; they acted on what was unseen as if it were seen, giving evidence that it was real.[b] Thus the objective meaning also fits. Their faith was a title deed or guarantee of what was hoped for, though they did not yet possess it.[c] In the same way, the faith of Christians is a title deed to the full realization of these blessings in the city that is to come (13:14).

a. The NAB translates *hypostasis* in Heb 3:14 as "reality" (giving it an objective sense), but most other English translations render it as "confidence" (a subjective sense).
b. Luke Timothy Johnson, *Hebrews: A Commentary*, New Testament Library (Louisville: Westminster John Knox, 2006), 279.
c. Albert Vanhoye, *A Different Priest: The Letter to the Hebrews*, trans. Leo Arnold, Series Rhetorica Semitica (Miami: Convivium, 2011), 342.

Verse 3 is the first of eighteen sentences that begin with the ringing refrain   **11:3** "By faith."[4] This first example of faith is not a specific individual but rather the foundational act of faith that underlies all other acts of faith: belief in God as creator of the universe. The first-person plural "we" accents our close link with the saints of old, with whom we share the same faith in the creator God. **By faith we understand that the universe was ordered by the word of God.** This clearly alludes to the creation account in Genesis 1, where God speaks all things into existence. As the psalm proclaims, "By the Lord's word the heavens were made; / by the breath of his mouth all their host. . . . / For he spoke, and it came to be, / commanded, and it stood in place" (Ps 33:6, 9; see Wis 9:1; Sir 42:15). Here the Greek word for "word" is not *logos*, as in the Gospel of John (1:1–3), but *rhēma*, "speech" or a spoken word, as in Hebrews 1:3: "he upholds the universe by the word of his power" (ESV). God "ordered" the universe in that, as Genesis tells us, God created by arranging all things in proper order: day and night, sky and sea, sea and dry land, and then all the inhabitants of each realm. The Greek word for "universe" is literally "ages," emphasizing that God's word brought into existence not only space but also time.

The next clause is harder to interpret: **so that what is visible came into being through the invisible.** As translated by the NAB, it seems to be saying that God made visible things out of invisible things, perhaps alluding to the formless wasteland that God created at first (Gen 1:1–2; see Wis 11:17). But the sentence could also be translated, "what is seen was not made out of things that are visible" (ESV). In that case, it is affirming the biblical doctrine of creation *ex nihilo*: God brought the world into existence out of nothing. As the heroic mother in 2 Maccabees declared to her son, "Look at the heavens and the earth and see all that is in them; then you will know that God did not make them out of existing things" (2 Macc 7:28). The main point there, as in Hebrews, is that the universe is totally dependent on God for its existence.

Reflection and Application (11:1–3)

A line from the classic movie *Miracle on 34th Street* captures well the idea of faith that is widespread in modern culture: "Faith is believing in things when common sense tells you not to." In this view, faith is a blind leap, believing against reason (like grown-ups believing in Santa Claus). It is the opposite of science, which is based on reason and hard evidence. For those who have this

---

4. This is the literary technique known as anaphora (see, in the introduction, the section "Literary Form and Features").

The Unity of Faith and Reason

The biblical understanding of faith, exemplified in Hebrews 11, recognizes a perfect harmony between faith and reason, since the God who created the visible universe is the same God who reveals himself in Scripture and salvation history. Catholic tradition has always upheld this unity of faith and reason, as was well expressed by Vatican Council I (*Dei Filius* 4):

> Although faith is above reason, nevertheless, between faith and reason no true dissension can ever exist, since the same God who reveals mysteries and infuses faith has bestowed on the human soul the light of reason; moreover, God cannot deny Himself, nor ever contradict truth with truth. . . .
>
> And, not only can faith and reason never be at variance with one another, but they also bring mutual help to each other, since right reasoning demonstrates the basis of faith and, illumined by its light, perfects the knowledge of divine things, while faith frees and protects reason from errors and provides it with manifold knowledge. Wherefore, the Church is so far from objecting to the culture of the human arts and sciences, that it aids and promotes this cultivation in many ways.

St. John Paul II reaffirmed this unity in his encyclical *Faith and Reason* (9):

> Based upon God's testimony and enjoying the supernatural assistance of grace, faith is of an order other than philosophical knowledge which depends upon sense perception and experience and which advances by the light of the intellect alone. Philosophy and the sciences function within the order of natural reason; while faith, enlightened and guided by the Spirit, recognizes in the message of salvation the "fullness of grace and truth" (cf. *Jn* 1:14) which God has willed to reveal in history and definitively through his Son, Jesus Christ (cf. *1 Jn* 5:9; *Jn* 5:31–32).

The idea that faith is at war with science is therefore based on a drastic misunderstanding of either faith or science, or both.

Santa Claus idea of faith, it is no wonder that religious faith appears irrational, even absurd.

But nothing could be further from the biblical understanding of faith. For Hebrews, as for the whole Bible, faith is a way of *knowing*. Faith is not against reason but beyond reason: it perceives that which cannot be perceived with the senses or deduced by logic, but which God has revealed. Faith is a reliable way of knowing because it is founded on the truthfulness of God himself. Understood rightly, it does not deny but rather complements and elevates the knowledge that we gain from human reason and science.

Hebrews also shows us how faith—or, more precisely, *acting* on faith—gives "evidence" of what is unseen. Those who live by faith give persuasive evidence to others that invisible things—such as Jesus reigning in glory (2:9), angels in joyful assembly on Mount Zion (12:22), and an unshakable kingdom (12:28)—are truly real. Faith is a title deed to the glorious inheritance promised us by God. If we live by faith, that inheritance is not merely a document filed away in an attorney's office; it is a reality that we can experience and a vast kingdom that we can explore.

The Faith of Abel, Enoch, and Noah (11:4–7)

⁴**By faith Abel offered to God a sacrifice greater than Cain's. Through this he was attested to be righteous, God bearing witness to his gifts, and through this, though dead, he still speaks. ⁵By faith Enoch was taken up so that he should not see death, and "he was found no more because God had taken him." Before he was taken up, he was attested to have pleased God. ⁶But without faith it is impossible to please him, for anyone who approaches God must believe that he exists and that he rewards those who seek him. ⁷By faith Noah, warned about what was not yet seen, with reverence built an ark for the salvation of his household. Through this he condemned the world and inherited the righteousness that comes through faith.**

OT: Gen 4:1–12; 5:18–24; 6:1–22; Wis 4:10–11; Sir 44:16–18; 49:14
NT: Matt 23:35; 1 Pet 3:20; 2 Pet 2:5; Jude 14–15
Catechism: necessity of faith, 161, 846–48; Abel, 58, 401, 2259, 2569; Enoch, 2569; Noah, 56–58, 845, 1080, 1219

The first three models of faith lived prior to Abraham, the father of the cho- **11:4**
sen people. First is Abel, who **by faith . . . offered to God a sacrifice greater than Cain's.** According to Genesis 4, the two brothers each brought the Lord an offering, and "The LORD looked with favor on Abel and his offering, but on Cain and his offering he did not look with favor" (Gen 4:4–5). This passage raises the obvious question: Why did God accept Abel's offering but not Cain's? Is this a case of arbitrary favoritism? The narrative itself gives us two clues to the answer. First, it states that whereas Cain simply brought produce from the field, Abel brought the *firstborn* lambs of his flock and their fat portions (Gen 4:3–4). This suggests that Abel offered to God what was most valuable, but Cain kept the best for himself, giving God the second best. Second, Genesis tells us that the Lord looked with favor on *Abel* and his offering, but not on *Cain* and

his offering—a signal that there was something wrong in Cain's interior disposition, since God sees into the heart (1 Sam 16:7). God's admonition to Cain confirms this interpretation: "If you act rightly, will you not be accepted?" (Gen 4:7). As a loving Father, God instructs Cain on what is needed for his sacrifice to be acceptable: not merely the material offering, but the right disposition of heart that it is meant to signify.

Genesis does not mention that Abel had faith, but his example (like all the others in Heb 11) sheds light on what faith means. To give God what is most costly, offering from one's substance and not merely one's surplus, is an act of faith. It bears witness that everything we have comes from God and that he will continue to provide for our needs. **Through this** sacrifice Abel **was attested to be righteous, God bearing witness to his gifts**. This sentence uses the verb *martyreō* ("attest, bear witness") twice to emphasize God's approval of Abel. It hints that in fact Abel, victim of the first murder, was in a sense the first martyr. God's acceptance of his offering attested that Abel was righteous (see Matt 23:35, where Jesus calls Abel "righteous"; 1 John 3:12).

Even more, Abel, like several of the other heroes of faith, foreshadows the resurrection of Christ, because **though dead, he still speaks**, which implies that he is in some sense alive. This alludes to Genesis 4:10, where Abel's blood cries out to God from the ground for vindication (Hebrews will later say that the blood of Christ "speaks more eloquently than that of Abel," 12:24). But here the focus is not on Abel's blood but on how his act of faith in offering a costly sacrifice speaks, even today, of the faithfulness of God. Abel's offering of his firstborn lambs can even be seen as a dim foreshadowing of God's own sacrifice of his firstborn Son (1:6).[5]

11:5   Genesis says very little about **Enoch**, the second example of faith in Hebrews 11, other than the mysterious statement that he "walked with God, and he was no longer here, for God took him" (Gen 5:24). To walk with God signifies intimate fellowship, recalling the intimate communion between God and man in Eden before the fall (Gen 3:8). Hebrews quotes the †Septuagint version of Genesis 5:24, which interprets "he walked with God" as "he pleased God": Enoch **was attested to have pleased God**. Hebrews takes this statement as clear evidence of Enoch's **faith**, which God rewarded by delivering him from death.

Although Genesis simply states that Enoch **was found no more because God had taken him**, Hebrews, in accord with Jewish tradition, interprets "taken" (the Greek literally means "transferred") as his being transferred from this

---

5. See Luke Timothy Johnson, *Hebrews: A Commentary*, New Testament Library (Louisville: Westminster John Knox, 2006), 280.

world to God's heavenly realm without experiencing **death**. Sirach says, "No one like Enoch has been created on the earth; / for he was taken up from the earth" (Sir 49:14 RSV; see also Sir 44:16; Wis 4:10–11). The Letter of Jude envisions Enoch as preaching judgment (Jude 14–15). Enoch and Elijah are the only two Old Testament figures who are said to be taken up without dying. As Abel foreshadowed Christ's death and resurrection, Enoch can thus be seen as mysteriously prefiguring Christ's ascension.[6]

Hebrews infers that Enoch had faith from the principle that **without faith it is impossible to please** God. This stark statement makes clear that what God desires from human beings is not merely virtuous living but a relationship with himself. That relationship begins with faith, which puts creatures in a right position of trust and dependence on the creator. **For anyone who approaches God must believe that he exists and that he rewards those who seek him**. To "approach God" is a term Hebrews often uses to refer to worship (see 10:1, 22); more broadly, it refers to living one's whole life in communion with God, as Enoch did. The minimum baseline for a relationship with God is, first, to believe that God exists (see James 2:19). Second, it is to believe that God rewards those who seek him: he answers prayers, delivers, forgives, guides, and blesses. This means that God is personal. He is not an impersonal force but a living God whose providence guides all things and who is passionately interested in the human beings he created. Ultimately, God's reward for those who seek him is nothing other than himself. "When you look for me, you will find me. Yes, when you seek me with all your heart, I will let you find me—oracle of the Lord" (Jer 29:13–14; see Gen 15:1).

11:6

The third example of **faith** is **Noah**, who was **warned about what was not yet seen** and so exemplifies the statement in verse 1 that faith is "evidence of things not seen." In his case, the thing not seen was the coming judgment by flood announced by God (Gen 6:12–22). Noah demonstrates that, as often emphasized in Hebrews, faith is inseparable from obedience. His faith in God's word was expressed in action: he "complied, just as the Lord had commanded" (Gen 7:5) and **with reverence built an ark for the salvation of his household**. According to Jewish tradition, Noah was ridiculed by his contemporaries as he built a boat on dry ground far from the sea.[7] He is thus a classic example of a person of faith living in an age of unbelief and corruption (Gen 6:5, 11–12), when faith entails the willingness to be a fool for God—to stake one's reputation or even one's life on the truthfulness of God's word.

11:7

6. Albert Vanhoye, *A Different Priest: The Letter to the Hebrews*, trans. Leo Arnold, Colección Rhetorica Semitica (Miami: Convivium, 2011), 342.
7. *Sibylline Oracles* 1.171–72.

Fig. 15. Twelfth- to thirteenth-century mosaic of Noah and the ark, St. Mark's Basilica, Venice

Through this Noah **condemned the world,** not directly but in the sense that his act of faith implicitly rebuked the unbelief and wickedness of his generation. Faith, simply by being itself, exposes the darkness and unbelief in the human heart (see John 3:19) and thereby often provokes hostility. Genesis calls Noah "a righteous man and blameless in his generation" (6:9), and Hebrews specifies that it was **the righteousness that comes through faith,** exemplifying the statement quoted above from Habakkuk (10:38). Paul uses similar language to emphasize that righteousness is a gift of God, not a human work.[8] That Noah **inherited** that righteousness links him with all the people of the old and new covenants who are heirs of God's promises (6:17; 11:9).

The Faith of Abraham and Sarah (11:8–12)

> [8]By faith Abraham obeyed when he was called to go out to a place that he was to receive as an inheritance; he went out, not knowing where he was to go. [9]By faith he sojourned in the promised land as in a foreign country, dwelling in tents with Isaac and Jacob, heirs of the same promise; [10]for he was looking forward to the city with foundations, whose architect and maker is God. [11]By faith he received power to generate, even though he was past the normal age—and Sarah herself was sterile—for he thought that the one who had made the promise was trustworthy. [12]So it was that there came forth from one man, himself as good as dead, descendants as numerous as the stars in the sky and as countless as the sands on the seashore.

OT: Gen 12:1–4; 15:4–5; 21:1–3; 22:17
NT: Rom 4:11–12
Catechism: Abraham our father in faith, 145–47
Lectionary: Heb 11:8, 11–12, 17–19: Solemnity of the Holy Family (Year B option)

---

8. Paul speaks of righteousness "of" faith (Rom 4:11, 13), "from" faith (Rom 9:30; see Rom 9:32), "through" faith (Rom 3:22), and "based on" faith (Phil 3:9), though without using the same preposition used in Heb 11:7.

By far the longest section in the roll call of biblical heroes is devoted to Abraham (11:8–22), the father of the chosen people who has become the father of all who believe (see Rom 4:11). It was through Abraham that God initiated the plan of salvation that unfolded through the Old Testament and culminated in the sending of his Son. Abraham is the supreme biblical model of faith, a faith that began with his response to God's call in Genesis 12 and endured through a lifetime of trials. The refrain "by faith" appears seven times in this section, applied to Abraham, his wife Sarah, and their offspring, the †patriarchs of Israel.

Hebrews highlights Abraham's faith in four key stages of his life (vv. 8, 9, 11, 17). First, **by faith Abraham obeyed when he was called to go out to a place that he was to receive as an inheritance**. Genesis 12:1–4 narrates the call of Abraham, emphasizing that it was a sovereign initiative of God. Out of all the peoples of the earth God chose this one man, not because of any prior merit on his part (Josh 24:2 describes Abraham as coming from a pagan background), but because of God's plan to bless the whole world through him. God asked of Abraham a threefold self-abandonment: "Go forth from your land, your relatives, and from your father's house to a land that I will show you" (Gen 12:1). To give up one's land, family, and inheritance was a radical act of trust in a world where family was the sole source of identity and security. But God promised something far greater in return: a great name, a new land, countless descendants, and blessing for the whole world.

11:8

Abraham's response is a model of obedient faith: **he went out, not knowing where he was to go**. That God did not initially tell him where to go meant that Abraham could not be self-sufficient; he would have to walk in constant dependence on God. He had to put one foot in front of the other and set out, trusting that God would eventually show him the destination. Just as in the call of Jesus' disciples, faith manifests itself in action. Faith means being willing to drop everything and follow the Lord, without yet knowing where he will lead (Mark 1:16–20; 2:14). All believers in Christ are, like Abraham, "those who are called" and who set out in faith (Heb 9:15).

Abraham's second act of **faith** was that **he sojourned in the promised land as in a foreign country**. God led him to Canaan, but despite the fact that this was the land God promised to him, Abraham never had a permanent dwelling there. He never owned a single plot of land except the cave that he purchased as a burial place for Sarah (Gen 23:17–20). He remained a sojourner or resident alien, roaming from place to place and **dwelling in tents** with his son **Isaac** and grandson **Jacob, heirs of the same promise**. To live in tents, with their flimsy protection against the elements, is an image of the impermanence and insecurity

11:9

of life on earth. The Gospel of John, referring to Christ's incarnation, says, "the Word became flesh / and made his dwelling [literally, "pitched his tent"] among us" (John 1:14). Thus Christ himself shared the human experience of never being fully at home on this earth, because our true home is elsewhere. The Greek word for "sojourner" (*paroikos*; see 1 Pet 2:11) is the root of the English words "parish" and "parochial," since members of the Church are sojourners on earth, looking forward to a heavenly homeland (Phil 3:20; Heb 10:34).

11:10   Abraham's whole life was a pilgrimage, a journey of faith. As Hebrews interprets it, his very lack of a permanent home propelled him to look beyond the transitory things of this world and stirred an expectation that God had something greater in store: **he was looking forward to the city with foundations, whose architect and maker is God.** For Abraham's descendants, the summit of the promised land was the holy city, Jerusalem. But even that city was only a shadow and anticipation of the glorious city prepared by God (v. 16), the city that is to come (12:22; 13:14). The book of Revelation describes that city and its foundations: "He . . . showed me the holy city Jerusalem coming down out of heaven from God. . . . The wall of the city had twelve courses of stones as its foundation, on which were inscribed the twelve names of the twelve apostles of the Lamb" (Rev 21:10, 14).

11:11   The third act of faith applies to both Abraham and Sarah. The Greek of this verse causes some difficulty for translators.[9] Although the NAB translation says **he** (i.e., Abraham) **received power to generate**, the sentence reads more naturally with Sarah as the subject, as in the Vulgate and most English translations (RSV, NJB, ESV, KJV). The difficulty is that "power to generate" is literally "power for the casting of seed," an expression normally used for the male role in procreation. However, seed is attributed to the woman in Genesis 3:15, the first promise of salvation, and in Revelation 12:17. Moreover, "past the age" applies more to a woman than a man (see Gen 18:11), especially in this case, since years later, after Sarah's death, Abraham remarried and had more children (Gen 25:1–2). The phrase can also be interpreted to mean that **by faith** Sarah received the power to "establish offspring." Sarah stands at the head of a long line of biblical women who suffered the stigma of infertility, including Rebekah, Rachel, Hannah, and Elizabeth. Yet in each case God intervened miraculously, enabling the birth of a child who turned out to play a pivotal role in the plan of salvation.

For Sarah, procreation seemed even more impossible because besides being **sterile**, she was **past the normal age**. When God first gave the promise, Abraham

---

9. See discussion in Johnson, *Hebrews*, 291–92; Philip Edgcumbe Hughes, *A Commentary on the Epistle to the Hebrews* (Grand Rapids: Eerdmans, 1977), 471–76.

was a venerable seventy-five and Sarah sixty-five, yet they had to wait another twenty-five long years before seeing the promise come to fruition in the birth of Isaac (Gen 12:4; 17:17). The Lord brought them to a point of totally giving up on human possibilities, so that it would be undeniably clear that the promise was fulfilled by his miraculous power.

Sarah is also best understood as the subject of the next clause: she **thought** (or "considered") **that the one who had made the promise was trustworthy**, just as the author of Hebrews wants his readers to consider God trustworthy (10:23). It is true that Genesis portrays both Abraham and Sarah as faltering in faith at times, for instance when they decided to use Sarah's maid Hagar as a surrogate womb (Gen 16:1–4), and when each of them laughed at God's promise (Gen 17:17; 18:12). But apart from these missteps, they clung to God's word, taking to heart his rhetorical question: "Is anything too marvelous for the LORD to do?" (Gen 18:14). And when the baby was born, the overjoyed couple fittingly named him Isaac, meaning "he laughs" (Gen 21:1–3).

So it was that, through the joint faith of Abraham and Sarah, God did the **11:12** impossible. **There came forth from one man** (literally, "from one"), **himself as good as dead**, countless descendants. The couple are considered as one, as in Isaiah 51:2: "Look to Abraham, your father, / and to Sarah, who gave you birth; / Though he was but one when I called him, / I blessed him and made him many." The phrase "as good as dead" refers to their inability to procreate children (see Rom 4:19). From this aged pair the Lord brought forth **descendants as numerous as the stars in the sky and as countless as the sands on the seashore**, as he had promised in Genesis 15:4–5; 22:17. These descendants are, first of all, the people of Israel (see Deut 1:10; 1 Kings 4:20). But the promise received a further, transcendent fulfillment in all those who believe in Christ, who have become Abraham's spiritual children (see Gal 3:7, 16, 29). Thus through Abraham and Sarah God brought life out of apparent death, in another foreshadowing of the resurrection of Christ.

Reflection and Application (11:8–12)

Pilgrimages of faith. The custom of pilgrimage, going on a journey to a sacred place such as the Holy Land, Rome, Santiago de Compostela, or the site of a Marian apparition, is an ancient Christian tradition that has its roots in the Old Testament. The story of God's dealings with his people began with a pilgrimage, Abraham and Sarah's journey to the promised land (Heb 11:8). Three times a year devout Israelites made pilgrimage to Jerusalem to celebrate the feasts of

Passover, Pentecost, and Tabernacles (Exod 23:14); and Jesus himself did so (Luke 2:41; John 2:13; 5:1). The tradition of pilgrimage expresses the recognition that our life on earth is itself a pilgrimage—a journey home to the Father. Ever since the expulsion of Adam and Eve from the garden, deep in the human heart there is a nostalgia for paradise that keeps us from being fully content with life on earth. Like Abraham, we are only sojourners, looking forward to "the city with foundations" that alone is our true permanent home (Heb 11:10). A pilgrimage, then, is not just a tour or vacation; it is an important Christian practice that puts life in true perspective and that is often the source of life-changing graces.

Called to go out. Hebrews emphasizes Abraham's steadfast trust in God through many years of waiting, wandering, and not yet seeing the fulfillment of God's promises. In the story of Abraham's call it is striking that God does not tell Abraham the destination but simply directs him to go forth "to a land that I will show you" (Gen 12:1). In the same way, God may call us to take a new step in life—a vocation, a job, a ministry, a relationship, or a move—but without showing us where it will ultimately lead, or even what the next step will be. We may wonder, "Why doesn't God just tell me where I'm going? Then I could get on with it!" But that would forfeit what is perhaps the most important part of the journey: the intimacy with God that comes from depending entirely on him, seeking his will anew day by day.

Dying in Faith (11:13–16)

> [13]**All these died in faith. They did not receive what had been promised but saw it and greeted it from afar and acknowledged themselves to be strangers and aliens on earth,** [14]**for those who speak thus show that they are seeking a homeland.** [15]**If they had been thinking of the land from which they had come, they would have had opportunity to return.** [16]**But now they desire a better homeland, a heavenly one. Therefore, God is not ashamed to be called their God, for he has prepared a city for them.**

OT: Gen 23:4; Ps 119:19
NT: Luke 9:26; John 8:56; 14:2–3; Rev 21:10, 14
Catechism: dying in faith, 1005–14
Lectionary: Mass for Refugees and Exiles

11:13–14   Verses 13–16 are a kind of interlude reflecting on the things "hoped for" and "not seen" (v. 1) that the patriarchs and matriarchs of Israel looked forward to in faith. **All these** heroes mentioned so far (with the exception of Enoch) **died**

in faith. That is, they died still steadfastly trusting in God's promises, looking to a fulfillment beyond this present world. Their faith was thus victorious even over death.[10] **They did not receive what had been promised, but saw it and greeted it from afar**. The partial fulfillment that they did see—for instance, the arrival in the promised land and the birth of Isaac—only showed more clearly that God had something more glorious in store when he promised an everlasting possession, countless descendants, and worldwide blessing (Gen 17:8; 22:17–18). They "saw" these future realities not literally but in faith, just as we "see Jesus" (Heb 2:9). Their faith laid hold of that which was not yet, and so became "evidence of things not seen" (v. 1). Jesus affirms this of Abraham: "Abraham . . . rejoiced to see my day; he saw it and was glad" (John 8:56).

They **acknowledged themselves to be strangers and aliens** (or "exiles," RSV) **on earth**. This alludes to Genesis 23:4, where Abraham says to the native inhabitants of Canaan, "I am a stranger and a sojourner among you" (RSV). In the Old Testament period, that acknowledgment grew into a deeper recognition that none of God's people are fully at home in this world. As the psalmist confesses, "I am a sojourner on earth" (Ps 119:19 RSV; see Ps 39:12). **Those who speak thus**—who demonstrate by their words and actions, and by the way they die, that they are exiles on earth—**show that they are seeking a homeland**. Their hopes and dreams are not confined to what can be obtained in this world, whether pleasure, possessions, power, privilege, or posterity. The longing for something beyond this world is a universal human experience. But those who trust in God live in confident hope that they will one day see that "homeland" (Greek *patris*, literally, "fatherland," the land of God the Father).

If Abraham and his family **had been thinking of the land from which they** **11:15–16** **had come**, Ur of the Chaldeans, **they would have had opportunity to return**. It is not easy to live as an exile among strangers. If the goal had been earthly comfort and security, they could have found an excuse to go back to Ur. But amid all the discomforts of a nomadic life, they persevered in obedience to God's call and in expectation of **a better homeland, a heavenly one**. This recalls the contrasting example of the faithless exodus generation of Israelites, who because of the hardships of the journey and the dangers of entering the promised land, hankered to go back to Egypt (Num 14:4; Heb 3:18; 4:3). It also alludes to the original readers of Hebrews, some of whom may have been tempted to return to the old covenant form of worship with which they were familiar.

Therefore, God is not ashamed to be called their God. This striking expression is a figure of speech known as a litotes, where a double negative is

---

10. Hughes, *Hebrews*, 477.

used for emphasis (as in 2:11).[11] The meaning, then, is that God is *honored* to be their God.[12] God, in fact, goes so far as to identify himself by the names of the patriarchs: "I am . . . the God of Abraham, the God of Isaac, the God of Jacob" (Exod 3:6; see Gen 28:13). As Jesus interprets it (Mark 12:26–27), the fact that God refers to himself as the God of these long-dead patriarchs proves their faith was not in vain, for they are actually not dead but alive and still awaiting the full realization of the promises.[13] When people trust God's word against seemingly impossible odds, it gives God glory and opens the way for him to display his omnipotence. On the other hand, when people distrust God and are unwilling to take a stand of faith, God is dishonored and withdraws his blessing (10:38).

For God's people to turn back to Ur—or back to Egypt, or, for the readers of Hebrews, back to life apart from Christ—would be to deprive themselves of their glorious inheritance. **For he has prepared a city for them**, the "city with foundations" mentioned in verse 10. Jesus declares, "In my Father's house there are many dwelling places. . . . And if I go and prepare a place for you, I will come back again and take you to myself" (John 14:2–3). In the book of Revelation God's preparation of the city is described as the adornment of a bride: "I also saw the holy city, a new Jerusalem, coming down out of heaven from God, prepared as a bride adorned for her husband" (Rev 21:2).

The Supreme Test of Faith (11:17–22)

[17]By faith Abraham, when put to the test, offered up Isaac, and he who had received the promises was ready to offer his only son, [18]of whom it was said, "Through Isaac descendants shall bear your name." [19]He reasoned that God was able to raise even from the dead, and he received Isaac back as a symbol. [20]By faith regarding things still to come Isaac blessed Jacob and Esau. [21]By faith Jacob, when dying, blessed each of the sons of Joseph and "bowed in worship, leaning on the top of his staff." [22]By faith Joseph, near the end of his life, spoke of the Exodus of the Israelites and gave instructions about his bones.

OT: Gen 27:27–40; 47:29–31; 48:13–20; 50:24–25; Sir 44:19–23
NT: Rom 8:32; James 2:21–23
Catechism: Abraham our father in faith, 145–47; test of faith, 1819

11. See, in the introduction, the section "Literary Form and Features."
12. Johnson, *Hebrews*, 291.
13. Hughes, *Hebrews*, 480.

Fig. 16. Mosaic depicting the binding of Isaac in the sixth-century AD synagogue at Beth Alpha, Israel. To the right, Abraham dangles Isaac over the fiery altar as he raises his hand to perform the sacrifice. In the middle is the ram caught in the thicket; to the left Abraham's servants and donkey. God is symbolized by the small fire-encircled hand in the upper center.

Verses 17–19 return to the story of Abraham, recounting his fourth and greatest act of faith (see vv. 8, 9, 11): his willingness to sacrifice his son.

By faith Abraham, when put to the test, offered up Isaac. By using the verb **11:17–18** "put to the test," Hebrews links Abraham with Jesus, who "himself was tested through what he suffered" and so "is able to help those who are being tested" (2:18). Genesis 22 recounts this supreme test, in which Abraham's faith was strained to the uttermost. Having promised Abraham a son through Sarah, and having miraculously given that son after a long wait, God required back the very object of the promise, the central love of Abraham's heart. The narrative emphasizes that God was fully aware of the anguish this demand entailed: "Take your son Isaac, your only one, whom you love, and . . . offer him up as a burnt offering" (Gen 22:2). The death of Isaac would mean not only the tearing apart of human bonds of affection but also the failure of all that God had promised by solemn oath (Gen 15:18; see Heb 6:13–14), everything that Abraham had staked his life on. Yet **he who had received the promises was ready to offer his only son.**[14] Although Abraham also had a son by Hagar, Ishmael, Isaac was

14. The Hebrew term for "only son" is often used in reference to an only son who is destined to die (Gen 22:2; Jer 6:26; Amos 8:10; Zech 12:10); the feminine form is likewise used for an only daughter who is destined to die (Judg 11:34; see Tob 3:10). The Septuagint translation for this term is *agapētos* ("beloved"), but Hebrews uses the more literal translation *monogenēs* ("unique" or "only"), perhaps to highlight that Isaac prefigures Christ, God's only Son (John 1:14, 18).

his "only son" in that the promise was specifically given in reference to him. God had said: **Through Isaac descendants shall bear your name** (Gen 21:12).[15]

That God would ask of Abraham that which was most precious to him, the gift that God himself had miraculously bestowed, vividly illustrates the fact that God seeks undivided and absolute love from the human heart (Deut 6:4–5). The Lord is "a jealous God" (Exod 34:14), a phrase that means he is impassioned or ardent in his love for us and his desire to be loved in return. Nothing whatsoever can claim a higher loyalty and affection than God himself. Yet this demand is not arbitrary or tyrannical. It is the only fitting response to the God who loves *us* with undivided and absolute love, "who did not spare his own Son but handed him over for us all" (Rom 8:32).

11:19   That Abraham was willing to carry out this drastic demand, not knowing why or understanding how it could possibly be compatible with God's sworn word, is the supreme biblical example of obedient faith. The Letter of James invokes it to illustrate that faith is inseparable from works: "Was not Abraham our father justified by works when he offered his son Isaac upon the altar? You see that faith was active along with his works, and faith was completed by the works. Thus the scripture was fulfilled that says, 'Abraham believed God, and it was credited to him as righteousness'" (James 2:21–23).

Abraham **reasoned that God was able to raise even from the dead**. Although Genesis does not say this directly, Hebrews may see it as implied in Abraham's words to his servants, "The boy and I . . . will worship and then come back to you" (Gen 22:5). Having experienced God's faithfulness in the birth of Isaac, Abraham stretched his faith yet further, trusting that God somehow had a solution to this terrible ordeal. And in the very act of sacrifice, when Abraham had totally given up his son, God intervened and gave back to him that which he had surrendered. So **he received Isaac back as a symbol**. Isaac's restoration to his father is a figure pointing to Christ, the only-begotten Son who was sacrificed not only in intention but in reality, and who was restored in his resurrection from the dead.

11:20   The last part of this section rapidly sums up the faith of the three generations of patriarchs following Abraham: Isaac, Jacob, and Joseph, who was one of Jacob's twelve sons. Here the focus is again on how they "died in faith" (see v. 13), looking beyond the grave to the future fulfillment of God's promises. **By faith regarding things still to come Isaac blessed Jacob and Esau**. The blessing of

---

15. Moreover, in the same verse God instructs Abraham to send Hagar and Ishmael away, underscoring the fact that Ishmael was not the promised heir, although God promised him blessing and numerous descendants as well.

The Testing of Abraham's Faith

LIVING TRADITION

Origen, a third-century Church Father, reflected on Abraham's struggle in a homily on the offering of Isaac:

> God . . . had kindled [Abraham's] soul, therefore, in love for his son not only because of posterity, but also in the hope of the promises. But this son, in whom those great and marvelous promises have been made, this son, I say, on whose account his name is called Abraham, he is ordered to offer as a holocaust to the Lord on one of the mountains.
>
> What do you say to these things, Abraham? What kind of thoughts are stirring in your heart? A word has been uttered by God which is such as to shatter and try your faith. What do you say to these things? What are you thinking? What are you reconsidering? Are you thinking, are you turning over in your heart that if the promise has been given to me in Isaac, but I offer him as a holocaust, that promise holds no hope? Or rather do you think of those well-known words, and say that "it is impossible for him who promised to lie" [Heb 6:18]?
>
> The apostle Paul . . . teaching by the Spirit what feeling, what plan Abraham considered, has revealed it when he says: "By faith Abraham did not hesitate, when he offered his only son, in whom he had received the promises, thinking that God is able to raise him up even from the dead" [Heb 11:17, 19]. . . . Abraham, therefore, hoped for the resurrection of Isaac and believed in a future that had not yet happened.[a]

a. Origen, *Homily VIII on Genesis* (translation adapted from Origen, *Homilies on Genesis and Exodus*, trans. Ronald E. Heine [Washington, DC: Catholic University of America Press, 1982], 137). Note that Origen, like most Greek Fathers, held that Hebrews expresses the thought of Paul even if written by someone else.

children before death was a solemn Israelite practice by which God's gifts were passed on to the next generation. Jacob, although he was the younger son, is mentioned first because he received the greater blessing normally reserved for the firstborn, both because it had been foretold before his birth (Gen 25:22–23) and because in conspiracy with his mother he obtained it by trickery (Gen 27). The reversal of the primacy of the firstborn is a theme that runs through Genesis, from Cain and Abel to Ishmael and Isaac, Esau and Jacob, and Joseph's sons Manasseh and Ephraim. God's choice of those who are less prominent from a human perspective is a sign that God's promises do not come about by human standards of worthiness.

By faith Jacob, when dying, blessed each of the sons of Joseph, Ephraim   11:21 and Manasseh. To the surprise of Joseph, the dying grandfather crossed his arms so that his right hand (the hand of greater blessing) rested on the head of

The Offering of Isaac

The story of the offering of Isaac (or, as Jewish tradition calls it, the binding of Isaac) has troubled readers from ancient times until now. What kind of God could ask such a thing? How could the God who forbids murder demand a human sacrifice? Is this a story about a cruel God who asks believers to do horrifying things to serve him?

In reality, the binding of Isaac is the means by which God demonstrates that he does *not* desire child sacrifice, which was a common practice of the pagan nations around Israel but which God declares an abomination (see Lev 18:21; Jer 7:31). At the last moment God stayed Abraham's hand and provided an animal substitute. This story illustrates, however, that God may ask of us that which we hold most dear, and that we need to be ready to trust and obey like Abraham. God alone must have first place in our heart (see Luke 14:26).

More significantly, through this event God revealed something of the mystery of his own self-giving love. The surrender of God's own beloved Son, the Lamb of God, is foreshadowed in the very wording of Abraham's reassurance to Isaac: "God will provide *himself the lamb* for a burnt offering, my son" (Gen 22:8 RSV, emphasis added).

---

the younger son (Gen 48:13–20), again reversing human expectations. Jacob's deathbed blessing, like that of Isaac, expressed his confident trust in the future realization of God's promises.

It was on a different occasion, when Jacob made Joseph swear to bury him not in Egypt but with his fathers in the promised land (Gen 47:29–31; see 50:12–14), that he **bowed in worship, leaning on the top of his staff**. The original Hebrew of this verse says Jacob "bowed at the head of the bed," which could seem to suggest age and weariness. But Hebrews, following the Septuagint, interprets it as an act of reverence toward God.[16] This event too demonstrates Jacob's confidence that, although the whole family had relocated to Egypt, God would indeed one day bring them back to Canaan. He died trusting God to accomplish his purposes, despite apparent digressions and setbacks.

11:22   **By faith Joseph, near the end of his life, spoke of the Exodus of the Israelites and gave instructions about his bones**. Joseph, in a gesture similar to his father's, prophesied the exodus and made his brothers swear to bring his remains back to the promised land: "I am about to die. God will surely take

---

16. The Hebrew word for "bow" can refer either to bowing physically or to worshiping. The Hebrew letters *mth* can be interpreted as either "bed" or "staff," depending on which vowels are placed with them.

care of you and lead you up from this land to the land that he promised on oath to Abraham, Isaac and Jacob. . . . When God thus takes care of you, you must bring my bones up from this place" (Gen 50:24–25). The Greek word for "spoke of" is literally "remembered." But how could Joseph "remember" an event that would not occur until four centuries later? This may mean he remembered that years earlier God had foretold the exodus to Abraham (Gen 15:13–14), and Joseph considered God's word so reliable that it was as if it had already occurred. When the exodus did occur, the oath concerning Joseph's bones was honored by Moses, who brought the bones along on the desert journey (Exod 13:19), and by Joshua, who later buried them in the promised land (Josh 24:32).

The Faith of Moses (11:23–29)

²³By faith Moses was hidden by his parents for three months after his birth, because they saw that he was a beautiful child, and they were not afraid of the king's edict. ²⁴By faith Moses, when he had grown up, refused to be known as the son of Pharaoh's daughter; ²⁵he chose to be ill-treated along with the people of God rather than enjoy the fleeting pleasure of sin. ²⁶He considered the reproach of the Anointed greater wealth than the treasures of Egypt, for he was looking to the recompense. ²⁷By faith he left Egypt, not fearing the king's fury, for he persevered as if seeing the one who is invisible. ²⁸By faith he kept the Passover and sprinkled the blood, that the Destroyer of the firstborn might not touch them. ²⁹By faith they crossed the Red Sea as if it were dry land, but when the Egyptians attempted it they were drowned.

OT: Exod 1:22; 2:1–3, 11–15; 3:1–2; 12:22–23; 14:10–31
NT: Matt 2:16; Acts 7:20–36

As verses 17–22 showed how faith conquers death, verses 23–29 illustrate how faith overcomes fear. This section on Moses, the great deliverer and law-giver of Israel, is the longest after the one on Abraham. Hebrews has already devoted considerable attention to Moses, who "was faithful in all God's house as a servant" (3:5 RSV). This section highlights five acts of faith by which Moses trusted God in the face of grave dangers.

First, **by faith Moses was hidden by his parents for three months after his** **11:23** **birth**. Here the faith is not that of Moses himself but of his parents—an indirect affirmation that children share in the faith of their parents and of the whole people of God to whom they belong.[17] At the time of Moses' birth Pharaoh had begun a campaign of genocide to wipe out the Hebrew people, ordering that all their male children be thrown into the Nile (Exod 1:22). But his parents **saw that he was a beautiful child**, perhaps intuiting from his unusual beauty that he was to have a special role in God's plan (see Acts 7:20, which says he was "beautiful before God," RSV). **They were not afraid of the king's edict**, which does not mean they did not experience the emotion of terror, but that they chose to act in faith rather than fear. At risk to their own safety they saved Moses' life by hiding him for three months, then putting him in a basket among the reeds on the river bank (Exod 2:2–3), where he was providentially found by the daughter of Pharaoh. Here there is an ironic reversal of the story of Isaac: as Abraham displayed obedient faith in being willing even to sacrifice his son, Moses' parents showed obedient faith by saving their son.[18]

For readers familiar with the Gospel of Matthew, there is an unmistakable parallel between Moses and Jesus, another baby who escaped a wicked ruler's attempt to kill the male children of Israel (Matt 2:16), who was saved by his parents' faithful obedience (ironically, by their taking Jesus *to* Egypt), and who grew up to become the great deliverer of God's people, in this case from the slavery of sin into the true promised land (Heb 2:15; 4:3; 11:16).

11:24   Moses' second act of **faith** was that **when he had grown up**, he **refused to be known as the son of Pharaoh's daughter**. Having been adopted and raised by Pharaoh's daughter, Moses enjoyed the privilege, wealth, and power that belonged to a royal prince. According to Jewish tradition, he had also received the benefits of a first-class Egyptian education (Acts 7:22). Yet Exodus indicates that Moses identified more with the despised tribe of slaves into which he had been born than with the ruling dynasty of Egypt. Hebrews alludes to, but without mentioning, the incident in which Moses came to the rescue of a Hebrew slave who was being beaten by an Egyptian taskmaster. In this first, well-meaning but wrongheaded attempt to save a fellow Israelite, Moses killed the Egyptian, necessitating his flight from the country (Exod 2:11–15).

11:25   In Moses' exemplary choice to identify with God's suffering people, Hebrews sees another foreshadowing of Christ, who became "like his brothers in every way" and "was tested through what he suffered" (2:17–18). Moses **chose to be ill-treated along with the people of God rather than enjoy the fleeting pleasure of sin**. Instead of distancing himself from the lowly and despised people he belonged to, Moses accepted the burdensome task of leading them through

---

17. This principle underlies the practice of infant baptism; see Catechism 1250–55.
18. Johnson, *Hebrews*, 299.

the desert to freedom. The "pleasures of sin" may refer to the decadent and luxurious lifestyle of Egypt's royal palace or, more likely, to the sin of Egyptian idolatry. Between the lines of this description of Moses is a clear exhortation to the readers of Hebrews: joyfully accept the suffering that comes with your Christian identity (10:32–34), including whatever loss of material comfort or social approval it entails.

Moses **considered the reproach of the Anointed** (literally, of "Christ") **11:26** **greater wealth than the treasures of Egypt**. In what sense could Moses have been aware of Christ? Hebrews is playing on the broad biblical meaning of the term Christ ("anointed one," "Messiah"). In the Old Testament every Israelite priest and king was an "anointed one," consecrated by God for his special office. But the whole people of God could also be called God's "anointed ones" (Ps 105:15), or even, collectively, God's "anointed one" (Hab 3:13). "The Messiah is one with the messianic people, bone of their bone and flesh of their flesh."[19] Moses considered solidarity with God's anointed people, cruelly subjugated yet the heirs of God's great promises, more valuable than all the earthly treasures of Egypt. In doing so, by anticipation he shared in the suffering of the Anointed One to come, Jesus Christ. The Greek word for "reproach" can mean humiliation or any kind of verbal abuse, as in 10:33. In a similar way, the audience of Hebrews had suffered insult and the loss of earthly possessions for the sake of Christ (10:32–33) but now needed to be encouraged again to willingly bear the reproach Christ bore (13:13). Moses did so because he **was looking** in faith beyond earthly circumstances **to the recompense** promised by God, believing that, as said above (10:35; 11:6), God has a glorious reward in store for those who seek him.

Moses displayed **faith** for the third time when he **left Egypt, not fearing the** **11:27** **king's fury**. Commentators are divided as to whether this statement refers to Moses' initial flight to Midian after killing the Egyptian or to the exodus forty years later. The first interpretation would seem to contradict Exodus, which specifically states that Moses fled in fear of Pharaoh (Exod 2:14–15), whereas he showed remarkable courage in his later confrontations with Pharaoh (Exod 5–10). On the other hand, mentioning the exodus in verse 27 before the Passover in verse 28 reverses the order of events. Still, the exodus option seems more likely, since Hebrews is not always concerned with strict chronological order (see 11:8–19, 32), and the Passover and exodus can be considered a single saving event.

19. F. F. Bruce, *The Epistle to the Hebrews*, rev. ed., New International Commentary on the New Testament (Grand Rapids: Eerdmans, 2012), 311.

In any case, throughout the exodus and the wilderness journey Moses **persevered as if seeing the one who is invisible**. Exodus records several occasions when Moses did see the invisible God, or at least his angelic representative: first and foremost at the burning bush on Mount Sinai (Exod 3:1–2), then at the later theophanies at the same mountain (Exod 19:20; 24:9–18; 33:11; 34:5–8, 27–35). But the point is that even apart from these extraordinary visions, Moses kept his attention focused on the faithfulness of God rather than on the dangers and troubles of his present circumstances.

11:28   Fourth, **by faith** Moses (and the whole people of Israel) **kept the Passover**, obeying God's instructions for the solemn banquet that first anticipated, and later celebrated, their dramatic rescue from Egypt. Hebrews had much to say in chapters 9–10 about the sprinkling of blood in the covenant ceremony at Sinai (Exod 24) and in the annual rites of the †Day of Atonement (Lev 16). Here for the first time it mentions the primordial blood-sprinkling event: the **blood** of the Passover lamb that every Israelite family **sprinkled** on the doorposts and lintel of their home so **that the Destroyer of the firstborn might not touch them** (Exod 12:22–23). Their doing so was no mere ritual; it was an act of obedient faith, trusting that the Lord would spare their lives while he punished their enemies. It is not difficult to see in this event a prefigurement of Christ, the "lamb of God" (John 1:29, 36), "our Passover lamb" (1 Cor 5:7 ESV), the "spotless unblemished lamb" (1 Pet 1:19) who has delivered us, God's firstborn children (see 12:23), by his own shed blood. Through his death Christ "destroyed the power of the devil, our spiritual Pharaoh, and delivered us from lifelong bondage (Heb 2:14f)."[20]

11:29   Finally, in the dramatic culmination of the exodus, **by faith** Moses and the whole Israelite people **crossed the Red Sea as if it were dry land**. The greatest test of faith in the Exodus narrative comes at the terrifying moment when the throng of Israelite men, women, and children found themselves trapped between the Red Sea and the furiously pursuing army of Pharaoh (Exod 14:9–10). In response to the people's fright Moses cried out, "Do not fear! Stand your ground and see the victory the LORD will win for you today" (Exod 14:13). In the midst of an impossible situation, by an awesome display of divine power the water was divided, and "the Israelites entered into the midst of the sea on dry land, with the water as a wall to their right and to their left" (Exod 14:22).

But when the Egyptians attempted it they were drowned. One and the same act of God was salvation for God's people and destruction for their enemies. Reflecting on this, the book of Wisdom observes, "Your creation, serving you,

20. Hughes, *Hebrews*, 500.

its maker, / grows tense for punishment against the wicked, / but is relaxed in benefit for those who trust in you" (Wis 16:24). God's spectacular act of deliverance led in turn to deeper faith, since Exodus records that when the people "saw the great power that the LORD had shown against Egypt . . . they believed in the LORD and in Moses his servant" (Exod 14:31). The Church sees in this event a figure of baptism (see 1 Cor 10:2), by which believers are brought through water from death to life. Once again, as in the example of Isaac above, God reveals his power to deliver his people from death.

The Faith of Other Israelite Heroes (11:30–40)

> [30]By faith the walls of Jericho fell after being encircled for seven days. [31]By faith Rahab the harlot did not perish with the disobedient, for she had received the spies in peace.
>
> [32]What more shall I say? I have not time to tell of Gideon, Barak, Samson, Jephthah, of David and Samuel and the prophets, [33]who by faith conquered kingdoms, did what was righteous, obtained the promises; they closed the mouths of lions, [34]put out raging fires, escaped the devouring sword; out of weakness they were made powerful, became strong in battle, and turned back foreign invaders. [35]Women received back their dead through resurrection. Some were tortured and would not accept deliverance, in order to obtain a better resurrection. [36]Others endured mockery, scourging, even chains and imprisonment. [37]They were stoned, sawed in two, put to death at sword's point; they went about in skins of sheep or goats, needy, afflicted, tormented. [38]The world was not worthy of them. They wandered about in deserts and on mountains, in caves and in crevices in the earth.
>
> [39]Yet all these, though approved because of their faith, did not receive what had been promised. [40]God had foreseen something better for us, so that without us they should not be made perfect.

OT: Josh 2; 6; Judg 4–16; Dan 3; 6; 1 Kings 17; 2 Kings 4; 2 Macc 7; 2 Chron 24:20–22
NT: John 15:19; Phil 2:15; 1 John 3:13
Catechism: Old Testament witnesses to faith, 147

The roll call of heroes of faith reaches a crescendo in this last section of chapter 11, where several named heroes are brought on stage, followed by a list of accomplishments of unnamed people. Their accomplishments include both mighty victories of faith and ordeals where faith prevailed even in apparent defeat.

11:30   Verse 30 skips from the exodus to the entry into the promised land forty years later, after the death of Moses. Under the leadership of Joshua, **by faith the walls of Jericho fell after being encircled for seven days**. This first battle in the land of Canaan was a powerful lesson in faith, since God's instructions for conquering the city entailed not a military assault but a liturgical procession. God commanded Joshua to have his troops, along with seven priests carrying the †ark of the covenant and blowing ram's horns, march around the city once a day for six days, then seven times on the seventh day. The last encirclement was to be followed by a blast of the horns and a loud shout from the people. The people faithfully obeyed these peculiar instructions, trusting in God's word: "I have delivered Jericho, its king, and its warriors into your power" (Josh 6:2). Once again faith made way for the Lord to work wonders. "When they heard the sound of the horn, they raised a tremendous shout. The wall collapsed, and the people attacked the city straight ahead and took it" (Josh 6:20).

11:31   Closely involved in the story of Jericho was the Canaanite woman Rahab, who sheltered and hid the Israelite spies who had come to scout out the city. **By faith Rahab the harlot did not perish with the disobedient, for she had received the spies in peace**. Rahab's faith is shown in her remarkable confession of faith in the Lord, the God of Israel, after hearing of his mighty deeds. She tells the scouts, "I know that the LORD has given you the land, that a dread of you has come upon us, and that all the inhabitants of the land tremble with fear because of you. . . . since the LORD, your God, is God in heaven above and on earth below" (Josh 2:9–11). She also trusts that kindness will be shown her in recompense for her kindness (Josh 2:14). Accordingly, at the fall of the city she and her family were "kept alive" (Josh 6:25, literal translation)—another example of faith bringing salvation from death.

Rahab's mention in Hebrews 11 is unusual for several reasons. First, she is the only woman named besides Sarah (who appears in close connection with Abraham), although anonymous women appear in verse 35. Second, she is the only Gentile mentioned subsequent to the time of Abraham. In fact, she was the first convert to faith in the God of Israel. According to the genealogy in the Gospel of Matthew, Rahab was later grafted into Israel through marriage and even became part of the family line of the Messiah (Matt 1:5). She thus foreshadows the ingathering of the Gentiles into God's people. Finally, she was a prostitute, at least before turning to faith in God, and thus an unlikely candidate for a list of heroes. But in that way she too prefigures Christ's redeeming grace toward sinners. In the Gospels Jesus shows a special care for women in that degrading lifestyle and declares to the religious leaders, "Amen, I say to you, tax collectors and prostitutes are entering the kingdom of God before you" (Matt 21:31). The Letter of James mentions Rahab along with Abraham as a model of faith that is expressed in works: "Was not Rahab the harlot also justified by works when she welcomed the messengers and sent them out by a different route?" (James 2:25).

The author catches his breath with a rhetorical pause before launching into **11:32** the final cascade of victories of faith. **What more shall I say?** He considers his theme, that faith is the realization of what is hoped for and evidence of things not seen (v. 1), to be sufficiently proven by the examples given so far. For lack of **time**, the rest will be rapidly mentioned without elaboration. This is not an exhaustive list but a representative sampling of biblical heroes, nor are they in chronological order. The first four named are from the period of the judges, after the conquest of the promised land but before the time of the kingship. **Gideon** was famous for defeating the invading army of Midianites with a tiny band of three hundred men, smashing jugs and blowing horns at God's command (Judg 6–8). **Barak** was summoned by the prophetess Deborah to engage in battle against the Canaanites under the command of Sisera, a force superior in numbers and in technology (Judg 4–5). He routed them, believing in God's word through Deborah: "This is the day on which the LORD has delivered Sisera into your power. The LORD marches before you" (Judg 4:14). **Samson**, with God-given supernatural strength, overthrew the Philistines (Judg 13–16). **Jephthah** vanquished the Ammonites, although this victory was marred by the horrendous act of sacrificing his daughter to fulfill a vow that he had rashly made (Judg 11).

David, who despite his grave sins was "a man after [God's] own heart" (1 Sam 13:14), unified the tribes of Israel, established Jerusalem as the holy city, and founded the royal dynasty from which came forth the Messiah, the King of kings (1 Sam 16–1 Kings 2; Sir 47:1–11). **Samuel** was the last of the judges and the prophet who anointed Israel's first kings, Saul and David (1 Sam 1–16; Sir 46:13–20). Following Samuel was a long line of biblical **prophets** who boldly proclaimed God's word and continually called the people back to covenant fidelity.

Verses 33–34 list three successes, three great escapes, and three military ex- **11:33–34** ploits accomplished **by faith**. Those who **conquered kingdoms** include Joshua (Josh 12); the judges already mentioned in verse 32; and David, who conquered the Philistines and other enemies of Israel. They **did what was righteous** (or "administered justice," NIV); the phrase may refer either to personal integrity and good works (Ps 15:2 †LXX) or to governing justly, as did Joshua (Josh 13) and other judges, as well as Samuel, David, and Solomon (1 Sam 12:3–5; 2 Sam 8:15; 1 Kings 10:9). Those who **obtained the promises**—that is, saw promises of God fulfilled—are everyone mentioned in Hebrews 11 and innumerable others. The starving widow of Zarephath, for example, saw God's promise through Elijah come true: "The jar of flour shall not go empty, nor the jug of oil run dry, until the day when the Lord sends rain upon the earth" (1 Kings 17:14).[21] The phrase should, however, be translated "obtained promises" (without the definite article "the"), since there is no definite article in the Greek, and in verse 39 Hebrews will explicitly say they did not obtain *the* promise—that is, the fulfillment in Christ of all that was symbolized and hoped for in the old covenant.[22]

Among the great escapes, Daniel is well known for his miraculous rescue from the lions' den into which King Nebuchadnezzar had thrown him, when God **closed the mouths of lions** (Dan 6:17–23). But Samson, David, and Benaiah, one of David's warriors, are also known for slaying lions (Judg 14:5–6; 1 Sam 17:34–36; 2 Sam 23:20). Those who **put out raging fires** are the three young men whom Nebuchadnezzar had thrown into the blazing furnace, from which God wondrously rescued them (Dan 3:13–27). Their defiant challenge became a classic expression of faith: "If it be so, our God whom we serve is able to deliver us from the burning fiery furnace; and he will deliver us out of your hand, O king. But if not, be it known to you, O king, that we will not serve your gods or worship the golden image which you have set up" (Dan 3:17–18 RSV). Those who **escaped the devouring sword** include the prophets Elijah and Elisha (1 Kings 19:2–3; 2 Kings 1:9–12; 6:18), David on numerous occasions (1 Sam 18:11; 19:10; 2 Sam 15:14), Jeremiah (Jer 26:23–24), and the people of Jerusalem during the invasion of Sennacherib (2 Kings 19).

Out of weakness they were made powerful. This phrase may apply especially to women of faith such as Jael, who slew the enemy general Sisera (Judg 4:21); Judith, who cut off the head of the enemy general Holofernes (Jdt 13:4–8); and Esther, who saved Israel from the malicious plotting of Haman (Esther 7). It may also apply to David, who as a mere youth slew the Philistine giant Goliath (1 Sam 17, and Samson, who had become weak but to whom the Lord granted one last burst of strength to topple the Philistine temple of Dagon (Judg 16:28–30). The faithful became **strong in battle** not out of their own strength but because they trusted God, who is "a mighty warrior, / the Lord, mighty in battle" (Ps 24:8 NAB). They **turned back foreign invaders**, including Sisera, Holofernes, Sennacherib, and most notably, the Seleucid tyrant Antiochus Epiphanes in the

---

21. See also, e.g., Moses in Exod 3:12; 19:17; Gideon in Judg 7:7, 22; Joshua in Josh 21:44–45.
22. See Vanhoye, *A Different Priest*, 355.

time of the Maccabees (1 Macc 3:23–26; 4:6–25; 5:21–36). Judas Maccabeus exemplifies the courageous faith of the Jews as they faced their powerful enemy:

> Do not fear their numbers or dread their attack. Remember how our ancestors were saved in the Red Sea, when Pharaoh pursued them with an army. So now let us cry to Heaven in the hope that he will favor us, remember the covenant with our ancestors, and destroy this army before us today. All the Gentiles shall know that there is One who redeems and delivers Israel. (1 Macc 4:8–11; see 3:18–19)

With this cry they "joined the battle" and "crushed the Gentiles" (1 Macc 4:14).

The most remarkable foreshadowings of the future victory of Christ—and of **11:35** the consolation of his mother—are the **women** who **received back their dead through resurrection**. This clearly refers to the widow of Zarephath, whose son was resuscitated by the prayers of Elijah as he stretched himself out on the dead boy (1 Kings 17:17–24), and the Shunammite woman, whose son was brought back to life by Elisha in a similar manner (2 Kings 4:32–37). Like God's restoration of Isaac to his father, and like Jesus' raising of Lazarus and others in the Gospels, these resurrections were a deferral of death, not the overcoming of death. Yet they point forward to the "better resurrection" won by Christ, which is not merely a return to earthly life but a share in God's own life.[23]

The examples so far have been of glorious triumphs of faith, but now there is a list of ordeals of faith. These are a very different kind of victory: faith remaining steadfast in the midst of terrible trials and cruel deaths.

Some were tortured and would not accept deliverance. Here again Hebrews refers to the horrific persecution in the time of the Maccabees, when many Jews endured torture rather than obey the king's edict to violate the laws of God. Most famous are the seven sons and their mother who were brutally tortured and killed for refusing to eat pork (2 Macc 7). They endured **in order to obtain a better resurrection** than the earthly resuscitations mentioned above. Before dying, the brothers confidently expressed their hope of this "better resurrection": "You dismiss us from the present life, but the King of the universe will raise us up to an everlasting renewal of life"; "One cannot but choose to die at the hands of men and to cherish the hope that God gives of being raised again by him" (2 Macc 7:9, 14 RSV). Likewise, the mother exhorted her youngest son: "Since it is the Creator of the universe who shaped the beginning of humankind and brought about the origin of everything, he, in his mercy, will give you back both breath and life, because you now disregard yourselves for the sake of his law" (2 Macc 7:23). Also worthy of mention is the elderly scribe Eleazar, who

---

23. Johnson, *Hebrews*, 308.

refused to deny his faith: "Preferring a glorious death to a life of defilement, he went forward of his own accord to the instrument of torture, spitting out the meat" (2 Macc 6:19–20).

11:36   The Maccabean martyrs were among the many heroes of faith who **endured mockery** (2 Macc 7:7, 10) and **scourging** (2 Macc 7:1, 37). The **chains and imprisonment** recall the prophet Jeremiah, who besides being mocked and scourged, was beaten, repeatedly imprisoned, put in the stocks, and thrown into a muddy cistern (Jer 20:2, 7–8; 37:15; 38:6). For the Christian readers of Hebrews, these descriptions cannot help but bring to mind the passion of Christ, who "endured the cross, despising its shame" (12:2), and willingly took his place in the long line of prophets who suffered for their fidelity to God's word (Luke 11:49–51; 13:33–34). It also calls to mind the sufferings of Christ's faithful apostle Paul, who spent much of his life in chains (2 Cor 11:23; Col 4:18; 2 Tim 1:16), and the original readers of Hebrews themselves, who had endured similar trials (10:32–34).

11:37   The priest Zechariah was **stoned** to death in the temple in retaliation for prophesying God's judgment (2 Chron 24:20–22; see Luke 11:51); Naboth, a layman, was stoned for refusing King Ahab's unjust demand (1 Kings 21:13). Jesus speaks of other prophets who suffered the same fate (Matt 23:37), perhaps referring to Jeremiah, who according to Jewish tradition was stoned by his fellow Jews in Egypt.[24] In the Christian era Stephen was stoned to death (Acts 7:58–60), while Paul survived stoning by hostile Jews after preaching the gospel in Lystra (Acts 14:19).

The biblical figure who was **sawed in two** was the prophet Isaiah, whose death is recounted not in Scripture but in the Jewish †intertestamental work *Martyrdom and Ascension of Isaiah* (5:1–14). Countless prophets and faithful Israelites were **put to death at sword's point** (1 Kings 19:10, 14; Jer 2:30). Elijah **went about in skins of sheep or goats** (2 Kings 1:8), and many others of God's people through the centuries were **needy, afflicted, tormented**.

11:38   A brief parenthetical remark expresses the paradox: although these faithful people were despised, disregarded, and dishonored by the world, **the world was not worthy of them**. As Paul says of the Philippian Christians, "In the midst of a crooked and perverse generation . . . you shine like lights in the world" (Phil 2:15). Their refusal to conform to the values of the world, in which only visible things count, arouses the world's fury. As the First Letter of John warns, "Do not be amazed, . . . brothers, if the world hates you" (1 John 3:13; see John 15:19).

24. See Tertullian, *Antidote for the Scorpion's Sting* 8; Hippolytus, *Demonstratio de Christo et antichristo* 31.

But though they appeared to be the losers, the glorious hidden reality is that they are the overcomers, for whom God is preparing a great reward (vv. 6, 16).

They wandered about in deserts and on mountains, in caves and in crevices in the earth. Those who had to take refuge in the wild, fleeing for their lives, include Israelites in the time of Gideon (Judg 6:2), David (1 Sam 22:1), Elijah (1 Kings 19:9), and the Maccabees (1 Macc 2:28; 2 Macc 6:11; 10:6). The readers of Hebrews, whose property had been confiscated (10:34), themselves knew what it is to experience homelessness. They endured it joyfully because "here we have no lasting city, but we seek the one that is to come" (13:14).

The concluding statement echoes what was said in verse 2, forming a frame **11:39–40** around the whole chapter: these saints of old were **approved** (*martyreō*)[25] **because of their faith. Yet**, in another paradox, **all these did not receive what had been promised**; literally, "they did not receive *the* promise," the full realization of God's plan through the once-for-all sacrifice of Jesus the high priest. This does not mean that the people of the old covenant are excluded from the promise; rather, **God had foreseen something better for us, so that without us they should not be made perfect**. In God's mysterious plan those who belonged to the time of "shadow" (10:1) and we who belong to the time of fulfillment would be "made perfect" together by the one sacrifice of Christ (10:14). What they had in anticipation we now have in reality. Yet Christians too walk by faith, since we too still await the full consummation of the promise (10:36).

Reflection and Application (11:30–40)

The roll call of biblical heroes in Hebrews 11 is an inspiring reminder of the legacy of faith that both Jews and Christians share. But we should not make the mistake of thinking that the roll call ended with the Old Testament or when Hebrews was written; it has continued throughout the centuries and into our own times. The Church in our age has witnessed countless miracles of faith and countless triumphs of unbroken faith in the midst of apparent defeat. Imitating Hebrews we might say, for instance:

By faith the Solidarity movement in Poland steadfastly resisted Soviet tyranny and state-imposed atheism in the face of impossible odds and eventually won, leading to the fall of the Iron Curtain.

By faith the people of the Philippines overthrew the oppressive Marcos regime peacefully, the whole nation engaging in fervent prayer as nuns and laypeople together prayed the rosary in front of tanks.

---

25. This is the same word translated "attested" in verses 2, 4, 5.

By faith Father Rick Thomas, founder of the Lord's Ranch, distributed food to the poor who scavenged on the garbage dump of Juárez, Mexico, often witnessing the multiplication of food and other miracles.

By faith an unknown Franciscan sister, Mother Angelica, with no financial resources, founded a television studio in a garage that became a worldwide evangelistic radio and television apostolate.[26]

By faith Protestant missionary Jackie Pullinger traveled to the dreaded Walled City of Hong Kong, alone and nearly penniless, and ended up bringing countless drug addicts, prostitutes, criminals, and gang members to faith in Christ and radical transformation of life.[27]

By faith thousands of sick people have been healed at the shrine of Our Lady of Lourdes and other shrines, and thousands more have been brought to deeper conversion or joy in the midst of their suffering.

By faith Cardinal Nguyen Van Thuan of Vietnam spent thirteen years in a communist reeducation camp, nine of them in solitary confinement, celebrating Mass in secret with a few drops of smuggled wine and a tiny piece of bread on the palm of his hand.[28]

By faith ordinary women like Asia Bibi in Pakistan and Mariam Yehya Ibrahim in Sudan showed extraordinary courage, refusing to renounce their faith in Christ even in the face of imprisonment and the sentence of death.

By faith the French Trappist monks of Tibhirine, Algeria, when threatened by Islamic extremism, chose to stay among the people they loved; all seven of them were martyred.[29]

What more shall I say? I have not time to tell of all the other heroes of faith of our time.

---

26. Raymond Arroyo, *Mother Angelica: The Remarkable Story of a Nun, Her Nerve, and a Network of Miracles* (New York: Doubleday, 2005).

27. Jackie Pullinger and Andrew Quicke, *Chasing the Dragon: One Woman's Struggle against the Darkness of Hong Kong's Drug Dens* (Grand Rapids: Chosen, 2007).

28. Francis Xavier Nguyen Van Thuan, *The Road of Hope: A Gospel from Prison*, trans. John Peter Pham (Hyde Park, NY: New City Press, 2013).

29. Their story is depicted in the 2010 film *Of Gods and Men*.

The Discipline of a Loving Father

Hebrews 12:1–29

The litany of heroes of faith that comprises Hebrews 11 actually culminates not with an Old Testament figure but with Jesus, "the leader and perfecter of faith" (12:2).[1] He is the only perfect model to imitate, the only one who has persevered in total fidelity to God and attained the glorious reward. But Jesus is not merely our example; he is also the source of our faith and the one who brings it to completion (see Phil 1:6). By gazing on him, instead of on the obstacles that stand in our way, we press on toward the goal with singleness of purpose. The ultimate lesson of the heroes of faith, then, is to "persevere . . . while keeping our eyes fixed on Jesus" (12:1–2).

In chapter 12 Hebrews presents three images that help us to see the Christian life in true perspective. First, our life is an *endurance race* in which we are striving toward the finish line, cheered on by those who have gone before us (12:1–4). Second, it is *growth toward maturity* through the discipline of a loving Father (12:5–13), which requires our free cooperation (12:14–17). Our sufferings have great value for training us in holiness and thus are a reason not for discouragement but for confidence in God's love for us. Third, our life is a joyous *liturgical assembly* on a holy mountain amid all the angels and saints (12:18–24). The last image becomes the occasion for a final solemn warning, in which the author urges readers not to turn away from God and thus forfeit such a heavenly reward (12:25–29).

---

1. Readers should keep in mind that chapter divisions were not created by the biblical authors but were added in the thirteenth century AD as an aid to readers. The roll call of faith in Heb 11 flows organically into Heb 12, and 12:1–4 serves as both the culmination of the roll call of faith and the beginning of a new section.

For the Sake of Joy (12:1–4)

¹Therefore, since we are surrounded by so great a cloud of witnesses, let us rid ourselves of every burden and sin that clings to us and persevere in running the race that lies before us ²while keeping our eyes fixed on Jesus, the leader and perfecter of faith. For the sake of the joy that lay before him he endured the cross, despising its shame, and has taken his seat at the right of the throne of God. ³Consider how he endured such opposition from sinners, in order that you may not grow weary and lose heart. ⁴In your struggle against sin you have not yet resisted to the point of shedding blood.

OT: Ps 110:1

NT: Rom 8:18; 2 Tim 2:12; Rev 3:21

Catechism: the cloud of witnesses, 165, 1161, 2683; communion of saints, 957; Christ's opposition from sinners, 598; martyrdom, 2473

For people of the ancient world, just as for people today, it is hard to think of a greater thrill than that of a star Olympic athlete, racing along the track toward the finish line, cheered on by the roar of a vast crowd. Such an exhilarating scene is a far cry from Christian life as the original readers of Hebrews had come to view it, discouraged as they were by persecutions and the daily struggle against sin. And yet, according to the preacher, this is the true though invisible reality: as disciples of Christ we are on a racecourse heading toward a triumphant goal. And all those biblical figures listed in chapter 11 are not just heroes from the distant past but our enthusiastic fans, our elder brothers and sisters in faith who are encouraging us on to the same victory they have won.

12:1   The word **therefore** signals a turn from examples to exhortation, showing us how to concretely apply the lesson on faith just given. As usual, the author includes himself in the exhortation by using the pronoun **we**. The whole section revolves around the image of the Christian life as an athletic contest, specifically a race—one of the favorite images of St. Paul.[2] As we run this race, we are **surrounded** by a **great cloud of witnesses**, as if filling the stands of a huge sports arena. They are the saints of the old covenant (now joined by those of the new covenant), who are rooting for us and passionately interested in the outcome of our lives. In chapter 11 God was said to "bear witness" to them (11:2, 4, 5, 39); here they themselves are "witnesses"—not in the sense of being spectators but in the sense that they testify to the faithfulness of God. The Greek word

2. 1 Cor 9:24–27; Gal 2:2; Phil 2:16; 3:14; 1 Tim 6:12; 2 Tim 2:5; 4:7; see Acts 20:24.

Fig. 17. The ruins of Corinth, site of the famous Isthmian games

for "witnesses" (*martyres*) later came to refer to those who give the ultimate testimony of shedding their blood for Christ (see Acts 22:20; Rev 2:13).

This great contest calls for a decisive response: first, to **rid ourselves of every burden**. The verb for "rid oneself" can also be translated "lay aside" (RSV) or "throw off" (NIV, NJB) and is often applied to what people have to discard when they become a disciple of Jesus: the works of darkness (Rom 13:12), the old self (Eph 4:22), falsehood (Eph 4:25), anger and gossip (Col 3:8), moral impurity (James 1:21), malice and deceit (1 Pet 2:1). Like disciplined athletes who shed all excess body weight as well as unnecessary clothing (in fact, ancient Greek athletes stripped naked to compete), we do well to remove any bulk or burden that might impede our progress. In light of Hebrews 10:32–34, this could include an excessive attachment to possessions or worldly security or the esteem of others. They especially include any **sin that clings to us**, or "entangles" or "obstructs" us, like an obstacle on the racetrack that could trip us up and hinder us from reaching the finish line.

Stripped of encumbrances, we are better able to **persevere in running the race that lies before us**. Perseverance, or endurance, is one of the essential qualities in the Christian life (see 10:36), both for individuals and for communities. It is the quality most often mentioned by the risen Jesus in commending the churches of Asia (Rev 2:2–3, 19; 3:10). This implies that the pilgrimage of faith is not a sprint but a distance race that will include some long, uphill climbs and stretches of rough terrain.

12:2   As Olympic athletes totally focus their attention on the finish line, so we are to keep **our eyes fixed on Jesus**, the runner who has reached the goal ahead of us (see 2:10). Stephen literally did so as he was being stoned (Acts 7:55). The titles given to Jesus here, **leader and perfecter** (Greek *archēgos* and *teleiōtēs*), are rooted in the words "beginning" and "end" (*archē* and *telos*) and imply that Jesus is the one who has blazed the trail **of faith** before us (as in 2:10) and will one day bring our faith to perfection (as in 10:14; see Phil 1:6). More than any of the biblical heroes praised in chapter 11, Jesus is our supreme exemplar of faith. Although as God's Son he had a totally unique relationship to God, characterized by knowledge rather than faith (see Matt 11:27; John 1:18; 6:46),[3] as man he was "like his brothers in every way" (2:17). He knew the human experience of darkness, temptation, and anguish (4:15; 5:7; see Mark 14:36), yet his whole life embodied trust in the Father (see Matt 27:43).[4]

Jesus himself fixed his eyes on the goal: **for the sake of the joy that lay before him he endured** (*hypomenō*) **the cross**. Our endurance (*hypomonē*, translated as "persevere" in v. 1) is rooted in *his* endurance. The joy that lay before him was the joy of completing the mission given him by the Father, to redeem fallen humanity and bring us into eternal life, so that his joy could be ours (John 15:11; 17:13). It is the overflowing joy felt in heaven over even one sinner who repents (Luke 15:7). Jesus considered that joy to far outweigh the anguish of the cross, **despising**, or thinking nothing of, **its shame**. For the ancient world, as appalling as was the physical torture of crucifixion, even more dreadful was the shame of that degrading punishment, reserved for only the basest of slaves and criminals. Yet Jesus, and his followers after him, disregarded this shame in view of the glorious victory it won. Thus Paul, the once-proud Pharisee, could say, "I am not ashamed of the gospel. It is the power of God for the salvation of everyone who believes" (Rom 1:16).

It is by looking at Jesus that we can glimpse the outcome of our own contest. The same Messiah who suffered the extreme disgrace—far worse than any afflictions we face—has now **taken his seat at the right of the throne of God**, the place of supreme honor and authority.[5] Just as believers share with him in the struggles of the race, so we will share with him in the glory of God's heavenly dwelling, "where Jesus has entered on our behalf as forerunner" (6:20). Paul

---

3. The New Testament never uses the verb "believe" (*pisteuō*) to describe Jesus' relation to God, although this verb is used 241 times. See Albert Vanhoye, *A Different Priest: The Letter to the Hebrews*, trans. Leo Arnold, Series Rhetorica Semitica (Miami: Convivium, 2011), 366.

4. The Greek word usually translated as "faith" (*pistis*) connotes trust, fidelity, and trustworthiness as well as belief.

5. This is the fifth time Hebrews has quoted Ps 110:1: see 1:3, 13; 8:1; 10:12.

exhorts Timothy along the same lines: "If we persevere [*hypomenō*] / we shall also reign with him" (2 Tim 2:12). And the risen Jesus promises in Revelation, "I will give the victor the right to sit with me on my throne, as I myself first won the victory and sit with my Father on his throne" (Rev 3:21).

Verse 3 focuses on another aspect of Jesus' interior suffering: the **opposition**   **12:3** (or "hostility," RSV) that he faced from those he came to save. A form of the same word is in Simeon's prophecy over the infant Jesus: "Behold, this child is destined . . . to be a sign that will be contradicted" (or "opposed," Luke 2:34). Few human experiences are more painful than being opposed and reviled by the very people you love. For Jesus, this suffering extended throughout his public ministry[6] and culminated in his being handed over to **sinners** who crucified him (see Mark 14:41). If we **consider how he endured** (*hypomenō*, as in v. 2) such intense hostility, it puts our own troubles in right perspective. The original readers of Hebrews, like so many Christians today, were in danger of losing heart and dropping out of the race.[7] By contemplating Jesus, we are strengthened against the temptation to discouragement and motivated to persevere.

"Cheer up! You haven't been martyred yet." This might seem a rather odd   **12:4** way to reassure the fainthearted, but it is precisely what Hebrews is saying in verse 4. **In your struggle against sin**—especially the sin of turning away from the faith because of cultural pressure or persecution—**you have not yet resisted to the point of shedding blood**. Not only Jesus but also many of the Old Testament saints and early Christians paid the ultimate price for refusing to sin. Having found the priceless treasure (Matt 13:44), they could say with Paul, "I consider that the sufferings of this present time are as nothing compared with the glory to be revealed to us" (Rom 8:18; see 2 Cor 4:17). For most of us, our struggles to keep the faith have been minor in comparison. How then could anyone consider so lightly throwing away such a great gift?

The Discipline of the Lord (12:5–13)

[5]**You have also forgotten the exhortation addressed to you as sons:**

> **"My son, do not disdain the discipline of the Lord**
> **or lose heart when reproved by him;**
> [6]**for whom the Lord loves, he disciplines;**
> **he scourges every son he acknowledges."**

---

6. See Mark 3:6, 21–22; 8:11; 11:18; 12:13; 14:1; 15:29; Luke 20:20.
7. See 2:1; 3:12; 4:1; 6:6; 10:25–26, 35, 39.

⁷Endure your trials as "discipline"; God treats you as sons. For what "son" is there whom his father does not discipline? ⁸If you are without discipline, in which all have shared, you are not sons but bastards. ⁹Besides this, we have had our earthly fathers to discipline us, and we respected them. Should we not [then] submit all the more to the Father of spirits and live? ¹⁰They disciplined us for a short time as seemed right to them, but he does so for our benefit, in order that we may share his holiness. ¹¹At the time, all discipline seems a cause not for joy but for pain, yet later it brings the peaceful fruit of righteousness to those who are trained by it.

¹²So strengthen your drooping hands and your weak knees. ¹³Make straight paths for your feet, that what is lame may not be dislocated but healed.

OT: Ps 119:67, 71; Prov 3:11–12; Isa 32:17
NT: Acts 14:22; Rom 8:28; 2 Cor 4:17; 1 Pet 4:12; 1 John 3:13
Catechism: the value of suffering, 1500–1505, 1508, 1521
Lectionary: Heb 12:2–13: Mass for Persecuted Christians

Most Christians are aware, at least on a theoretical level, that suffering is an unavoidable part of Christian life—and of human life. Yet we tend to be taken aback and disheartened when we actually encounter it. Thus Peter had to remind the early Christians, "Beloved, do not be surprised that a trial by fire is occurring among you, as if something strange were happening to you" (1 Pet 4:12). And 1 John exhorts, "Do not be amazed, . . . brothers, if the world hates you" (1 John 3:13). Here Hebrews gives a similar exhortation, showing the right way to understand our sufferings: they are the *discipline* of a loving Father, who is preparing us to share in his own divine glory. Suffering is training in sonship. Rather than being discouraged, we should be thrilled, as Jesus said in the Gospel: "Blessed are you when people hate you, / and when they exclude and insult you, / and denounce your name as evil / on account of the Son of Man. Rejoice and leap for joy on that day!" (Luke 6:22–23).

The key word throughout this section is "sons" (inclusive, of course, of both sons and daughters). The author has spent much time talking about the passion and exaltation of Christ, boldly affirming that Jesus was made "perfect through suffering" (2:10) and that "he learned obedience from what he suffered" (5:8). It was Jesus' filial trust and obedience in the face of unbearable suffering that refined his human nature to infinite perfection. Now Hebrews shows more concretely how Jesus' perfection relates to us. Redemption is not a mere paying of a price on our behalf, a kind of commercial exchange; rather, Jesus is the "leader," the pioneer, who is "bringing many children to glory" (2:10)[8] through our union with him in his passage from suffering to glory. Paul took every occasion to teach this principle: we are "heirs of God and joint heirs with Christ, if only we suffer with him so that we may also be glorified with him" (Rom 8:17; see Phil 3:10–11; 1 Pet 1:6; 5:10).

God's fatherly discipline, painful though it sometimes is, transforms us into **12:5** faithful, obedient sons and daughters. The Old Testament testifies to this reality, as the preacher reminds his audience: **You have also forgotten the exhortation addressed to you as sons**. This statement could be translated as a question: "Have you forgotten . . . ?" The passage he is about to quote, Proverbs 3:11–12, is a word of "exhortation" or "encouragement" (*paraklēsis*), like the Letter to the Hebrews itself (13:22). Like other biblical texts, it is a living word in which God addresses us in the present. **My son, do not disdain the discipline of the Lord / or lose heart when reproved by him**. This proverb cautions against two wrong responses to God's "discipline" (*paideia*, which can mean, more broadly, "training" or "education").[9] The first, to "disdain," is exemplified by a child who laughs off correction without any intention of changing his or her behavior. The second, to "lose heart," is exemplified by a child who becomes dejected and discouraged at correction. It is the latter to which the readers of Hebrews are tempted, as the same verb "lose heart" in verse 3 shows. But in either case, one misses out on the educational value of the discipline.

The proverb continues by giving the reason we should highly value our **12:6** sufferings: because they are a sign of God's love for us. **For whom the Lord loves, he disciplines; / he scourges every son he acknowledges**. God allows suffering because he deeply cares about his children growing to full maturity. The people of Israel had to learn to understand suffering in this light. Moses had said of their hunger and other hardships during the forty years in the desert, "You must know in your heart that, even as a man disciplines his son, so the LORD, your God, disciplines you" (Deut 8:5). The psalmist confesses to God that he sees how his sufferings changed him: "Before I was afflicted I went astray, / but now I hold to your promise" (Ps 119:67); "It was good for me to be afflicted, / in order to learn your statutes" (Ps 119:71). For the same reason the book of Proverbs repeatedly admonishes parents not to neglect disciplining their children: "He who spares the rod hates his son, / but he who loves him is diligent to discipline him" (Prov 13:24 RSV).[10]

---

8. The word for "children" in 2:10 (*huioi*) is the same as the word for "sons" in 12:5–8.

9. This word derives from *pais*, the Greek word for "child."

10. See also Prov 19:18; 22:15; 23:13–14; 29:15, 17. The "rod" should not be seen only as physical punishment, and certainly not as abusive punishment, but rather whatever form of discipline is appropriate, firm, and loving.

12:7–8   This is how, then, we should regard the troubles that come from Christian witness in a hostile world, and any other sufferings: **Endure your trials as "discipline."**[11] They are signs that **God** is treating us **as sons.** This analogy does not mean that God is simply treating us the same way a human father treats his children; rather, God is treating us as *his own* sons and daughters. The analogy moves not upward but downward: it is not that God acts like human fathers, whose conduct often falls far short, but that wise, firm, and loving fathers give us a glimpse of what God is like.[12] God uses all the adverse events in our lives to "perfect" us—to prepare us for the unimaginable glory of divine life—as Jesus himself, the firstborn Son, was "made perfect through suffering" (2:10; see 12:23).

For what "son" is there whom his father does not discipline? The implied answer is "none." In the ancient world the education of sons, preparing them for full participation in the life of society, was considered a paramount duty of fathers. If adolescents were observed growing up without parental discipline, one would assume they were **not** legal **sons** but illegitimate children who, in ancient society, had no rights of inheritance. Therefore, the author reasons, we would have grounds to be concerned only if we were **without discipline**! But God, the infinitely wise Father, does not leave any of his children without the correction that brings us to spiritual maturity. **All have shared** in these lessons of sonship, including the biblical heroes of chapter 11, Christian believers (10:32–34), and most of all, Jesus himself, the firstborn Son.

12:9   Verse 9 deploys the same kind of rabbinic argument used in 2:2 and 9:13–14, reasoning from the lesser to the greater (†*qal wahomer*). If **we respected** our human parents, who disciplined us imperfectly, **all the more** should we trustingly **submit** to our heavenly Father, who disciplines us with perfect wisdom and love. The Greek phrase for **earthly fathers** is literally "fathers of flesh." God, in contrast, is **the Father of spirits**. This is an unusual title for God.[13] Here it probably means that God is the source of our spiritual life, our capacity to relate to him, whereas our earthly parents are the source of only our natural life. If we submit to God's discipline, as hard as it may seem at the time, we will **live**—that is, share in God's own eternal life (see 7:16).

12:10   Our earthly parents **disciplined us for a short time**, literally, "for a few days," **as seemed right to them**. Even the best parents cannot see into the hearts of their children. Their discipline will at times be unfair, too strict or too lenient, or not

---

11. The phrase "your trials" is not in the Greek but is supplied by the NAB. The word "endure" (*hypomenō*) is the same key word from Heb 12:1–4.

12. Luke Timothy Johnson, *Hebrews: A Commentary*, New Testament Library (Louisville: Westminster John Knox, 2006), 321.

13. There is some precedent in the title "God of the spirits of all flesh" (Num 16:22; 27:16 RSV).

St. Isaac Jogues on Enduring Trials

LIVING TRADITION

St. Isaac Jogues, one of the heroic French Jesuit missionaries to North America, suffered months of captivity and torture by the Mohawks before being martyred in 1646. During this period the only book he possessed was the Letter to the Hebrews, and in it he found his greatest consolation. He wrote to his provincial:

> Amid this frequent fear and death, while every day I die, or rather drag on a life more bitter than any death . . . God my stout Helper often by his unfailing goodness roused my drooping spirits. I had recourse to the Holy Scriptures, my only refuge in the tribulations that were heaped upon me. These did I venerate; with these I wished to die. Of all the books which we were carrying for the use of the Frenchmen living among the Hurons, none had fallen into my hands but the Epistle of St. Paul to the Hebrews. . . . This little book, with a picture of St. Bruno . . . and a rude wooden cross I had made, I always carried about me, so that whenever death, which was ever present before my eyes, should strike me down, I could most cheerfully die with the Holy Scriptures which had ever been my greatest consolation, with the graces and indulgences of my most holy Mother the Church, whom I had always greatly, but now most tenderly loved, and with the cross of my Lord and Savior.[a]

a. Translation adapted from John Gilmary Shea, *Perils of the Ocean and Wilderness: or, Narratives of Shipwreck and Indian Captivity; Gleaned from Early Missionary Annals* (Boston: P. Donahoe, 1857), 45–46.

well suited to the child's unique personality. But God **does so for our benefit**. His discipline is always to our advantage. As Paul affirms, God orchestrates all the events in our life, including the most pleasant and the most painful, for our good: "We know that all things work for good for those who love God, who are called according to his purpose" (Rom 8:28). God's ultimate purpose is **that we may share his holiness**.[14] Hebrews said earlier that we "have been made holy" by the once-for-all sacrifice of Christ (10:10), and yet in this life we "are being made holy" (10:14). Here the author is elaborating on that second dimension: the gradual sanctification of our thoughts, words, and actions that takes place through God's discipline.

In Scripture God's holiness is synonymous with God himself; to say "The Lord God has sworn by his holiness" is the same as "The Lord God has sworn by his very self" (Amos 4:2; 6:8).[15] That we will "share his holiness" is therefore

---

14. This theme appears throughout Scripture: see Lev 19:2; Num 15:40; Joel 3:17; Eph 1:4; 1 Thess 4:3; 1 Pet 1:15–16.

15. As the Catechism affirms, "The holiness of God is the inaccessible center of his eternal mystery" (2809).

the same as saying we will "share in the divine nature" (2 Pet 1:4) or will be "divinized," as the Church Fathers put it. God's purpose is to communicate his own nature to us, preparing us for a destiny far beyond "all we ask or imagine" (Eph 3:20). However, this can take place only through a radical purification and transformation of our own nature. Thus Paul affirms in Acts, "It is necessary for us to undergo many hardships to enter the kingdom of God" (Acts 14:22)—an insight he expressed after being stoned in Lystra (Acts 14:19). And he tells the Christians in Thessalonica, "The afflictions you endure [are] . . . evidence of the just judgment of God, so that you may be considered worthy of the kingdom of God for which you are suffering" (2 Thess 1:4–5).[16] If we are tempted to see troubles as a sign of God's disfavor, we should, on the contrary, recognize them as a sign of God's surpassing fatherly love. Even those troubles that follow directly or indirectly from our bad behavior (for instance, broken health due to drug abuse, or a broken relationship due to selfishness) will be used by God as remedial discipline that ultimately will make us holy, if we trust him.

12:11   Hebrews applies to the spiritual life a principle universally recognized in sports: no pain, no gain.[17] **At the time, all discipline seems a cause not for joy** (*chara*) **but for pain** (*lypē*).[18] Correction never feels good at the time, but Hebrews is careful to say that that negative sensation is based on what *seems* to be. We must avoid the temptation to resentment or self-pity when troubles come our way. Only **later** are we able to perceive the abundant positive results of God's discipline: **it brings the peaceful fruit of righteousness to those who are trained by it.** The Greek word for "trained" (*gymnazō*) shows that our author still has in mind the sports imagery that began in verse 1: Christians are athletes in training for eternal life. The fruit of that training is "righteousness" that is "peaceful" because it includes both the inner serenity and the external harmony in relationships that come from having one's life in right order. These two qualities are inextricably linked: "The effect of righteousness will be peace" (Isa 32:17 RSV; see Ps 85:11).

12:12   Like a coach shouting encouragement to a cross-country team as they enter the final stretch (see vv. 1–2), the preacher rallies his hearers: **So strengthen** (*anorthoō*; literally, "straighten up") **your drooping hands and your weak** (or "paralyzed") **knees.** This line is from a passage in Isaiah (35:3–6), in which the

---

16. See also Rom 8:16–17; 2 Cor 4:17; Phil 3:10–11; 2 Tim 2:11–12; James 1:2–4, 12; 1 Pet 1:3–7; 4:12–14.

17. An ancient version of this principle as applied to education is attributed to Aristotle: "The roots of discipline are bitter, but its fruit is sweet" (Diogenes Laertius, *Lives and Opinions of Eminent Philosophers* 5.18).

18. Jesus uses the same contrast in reassuring his disciples at the Last Supper as they are about to face the painful events of his passion: "You have sorrow [*lypē*] now, but I will see you again and your hearts will rejoice, and no one will take your joy [*chara*] from you" (John 16:22 RSV).

prophet encourages the Jews who are weary and disheartened by the sufferings of their exile in Babylon:

> Strengthen hands that are feeble,
>   make firm knees that are weak,
> Say to the fearful of heart:
>   Be strong, do not fear!
> Here is your God,
>   he comes with vindication;
> With divine recompense
>   he comes to save you.
> Then the eyes of the blind shall see,
>   the ears of the deaf be opened;
> Then will the lame shall leap like a stag,
>   and the mute tongue sing for joy.

The heart of the passage, and the primary reason for taking courage, is the promise in Isaiah 35:4: "Here is your God, / . . . he comes to save you" (similar to the promise of Habakkuk quoted above at 10:37). Our confident hope in God's promise is what enables us to summon our energies and press on.

The next line, **Make straight paths for your feet**,[19] is from Proverbs 4:26–27:   **12:13** "Keep straight the path of your feet, / and all your ways will be sure. / Do not swerve to the right or to the left; / turn your foot away from evil" (NRSV). This picks up on the same Greek root for "straight" (*orth-*) as in the exhortation to straighten up hands and knees in verse 12. The point is to avoid being wobbly or wavering Christians who might easily trip and suffer even greater injury. **What is lame** may refer to areas of personal weakness and vulnerability to temptation, or to members of the church who have become confused, discouraged, or even tempted to abandon the faith. If every member strives to keep moving straight toward the goal (see 6:19–20), that portion of the community that is struggling will **not be dislocated but healed**, in accord with God's promise to heal the lame in the Isaiah passage quoted above (Isa 35:6).

Reflection and Application (12:5–13)

Contemporary society has something of an allergy to parental discipline. This is partly because some people have been hurt by parental discipline that

---

19. The word for "paths" (*trochias*) is related to "run" (*trechō*) in Heb 12:1, continuing the race metaphor.

was administered harshly or arbitrarily, or even abusively, motivated more by annoyance at the child's behavior than by love. Such uncharitable discipline can leave deep wounds in the heart of a child, often leading to dysfunctional behavior as an adult. But many parents forget that the reverse is also true. A child who does not receive consistent, loving discipline experiences a lack of appropriate boundaries, which causes insecurity. Such a child becomes a slave to his or her own selfish whims and grows up lacking in self-control, which in turn deprives him or her of the happiness that comes from relationships of self-sacrifice and self-giving love. Such a person is also unprepared to receive correction from other authorities or from God himself, and may misinterpret discipline as rejection. On the other hand, children who receive consistent and loving discipline from their parents are formed in character and, more importantly, are shown an image of their infinitely more wise and loving heavenly Father.

Peace and Holiness (12:14–17)

---

¹⁴**Strive for peace with everyone, and for that holiness without which no one will see the Lord. ¹⁵See to it that no one be deprived of the grace of God, that no bitter root spring up and cause trouble, through which many may become defiled, ¹⁶that no one be an immoral or profane person like Esau, who sold his birthright for a single meal. ¹⁷For you know that later, when he wanted to inherit his father's blessing, he was rejected because he found no opportunity to change his mind, even though he sought the blessing with tears.**

OT: Gen 25:29–34; 27:34–38; Prov 4:26–27; Isa 35:3–6
NT: Matt 5:8–9; Rom 12:18; 1 John 3:2–3; Rev 21:27
Catechism: pursuing peace, 2304–5; holiness and seeing God, 1720–24

Verses 1–13 were an exhortation to endure the trials that come our way; here the emphasis shifts to the proactive steps we should take to attain the goal of eternal life, the city that is to come (11:10). Specifically, we ought to strive for "peace" in our human relationships and "holiness" toward God. These verses are a reminder that we progress toward the goal not as isolated individuals but as a community. We are to help one another reach the finish line.

12:14   The two lines of verse 14 recall two of the Beatitudes, in inverse order: "Blessed are the clean of heart, / for they will see God. / Blessed are the peacemakers . . ."

(Matt 5:8–9). First, **strive for peace with everyone**.[20] Peace in the biblical sense is not a mere absence of conflict but full harmony in relationships with others. This is a tall order because it includes peace not only with members of the church (as in Mark 9:50) but also with people in society at large, even those who have inflicted terrible injustices (see Heb 10:32–34). As Paul acknowledges, complete peace requires the good will of both parties in a relationship, and we are responsible only for our part: "If possible, on your part, live at peace with all" (Rom 12:18). The conduct of Christians should always be peaceable, always fostering reconciliation, never fueling tensions, so that our God-given peace might touch the lives of those around us. Such peace, in ourselves and in the church, is the fruit of God's fatherly discipline (v. 11).

Second, pursue **that holiness without which no one will see the Lord**. We have already been made holy by Christ's blood, shed on the cross (9:14; 10:10), but here the point is that we must allow that holiness to pervade and transform every aspect of our lives. The same paradox appears in Paul's first letter to the Corinthians: "you who *have been made holy* in Christ Jesus, *called to be holy*" (1 Cor 1:2, literal translation). Both Hebrews and Paul are saying, in effect: Christians, become what you are! There is an implicit warning that those who are not pure in heart and life will not be able to enter the presence of the Lord. Revelation says of the heavenly city, "Nothing unclean will enter it, nor any[one] who does abominable things or tells lies" (Rev 21:27; see 1 Cor 6:9–11; Gal 5:19–21; Eph 5:5). But there is also an implicit promise: the glorious goal toward which we are heading—the fulfillment of the deepest desire of the human heart (Ps 17:15; 42:3)—is to see our God face-to-face (1 Cor 13:12).[21] Then "we shall be like him, for we shall see him as he is. Everyone who has this hope based on him makes himself pure, as he is pure" (1 John 3:2–3).

The Greek verb for **see to it** (*episkopeō*) is related to the word for "overseer" **12:15** or "bishop" (*episkopos*) but is used here for the responsibility that all members of the church have for one another. The concern of each should be **that no one be deprived of the grace of God**. The grace of God is God's free gift of his own divine life, always available to us from the "throne of grace" (4:16). However, a person can be deprived of it by forsaking faith in God (3:12) and dropping out of the race (12:1), or by the sins that Hebrews is about to mention.[22]

---

20. In 1 Peter we find the same instruction: "seek peace and pursue it" (1 Pet 3:11 RSV, quoting Ps 34:15); see also Rom 14:19; 2 Tim 2:22.

21. Since "the Lord" refers to Christ, in whom we see the face of God (John 14:9), it is possible that Hebrews is referring to seeing the Lord in this life with the eyes of faith (see 2:9; 2 Cor 3:18).

22. See 2:1–3; 4:1; 6:4–6; 10:29, 35, 39; 12:25.

All must be on guard **that no bitter root spring up and cause trouble, through which many may become defiled**. This phrase is borrowed from Deuteronomy, where Moses warns of the grave damage done by those who fall into idolatry: "Beware lest there be among you a man or woman or family or tribe whose heart turns away from the LORD our God to go and serve the gods of these nations; lest there be among you a root bearing poisonous and bitter fruit" (Deut 29:18 RSV). Apostasy and any other serious sins rarely occur in isolation. Even one person whose heart has become bitter through resentment or any other sin can poison others and thus have a devastating effect on the whole community, as one rotten apple can spoil the barrel.

12:16   The author highlights what is at stake by bringing out the counterexample of **Esau**, an exact contrast to the heroes of faith in chapter 11. Esau is the classic biblical example of a person who forfeited what is truly valuable for the sake of instant, short-term gratification. Genesis 25:29–34 recounts how Esau, coming in from the field one day, craved some of his brother Jacob's stew and agreed to give up his birthright—his right as firstborn to the greater share of the inheritance—in exchange for it. Esau thus appears as a man enslaved to his own appetites, who **sold his birthright for a single meal**. Hebrews calls him **profane** (or "godless," "irreligious") because this was not merely an act of stupidity; it was an act of disregard for his inheritance in the family of Abraham, a sacred gift from God. Esau traded in this divine gift for a moment of fleeting pleasure.

Although Genesis does not speak of Esau as **immoral** (Greek *pornos*), it does mention that he married two pagan women, who "became a source of bitterness" to his parents (Gen 26:35). The implication may be that his lack of self-control in one area, food, was also manifested in the area of sex. Throughout Scripture sexual immorality is closely linked with idolatry.[23] Marriage is the most profound earthly image of God's covenant relationship with his people. Conversely, sexual immorality is both a symbol of and a concrete act of covenant-breaking: it is to worship pleasure as a false god.[24] It is the antithesis of "that holiness without which no one will see the Lord" (v. 14; see 1 Thess 4:3–7). That some of the readers of Hebrews were in danger of falling into precisely this sin is suggested by the admonition in 13:4: "Let marriage be honored among all and the marriage bed be kept undefiled, for God will judge the immoral [*pornos*] and adulterers."

---

23. The link was manifested in that (1) the Israelites were often led into idolatry through liaisons with foreign women, and (2) pagan worship often involved cult prostitution and other sexually disordered practices (e.g., Num 25:1–2; 1 Kings 14:24). Esau was the ancestor of Edom (Gen 36:1), a nation that Jewish tradition regarded as the epitome of sexual promiscuity and idolatry (see Johnson, *Hebrews*, 325).

24. See Deut 31:16 RSV; Jer 2:20; Ezek 16; 23; Hosea 1:2; Rev 17:1–2.

Although Esau later regretted his rash act, the consequences were irrevers- **12:17** ible. **For you know that later, when he wanted to inherit his father's bless- ing, he was rejected**. This refers to the incident in which Jacob, at his mother's instigation, tricked Esau out of his dying father's blessing—in particular, the special blessing reserved for the firstborn son (Gen 27). The implication here is that this happened precisely because of Esau's earlier failure to value his sacred birthright. The "blessing" he desired was God's blessing given to Abraham (Gen 12:2–3) and passed down through each generation. When Esau found to his dismay that Isaac had already bestowed on Jacob the **blessing** of the firstborn, he begged him **with tears**, "Father, bless me too!" (Gen 27:34, 38). But it was too late; what was done could not be undone.[25]

Esau **found no opportunity to change his mind**, or "no chance for repen- tance." The account in Genesis does not indicate that Esau sincerely repented of his disdain for the sacred inheritance; rather, it seems that his regret was only for what he had lost. The implication for Christian readers is clear: we are the "firstborn" (12:23) who are heirs of an "eternal inheritance" (9:15) infinitely greater than that of the land of Israel (see 3:8–9). Yet we too, like Esau, could forfeit that inheritance by a rash decision from which there is no turning back (6:4–8; 10:26–27). As N. T. Wright points out, many a public figure embroiled in scandal has demonstrated that "it is indeed possible to do things which bring our character crashing down in ruins and to discover that there is no way back."[26]

Reflection and Application (12:14–17)

The first part of Hebrews 12 is full of practical wisdom on how to respond to sufferings that come our way, no matter what the cause. These exhortations summon us to understand our trials in the light of faith and to trust that God is using them to bring us to full maturity as his sons and daughters. Here is a brief summary of the author's prescription for enduring trials:

- Look to Jesus; remember his suffering and the reward that he received (v. 2).
- In this light, make up your mind to endure (vv. 1, 3).
- Remember that God's discipline is a sign of his fatherly love for us, and that, appropriately accepted and endured, it produces good character (v. 5–11).

25. Esau did receive a secondary blessing from Isaac in Gen 27:39–40; in fact, Hebrews mentions this in 11:20. But it was far inferior to the blessing of God's covenant with Abraham, which would now be passed down through the line of Jacob.
26. N. T. Wright, *Hebrews for Everyone*, New Testament for Everyone (Louisville: Westminster John Knox, 2004), 155.

- Do not lose heart and give up; instead, do what you know is right (vv. 12–13).
- Seek to be at peace with everyone; root out all bitterness (vv. 14–15).
- Seek to be holy in all your conduct (vv. 14, 16).

Mount Sinai and Mount Zion (12:18–24)

[18]You have not approached that which could be touched and a blazing fire and gloomy darkness and storm [19]and a trumpet blast and a voice speaking words such that those who heard begged that no message be further addressed to them, [20]for they could not bear to hear the command: "If even an animal touches the mountain, it shall be stoned." [21]Indeed, so fearful was the spectacle that Moses said, "I am terrified and trembling." [22]No, you have approached Mount Zion and the city of the living God, the heavenly Jerusalem, and countless angels in festal gathering, [23]and the assembly of the firstborn enrolled in heaven, and God the judge of all, and the spirits of the just made perfect, [24]and Jesus, the mediator of a new covenant, and the sprinkled blood that speaks more eloquently than that of Abel.

OT: Exod 19:12–19; 20:18–21; Deut 4:11; 5:22–26; 9:19
NT: Luke 10:20; 2 Cor 3:6–11; Gal 4:24–26
Catechism: angels, 334–36; our share in the festal gathering, 2188; God as judge, 1021–22; 1038–50

The contrast between the old covenant and the new, a theme that has run throughout Hebrews, is vividly portrayed in this passage. The contrast is symbolized by two mountains: Sinai, the forbidding mountain in the wilderness where the law was given through Moses, and Zion, the joyful mountain of the heavenly city where God dwells in the midst of his people. The most striking feature of this passage is that it depicts the heavenly Jerusalem not as something in the remote future but as a *present reality* that Christians already enjoy.

12:18–19   Verses 18–21 present the Sinai side of the contrast. Although Sinai is not explicitly mentioned, Hebrews is clearly drawing from the accounts of the Sinai †theophany in Exodus and Deuteronomy. This climactic event of the giving of the law at Sinai stands for the old covenant as a whole, with its earthly tabernacle, †levitical priesthood, and animal sacrifices. As Hebrews describes it here, the whole atmosphere is stern and terrifying. God is not even mentioned. This passage emphasizes the inferior status of the former age of salvation history:

272

what Christians **have not approached**, in contrast to the glorious heavenly reality that they "have approached" (v. 22) and are continually invited to approach (4:16; 7:25; 10:22).

The audiovisual phenomena of the Sinai event are described in seven vivid phrases. (1) The whole experience involved **that which could be touched**, because as dramatic as this encounter with God was, it remained on an earthly, physical level. (2) There was a **blazing fire**, as recounted in Exodus 19:18: "Mount Sinai was completely enveloped in smoke, because the LORD had come down upon it in fire. The smoke rose from it as though from a kiln." Moses later recalls the frightening scene: "You came near and stood at the foot of the mountain, while the mountain blazed to the heart of the heavens with fire and was enveloped in a dense black cloud" (Deut 4:11; see 5:22). There was (3) **darkness** that was (4) **gloomy** (literally, "darkness and gloom") and (5) a **storm** (or "whirlwind"): "peals of thunder and lightning, and a heavy cloud over the mountain" (Exod 19:16; see 19:18). Significantly, the words "touch," "darkness," and "storm" also appear in the account of the ninth plague of Egypt—"darkness that can be felt," "a storm over the whole land of Egypt" (Exod 10:21, 22 †LXX)—suggesting that Israel's experience of God was in certain ways not unlike that of their enemies.

(6) God's voice like a **trumpet blast** at Sinai was such that both the people and the earth quaked: there was "a very loud trumpet blast, so that all the people in the camp trembled. . . . The whole mountain trembled violently. . . . The trumpet blast grew louder and louder, while Moses was speaking and God answering him with thunder" (Exod 19:16, 18–19 NAB). (7) From the midst of the blazing mountain they heard **a voice speaking words** (Deut 4:12; see 5:24–26)—a voice so fearsome **that those who heard begged that no message be further addressed to them**. This response exemplifies the human reaction to a theophany. To be confronted with the overwhelming majesty and holiness of God is at the same time to be confronted with one's own *un*holiness, smallness, and fragility.[27] Thus the people implored Moses, "You speak to us, and we will listen; but do not let God speak to us, or we shall die" (Exod 20:19; see Deut 5:24–27). Although God approved of this request (Deut 18:16–17), their refusal to hear God was symbolic of the general hardness of heart of that exodus generation, who continually rebelled against God, as recounted in Hebrews 3–4.

The people's alarm was intensified by **the command: "If even an animal touches the mountain, it shall be stoned."** God himself had solemnly warned them not to come too near: "Take care not to go up the mountain, or even to

12:20

---

27. Such was the experience of Abraham (Gen 15:12), Isaiah (Isa 6:5), Daniel (Dan 10:9), Peter (Luke 5:8), the three apostles at Jesus' transfiguration (Matt 17:6), and John the seer (Rev 1:17).

touch its edge. All who touch the mountain must be put to death" (Exod 19:12; see 19:21). Any person or beast who violated the prohibition was to be executed by stoning or arrows—that is, from a safe distance.

12:21   Finally, the inferior status of the old covenant is strikingly underscored by the fact that even Moses, the mediator of the covenant, the man who spoke with God face-to-face (Exod 33:11), admitted that he was **terrified and trembling** at the **spectacle**. Significantly, this phrase echoes Deuteronomy 9:19, where Moses is referring not to the Sinai theophany itself but to his fear of God's wrath in response to the people's idolatry of the golden calf: "I am terrified of the fierce anger of the Lord against you: his wrath would destroy you."[28]

The overall effect of this description of the Sinai theophany is to powerfully accent the unapproachability of God in the old covenant. For a people not yet redeemed in Christ, to draw near to the all-holy God was not safe.

12:22   Against this dark background the joyous and welcoming reality that Christians *have* **approached** stands out all the more. The perfect tense of the verb "approached" expresses the present result of a past action: our nearness to God as a result of our conversion to Christ through faith and baptism.[29] As Hebrews has shown at length, through the sacrifice of Jesus we are able to approach God with full confidence (4:16; 7:25; 10:22). "Approach" often has the nuance of "worship," to enter with God's people into his holy presence. The scene depicted here is the heavenly †liturgy (like that of John's vision in Rev 4–5), in which the Christian liturgy on earth mystically participates.

The Zion side of the contrast too is described in seven phrases. Whereas the Sinai phenomena were visible and palpable, the new covenant has to do with unseen spiritual realities. Yet they are not less real but *more* real; they are the realities in contrast to the shadows (Heb 10:1). (1) First there is **Mount Zion and the city of the living God, the heavenly Jerusalem**. These are three ways of saying the same thing. Mount Zion, one of the hills on which Jerusalem was built, had become synonymous with the city itself (see Ps 147:12–13). As the site of the temple it was the holy city, beloved by God, where God had promised to dwell forever (Ps 87:1–2; 132:13–14). There David had reigned, and the prophets foretold that one day God himself would reign in Jerusalem (Isa 24:23). The psalm that has been quoted most often in Hebrews, Psalm 110, envisions the Messiah's kingdom as centered in Jerusalem: "The scepter of your might: / the Lord extends your strong scepter from Zion" (Ps 110:2; see Rev 14:1).

---

28. Author's translation. Stephen's speech in Acts also refers to Moses' "trembling" at the burning bush encounter (Acts 7:32; see Exod 3:6).
29. Vanhoye, *A Different Priest*, 391.

Fig. 18. The oldest known map of Jerusalem, part of a sixth-century mosaic floor map in the Byzantine church of Saint George, Medeba, Jordan

As the earthly tabernacle was only a copy of the heavenly sanctuary (8:5), so the earthly Jerusalem is the lesser counterpart of the heavenly city, "whose architect and maker is God" (11:10). Paul draws a similar analogy in Galatians: Mount Sinai symbolizes the earthly Jerusalem and the old dispensation as a whole, with all its failures and imperfections, in contrast to "the Jerusalem above" (Gal 4:26). Christians already have their true citizenship in that heavenly city (Phil 3:20), even though in the fullest sense it is still to come (Heb 13:14; see Rev 21:2).

As the dwelling place of "the living God," the heavenly city is filled with life and overflowing joy. (2) The second characteristic of Mount Zion is that there are **countless** (literally, "myriads of") **angels in festal gathering**. A myriad equals ten thousand and was the greatest quantity for which there was a word in Greek. This throng of heavenly beings recalls Daniel's vision of the throne of God: "Thousands upon thousands were ministering to him, / and myriads upon myriads stood before him" (Dan 7:10).[30] Hebrews earlier described angels as those who minister to God's people (1:14), but here the angels' main activity is worship. As in John's vision in Revelation, they are jubilantly celebrating the glorious victory that God has won in Christ (Rev 5:11–12).

(3) The angels are joined by the saints, **the assembly** (*ekklēsia*, literally, "church") **of the firstborn enrolled in heaven**. This is another subtle contrast **12:23**

---

30. There may also be an implied contrast with the "ten thousands of holy ones" who, according to Deut 33:2 (RSV), accompanied God at Mount Sinai.

New Revelation on a New Mountain

BIBLICAL BACKGROUND

Throughout Scripture, mountains are places of encounter with God. The lonely desert mountain, Sinai, was the site of the high point of Old Testament revelation, where God gave the covenant and the law. Mount Sinai was symbolic of all the barriers that the law had erected to set Israel apart from other nations: the kosher laws, the ritual purity laws, the laws of sabbath and sacrifice. But the prophets foretold that in the end times Mount Zion would, in contrast, be the place from which God's revelation would go out to the whole world.

> Many peoples shall come and say:
> "Come, let us go up to the LORD's mountain,
>   to the house of the God of Jacob,
> That he may instruct us in his ways,
>   and we may walk in his paths."
> For from Zion shall go forth instruction,
>   and the word of the LORD from Jerusalem.
>
> (Isa 2:3; see Isa 56:6–7; Mic 4:2)

The New Testament reveals the fulfillment of that prophecy beginning at Pentecost, when the disciples gathered in the upper room on Mount Zion were filled with the Holy Spirit and then propelled by the Spirit to bring the good news of Jesus Christ, the fullness of God's revelation, to every corner of the earth (Acts 1:8; 2:1–11).[a]

a. "Mount Zion" originally referred to the northern hill in Jerusalem on which the temple stood. By the first century, the name had migrated to the western hill, the probable site of the upper room. But in both the Old and New Testaments "Zion" could be used as a poetic name for the whole city (e.g., Ps 97:8; 102:22).

with Israel, the assembly (*ekklēsia*) of God's people at Sinai (Deut 9:10 LXX). Hebrews earlier ascribed to Jesus the status of God's firstborn (1:6); now all believers share that same exalted status. After the exodus God directed that the firstborn in every family was to be consecrated to him, to belong to him in a special way (Exod 13:2, 15); now all Christians have that privilege (see Heb 10:10, 14). Being the "firstborn" (*prototokos*) also calls to mind the "birthright" (*prototokia*)—the sacred inheritance that Esau had so foolishly bartered away (12:16). That we are "enrolled in heaven" means that a place is reserved for us there. Jesus had promised his apostles, "Your names are written in heaven" (Luke 10:20), and both Paul and Revelation speak of Christians as those whose names are written in "the book of life" (Phil 4:3; Rev 21:27; see Ps 69:29; Dan 12:1).

(4) At first glance, the mention of **God the judge of all** might seem to introduce a more ominous note into this festive scene. It is a reminder that God is the one to whom every creature will have to render an account (Heb 4:13; see 10:30; Gen 18:25), and that every deed, good or evil, will receive its just recompense (Rom 2:5–8; 1 Pet 1:17). But for believers, this is reason for confident hope, even joy. Whoever has read Hebrews up to this point realizes that the God who judges is the same God who has atoned for our sins and given believers a share in his own holiness through the one perfect sacrifice of Jesus Christ.

(5) **The spirits of the just made perfect** may refer to the saints of the old covenant, exemplified by the heroes of faith in chapter 11. But more likely, the phrase refers to all the deceased faithful of both the old and the new covenant eras, those who died looking forward in faith (11:13) and those who have fallen asleep in Christ (1 Cor 15:18). In biblical thought the just, or "righteous," are those who live in right relationship with God and neighbor. Now the saints of the old covenant and the new, having been perfected by Christ's grace, are rejoicing together before the throne of God. The term "spirits" is here synonymous with "souls" (as in Wis 3:1), referring to souls that have been separated from the body. They are still looking forward to the final consummation of God's plan, the resurrection of the dead.

(6) At the climax of the series is **Jesus**. The mention of his human name **12:24** accents his shared humanity with ours. It is because of his self-offering on the cross that the throng of angels and saints are joyously worshiping before God's throne. His being made "perfect through suffering" is what has brought "many children to glory" (2:10). As Hebrews already showed, he is **the mediator of a new covenant** (9:15), the better covenant (7:22; 8:6), which can never be broken because it brings about a radical and permanent transformation in the recipients. Here the phrase "new covenant" uses a different Greek word for "new" (*nea*, meaning "fresh" or "young," instead of *kainē* as in 8:8, 13; 9:15). As one biblical scholar notes, "The covenant founded by Jesus is not only of a new kind; it is at the same time radiant with youth, springing up like a source of fresh water."[31]

(7) That believers have "approached" (v. 22) **the sprinkled blood** of Jesus means that they have been sprinkled by that blood which, unlike the animal blood with which the Israelites were sprinkled (9:19–21), has power to "cleanse our consciences from dead works to worship the living God" (9:14; see 10:22). This blood **speaks more eloquently** (literally, "better") **than that of Abel**, the first victim of murder. According to Genesis, Abel's blood cried out to God from the ground (Gen 4:10; see Heb 11:4), and in response God punished the

---

31. Vanhoye, *A Different Priest*, 395.

perpetrator, Cain, for his crime. Whereas Abel's blood called for retribution, the blood of Jesus, innocent victim of an infinitely worse crime, cries out for mercy and forgiveness. Instead of bringing a curse (see Gen 4:11), it brings the blessing of eternal redemption (Heb 9:12) and victory over death.

The mention of the covenant and sprinkled blood again calls to mind the Sinai theophany, sharpening the contrast between the old and new. The former covenant, mediated by Moses, was established by sprinkling animal blood on the altar, representing God, and on the people (Exod 24:6–8; see Heb 9:19–21). But a bond forged by the blood of animals was fragile at best, "for it is impossible that the blood of bulls and goats take away sins" (Heb 10:4). The new covenant, in contrast, is founded on Jesus, who shared our human nature (2:14) and freely chose to shed his blood out of love for us. "Covenant" and "blood" also call to mind the Last Supper, where Jesus instituted the great sacrament of the new covenant: "This cup is the new covenant in my blood, which will be shed for you" (Luke 22:20). This allusion strengthens the liturgical overtones of the whole passage. It is at the Eucharistic liturgy that Christians most fully enter into the wondrous celebration of Christ's triumph that goes on eternally before God's throne in heaven.

The Unshakable Kingdom (12:25–29)

> [25]See that you do not reject the one who speaks. For if they did not escape when they refused the one who warned them on earth, how much more in our case if we turn away from the one who warns from heaven. [26]His voice shook the earth at that time, but now he has promised, "I will once more shake not only earth but heaven." [27]That phrase, "once more," points to [the] removal of shaken, created things, so that what is unshaken may remain. [28]Therefore, we who are receiving the unshakable kingdom should have gratitude, with which we should offer worship pleasing to God in reverence and awe. [29]For our God is a consuming fire.

OT: Exod 19:18; Deut 4:24; Judg 5:5; Ps 68:9; Hag 2:6–7
NT: Rom 12:1; 1 Cor 10:5–6; Rev 21:1
Catechism: reverence and awe, 2777–78
Lectionary: Heb 12:18–19, 22–24: Anniversary of the Dedication of a Church; Mass of the Most Holy Eucharist; Mass of the Most Precious Blood of Our Lord Jesus Christ

This section is the author's final solemn warning (similar to 6:4–8 and 10:26–31) and his final use of a lesser-to-greater argument (†*qal wahomer*) comparing the old covenant with the new. He is bringing his whole homily full circle by restating the comparison made in 2:2–4: If those who were unfaithful to the former covenant received a just penalty, how much more so will those who refuse the overflowing grace and mercy of the new covenant? This passage decisively refutes a common misunderstanding of the gospel: the idea that God is like a permissive parent who is not terribly concerned about his children's conduct. Rather, this passage, and the whole Letter to the Hebrews, affirms that the God we worship is the same holy and awesome God who thundered at Mount Sinai. God has not changed; rather, *we* are changed by the atoning †sacrifice of Jesus. We are empowered to live a holy life, offered as a pleasing sacrifice to God.

The admonition of verse 25, **See that you do not reject the one who speaks**, echoes that of 3:12: "See to it, brothers, that none of you may have an evil and unfaithful heart, so as to forsake the living God" (literal translation). The "one who speaks" links this statement with the previous verse: God is speaking through the blood of Jesus (v. 24), offering forgiveness and redemption. It also recalls the very beginning of Hebrews: "In these last days, he spoke to us through a son" (1:2). **12:25**

The Israelites **did not escape**—as Paul says, they were "struck down in the desert" (1 Cor 10:5)—**when they refused the one who warned them on earth**. A difficulty with this line is that Exodus clearly states that at Sinai God spoke *from heaven* (Exod 20:22; Deut 4:36). But Hebrews may mean that the warnings that accompanied the Sinai covenant were given on an earthly mountain, whereas now the readers of Hebrews stand in the very presence of God, who **warns from heaven**, speaking to us through the blood of Christ shed in love for us. Reasoning from the lesser to the greater, the author asks: If **we turn away from** such a gracious offer of salvation, **how much more** severely will we be judged? The incomparably greater grace of the new covenant entails a greater accountability. "From everyone to whom much has been given, much will be required; and from the one to whom much has been entrusted, even more will be demanded" (Luke 12:48 NRSV).

God's **voice shook the earth at that time**, as Exodus relates: "the whole mountain trembled violently" (Exod 19:18). That awesome display of divine power was deeply engraved on Israel's memory and commemorated in the Psalms: "The earth quaked, the heavens poured, / before God, the One of Sinai, / before God, the God of Israel" (Ps 68:9; see Judg 5:5; Ps 77:19).[32] In the Old Testament, prophecies about "the day of the LORD," the day when God will decisively act to overthrow the wicked, often include earthquake imagery (see **12:26**

32. F. F. Bruce, *The Epistle to the Hebrews*, rev. ed., New International Commentary on the New Testament (Grand Rapids: Eerdmans, 2012), 363.

Isa 13:13; Ezek 38:19–20). Hebrews quotes one of these, from Haggai 2:6: **I will once more shake not only earth but heaven**. In its context this promise was an encouragement to the Jewish exiles who had returned from Babylon and were trying to rebuild the temple in adverse economic and political circumstances. The prophecy continues (Hag 2:7, 21–22),

> I will shake all the nations,
>> so that the treasures of all the nations will come in.
> And I will fill this house with glory—
>> says the Lord of hosts. . . .
> I will shake the heavens and the earth;
>> I will overthrow the thrones of kingdoms,
>> and destroy the power of the kingdoms of the nations.

Haggai is assuring the people that God's demolition of hostile kingdoms will lead all peoples to acknowledge and revere him as the true God in his temple in Jerusalem.

12:27   Hebrews interprets a **phrase** in the Haggai prophecy, **once more**, as indicating that this will be a final, †eschatological "shaking." It will cause the **removal of shaken, created things**, literally, "the removal of what is shaken, as of what has been made" (RSV). The shaking of heaven and earth signifies a kind of undoing of the created order, in which all that is tainted, imperfect, and corruptible will be removed. This promise recalls the quotation from Psalm 102 at the beginning of Hebrews, where God declares that the heavens and the earth will be rolled up like a cloak and changed like a garment (1:10–12). Christ's passion is the beginning of a new creation, which portends the end of the old: "Then I saw a new heaven and a new earth. The former heaven and the former earth had passed away" (Rev 21:1; see 2 Pet 3:10–13). What will **remain** in the new creation is only **what is unshaken**—the blessings of our eternal inheritance in Christ, which can never be taken away (see 9:15; Eph 1:14). There is an implied contrast with the sacrificial system of the old covenant, which "has become obsolete" and "is close to disappearing" (8:13). If Hebrews was written in the mid 60s, as seems likely, the earthly temple was in fact soon to be reduced to rubble and the †levitical priesthood and sacrifices brought to an end.

12:28   For Christians, however, the prospect of cosmic upheaval is reason not for fear but for eager expectation (see 9:29). For we **are receiving the unshakable kingdom**—the everlasting kingdom that God promised to David: "I will raise up your offspring after you . . . and I will establish his kingdom. . . . And I will establish his royal throne forever" (2 Sam 7:12–13). Hebrews reminded us

St. Augustine on the Worship We Offer God

LIVING TRADITION

In *The City of God*, St. Augustine writes,

> To this God we owe our service—what in Greek is called *latreia*—whether in the various sacraments or in ourselves. For we are his temple, collectively, and as individuals. . . . When we lift up our hearts to him, our heart is his altar. We propitiate him by our priest, his only-begotten Son. We sacrifice blood-stained victims to him when we fight for truth "as far as shedding our blood" [Heb 12:4]. We burn the sweetest incense for him when we are in his sight on fire with devout and holy love. We vow to him and offer to him the gifts he has given us, and the gift of ourselves. And we have annual festivals and fixed days appointed and consecrated for the remembrance of his benefits, lest ingratitude and forgetfulness should creep in as the years roll by. We offer to him, on the altar of the heart, the sacrifice of humility and praise [Ps 116:17], and the flame on the altar is the burning fire of charity. To see him as he can be seen and to cleave to him, we purify ourselves from every stain of sin and evil desire and we consecrate ourselves in his name. For he himself is the source of our bliss, he himself the goal of all our striving.[a]

a. *The City of God* 10.3.

early on that this promise is fulfilled in Jesus, of whom Scripture says, "Your throne, O God, stands forever and ever" (1:8; see Luke 1:33). This kingdom will be manifested in its full splendor only at his second coming (10:37), yet it is already present because Jesus the King is seated in majesty at God's right hand (1:3; 8:1; 10:12). Christians "are receiving" it (present tense) because we "have approached" (perfect tense) the heavenly Zion (v. 22).

The right response is overflowing **gratitude**, as Paul counsels: give thanks "always and for everything in the name of our Lord Jesus Christ to God the Father" (Eph 5:20). Gratitude impels us to **offer worship pleasing to God in reverence and awe**. As Hebrews showed earlier (10:14, 19), Christ has consecrated all those who believe in him as a holy priesthood, qualified to enter the †Holy of Holies and offer †sacrifices acceptable to God.[33] As chapter 13 will show, these sacrifices are our own lives offered in loving service to God and neighbor, as Paul says: "Offer your bodies as a living sacrifice, holy and pleasing to God, your spiritual worship" (Rom 12:1). And the mention of worship also brings to mind the central Christian act of worship, the Eucharistic liturgy (see

33. See Peter J. Leithart, "Womb of the World: Baptism and the Priesthood of the New Covenant in Hebrews 10.19–22," *Journal for the Study of the New Testament* 78 (2000): 63–64.

Our God Is a Consuming Fire

LIVING
TRADITION

Origen, a third-century Church Father, wrote this about the divine fire:

> "Our God is a consuming fire." What is this fire which tests our works? What is this fire so wise that it guards my gold and shows forth my silver more brilliantly, that it leaves undamaged that precious stone in me and burns up only the evil I have done, the wood, hay and straw that I have built over it (1 Cor 3:12–15)? What is this fire? "I came to cast fire on the earth; and would that it were already enkindled!" (Luke 12:49). Jesus Christ says: "How I wish that it were already enkindled!" For he is good, and he knows that if this fire is enkindled, wickedness will be consumed. This means that fire is sent forth upon your sinful works so that you will be glorified.[a]

a. Origen, *Homilies on Ezekiel* 1.3.

comments on 12:24), in which we unite ourselves with Christ in his eternal self-offering to the Father.

12:29   It may seem paradoxical that Christians are to worship "with reverence and awe," since Hebrews has constantly encouraged us to draw near to God with boundless trust and confidence (4:16; 7:19, 25; 10:19–22). But this paradox is at the heart of the gospel, for our God is the same holy God whom the Israelites encountered on Mount Sinai. **Our God is a consuming fire**. Hebrews is quoting Moses' solemn words to the Israelites: "The LORD, your God, is a consuming fire, a jealous God" (Deut 4:24; see Deut 9:3). That he is jealous refers not to petty or vindictive jealousy but rather to the zeal of a lover who has given himself totally to the beloved and who desires to be loved totally and exclusively in return (see Song 8:6). In the light of Christ, we can see more fully that the "consuming fire" is the fire of divine love (see 1 John 4:8). We are able to stand in the presence of that fire not because God's holiness is compromised but because we have been purified and transformed by the sacrifice of Christ. In worshiping God with both childlike confidence and holy awe, we imitate Jesus, the firstborn Son, who prayed to God with reverence (Heb 5:7).

Pleasing Sacrifices in Day-to-Day Life

Hebrews 13:1–25

In this last chapter Hebrews turns to some very practical, concrete instructions on life in the Christian community. At first sight, chapter 13 seems a kind of addendum to the rest of the letter, with a hodgepodge of loosely related moral exhortations. But if we pay closer attention, we see that these exhortations follow directly from the call to "offer worship pleasing to God in reverence and awe" in 12:28. The whole letter has been a compelling demonstration that Christ's sacrifice has qualified us to be a priestly people who can enter with joyful confidence into the very throne room of God and offer worship pleasing to him through Christ our high priest. What is the pleasing worship that we offer? Our whole life! It is not coincidental that the words "pleasing" and "sacrifice" reappear several times in this chapter (vv. 15, 16, 21) to describe daily life in the Christian community. Our worship of God in his heavenly sanctuary is concretely expressed in our acts of love on earth. The author thus tightly ties together the twofold commandment of love for God and love for neighbor, just as Jesus did (Matt 22:37–40; see 1 John 4:21).

Exhortations to Love, Chastity, and Simplicity of Life (13:1–6)

¹Let mutual love continue. ²Do not neglect hospitality, for through it some have unknowingly entertained angels. ³Be mindful of prisoners as if sharing their imprisonment, and of the ill-treated as of yourselves, for you also are in the body. ⁴Let marriage be honored among all and the marriage bed be kept undefiled, for God will judge the immoral and adulterers. ⁵Let

your life be free from love of money but be content with what you have, for he has said, "I will never forsake you or abandon you." ⁶Thus we may say with confidence:

> "The Lord is my helper,
> [and] I will not be afraid.
> What can anyone do to me?"

OT: Gen 18:1–2; Josh 1:5; Ps 118:6; Sir 23:18–19
NT: Matt 22:37–39; 25:35–36; John 13:34; 1 Tim 6:10; 1 Pet 1:22; 4:9
Catechism: visiting prisoners, 2447; honoring marriage, 1641–48; love of money, 2534–37
Lectionary: Heb 13:1–4a, 5–6b: Sacrament of Marriage; Heb 13:1–2, 7–8, 17–18: Mass for the Blessing of Abbots and Abbesses; Heb 13:1–3, 14–16: Mass for Refugees

13:1 The first exhortation, **Let mutual love continue**, is literally "let brotherly love [*philadelphia*] continue." Jesus' command for his disciples to love one another is his "new commandment" (John 13:34)—new because it is made possible by the love with which he first loved us (1 John 4:19). Love is, as Paul teaches, the commandment that sums up the entire law (Gal 5:14) and the virtue that perfects all others (Col 3:12–14). By placing this exhortation immediately after the call to offer pleasing worship to God (12:28), the author of Hebrews expresses in his own way the unity of the two great commandments—love of God and love of neighbor (Matt 22:37–40; see 1 John 4:20–21). We worship God precisely by loving our brothers and sisters, just as the sacrifice Jesus offered was not a ritual act performed in sacred isolation but an act of self-giving love and total solidarity with us.[1] Hebrews calls Christians' love for one another "brotherly" love because in Christ we have become sons and daughters of God, members of one family of God, united by bonds much deeper than those of friendship or common interests (see 2:11–14; Gal 3:26). The Christian community is meant to be characterized by this mutual love that is intense and full of affection (Rom 12:10; 1 Pet 1:22).

The addressees are not asked to *have* this brotherly love but rather to let it *continue*, because they have already been showing love for one another through concrete acts of service (6:10) and sympathy (10:33–34). The Greek word for "continue" is the same as the word for "remain" in 12:27, suggesting that the intense love of Christians for one another is one of those things that will remain when all else is shaken.[2]

13:2 There is a neat parallel between verse 1 and verse 2 that is difficult to render in English. Whereas verse 1 calls for love of brothers and sisters (*philadelphia*),

---

1. Albert Vanhoye, *A Different Priest: The Letter to the Hebrews*, trans. Leo Arnold, Series Rhetorica Semitica (Miami: Convivium, 2011), 404.
2. Luke Timothy Johnson, *Hebrews: A Commentary*, New Testament Library (Louisville: Westminster John Knox, 2006), 339.

verse 2 calls for love of strangers (*philoxenia*)—that is, **hospitality**. Hospitality was valued extremely highly in the ancient world, especially among Christians. Itinerant missionaries and even Christians traveling on other business would be in need of food, lodging, and a warm welcome wherever they went.[3] Thus 1 Peter exhorts Christians to "be hospitable to one another without complaining" (1 Pet 4:9), and Paul mentions hospitality as an essential quality of Christian leaders (1 Tim 3:2; Titus 1:8).

Hebrews adds a new motive to this common exhortation by asserting that through hospitality **some have unknowingly entertained angels**. Readers familiar with the Scriptures would recognize an allusion to Old Testament figures such as Abraham, who was visited by the Lord God himself in the form of three men, two of whom are identified as angels (Gen 18:1–2; 19:1).[4] Abraham showed extraordinary hospitality, bowing to the ground and hurrying to bring water to bathe their feet and prepare a rich banquet. Lot welcomed the same angels into his home (Gen 19:2). Gideon set choice foods before the angel who came to him (Judg 6:19), and Manoah, the father of Samson, offered a meal to an angel (Judg 13:15–16), neither of them at first recognizing the heavenly identity of the visitor. Tobit warmly greeted the angel Raphael (Tob 5:4–14), whom he too did not recognize as a messenger of the Lord. Christian hospitality is not just an act of kindness but a way of receiving the Lord himself into one's home, as Jesus indicates in the Gospel: "I was . . . a stranger and you welcomed me. . . . Whatever you did for one of these least brothers of mine, you did for me" (Matt 25:35, 40).

The next exhortation, **Be mindful of prisoners as if sharing their imprisonment**, again recalls Jesus' words in the Gospel, "I was . . . in prison and you visited me" (Matt 25:35–36). Whereas hospitality entails receiving those who come, care for prisoners entails actively going out to those who cannot come, by praying for them and, if possible, ministering to their needs. It was, and still is in many areas of the world, common for Christians to be thrown into prison for their faith. Yet it is all too easy for those in relative safety to forget about their suffering fellow believers or, worse, to tacitly ignore them for fear of sharing their fate. In their early days the readers of Hebrews had shown admirable care for the imprisoned (10:34); now they are urged to continue this practice.

13:3

Likewise, their concern for **the ill-treated** (or "tortured," NRSV) is to be just as strong as if they themselves were the ones being mistreated. It was, and still is, also common for God's people to be subjected to horrendous tortures

---

3. See Acts 16:15; 21:4; 28:2; Rom 12:13; 16:1–2; Gal 4:14; Phil 2:29; Col 4:10; James 2:25; 3 John 1:5.

4. The third guest is identified as the Lord God (Gen 18:13, 17, 20, 22, 26–33). In this case, Abraham seems to have been fully aware of the identity of his exalted guests from the start (see Gen 18:2).

and abuses, like the Jewish martyrs of old (11:35–37). That we **also are in the body** means that we should identify with the ill-treated because we share the same frail human nature. If Hebrews is speaking specifically of Christians, this phrase may refer to their membership in the body of Christ. Such is the unity of that body that "if one member suffers, all suffer together" (1 Cor 12:26 RSV).

13:4   The next two exhortations have to do with disordered desires in two perennially troublesome areas: sex and money (both exemplified by Esau in 12:16). First, **let marriage be honored among all** (or "in every respect"). The call to honor marriage strikes against two opposite errors. On the one hand, some early Christian heresies, especially forms of †Gnosticism, condemned marriage on the grounds that matter is evil and bodily pleasure is unworthy of those who seek to be spiritual. Paul's Letters vigorously combatted this error, affirming the exalted dignity of marriage as a sign of Christ's own relationship with his bride, the Church (Eph 5:31–32; see 1 Cor 7:7, 28; 1 Tim 4:3–5). The opposite error, which is much more characteristic of Western culture today, is to condone various forms of sexual activity outside marriage, on the grounds that what one does with the body is insignificant. The language used by Hebrews, let **the marriage bed be kept undefiled**, implies that the sexual union of spouses is something intrinsically holy that we must take care not to defile.

Hebrews adds a solemn warning: **God will judge the immoral and adulterers**. The "immoral" (*pornoi*) refers to those who engage in any sexual activity outside marriage; adulterers are those who commit the additional sin of violating the marriage covenant. Scripture is filled with similar warnings. Sirach 23:18–19 says,

> The man who dishonors his marriage bed
>   says to himself, "Who can see me? . . .
>   Who can stop me from sinning?"
> He is not mindful of the Most High,
>   fearing only human eyes.
> He does not realize that the eyes of the Lord,
>   ten thousand times brighter than the sun,
> Observe every step taken
>   and peer into hidden corners.

Paul includes serious sexual sin among those grave offenses that, if unrepented, will exclude people from the kingdom of God: "Be sure of this, that no immoral or impure or greedy person, that is, an idolater, has any inheritance in the kingdom of Christ and of God" (Eph 5:5).[5]

5. See also 1 Cor 6:9–10; Col 3:5–6; 1 Thess 4:4–6; Rev 21:8; 22:15.

Let your life be free from love of money (literally, "un-money-loving"). **13:5**
Like sexual self-indulgence, money promises happiness and then leaves those
who pursue it miserable and enslaved. As Scripture often warns, greed leads
to other sins. "The lover of gold will not be free from sin; / whoever pursues
money will be led astray by it" (Sir 31:5; see 27:1). Paul warns Timothy, "The
love of money is the root of all evils, and some people in their desire for it have
strayed from the faith and have pierced themselves with many pains" (1 Tim
6:10). Instead of accumulating wealth, God's people are to store up treasure in
heaven by giving alms (Matt 6:19–21; Tob 12:8). Jesus taught a radical detachment from money and possessions: "Take care to guard against all greed, for
though one may be rich, one's life does not consist of possessions" (Luke 12:15).
"You cannot serve God and mammon" (Matt 6:24).

The antidote to being money-loving, and the authentic Christian disposition,
is to **be content with what you have**. John the Baptist gave this very practical advice as he called people to repentance in preparation for the Messiah
(Luke 3:14). Paul likewise counsels Timothy to be content with having food
and clothing, the necessities of life (1 Tim 6:6–8). Paul exemplified in his own
life the happiness that comes from detachment: "I have learned, in whatever
state I am, to be content" (Phil 4:11 RSV), "having nothing and yet possessing
all things" (2 Cor 6:10). This advice may have been especially challenging to
the original readers of Hebrews, who had suffered the trauma of having their
property plundered (10:34). So the author reminds them of the true basis of
their security: the God who has given them an unshakable kingdom (12:28).
God's promise, **I will never forsake you or abandon you**, was given to Joshua
(Josh 1:5) and in similar words to Jacob (Gen 28:15), Solomon (1 Chron 28:20),
and the whole people of Israel as they entered the promised land (Deut 31:6). It
now applies to every believer in Jesus, the new Joshua who leads us into God's
eternal rest (Heb 4:8–11): the Lord will never let go of us but will guard us until
he has accomplished everything he promised (see Gen 28:15).

The Christian attitude, then, is one of victorious **confidence** in the face of **13:6**
every adverse circumstance. **Thus we may say** with the psalmist: **The Lord is
my helper, / [and] I will not be afraid. / What can anyone do to me?** This
quotation is from Psalm 118:6, one of the Hallel psalms sung at the Passover
festival, in which the psalmist expresses joy and confident trust in God's great
victory. Jewish readers familiar with the psalm probably called to mind the
wider context, which contains a line that especially resonates with the advice
given in Hebrews 12: "The Lord disciplined me severely, but did not hand me
over to death. Open the gates of victory; I will enter and thank the Lord" (Ps

118:18–19).[6] Hebrews explained earlier that Jesus is able to help us because he has been tested just as we have (2:18), and that it is from the throne of grace that we find help in time of need (4:16). Knowing that the Lord is our helper is what frees Christians from every fear of want or of human opposition.

Reflection and Application (13:1–6)

Being mindful of persecuted Christians. Christians in the Western world are rightly disturbed by the increasing cultural hostility to Christianity and government pressure on believers to privatize faith and conform to an aggressive secularist agenda. But we are often less cognizant of the fact that in other parts of the world Christians are subjected to outright violence in staggering numbers. The Center for the Study of Global Christianity at Gordon-Conwell Theological Seminary estimates that in the early twenty-first century an average of 100,000 Christians have been killed every year in religious persecution.[7] In addition, Christians in many countries are deprived of fundamental rights, sidelined from public life, and subjected to threats and violent attacks against their churches and homes. According to 2011 data from the Pew Forum, Christians face harassment in an astounding total of 130 countries, more than two-thirds of all nations, including many where Christians are a majority.[8] Some of the main sources of anti-Christian hostility are Islamic, Hindu, and Buddhist radicalism; communist totalitarianism; aggressive secularism; and organized crime. Those of us who live in relative freedom have a grave obligation to pray for the victims of persecution, to provide moral and financial support where possible, to put pressure on governments to stop human rights abuses, and to let our suffering brothers and sisters know they are not forgotten.

Jesus Is the Same Yesterday, Today, and Forever (13:7–14)

[7]**Remember your leaders who spoke the word of God to you. Consider the outcome of their way of life and imitate their faith.** [8]**Jesus Christ is the same yesterday, today, and forever.**

[9]**Do not be carried away by all kinds of strange teaching. It is good to have our hearts strengthened by grace and not by foods, which do not**

---

6. Author's translation. In Ps 118:18 †LXX the word for "discipline" (*paideuō*) is the same as in Heb 12:6, 7, 10.

7. http://www.gordonconwell.edu/resources/documents/StatusOfGlobalMission.pdf. See line 28.

8. http://www.pewforum.org/2011/08/09/rising-restrictions-on-religion2.

benefit those who live by them. ¹⁰We have an altar from which those who serve the tabernacle have no right to eat. ¹¹The bodies of the animals whose blood the high priest brings into the sanctuary as a sin offering are burned outside the camp. ¹²Therefore, Jesus also suffered outside the gate, to consecrate the people by his own blood. ¹³Let us then go to him outside the camp, bearing the reproach that he bore. ¹⁴For here we have no lasting city, but we seek the one that is to come.

OT: Exod 33:7; Lev 16:27
NT: John 15:20; 19:20; 1 Cor 11:1; Gal 1:6–7; Eph 4:14; Col 2:16; 1 Tim 4:2–3
Catechism: altar of the new covenant, 1182; the city to come, 1042–47
Lectionary: Dedication of an Altar

Hebrews 11 held up the Old Testament saints as models of faith. Here the **13:7** author proposes models much closer in time to his readers, those whom they knew personally. **Remember your leaders who spoke the word of God to you.**[9] Verses 17 and 24 will speak of the current leaders of the local church, but here the reference is to the earliest leaders, now deceased. Then as now, the primary role of Christian leaders is to preach the word of God, since preaching gives birth to faith, the necessary foundation on which sacramental and ecclesial life is built.[10] These early leaders apparently practiced what they preached, so that not just their words but their whole lives were a lesson in faith. So the readers are urged to **consider the outcome of their way of life and imitate their faith**. This is a natural extension of the exhortation to fix our eyes on Jesus (12:2), since by looking at those who closely conformed their lives to Jesus, we can more clearly see *him*. Thus Paul taught, "Be imitators of me, as I am of Christ" (1 Cor 11:1). The "outcome" of their lives may refer to the martyrdom of some or, more likely, to the holiness and fidelity to Christ of all of them, even to the very last breath. The exhortation to "remember" these exemplary leaders, thereby rekindling one's own fervor, is part of the foundation for Catholic veneration of the apostles, fathers, and doctors of the Church, and saints and martyrs of every era.

Verse 8 may be the most well-known and well-loved sentence in the entire **13:8** letter. **Jesus Christ is the same yesterday, today, and forever.** Although it is often quoted as a stand-alone statement, it is closely tied to both what goes before and what comes after (vv. 7, 9). The Jesus whom those early leaders

---

9. Only here in the New Testament is the generic title "leaders" used for pastors of the Christian community instead of the more common terms "elders" (*presbyteroi*) and "overseers" (*episkopoi*).

10. As St. John Paul II wrote, "The priest is first of all a minister of the word of God. He is consecrated and sent forth to proclaim the good news of the kingdom to all, calling every person to the obedience of faith" (*Pastores Dabo Vobis* 26).

preached and staked their lives on is the same Jesus who is alive in the Church today. He has not changed. He is the same all-powerful redeemer and Lord who "yesterday" provided the all-sufficient atonement for our sins (1:3; 9:26) and "today" is enthroned in heaven as God's Son (1:5, 13; 5:5) and "forever" lives to make intercession for us so we are able to overcome every adversity and temptation (2:18; 4:16; 7:25). In a time of social turmoil and political instability such as the original setting of Hebrews, this truth of Christ's unchangeability provides the deepest possible assurance to his followers. Jesus cannot go back on what he has promised; he will bring it to completion (6:17–18; see Phil 1:6). This verse echoes the quotation from Psalm 102 at the beginning of Hebrews, which similarly applied God's attribute of immutability to Jesus: "But you are the same, and your years will have no end" (1:12; see James 1:17).

13:9   Verse 8 also leads into the next exhortation, because the fact that Jesus is unchanging means the truth concerning him is also unchanging.[11] As Paul emphatically declared to the Galatians, there is no other gospel than the one that has already been preached (Gal 1:6–7). Therefore Christians must beware **not** to **be carried away by all kinds of strange teaching**. A danger against which the New Testament constantly warns is that of false teachings, theological fads that have a certain appeal but are incompatible with the gospel.[12] Being persuaded by such alien teachings seems to have been one way the original readers were in danger of being "carried away" from fidelity to Christ (2:1). As Paul admonishes, embracing heretical teachings is a sign of spiritual immaturity and instability: we must "no longer be infants, tossed by waves and swept along by every wind of teaching arising from human trickery" (Eph 4:14; see Rev 2:15–16).

What precisely were these false teachings? The second half of the verse gives a clue. **It is good to have our hearts strengthened by grace and not by foods, which do not benefit those who live by them**. Most likely, "foods" refers to the food laws of the Torah or to additional stringent rules that had been imposed by Jewish oral tradition.[13] (The verb "live by" is literally "walk by," a common expression for keeping the †Torah.) The author spoke earlier of the spiritual ineffectiveness of these Mosaic food laws, which he called "regulations concern-

---

11. Philip Edgcumbe Hughes, *A Commentary on the Epistle to the Hebrews* (Grand Rapids: Eerdmans, 1977), 571.

12. See Matt 7:15; Acts 20:30; 2 Cor 11:4; Col 2:8; 1 Tim 4:1; 2 Tim 2:14–18; 2 Pet 2:1; 1 John 4:1–6; 2 John 7–9; Rev 2:15.

13. It is possible that, as some scholars hold, "foods" refers to the portion of temple sacrifices eaten by priests (see 1 Cor 9:13), but this interpretation does not as easily fit the description of "strange teachings." Besides, the common temptation for early Jewish Christians was to regard the observance of dietary laws as having spiritual "benefit."

ing the flesh, imposed until the time of the new order" (9:10). They have been set aside by Christ (see Mark 7:15–19; Eph 2:15), whose one perfect sacrifice superabundantly fulfills the law. Yet the belief that spiritual perfection could be attained through strict dietary observances was a continuing problem in some of the early Christian communities, as the Letters of Paul attest. He admonishes the Colossians, "Let no one . . . pass judgment on you in questions of food and drink or with regard to a festival or new moon or sabbath" (Col 2:16; see 2:21). He warns Timothy of "liars" who "require abstinence from foods which God created to be received with thanksgiving by those who believe and know the truth" (1 Tim 4:2–3), and he reminds the Roman Christians that "the kingdom of God is not a matter of food and drink, but righteousness, peace, and joy in the Holy Spirit" (Rom 14:17; see 1 Cor 8:8).

As Jesus taught, food in itself has no moral significance, since it "enters not the heart but the stomach and passes out into the latrine" (Mark 7:19). Rather, sin is what defiles, and grace, the free gift of God lavished on us through the sacrifice of Christ, is what purifies and strengthens the human heart.

The whole Letter to the Hebrews has been a demonstration of the infinite **13:10** superiority of the new covenant over the old. But now that truth is expressed in a new way: **We have an altar from which those who serve the tabernacle have no right to eat.** What does this "altar" refer to? Scholars have proposed various possibilities.[14] Most likely, the altar is the cross of Jesus, standing for the whole †paschal mystery in which he offered himself to God on our behalf. Christians have the awesome privilege of "eating" from this altar, in the sense of partaking in the divine life that flows from it (see 6:4), especially through the Eucharist, in which we truly eat the body and drink the blood of the risen Lord (see Matt 26:26–27; John 6:54). Thus the altar also alludes to the Eucharist.[15] Those who "serve the tabernacle," who worship in the earthly temple and have not come to believe in Christ,[16] have no access to this heavenly gift.

---

14. For example, it refers to the heavenly sanctuary (N. T. Wright, *Hebrews for Everyone*, New Testament for Everyone [Louisville: Westminster John Knox, 2004], 174), or to the Eucharistic altar of the Church (Scott Hahn and Curtis Mitch, *The Letter to the Hebrews*, Ignatius Catholic Study Bible [San Francisco: Ignatius Press, 2007], 436), or to the human heart (Johnson, *Hebrews*, 348).

15. See the Catechism 1182, which cites Heb 13:10: "The *altar* of the New Covenant is the Lord's Cross, from which the sacraments of the Paschal mystery flow. . . . The altar is also the table of the Lord, to which the People of God are invited." Thomas Aquinas wrote, "That altar is either the cross of Christ, on which He was immolated for us, or Christ Himself, in Whom and through Whom we offer prayers" (*Commentary on the Epistle to the Hebrews*, trans. Chrysostom Baer [South Bend, IN: St. Augustine's Press, 2006], 302).

16. Hebrews routinely speaks of the †tabernacle, the sanctuary set up by Moses in the desert, rather than the Jerusalem temple that eventually replaced it and probably was still standing in his day. He probably does so to focus on the original pattern for worship established by God, as well as to delicately avoid a direct criticism of the Jerusalem temple.

13:11   The mention of the earthly tabernacle leads into one more contrast—the final one in the letter—between the ineffective sacrifices of the old covenant and the one perfect sacrifice of Christ. The book of Leviticus specifies that **the bodies of the animals whose blood the high priest brings into the sanctuary as a sin offering are burned outside the camp** (Lev 4:12, 21).[17] The author probably has in mind the sin offerings of †Yom Kippur, the Day of Atonement, the one day when the high priest carried out his unique task of bringing blood into the sanctuary and sprinkling it on the †mercy seat in †atonement for Israel's sins (Lev 16:14–15, 27). Unlike most other sacrificial victims, the bull and goat whose blood was used for this ritual were not to be eaten but instead brought outside the camp and completely burned (Lev 16:27; see 6:23). But what is the point of this observation, and what does it have to do with Christ?

13:12   Verse 12 completes the thought with a surprising twist: **Therefore, Jesus also suffered outside the gate, to consecrate** (or "sanctify") **the people by his own blood**. With this statement Hebrews reveals another way, not previously mentioned, that the rituals of Yom Kippur prefigured the sacrifice of Christ. Jesus' crucifixion took place outside the walls of the city (John 19:17, 20) as was typical of public executions, either to highlight the disgrace of the punishment or to avoid ritual defilement.[18] The law of Moses directs that objects and activities connected with sin and death be symbolically excluded from the community by being placed outside the camp (e.g., Exod 29:14; Lev 14:40–45; Num 15:35). Yet precisely in this *unholy* setting Jesus offered the once-for-all sacrifice that makes God's people holy (see 10:10).

Even though his death looked like the furthest thing from a sacrifice—it was not in the temple and was not offered by †levitical priests—in reality it is the one perfect sacrifice that fulfills and infinitely surpasses Yom Kippur. The correspondence is not a wooden, point-by-point parallel, however. Jesus' body was not "burned" outside the city, but through his passion his human nature was set ablaze by the "eternal Spirit" (see comments on 9:14). He offered not the blood of animals but his own blood, which alone is able to purify the human conscience (9:12–14). His blood was sprinkled not in the earthly sanctuary but in the true sanctuary that is heaven itself (9:24). And his sacrifice was offered not by the levitical high priest but by Jesus himself, the great high priest who brings about everlasting communion between God and human beings (7:26–28; 9:15).

---

17. For an explanation of the sin offering and other types of sacrifice, see sidebar, "How Jesus Fulfills the Sacrifices of the Old Covenant," p. 152.

18. See Lev 24:14, 23; Num 15:35–36; 1 Kings 21:13; see also the parable of the wicked vineyard tenants, in which Jesus predicts the manner of his death (Matt 21:39).

Pope Leo the Great on Jesus' Suffering "Outside the Gate"

Pope Leo the Great said in regard to Jesus' suffering,

> When Christ offered himself to the Father, a new and true sacrifice of reconciliation, he was crucified not in the temple, whose worship was now at an end, and not within the confines of the city, which for its sin was doomed to be destroyed, but outside, "outside the camp," so that, on the cessation of the old symbolic sacrifices, a new Victim might be placed on a new altar, and the cross of Christ might be the altar not of the temple but of the world.[a]

a. *Sermon* 59.5.

Moreover, by describing Christ's death as a sin offering (as Paul also implies in 2 Cor 5:21), Hebrews gives a further insight into his passion. The underlying rationale of a sin offering is that the contamination of the offerers' sins is transferred to the animal victim, and the removal and complete destruction of the animal eliminates the sins.[19] That Jesus is compared to these animals contaminated by sin implies that he has absorbed the guilt of our sins and removed it from us.

Finally, the phrase "outside the camp" may also allude to Exodus 33:7, which implies that the tent of meeting was moved outside the camp because the camp had been defiled by Israel's worship of the golden calf. If the author intends this allusion, he is suggesting that the city of Jerusalem had become like the camp: "What was formerly sacred was now unhallowed, because Jesus had been expelled from it; what was formerly unhallowed was now sacred, because Jesus was there."[20]

Verse 13 hones in on the practical application of this truth for Christians. **Let** **13:13** **us then go to him outside the camp**. What does it mean to go to him outside the camp? On one level, the "camp" is Israel's camp in the desert (as in v. 11) and the entire old covenant dispensation that it stands for. The original readers of Hebrews had to resist the temptation to revert to their former dependence on the levitical system with its animal sacrifices and detailed food laws. The time of the old order was ended (see 8:13), its purpose accomplished, now that

19. See Baruch A. Levine, *Leviticus: The Traditional Hebrew Text with the New JPS Translation*, The JPS Torah Commentary (Philadelphia: Jewish Publication Society, 1989), 21.

20. F. F. Bruce, *The Epistle to the Hebrews*, rev. ed., New International Commentary on the New Testament (Grand Rapids: Eerdmans, 2012), 382.

the perfect fulfillment it prefigured had come. And its city and temple were about to be reduced to rubble, as Jesus had prophesied (Mark 13:2). The old order was what can be shaken, in contrast to the eternal kingdom that cannot be shaken (12:27–28).

In a broader sense, to go to Jesus "outside the camp" means to separate oneself from the world and all its security systems, values, and behaviors that are contrary to the gospel (see Eph 4:17–18; 1 Pet 4:3–4). It means enduring the world's hostility and mockery, **bearing the reproach** (or "abuse," RSV; "disgrace," NIV) that Jesus **bore**. It means even rejoicing at that persecution, as the apostles had (Acts 5:41; see Luke 6:22–23), and as Moses "considered the reproach of the Anointed greater wealth than the treasures of Egypt" (Heb 11:26). Jesus had taught, "'No slave is greater than his master.' If they persecuted me, they will also persecute you" (John 15:20); "Whoever does not take up his cross and follow after me is not worthy of me" (Matt 10:38). The original audience of Hebrews had known such abuse in the past (see 10:33). Stephen the martyr fulfilled this exhortation in a literal sense, bearing abuse for Christ and being executed outside the city (Acts 7:58).

13:14   Just as Abraham looked forward to "the city with foundations, whose architect and maker is God" (11:10), so Christians are aware that **here we have no lasting city, but we seek the one that is to come**. Like God's people of old, we recognize that we are only pilgrims and sojourners on earth (11:13). Our home is not here but in "the city of the living God, the heavenly Jerusalem" (12:22; see Phil 3:20). This city is "to come," not in the sense that it does not yet exist—it does exist, because God has prepared it (11:16)—but in the sense that we still await its full manifestation (see Rev 21:2). With our hearts anchored in this hope (Heb 6:19), Christians are enabled to meet all the challenges of this present life with courage and confidence.

Reflection and Application (13:7–14)

Being a disciple of Christ means never being fully at home in this world, because our hope is set on the city that is to come. Because of this hope Christians are sometimes accused of being "so heavenly minded they're no earthly good." This criticism has at times been justified; some have taken the hope of heaven as an excuse to withdraw from the world into a kind of religious ghetto, abandoning the world to its fate and despairing of making any positive change through social or political engagement. But understood rightly, the hope of heaven actually allows for deeper engagement with the world, since it frees us from being dominated by earthly aspirations to wealth, success, or power. It motivates us to go out into the world, bringing the good news of Christ into every part of society. Pope Francis spoke of this movement outward in an address to bishops, priests, and seminarians:

> It is . . . in the slums that one must go to seek and to serve Christ. . . . We cannot keep ourselves shut up in parishes, in our communities, when so many people are waiting for the Gospel! It is not enough simply to open the door in welcome, but we must go out through that door to seek and meet the people! Let us courageously look to pastoral needs, beginning on the outskirts, with those who are farthest away, with those who do not usually go to church.[21]

Sacrifices of Praise, Obedience, and Prayer (13:15–19)

[15]**Through him [then] let us continually offer God a sacrifice of praise, that is, the fruit of lips that confess his name.** [16]**Do not neglect to do good and to share what you have; God is pleased by sacrifices of that kind.**

[17]**Obey your leaders and defer to them, for they keep watch over you and will have to give an account, that they may fulfill their task with joy and not with sorrow, for that would be of no advantage to you.**

[18]**Pray for us, for we are confident that we have a clear conscience, wishing to act rightly in every respect.** [19]**I especially ask for your prayers that I may be restored to you very soon.**

OT: Ps 50:14; 107:22; 116:17; Sir 35:2
NT: Acts 2:42; 2 Cor 1:11–12; 1 Thess 5:12–13, 18; 1 Pet 2:5; 5:1–5
Catechism: the Eucharist as sacrifice of praise, 1359–61; obeying leaders, 1269

In this last series of exhortations Hebrews returns to the theme that unites all the moral instruction of chapter 13: the Christian life as worship that is pleasing to God (see 12:28). As in 12:28–13:6, this worship has both a vertical dimension (praise of God) and a horizontal dimension (doing good to one's neighbor).[22] Any parish whose members follow the advice given here will likely be a vibrant, flourishing community. Such a community will have the same essential characteristics as the early Christian community in Jerusalem: "They devoted themselves to the teaching of the apostles and to the communal life, to the breaking of the bread [i.e., the Eucharistic liturgy] and

21. Homily in the cathedral at Rio de Janeiro, July 27, 2013 (translation adapted).
22. Vanhoye, *A Different Priest*, 418.

to the prayers" (Acts 2:42). Here in Hebrews these same four characteristics are expressed as

- deferring to leaders (v. 17);
- sharing with one another (v. 16, where the Greek word for "share" [*koinōnia*] is the same word translated "communal life" in Acts 2:42);
- praise of God, especially in liturgical worship (v. 15); and
- prayer (v. 18).[23]

13:15   Since Jesus is our high priest and mediator of the new covenant (9:15; 12:24), all of our worship is now offered **through him**. This implies that all of our worship is a participation in his self-offering on the cross, a sacrifice that was infinitely pleasing to God because it came from the Son, whose whole heart was set on doing the Father's will (10:7–10). Hebrews has already alluded to the Eucharist (6:4; 10:19–20, 25), the Church's highest expression of praise and thanks to God (the Greek word *eucharistia* means "thanksgiving"). This passage now speaks of the extension of that praise in daily life: **let us continually offer God a sacrifice of praise**. "Continually" implies that the whole Christian life is to be lived as an unceasing song of praise. We are to lift up prayers of gratitude not just occasionally, or even frequently, but at *all* times and in *all* circumstances, as Paul taught: "In all circumstances give thanks, for this is the will of God for you in Christ Jesus" (1 Thess 5:18; see Eph 5:20; Col 3:17).

In the Old Testament a "sacrifice of praise" (in Hebrew, a *todah* sacrifice) was an animal sacrifice. It was one form of the peace offering (Lev 7:12), offered to thank God for some special blessing or to celebrate a joyful occasion, after which the worshiper and his family would eat the meat of the sacrifice (Lev 3).[24] The Psalms teach that it is not the animal alone but the praise offered by a heart full of gratitude that is most pleasing to God. Hebrews 10:8 alluded to one of these psalms, where God asks, "Do I eat the flesh of bulls / or drink the blood of he-goats? / Offer praise as your sacrifice to God; / fulfill your vows to the Most High" (Ps 50:13–14). Another, Psalm 107, exhorts all those who have experienced God's help or deliverance, "Let

---

23. These four characteristics are also reflected in the four pillars of the Catechism: the creed (apostolic teaching), the sacraments (worship of God), the commandments (how we are to live in communion with God and neighbor), and prayer.

24. James Swetnam makes the intriguing suggestion that Heb 13:7–17 is centered on the Christian version of the *todah* (i.e., the Eucharist), since three essential aspects of the *todah* are mentioned: "Verses 9–10 refer to the ritual consumption of the bread; vv. 11–13 refer to the bloody sacrifice [the passion of Jesus]; vv. 15–16 refer to the accompanying hymns and prayers" ("A Liturgical Approach to Hebrews 13," *Letter & Spirit* 2 [2006]: 166).

St. Augustine on Sacrifices of Praise

LIVING TRADITION

St. Augustine frequently exhorted his congregation to praise God with their hearts and voices and lives, as in this sermon:

> Thanks be to the Lord our God, and wave upon wave of praise to that God to whom praise songs are due in Zion. Thanks be to him to whom we have been singing with devoted hearts and mouths—God, *who is like you?* (Psalm 83:1)—because we can feel the holy love of him deeply ensconced in your hearts, because you revere him as Lord, love him as Father. Thanks be to him who is desired before he is seen and whose presence is felt, and whose coming is hoped for. Thanks be to him, fear of whom is not shaken off by love, love of whom is not paralyzed by fear. Him we bless, him we honor, both for us and in us. For the temple of God is holy, which is what you are (1 Cor 3:17). Now consider what kind of life, what intensity of life must be his, when the very stones of his temple are living in this way.[a]

a. *Sermon* 24.1 (translation adapted from Augustine, *Sermons [20–50]: On the Old Testament*, trans. Edmund Hill, OP, ed. John E. Rotelle, Works of Saint Augustine III/2 [Brooklyn, NY: New City Press, 1990], 72).

them offer a sacrifice in thanks, / recount his works with shouts of joy" (Ps 107:22; see Ps 116:17).

Such praise is **the fruit of lips that confess his name**—that publicly acknowledge the name of Jesus (see 4:14; 10:23). The expression "fruit of lips" is from a prayer of repentance in the †Septuagint version of Hosea 14:3. The original Hebrew can be rendered, "We will render the bulls of our lips," a strange expression that is a biblical way of saying, "We will offer you not just animal sacrifices but joyful praise from hearts filled with gratitude!" Such gratitude is the essential characteristic of Christian prayer.

Authentic worship is not just with our lips but with our lives. So Hebrews **13:16** reaffirms that love of God is inseparable from love of neighbor (as above at 12:28–13:1): **Do not neglect to do good and to share what you have; God is pleased by sacrifices of that kind**. Acts of charity to the needy are genuine sacrifices, as the Old Testament teaches: "By works of charity one offers fine flour, / and one who gives alms presents a sacrifice of praise" (Sir 35:3–4; see 3:3, 30). Now that Christ has offered the once-for-all sacrifice of himself (9:12; 10:10), the whole life of Christians is offered to God by virtue of and in union with his infinitely pleasing sacrifice—all our prayers, works, joys, and sufferings, and all our giving to others (see Rom 12:1, 13; Phil 4:18). As 1 Peter teaches, we have become "a holy priesthood to offer spiritual sacrifices acceptable to God through Jesus Christ" (1 Pet 2:5).

13:17   Since the Christian community has a leadership structure willed by God (see Acts 20:28; Eph 2:20; 4:11–12), as did Israel (Heb 3:2), Christians are to have a special esteem for those in pastoral authority. To **obey your leaders and defer to them** is part of the mutual love called for in verse 1. These present leaders are evidently the successors of the original leaders mentioned in verse 7, who first preached the gospel to this local church. Their role is to **keep watch over you**, a phrase that literally means to "lose sleep over your souls," like shepherds keeping watch over their flock by night (see Luke 2:8). Leaders are to be vigilant in caring for the spiritual condition of the souls entrusted to them, even to the disregard of their own comfort and convenience, as Jesus often taught (see Mark 10:42–45; Luke 12:41–48). As Hebrews solemnly adds, they **will have to give an account** to God, from whom nothing is concealed (see 4:13).

The respective responsibilities of leaders and members of the Church are delicately balanced in this exhortation, just as in 1 Peter 5:1–5. Members, for their part, should do their best to see that leaders **may fulfill their task with joy and not with sorrow** (literally, "not groaning"). Thus Paul appealed to the Thessalonians, "We ask you, brothers, to respect those who are laboring among you and who are over you in the Lord and who admonish you, and to show esteem for them with special love on account of their work" (1 Thess 5:12–13). For members to grumble, gripe, grouse, or resist the initiatives of their pastors not only makes life difficult for pastors but also is **of no advantage** to the members themselves. On the other hand, where there is mutual trust, respect, and collaboration between leaders and members, the church flourishes. Such was the Christian community in Philippi, whom Paul addressed as "my joy and crown" (Phil 4:1; see 3 John 4).

13:18   In the last two exhortations we get a glimpse, though only the tiniest glimpse, into the author of Hebrews and his situation. As Paul so often does in his letters,[25] he begs for prayers: **Pray for us** (the plural "us" may include his fellow ministers). It may seem odd that, as a motive for prayer, he says **we are confident that we have a clear** (or "honorable") **conscience, wishing to act rightly** (or "honorably") **in every respect**. This could imply that he (and other leaders?) has been involved in some controversy in which his motives have been impugned. Or it could simply be a way of emphasizing that this letter, with its occasional stern admonitions, has been absolutely free of self-interest and is motivated by pure love. Paul appeals for prayer in a similar way: "Help us with prayer. . . . For our boast is this, the testimony of our conscience that we have conducted ourselves in the world, and especially toward you, with the simplicity and sincerity of God" (2 Cor 1:11–12; see also Acts 20:18–21).

---

25. Rom 15:30; Eph 6:18–19; Phil 1:19; Philem 22.

In verse 19 the author becomes more personal by switching to "I" and con-   **13:19**
veying his desire to be reunited with his addressees. **I especially ask for your**
prayers that I may be restored to you very soon. He evidently is familiar with
them, possibly having been one of their past leaders, but is now some distance
away. It is impossible to know what obstacle he wished their prayers to overcome in order that he be restored to them. But it is evident that he holds them
in great affection. The letter has not been an exercise in abstract theology; it is
a personal communiqué from a pastor who cares deeply for them.

Reflection and Application (13:15–19)

Hebrews 13:15 exhorts us: through Jesus "let us continually offer God a sacrifice of praise." Catholics are accustomed to praising God in a liturgical context,
especially at Mass, but we may be less familiar with letting that act of worship spill
over into all of life. As Scripture constantly attests, God desires us to praise him
at all times, for every detail in our lives. "Rejoice always. Pray without ceasing.
In all circumstances give thanks" (1 Thess 5:16–18), "giving thanks always and
for everything in the name of our Lord Jesus Christ to God the Father" (Eph
5:20).[26] In fact, we "exist for the praise of his glory" (Eph 1:12). It is relatively easy
to praise God when things are going well; it is in times of difficulty—debilitating
illness, broken relationships, humiliation, or persecution—that praise becomes
especially precious as an act of faith. To praise and thank God in the midst of
painful trials is to acknowledge him as sovereign Lord and to trust that he has
permitted these circumstances in love as part of his perfect plan for us. And the
miracle is that as we do so, our minds begin to change, joy and gratitude become a
habit, and the way is opened for God to work more deeply in our hearts and lives.

The antithesis of giving praise is to grumble and rebel, as did the wilderness
generation (3:15–19). Grumbling is rooted in unbelief—in the suspicion that
God does not have our best interests in mind and is not working for our good.
The solution is to repent, trust God, and choose to be thankful from now on. A
spirit of gratitude leads to contagious joy, which in turn attracts others to Christ.

Final Blessing (13:20–21)

---

[20]May the God of peace, who brought up from the dead the great shep-
herd of the sheep by the blood of the eternal covenant, Jesus our Lord,

---

26. See Luke 6:22–23; Rom 15:9–11; Col 3:17; James 1:2; 1 Pet 4:13.

²¹**furnish you with all that is good, that you may do his will. May he carry out in you what is pleasing to him through Jesus Christ, to whom be glory forever [and ever]. Amen.**

OT: Exod 24:8; Jer 32:40; Zech 9:11
NT: John 10:11–14; Rom 8:11; Phil 2:13; 1 Pet 5:4
Catechism: the great Shepherd, 754; Jesus' resurrection, 648–55

The homily to the Hebrews concludes with a majestic blessing that compactly sums up its key themes, followed by a postscript in verses 22–25. The blessing is a single sentence: verse 20 contains the subject, "God," and verse 21 contains the predicate, with the main verb "furnish." It expresses the author's fervent hopes and desires for his audience, as Paul often does at the end of his letters.[27]

13:20   The blessing begins by invoking **the God of peace**, meaning "peace" in its biblical sense of the fullness of well-being and harmony in relationships (in the Old Testament, *shalom*). God is the source of peace because he has established peace between himself and humanity by the blood of Christ (see John 14:27; Col 1:20). Ever since Christ's †paschal mystery, a primary way to describe God is that he is the God who raised Jesus from the dead (see Rom 8:11), **who brought up from the dead the great shepherd of the sheep**. Surprisingly, this is the first time the author has directly mentioned Jesus' resurrection, although he has alluded to it several times (1:3; 7:11, 15–16). He does not use the usual New Testament verb for "raise" but instead a word that literally means "bring up from below," as in Psalm 30:4 †LXX: "Lᴏʀᴅ, you *brought* my soul *up* from Sheol; / you let me live, from going down to the pit" (see also Rom 10:7). The phrase evokes Isaiah 63:11 LXX: "Then they remembered the days of old, of Moses, his servant: Where is the one who brought up out of the sea / the shepherd of his flock?" God brought up the former shepherd, Moses, from the Red Sea, but God has done something infinitely greater with the "great shepherd," Jesus: he brought him up from the dead. Jesus' title as shepherd comes from his parables (Matt 25:32; Luke 15:4–7) and especially his self-identification as the good shepherd who lays down his life for his sheep (John 10:11–14). He is the *great* shepherd, the "chief Shepherd" (1 Pet 5:4), as he is the *great* high priest (Heb 4:14): all other priesthood and leadership is subordinate to his.

Jesus' blood—that is, his passion and death—is **the blood of the eternal covenant** because it brought about the everlasting covenant between God and man. This phrase sums up the whole central part of the letter (chapters 5–10). The phrase "blood of the covenant" appears twice in the †Septuagint: in Exodus

---

27. Rom 15:13, 33; 2 Cor 13:13; 1 Thess 5:23; 2 Thess 3:16.

24:8, where God established the covenant with Israel at Mount Sinai (see Heb 10:20), and in Zechariah 9:11, where God obliquely promises to raise the dead ("Because of the blood of my covenant with you, I will set your captives free from the waterless pit," RSV). Most significantly, at the Last Supper Jesus used this phrase for the great sacrament of the new covenant, the Eucharist (Mark 14:24): "this is my blood of the covenant." That it is an "eternal" covenant (as promised in Jer 32:40) means that those who share in it will, like **Jesus our Lord**, rise from the dead and live forever.

Verse 21 gives the content of the prayer: that by Christ's blood God may **13:21** **furnish you with all that is good, that you may do his will**. The Greek word for "furnish" (*katartizō*) is better translated "equip." It conveys complete preparation, training, or outfitting with everything needed (as in Luke 6:40; Eph 4:12). Just as God "prepared" (*katartizō*) a human body for the Son so that the Son could do his will (10:5), which was to lay down his life on the cross, so God prepares (*katartizō*) us to do his will, which is to love God and neighbor and do all the other good works mentioned in chapter 13. As Israel learned through long, hard experience, doing God's will is impossible by human resources alone. But the grace of the new covenant is that **through Jesus Christ** God himself is at work in us to **carry out ... what is pleasing to him**. This is the new law written on the heart rather than on tablets of stone (8:10; 10:16). As Paul reminded the early Christians, "God is the one who, for his good purpose, works in you both to desire and to work" (Phil 2:13). "For we are his handiwork, created in Christ Jesus for the good works that God has prepared in advance, that we should live in them" (Eph 2:10).

The blessing concludes with a doxology, an exclamation of praise: **to whom be glory forever [and ever]. Amen**. It is not clear whether "whom" refers to God or Jesus; it may be intentionally ambiguous. God has glorified Jesus by raising him from the dead (2:7), and Jesus has glorified God by carrying out his plan of salvation and bringing "many children to glory" (2:10).

Fig. 19. A page of the oldest surviving copy of Hebrews, showing Hebrews 2:3–11, from the Papyrus Collection at the University of Michigan

Final Exhortation and Greetings (13:22–25)

²²**Brothers, I ask you to bear with this message of encouragement, for I have written to you rather briefly.** ²³**I must let you know that our brother Timothy has been set free. If he comes soon, I shall see you together with him.** ²⁴**Greetings to all your leaders and to all the holy ones. Those from Italy send you greetings.** ²⁵**Grace be with all of you.**

NT: Acts 16:1–3; 2 Cor 12:19

The letter closes with a postscript that again gives us only tantalizing tidbits of information about the author and his audience. It includes an appeal to receive the message, a news item about Timothy, greetings, and a final blessing.

13:22 The term **brothers** conveys both the author's affection for his audience and the deep kinship bond that unites believers, because Jesus "is not ashamed to call them 'brothers'" (2:11). He begs them to **bear with** what he has written, perhaps as a gentle way of acknowledging that not all of it has been easy to hear. At the end of a similarly stern but affectionate letter Paul reassured the Corinthians, "In the sight of God we are speaking in Christ, and all for building you up, beloved" (2 Cor 12:19). The author calls his letter a **message of encouragement** (literally, "word of exhortation"), an apt description of this homily-in-writing that continually interweaves doctrine with practical exhortation. The same phrase is used for Paul's sermon in the synagogue at Antioch of Pisidia (Acts 13:15), which in twenty-six short verses covered Old Testament salvation history, the good news of Christ, and a call to conversion.

We might smile at the claim **I have written to you rather briefly**. If this letter is brief, what would a long one look like?[28] But the author did distill an amazing breadth and depth of revelation into a composition that can be read aloud in less than an hour. Like all Scripture, it has an inexhaustible richness that two thousand years of study, reflection, and commentary have not fully plumbed. At several points along the way he hinted that he would have liked to say more (5:11; 6:3; 9:5; 11:32).

13:23 A piece of information that would apparently be welcome news to the readers is that **our brother Timothy has been set free**. The only Timothy known in the New Testament is Paul's disciple and trusted coworker, who coauthored six of Paul's Letters.[29] The implication is that Timothy is well known to the readers, and that he was imprisoned (probably for his witness to Christ) but has now

28. Wright, *Hebrews*, 178.
29. Second Corinthians, Philippians, Colossians, 1–2 Thessalonians, and Philemon.

been released. Since Timothy traveled extensively and often served as Paul's delegate to local churches,[30] this information is not much help in narrowing down the possible location of the audience. The author hopes to be reunited with Timothy **soon** and to visit the community **together with him**. In a similar way, Paul often expresses his desire to **see** in person the disciples to whom he is writing[31]—another sign of the deep bonds of affection that united the early Christians.

The closing **greetings** that are common in the New Testament letters testify **13:24** to the early Christians' awareness of belonging to a worldwide body of believers and not merely a local church. Greetings are conveyed first to the **leaders**, those responsible for preaching the word of God and keeping watch over the church (13:7, 17). The plural suggests that at this early stage the local church was overseen by a group of leaders (as in Acts 14:23; 20:17). The **holy ones**, or "saints," are all Christians (as in Rom 16:15; Eph 1:1; Phil 4:22), made holy by Christ's once-for-all atoning sacrifice (10:10), as Hebrews has so powerfully demonstrated.

Greetings are also conveyed from fellow believers **from Italy**. Does this mean the author is in Italy writing to another location, or that he is writing to Italy from another location where some Italian Christians are present, possibly because they were expelled from Rome by the decree of the emperor Claudius (Acts 18:2)?[32] It is impossible to say.

The ending is simple but elegant: **Grace be with all of you**. This ending is **13:25** identical to that of Titus 3:15 and similar to those of all of Paul's Letters, as well as Revelation 22:21. "Grace" sums up in a word the entire content of Hebrews: the free gift of God's own divine life, given to us because of Christ's atoning sacrifice (2:9), flowing freely from the throne of grace (4:16) to strengthen our hearts (13:9) until we reach the goal of our pilgrimage, the city that is to come (13:14).

---

30. Acts 16:1–3; 17:14–15; 18:5; 19:22; 20:4; 1 Cor 4:17; 16:10; Phil 2:19; 1 Thess 3:2, 6.

31. Rom 1:11; 15:23–24; 1 Cor 16:5–7; Phil 2:23–24; Philem 22.

32. The author could, of course, be writing both to and from a place other than Italy, but then it becomes harder to explain why the greetings single out Italian Christians.

Suggested Resources

From the Christian Tradition

Heen, Erik M., and Philip D. W. Krey, eds. *Hebrews*. Ancient Christian Commentary on Scripture 10. Downers Grove, IL: InterVarsity, 2005. Selections from patristic writings on every passage of the biblical text.

Thomas Aquinas. *Commentary on the Epistle to the Hebrews*. Translated and edited by Chrysostom Baer. South Bend, IN: St. Augustine's Press, 2006. A highly systematic theological exposition of the argument of Hebrews in light of Scripture and tradition.

Scholarly Commentaries

Attridge, Harold W. *The Epistle to the Hebrews: A Commentary on the Epistle to the Hebrews*. Edited by Helmut Koester. Hermeneia. Philadelphia: Fortress, 1989. A carefully researched analysis of the text from a historical-critical perspective.

Bruce, F. F. *The Epistle to the Hebrews*. Rev. ed. New International Commentary on the New Testament. Grand Rapids: Eerdmans, 2012. A scholarly yet accessible commentary from an Evangelical perspective.

Hughes, Philip Edgcumbe. *A Commentary on the Epistle to the Hebrews*. Grand Rapids: Eerdmans, 1977. A rich, detailed, and profoundly theological commentary by an Evangelical Anglican priest.

Johnson, Luke Timothy. *Hebrews: A Commentary*. New Testament Library. Louisville: Westminster John Knox, 2006. A balanced, scholarly commentary that yields insights especially from rhetorical and literary analysis.

Vanhoye, Albert. *A Different Priest: The Letter to the Hebrews*. Translated by Leo Arnold. Series Rhetorica Semitica. Miami: Convivium, 2011. An interpretation of Hebrews by a cardinal and internationally renowned Hebrews scholar that pays very close attention to the structure of the text.

Popular Commentaries or Study Bibles

Barclay, William. *The Letter to the Hebrews*. Rev. ed. Daily Study Bible Series. Philadelphia: Westminster, 1976. A commentary by a minister of the Church of Scotland that conveys the theological and pastoral significance of the text and is useful for homily preparation.

Hagner, Donald. *Encountering the Book of Hebrews: An Exposition*. Encountering Biblical Studies. Grand Rapids: Baker Academic, 2002. A readable, balanced study that is designed for students; includes a wealth of sidebars and word studies.

Hahn, Scott, and Curtis Mitch. *The Letter to the Hebrews*. Ignatius Catholic Study Bible. San Francisco: Ignatius Press, 2007. The biblical text supplemented with succinct and informative footnotes, often citing the Fathers or Church doctrine.

Wright, N. T. *Hebrews for Everyone*. New Testament for Everyone. Louisville: Westminster John Knox, 2004. Short, highly readable commentary by a prominent Evangelical Anglican biblical scholar and bishop.

Special Studies

Harrington, Daniel J. *What Are They Saying about the Letter to the Hebrews?* WATSA Series. Mahwah, NJ: Paulist Press, 2005. A brief synopsis of important recent commentaries and studies on Hebrews, extremely useful as a tool for further study.

Milligan, George. *The Theology of the Epistle to the Hebrews: With a Critical Introduction*. Edinburgh: T&T Clark, 1899. Over a century old yet still worth consulting; available online at https://archive.org/details/theologyofepistl00mill.

Vanhoye, Albert. *Old Testament Priests and the New Priest: According to the New Testament*. Translated by Bernard Orchard. Rev. ed. Leominster: Gracewing, 2009. A readable, insightful study of biblical teaching on the priesthood of Christ and its implications for the Catholic priesthood.

Glossary

aorist: a Greek verb tense that (when used in the indicative mood) indicates a past event without reference to its completeness, duration, or repetition.

apostasy: a turning away from or abandonment of faith in God.

Aramaic: a Semitic language related to Hebrew, adopted by Jews after their exile in Babylon and spoken by most Jews in first-century Palestine.

ark of the covenant: the sacred chest made of acacia wood overlaid with gold, built by God's command during the exodus (Exod 25:10-22) and housed in the †Holy of Holies.

atonement: a term often used in the †Torah for the removal of sin through sacrifice. The original meaning of the verb "make atonement" (Hebrew *kipper*) may have been either "cover" or "purge." The English word "atonement" (from "at-one-ment") actually expresses the *result* of the removal of sin: reconciliation between God and humanity.

boldness (Greek *parrēsia*): confidence, fearlessless; filial assurance and trust before God (see Catechism 2778).

catena: a string of related biblical quotations, which was a common feature of biblical interpretation in the ancient world.

chiasm: a literary device in which words or phrases are placed in sequence and then inverted sequence, forming a concentric pattern; for example, A–B–C–C′–B′–A′. The word "chiasm" comes from the Greek letter *chi* (X), which reflects the mirror structure.

Christology, christological: referring to doctrine or understanding of the identity and mission of Jesus Christ.

covenant: a sacred kinship bond established by solemn oath. Hebrews refers to the "first covenant" (Heb 8:7) as that which God established with Israel through Moses at Mount Sinai (although there were earlier covenants with Noah and Abraham). Through his passion, death, and resurrection Jesus established the new and eternal covenant, which fulfills the old one (Jer 31:31–33; Heb 8:7–13).

cultic: relating to priesthood, sacrifice, or other elements of ritual worship.

Day of Atonement (Hebrew *Yom Kippur*): Israel's annual day of fasting and penance, when the high priest would cleanse the †tabernacle (later the temple) of the pollution caused by the people's sins. The sacred rites included the scapegoat ritual and sprinkling the blood of a sacrificed bull and goat on the †mercy seat within the †Holy of Holies (Lev 16; 23:27–32).

eschatological: having to do with the last things—God's decisive intervention in history to bring the former age to an end and begin the new and final age of salvation history. For the New Testament, the last things were inaugurated by Jesus' passion and resurrection.

gezerah shawa: a rabbinic principle of biblical interpretation that draws a connection between two Scripture passages by means of a key word that appears in both. Hebrews 4:3–4, for instance, connects Psalm 95:7–11 with Genesis 2:2 based on the words "rest," "work," and "day."

Gnosticism: an early Christian heresy that held that the material world is evil or worthless, and that salvation consists of liberation from the material world, attained by esoteric knowledge (Greek *gnōsis*). Gnosticism as an organized system arose in the second century, but early forms of it already existed in the New Testament period.

Great Shema: Israel's confession of faith, from Deuteronomy 6:4–9: "Hear, O Israel! The LORD is our God, the LORD alone! . . ."

Hellenists: Jews who lived or had lived in Hellenistic cultures outside Palestine and whose native language was Greek.

holocaust (also translated as "burnt offering" or "whole burnt offering"): a sacrifice in which the victim is entirely burnt on the altar, in contrast to other sacrifices in which all or part of the meat is eaten (Lev 1).

holy: (1) set apart from all that is worldly or †profane; (2) morally pure, upright, and just. God is intrinsically holy; for human beings, holiness is both a gift from God and a task (Heb 3:1; 12:14): "Be holy, for I, the LORD your God, am holy" (Lev 19:2).

Holy of Holies: the inner room of the †tabernacle (and later the temple), where the †ark of the covenant was kept and God dwelt in the midst of his people.

Holy Place: the outer room of the †tabernacle (and later the temple), where the lampstand, altar of incense, and altar of the bread of the Presence stood.

intertestamental writings: Jewish writings composed between the period of the Old and New Testaments (roughly 400 BC to AD 50).

law, law of Moses, Mosaic law: see **Torah**.

levitical: relating to the Levites, members of the tribe of Levi, who had the sacred duty of caring for the sanctuary and its furnishings. Levitical priests were those belonging to the family of Aaron within the tribe of Levi.

liturgy (Greek *leitourgia*): the public worship offered by God's people, consisting of ritual words and actions carried out in God's presence. *Leitourgia* originally referred to a public service; the †Septuagint uses it for the "public service" of Israel's worship (Num 8:22; 16:9).

LXX: see **Septuagint**.

mercy seat (Hebrew *kapporet*, also translated as "place of expiation" or "propitiatory"): the golden cover of the †ark of the covenant, upon which stood two gold statues of winged cherubim (Heb 9:5; Exod 25:18–21), and which on the †Day of Atonement was sprinkled with blood in expiation for the people's sins (Lev 16). It is often translated as "mercy seat" because God is said to be "enthroned on the cherubim" (1 Sam 4:4; Ps 99:1), and there he manifests his limitless mercy (Exod 25:22).

Messiah (from Hebrew *mashiah*, "anointed one"): the future descendant of King David promised by God, whose reign would endure forever (2 Sam 7:12–13).

parousia (Greek *parousia*, "coming" or "presence"): Jesus' promised return in glory at the end of the world (1 Cor 15:23; 1 Thess 4:15; see Heb 9:28).

paschal mystery (from Hebrew *pesah*, "passover," Exod 12:27): Jesus' passion, death and resurrection, in which he fulfilled the meaning of the Jewish Passover and passed over from death to eternal life with the Father (see Catechism 542, 571–72, 647, 1340).

patriarchs: the ancestors of the nation of Israel, especially Abraham, Isaac, Jacob, and Jacob's twelve sons.

Pentateuch: see **Torah**.

place of expiation: see **mercy seat**.

profane: that which is common or earthly in contrast to that which is holy or set apart for God (Heb 12:16). "Profane" is also used as a verb, meaning "desecrate" (e.g., Lev 21:12).

qal wahomer (Hebrew for "light and heavy"): a form of argument common among the ancient rabbis, similar to an *a fortiori* argument. It generally took the form "If X is true for the lesser, then how much more for the greater."

rhetoric: the art of persuasive speech or writing, a highly prized skill in the ancient world.

sacrifice: the offering of something costly to God through the mediation of a priest, to unite God's people in holy fellowship with him. The †Torah prescribed five main types of sacrifice (see sidebar, "How Jesus Fulfills the Sacrifices of the Old Covenant," p. 152).

sanctuary (literally, "the holy" or "the holies"): general term for a sacred space where God is present, used in Hebrews to refer to the entire †tabernacle, or to the †Holy Place or the †Holy of Holies.

Septuagint (abbreviated LXX): a translation of the Hebrew Bible into Greek, made around 250 BC by Jews in Alexandria, Egypt.

tabernacle: the sacred tent that God commanded Moses to construct during Israel's desert journey, to house the †ark of the covenant and serve as Israel's place of worship (Exod 25:8–9). The tabernacle was a precursor to the Jerusalem temple.

Talmud: a compilation of Jewish oral traditions put in writing between roughly AD 200 and 600, consisting of the Mishnah (the codification of Jewish religious and legal norms) and the Gemara (discussions and explanations of the Mishnah).

tamid: the "perpetual" sacrifice that God prescribed for Israel in Exodus 29:38–42 (translated as "regularly" in Exod 29:38 NABRE), consisting of the burnt offering of a lamb every morning and evening, together with flour, oil, and wine.

tent: see **tabernacle**.

theophany (Greek for "divine appearance"): a visible manifestation of God's holy presence, causing human awe, fear, and trembling.

Torah (Hebrew for "law" or "instruction"): the first five books of the Bible, traditionally attributed to Moses and thus also called the "law of Moses," the "books of Moses," or the "Pentateuch." "Torah" is also used more broadly to refer to all God's instruction on how to live an upright life in covenant relationship with him.

type, typology: typology is the recognition of how persons, things, and events at an earlier stage of biblical history prefigure God's future deeds, especially the culmination of his plan in Jesus Christ. The "type" is the sign (e.g., the Passover lamb); the "antitype" is that to which the type points (e.g., Christ the Lamb of God).

Yahweh: God's holy name, revealed to Moses at the burning bush (Exod 3:14–15). According to ancient custom, Jews refrain from pronouncing the divine name out of reverence; when reading the Scriptures aloud they substitute the title "the LORD" (Hebrew *Adonai*, Greek *Kyrios*) for the divine name. The form "YHWH" (known as the Tetragrammaton) is used because Hebrew script has no vowels; the form "Yahweh" is sometimes used to approximate the original pronunciation.

YHWH: see **Yahweh**.

Yom Kippur: see **Day of Atonement**.

Index of Pastoral Topics

This index indicates where topics are mentioned in Hebrews that may be useful for evangelization, catechesis, apologetics, or other forms of pastoral ministry.

Index of Sidebars